Anticipations and Experiences
in the Locality

Mutiny at the Margins
New Perspectives on the Indian Uprising of 1857
Series Editor: Crispin Bates

Mutiny at the Margins

New Perspectives on the Indian Uprising of 1857

Volume 1
Anticipations and Experiences in the Locality

Edited by
Crispin Bates

⑤SAGE   www.sagepublications.com
Los Angeles • London • New Delhi • Singapore • Washington DC

First published in 2013 by

 SAGE Publications India Pvt Ltd
B1/I-1 Mohan Cooperative Industrial Area
Mathura Road, New Delhi 110 044, India
www.sagepub.in

SAGE Publications Inc
2455 Teller Road
Thousand Oaks, California 91320, USA

SAGE Publications Ltd
1 Oliver's Yard, 55 City Road
London EC1Y 1SP, United Kingdom

SAGE Publications Asia-Pacific Pte Ltd
33 Pekin Street
#02-01 Far East Square
Singapore 048763

Published by Vivek Mehra for SAGE Publications India Pvt Ltd, Phototypeset in 10.5/12.5 Minion by Tantla Composition Pvt Ltd, Chandigarh and printed at Saurabh Printers, New Delhi.

Library of Congress Cataloging-in-Publication Data

Mutiny at the margins: new perspectives on the Indian uprising of 1857.
    volumes cm
  Includes bibliographical references and index.
  1. India—History—Sepoy Rebellion, 1857–1858. I. Bates, Crispin, 1958– editor of compilation. II. Major, Andrea. !II. Carter, Marina. IV. Rand, Gavin.

DS478.M87   954.03'17—dc23   2013   2013001632

ISBN: 978-81-321-0970-9 (HB)

The SAGE Team: Shambhu Sahu, Punita Kaur Mann, Anju Saxena and Dally Verghese

Series Note

THE volumes in this series take a fresh look at the Revolt of 1857 from a variety of original and unusual perspectives, focusing in particular on traditionally neglected socially marginal groups and geographic areas that have hitherto tended to be unrepresented in studies of this cataclysmic event in British imperial and Indian historiography.

Thank you for choosing a SAGE product! If you have any comment, observation or feedback, I would like to personally hear from you. Please write to me at <u>contactceo@sagepub.in</u>

—Vivek Mehra, Managing Director and CEO,
SAGE Publications India Pvt Ltd, New Delhi

Bulk Sales

SAGE India offers special discounts for purchase of books in bulk. We also make available special imprints and excerpts from our books on demand.

For orders and enquiries, write to us at

Marketing Department
SAGE Publications India Pvt Ltd
B1/I-1, Mohan Cooperative Industrial Area
Mathura Road, Post Bag 7
New Delhi 110044, India
E-mail us at <u>marketing@sagepub.in</u>

Get to know more about SAGE, be invited to SAGE events, get on our mailing list. Write today to <u>marketing@sagepub.in</u>

This book is also available as an e-book.

Contents

Preface

THE seven-volume *Mutiny at the Margins* series published by SAGE is the product of a research project of the same name undertaken at the University of Edinburgh in Scotland, with funding from the UK Arts and Humanities Research Council. Taking place 150 years after the Indian Uprising of 1857–1858, the *Mutiny at the Margins* project was created to challenge conventional understandings of the uprising through thematic, collaborative research, a network of scholars centred on Edinburgh and international conferences. This innovative project aimed to confront some of the many myths surrounding popular and academic conceptions of the revolt, to move beyond traditional nationalist and imperialist perspectives, and to explore previously neglected margins in the history of this tumultuous event.

Marginality is invoked in several ways throughout the series. It is presented in the telling of tales that fall outside the mainstream historiography of the period and pursued chronologically as the historical context of the Indian Uprising is enlarged in an exploration of both the progenitors and consequences of 1857. The series ventures into overlooked geographical margins, both within India and overseas, with the global impact of the revolt being examined in Volume 3. Finally, a core purpose of the series is to emphasise the critical roles played by socially marginal groups in the uprising and to use this to highlight new areas of current research.

Independent scholars from across the globe came together for the *Mutiny at the Margins* project. This collaboration fostered ground-breaking research, aided by three international conferences held in Edinburgh, London and Jamia Millia Islamia in New Delhi, and four workshops held in Edinburgh and at the Royal Asiatic Society in London. Altogether, some thirty leading Indian and Pakistani researchers were involved, along with a dozen academics from the United States and twice that number of participants drawn from universities across the United Kingdom and Europe. A majority of the chapters in the series are the product of the cooperative, committed and original endeavour of these scholars. The *Mutiny at the Margins* project was accompanied by a high level of public engagement, including a programme of public lectures, collaborative exhibitions, seminars and workshops in Edinburgh and London. A number of source materials were published online, for the benefit of students and future researchers. These are to be found at www.csas.ed.ac.uk/mutiny.

The original research carried out by the Edinburgh-based scholars of the *Mutiny at the Margins* project forms a key part of the material for this series. It led to new insights into the British experience of 1857 regarding the experiences of white subalterns (men and women) and of the often overlooked British communities in areas peripheral to the revolts, as well as British attempts to explain the meaning of the uprising. The research of the Edinburgh team—comprising Crispin Bates, Markus Daeschel, Andrea Major, Marina Carter and Kim A. Wagner—addressed the involvement of Muslims and Dalits and the long-term impact of the events of the mid-nineteenth century for the development of Islamic political culture and identity. In addition, new investigations scrutinised the role of Indian Adivasis (or tribals) in 1857 as well as the economic consequences of 1857 in north India and in particular the huge impetus it gave to labour migration within India and overseas in subsequent years. Kim A. Wagner undertook further innovative work concerning the mutiny of the regiments at Meerut in May 1857 and description of the impact of 1857 within European literature.

The series comprises seven volumes, each with a distinct thematic focus:

- Volume 1, *Anticipations and Experiences in the Locality*, centres on unrest and disorder in the long history of resistance to colonial rule (the *belli Britannica*) prior to 1857 and the impact of the revolt itself in diverse localities within India.
- Volume 2, *Britain and the Indian Uprising*, looks at the varied responses of British missionaries, colonial leaders and working-class voices and how they reveal the multiplicity of British reactions to the revolt.
- Volume 3, *Global Perspectives*, widens the geographical remit of the series and examines the global dissemination and portrayal of the events of the uprising in the international press and literature. It also examines the impact of the events of 1857 and the socio-economic impact of displaced mutineers and their experiences in the broader colonial world.
- Volume 4, *Military Aspects of the Indian Uprising*, deals with how battles were won and lost and how the army reorganised itself after the revolt. It also touches on the thorny issue of how to define the events of 1857—a rebellion, a national uprising or a small war of the kind experienced in many colonial states.
- Volume 5, *Muslim, Dalit and Subaltern Narratives*, addresses the role of marginal and Muslim groups, respectively. The first half of the volume explores minority perceptions of the uprising, including Dalit narratives and the use of 1857 in their invented histories; the second half looks into the response and involvement of different Muslim social groups, from

civil servants, philosophers and logicians to the mujahidin, as well as exploring the experience of indigenous participants in their own words.

- Volume 6, *Perception, Narration and Reinvention: The Pedagogy and Historiography of the Indian Uprising*, moves into the territory of hagiography, historiography and pedagogy. It covers the reaction of people to the revolt and the various ways in which historians and the wider public in India have sought to understand, categorise, and at times distort or exaggerate, salient aspects and particular events.
- Volume 7, *A Source Book: Documents of the Indian Uprising*, is both a research tool and a teaching resource. This collection of documents drawn from the extensive research conducted during the *Margins* project employs images and texts to offer a unique range of 1857 sources, emphasising a subaltern perspective and designed to complement the previous six volumes of the series.

Collectively, the series presents the most comprehensive collection to date of historical writings on the Indian Uprising of 1857. It is hoped that it will provide a benchmark of research to inform and inspire future scholars and encourage new perspectives on the Indian Uprising of 1857 that are both respectful of previous interpretations and permitting of re-imaginings of the past that are suited to the twenty-first century. The body of research and writings contained in the seven-volume set is much more than a collection about the 'revolt'; it demonstrates that the events of 1857 were, in their origins, progress and impact, vastly more significant than is implied by the usual emphasis on a unique historical event, with ramifications that reach forward into the present day.

Acknowledgements

THIS project was undertaken and completed with support from the UK Arts and Humanities Research Council (AHRC), the British Academy, the Royal Asiatic Society of London, Jamia Milia Islamia, the Indian Council for Historical Research, the Royal Society of Edinburgh, the National Library of Scotland, and the Centre for South Asian Studies and the School of History, Classics and Archaeology at the University of Edinburgh. Personal thanks for assistance with copy-editing go to Rosalind Parr, Lauren Wilks, Ben Thurman and Jessica Robinson, and also to the indefatigable group of researchers involved in the *Mutiny at the Margins* project: Marina Carter, Marcus Daechsel, Andrea Major and Kim A. Wagner. Thanks, finally, and above all, to the many scholars who have contributed to this series, thereby making it possible, as well as to Sugata Ghosh, Rekha Natarajan, Shambhu Sahu and other members of the extremely patient and hard-working editorial team at SAGE, New Delhi.

Introduction

Crispin Bates

THIS book is the first volume in the *Mutiny at the Margins* series from SAGE Publications, which takes its name from a research project at the University of Edinburgh in Scotland, funded by the UK Arts and Humanities Research Council. The project aimed to provide new insights into the Indian Uprising of 1857–1858 through thematic and collaborative research, a network of scholars centred in Edinburgh, and international conferences. Timed to coincide with the 150th anniversary of the Indian Uprising—an event commonly known in Britain as the Indian Mutiny—the project aimed to bring dynamic insights to old stories. Its purpose was to challenge conventional nationalist and imperialist perspectives and to dispel some of the myths that often still dominate popular and academic accounts.

The first sense in which marginality is invoked in the *Mutiny at the Margins* series is the telling of tales which fall outside the mainstream historiography on the period, including interpretations which employ unusual methodologies or perspectives. A second margin which the series pursues is chronological: the attempt being made to situate the great Indian Uprising in a broader historical context than is commonly conceived. In other words, the aim was to view 1857 as something beyond a single event by exploring its progenitors and consequences. This exploration continues even to the present day, with consideration being given in the final volume of the series (Volume 7) to the historiography and pedagogy of 1857 and its contemporary significance. A third intention is to explore some of the neglected geographical margins of the revolt. This is most notably undertaken in Volume 3 of the series, which explores the global impact of the Indian Uprising. A final key purpose is to highlight the critical role played by socially marginal groups—ranging from criminals to tribal peoples to white subalterns—in the events of 1857 and to thereby attempt to challenge prevailing historiography that has often become far removed from the most exciting new work in this field.

As part of the *Mutiny at the Margins* project, original research was carried out by Edinburgh-based scholars on specific aspects of 1857. The results of this were new insights into the British experience of 1857, including that of white subalterns (men and women), the various British attempts to explain the meaning of the revolt and the experiences of the often ignored British communities in areas on the peripheries of the revolt (the subject of Volume 2 in the series). The Edinburgh team also explored the involvement of Muslims and Dalits and the long-term impact of events of the mid-nineteenth century for the development of Islamic political culture and identity (the subject of Volume 5 in the series). Research was further undertaken on the involvement of Indian Adivasis (or tribals) in 1857 and the economic consequences of 1857 in north India—in particular the huge impetus it gave to labour migration within India and overseas in subsequent years. This research involved work in archives as far flung as Trinidad, Mauritius, Singapore and Guyana. The results of this endeavour are reflected in the chapters within the volumes of this series as well as in future publications to come.

Further innovative research on the mutiny of the regiments at Meerut in May 1857 was undertaken by Kim A. Wagner, employing methodologies of the Annales school in an attempt to unfold the 'basic dynamic of escalation' and to move beyond the general context of the uprising to explain precisely when and why the Indian Uprising happened at a key point of its instigation.[1] There was, finally, a high level of public engagement associated with the research project, with public lectures and collaborative exhibitions organised in Edinburgh as well as seminars and workshops in Edinburgh and London. A number of useful source materials were also published online for the benefit and encouragement of future researchers.[2]

Of particular relevance to this series, the *Mutiny at the Margins* project brought together cutting-edge research by a wide variety of independent scholars from across the globe. These collaborators attended three international conferences held in London, Edinburgh and Jamia Millia Islamia in New Delhi, as well as a total of four workshops held in Edinburgh and at the Royal Asiatic Society in London. In total, some thirty leading Indian and Pakistani researchers were involved, along with a dozen academics from the United States, and twice that number of participants drawn from universities across the United Kingdom and Europe. It is the collective, original and committed endeavour of these scholars that has produced a majority of the chapters in the volumes of the *Mutiny at the Margins* series, of which this is the first volume.

The Historiography of 1857

The Great Uprising of 1857 began with a mutiny within the ranks of the Bengal army of the East India Company, but was soon accompanied by widespread civil unrest affecting the North-west Provinces, Awadh, western Bihar and regions further afield. In total more than 100,000 native infantry, or sepoys (from the Persian *sipahi*), and *sowar*s (cavalrymen) turned against their British commanders. In the civil insurrection that followed the collapse of company rule, the British *firangi* (foreigners) were almost completely expelled from the Indo-Gangetic plains of north India. A vast army had to be mobilised to recapture this territory, including Scottish and English soldiers and sailors, European civilian residents and regiments of Sikhs recruited in the Punjab. In the process, whole cities were laid waste, and in the destruction, chaos and subsequent famine that followed, Indian civilian casualties (never properly enumerated) most probably ran into the millions.

Conventionally, the mutiny is attributed to anxieties amongst the volunteer infantry (sepoys) of the Indian army concerning the issue of greased cartridges for use with the new Lee Enfield rifle, which the East India Company was planning to distribute to its regiments in India. It was rumoured that these cartridges were greased with the fat of cows and of pigs in order to defile and undermine the ritual practices of both Hindu and Muslim sepoys. In narrative terms this explanation is expedient, yet simplistic. It is now widely understood that although sepoys in the company's regiments were trained in advance in how to use the new weapons, in the first instance the Lee Enfield rifles were only issued to European regiments. This suggests that although this issue proved to be in some cases the cause célèbre, as, for example, when the regiments first rebelled at Meerut in May 1857, there were clearly larger and more complex causes of unrest within the company's Bengal armies, as well as in the wider civilian population, which in many parts of India erupted, either opportunistically or in support of the army mutineers. The issue of the greased cartridges, however, figured large in subsequent colonial writings on the insurrection, such as Charles Ball's *The History of the Indian Mutiny* (1858), or most famously in John W. Kaye and George Malleson's comprehensive *History of the Indian Mutiny*, published in six volumes in 1878 (with an index volume added in 1880), which became the source for many later writings on the subject.[3]

The convenience of the greased cartridge theory was that it posited an entirely irrational and religious cause for the insurrection, which obviated the need to enquire too deeply into the malpractices, maladministration and exploitative practices of the East India Company's rule in north India. It was a single incident, with no prehistory. It also conveniently implied that the uprising was rooted in religious fanaticism and indiscipline within just one of the armies of the three presidencies (based in Madras, Bombay and Bengal) of the company's rule in India and did not enjoy any larger support. Furthermore, it enabled the uprising to be depicted as an early example of the 'clash of civilisations': a theme which has subsequently been employed to explain many other colonial and imperial misadventures.[4] In this clash of civilisations, particular suspicion was cast upon the motives of Indian Muslims. This was because the 3rd Light Cavalry and 20th Native Infantry who mutinied at Meerut in May 1857 had determined to dash the 40 miles to Delhi and attempt to restore the rule of the ailing 'puppet' Mughal Emperor Bahadur Shah II. Attention was focused in addition on the Indian princes who joined the revolt, notably the *taluqdar* aristocracy of the kingdom of Awadh: a formerly loyal ally of the East Indian Company, which had been peremptorily seized the year before in order to enlarge the company's territories. It was in Awadh that some of the fiercest fighting occurred, and also in central India, where the Rani of Jhansi belatedly joined the revolt. Considerable attention was also paid to the alleged atrocities of the rebels, focusing primarily on the massacre of civilians at Kanpur (or 'Cawnpore' as the British spelled it at the time).

Ironically, many of the allegations of brutality levelled against the rebels—notably that of raping European women—were subsequently found to be exaggerated, or simply untrue.[5] Nonetheless, in 1857, the British government was persuaded to send troops to India to support the East India Company on a mission to defend the honour of British women and to bring an end to barbarity, anarchy and fanaticism. Their success in this was seen as measure of the superiority of Christian civilisation and not merely (as it in fact was) a result of the bloody massacres that resulted from the troops' use of indiscriminate force, troops battle-hardened from the Crimean War and superior firepower.

Early Indian attempts to communicate their experience of 1857 were often cautiously disguised in the language of loyalty. Examples included Syed Ahmad Khan's *The Causes of the Indian Revolt*, published in 1860 (see also the chapter by Jalil in this volume). In 1909, V.D. Savarkar's highly influential *The Indian War of Independence* was immediately banned by the British government in India. This work has been described as the first nationalist Indian account of 1857; however, it was self-confessedly based upon Kaye and Malleson's account, with the heroines, heroes and villains and the moral judgements reversed. It was only after independence that a more subtle and original Indian perspective began to emerge. During the centenary celebrations of 1957, the central government sought to maintain good relations with the former colonising power by tempering any anti-imperialist rhetoric. In successive speeches and public pronouncements, the government stressed that 1857 was, above all else, a model of Hindu–Muslim cooperation, to be imitated by present generations.[6] Meanwhile, individual state governments made great efforts to commission publications using relevant material unearthed from their archives. Historian Surendranath Sen, who was drafted in to write an official history of the insurrection, clearly saw symptoms of nationalism in the activities of the mutinous sepoys and their civilian allies. Sounding a note of dissent, both R.C. Majumdar and H.P. Chattopadhyay rejected the notion that nationalism or patriotism in the modern sense was relevant in 1857, and characterised it as 'a popular movement on a regional basis'.[7] In their collective search for new (predominantly Hindu) heroes of 1857, these scholars brought about a fresh understanding of the great diversity of actors who were involved, but there was not, as yet, any great paradigmatic shift in approaches to the uprising.

During this period, there emerged a divergence between nationalist historians and authors who were influenced by the Marxist tradition and thus were far more inclined to downplay the significance of religion and to depict 1857 as a peasant revolt, albeit one involving an element of feudal leadership. There was at that time, however, limited evidence of what happened at the grass-roots level. In part this arose from neglect—for various reasons—of the voluminous Urdu and Persian records concerning the uprising at the village level in north India, which were—and still are—held in the regional archives in Allahabad, records in regional languages elsewhere. To fill this gap, historians resorted to the metonym of the sepoy as a 'peasant in uniform' whose actions therefore represented the feelings and sentiments those in the surrounding countryside. However, this representation somewhat conflicted with the evidence of the very high degree of professionalisation of military service in the Indo-Gangetic plain and offered little help in explaining the strength of support for the insurrection outside of the core recruiting districts (notably Awadh) that were employed by the British.[8] Amongst other limitations, these studies tended to accept without serious contestation the pretension of the British to have imposed a 'pax Brittania' before and after the 1857 insurrection. With the notable exception of S.B. Chaudhuri's *Civil Disturbances during the British Rule in India (1765–1857)*, published in 1955, there was little consideration given to the longue durée of small and large anti-colonial struggles (dismissed by the colonial authorities as criminal activities or riots) that went on in towns and cities as well as in remote and rural areas, amongst groups of artisans, peasants and Adivasi or tribal peoples.

The remaining lacunae and problematics in the contemporary historiography of 1857 will be considered in depth in the final volume of the *Mutiny at the Margins* series. It will suffice here to note that this series takes its inspiration from the path-breaking work of P.C. Joshi, Eric Stokes, Rudrangshu Mukherjee, Gautam Bhadra and Tapti Roy who in recent decades have begun to break the logjam imposed by the dead weight of nationalist and colonialist interpretations in studies of the Indian Uprising. The work of these scholars represents the beginnings of an attempt to explore the diversities of experience at the grass-roots level and the use of new methodologies, notably in Mukherjee's imaginative reconstruction of the Kanpur massacres, and in the use of land revenue and judicial records (rather than mere military proceedings), as well as vernacular sources. They have emphasised the widespread involvement of the peasantry in the insurgency, the frequency with which rural towns were plundered and government officials and symbols of authority were targeted, as well as mahajans (moneylenders) and others who were seen as supporters of the colonial regime. In the case of Rudrangshu Mukherjee's work on Awadh, the role of elite, *taluqdari* leadership was importantly qualified through an exploration of the agency and activism of the peasantry. Attention has also been paid to rumour and as indicators of popular involvement. Otherwise, as in the case of Rajat Ray's

The Felt Community and Ranajit Guha's *Elementary Aspects of Insurgency*, the attempt has been made to provide an explanation of the popular mentalities of territoriality, community and patrie, if not of nation, that lay behind the actions of many of the insurgents.

1857 in the Locality

All of the original and leading scholars who are contributors to this volume have endeavoured to take a further step forward, employing the new methodologies pioneered by early subaltern and postcolonial historiography with an emphasis on issues on the margins of the history and historiography of 1857. The chapters primarily concern anticipations of revolt in the early nineteenth century and experiences of revolt in the locality and attempt to raise new questions about the spatiality and temporality of events. Some of the chapters also touch upon issues returned to in greater detail in later volumes in the series. The theme which unites them is an attempt to transcend the malaise of dualism and the conventional meta-narratives that formerly dominated the historiography of 1857 by exploring events prior to the uprising and the multiple and varied meanings of insurrection as it unfolded within different regions of the subcontinent. In this endeavour, an attempt is made by the contributors to avoid simply mapping general explanations onto events at a local level, but instead to explore the dynamics of locality and period within their own terms.

The first chapter in this collection boldly questions whether, in terms of governance, the Uprising of 1857 was quite the turning point that many have claimed it to be. Thus, it is often argued that following the insurrection, the East India Company's administration was straightforwardly replaced on 1 November 1858 by a bureaucratic colonial government ruling directly from London, which acted upon and intervened with far more rigour than hitherto had been possible. It is correspondingly assumed that this introduced 'a modern regime of power' which, in Foucauldian terms, heralded the succession over sovereign power of governmental strategies and technologies concerned with the disciplinary reconstitution of the Indian subject, from roughly coerced bodies into self-policing minds. This explanatory arc is rigorously questioned by Thomas Lloyd, who argues that, in central India, the Anti-Thuggee Campaign of the 1830s saw the elaboration of many of the ideas of sovereignty peculiar to the modern state, a generation before the Mughal emperor was stripped of his status and the East Company was dissolved. Lloyd suggests that the trials and legal proceedings involved in the Anti-Thuggee Campaign anticipated the legalistic arguments invoked in the trial of Bahadur Shah II. In both cases, the British defined themselves as serving the interests of an abstract state, imagined in opposition to the novel entity of the population, and claimed the extra-legal right to make sovereign decision about whom to except and who to protect under the rule of law.

According to Lloyd, the practices that sustained the Anti-Thuggee Campaign and other similar episodes in the early nineteenth century marginalised a certain portion of 'the population' as irredeemably criminal, whilst making their marginality the highly visible business of the company's officials. These practices were midwife to the nascence of the effects of a state that effectively placed sovereignty in British hands well before the 1857 uprisings. Lloyd concludes that the trial of the last Mughal was not in terms of the transfer of power into British hands, the watershed, that some (such as Pramod Nayar)[9] have assumed, but was instead merely a show trial, or purely political spectacle, designed to reassure the morale of the British in India and at home.

The exceptionalism of 1857 is again questioned in the substantial and detailed second chapter in this collection, by Dirk Kolff. This chapter discusses a series of minor insurgencies and small wars that took place in 1824, particularly around the time of the Dasahra festival of that year, when the news of a British military disaster in Burma had excited the whole of Hindustan and the Punjab. The war conference of Jat, held by although Gujar and other leaders at Bharatpur during the monsoon of 1824 reveals that some of these actions were isolated events or based on the charisma of a local leader, most were rationally planned and revealed an awareness of the regional distribution of power. Unlike in 1857, in 1824 the core recruitment area of the company's Purbiya army in eastern Hindustan was not affected by the disturbances, which mainly took place in independent Indian states and in some peripheral districts that had relatively little experience of British rule. As in 1857, however, British management of the situation was characterised by a significant 'cognitive dissonance' and misunderstanding of Indian motives, and a conviction that rather than negotiating, the status quo ante could only be restored by the use of overwhelming force. What 1824 revealed, however, was a random cross section of, by no means exclusively anti-British, endemic political aspirations in Hindustan that simply became more than usually visible as a result of the sudden insecurities created by the news from Burma.

One of the best known shibboleths of 1857 is tackled by Andrea Major, who argues that British assumptions about the dangers of religious interference that solidified during the debate over the abolition of Sati in 1829 had a major impact on determining how the Uprising of 1857 was interpreted. Gayatri Spivak famously characterised the colonial reaction to Sati as 'White men saving brown women from brown men' and in subsequent British narratives (notably that of Sir John Kaye), the prohibition of Sati is frequently portrayed as a cause of Indian discontent in 1857, despite glaring disjunctures and discontinuities between the two events. However, Major argues that Sati was at best a marginal issue in 1857, and that British appropriation of it as a causal factor reveals more about the assumptions and agendas that informed the construction of colonial discourses on 1857 than it does about the reality of the event.

Another fresh perspective on the mythography of 1857 is offered by William R. Pinch, who examines judicial records on prostitute involvement in crime (more often than not as victims) in order to enquire into the not entirely unjustified claim that prostitutes played a key role in sparking the Mutiny/ Rebellion of 1857. His investigation takes us into an exploration of the regimental and cantonment bazars of the mid-nineteenth century and the cultural and political meanings of sex-slavery during the years of transition to British rule. He examines the changing legal status of the prostitute as the role conceived for the British colonial state was transformed from one of 'benevolent paternalism' to that of distant guarantor of individual prostitute rights and freedoms—a process still not complete by the 1850s. Most importantly, the prostitutes themselves, such as the famous Mees Dolly, emerge as key figures in the cantonment towns of mid-nineteenth century north India, perhaps explaining how they might indeed have come both to prompt Indians to mutiny in Meerut and to warn Britons (as it is said) of their impending catastrophe.

The mobilisation of insurrection at the grass-roots level is the focus of Amaresh Misra's chapter, in a homage to the pioneering research on the revolt in rural north India undertaken by Eric Stokes. Misra argues that despite the peasant background of many of the Bengal army sepoys who revolted in 1857, the effect of various Indian tenure structures on rural behaviour and peasant responses in 1857 has been little studied. Building upon Eric Stokes' work on the districts of the Upper Doab, Misra summarises the tenure structures in the areas of north India, where fighting was organised and intense, and contrasts them with the regions where popular support was more sporadic. The argument is advanced that key features in the Permanent Settlement, Malguzari and Ryotwari land settlements determined peasant mobilisation, and that the north Indian *pattidari– bhaichara–hissedari–biswedari* tenure in particular—which Charles Metcalfe famously described as constituting the basis of 'mini Asiatic republics'—was an important factor enabling the most determined and revolutionary activism among the peasantry. This tenure was symptomatic, he argues, of the dynamism and strength of local communitarian peasant associations, and in particular of the pattidar, or proprietary brotherhoods, which held large tracts of land on behalf of their extended family, or *gotra*. Altering Indian tenure structures was a major part of British attempts at social control, and where successful (from a British point of view), it was devastatingly destructive of local rural polities and social organisation. Where proprietary brotherhoods managed to survive, among particular castes and tribes that are identified by Misra, the potential for organised resistance was far stronger and more conspicuous. This factor in the political economy of rural India has enduring force even into the present day, Misra maintains, and requires more serious attention from historians.

Examining yet more closely the unfolding of the revolt in the locality, Mahmood Farooqui draws upon his researches amongst the Delhi Mutiny papers stored in the National Archives of India to tell the story of the role of the

Delhi city police. These documents, collected together by the British from the kotwali (police station), the secretariat, homes, and the despatches of spies and agents, are mostly written in Shikasteh Urdu, some in Persian and a few in Urdu. Hitherto little used by historians, they provide dense descriptions of a city at war and at work, of administration and anarchy, of desperation and of deceit. The bulk of the documents consist of petitions from ordinary citizens, shopkeepers, tenants, soldiers, sepoys and correspondence to and from the kotwal, which allow us to glimpse the day-to-day functioning of the city and the order and chaos that quickly followed upon one another. Just as in contemporary India, Farooqui shows how the police were used as the strong arm of the state, even as the fragile administrative authority established at the court of the Mughal emperor was forced to acknowledge the power of public opinion. Remarkably, in a time of conflict and chaos, the majority of the police chose to remain at their posts, even when unpaid, and worked hard to resolve the many disputes and problems that arose during the period of the siege. They zealously carried out their orders to the best of their abilities and did so with tact and consideration, even when asked to commander labour and resources, to do forcible searches and make arrests. Was this sheer professionalism? Or did it derive from a passionate engagement with the cause of the revolt? The question is unanswered, but the British were sufficiently suspicious of the Delhi police to insist upon a wholescale 'reform' once they had recaptured the city and resumed control.

To move beyond the official British narrative of events in 1857, historians have employed an increasing diversity of both vernacular and extra-archival sources. Literary texts in particular can often provide a far more nuanced understanding of historical events in the locality than official records and documents. Before 1857, poets dominated Delhi's cultural and intellectual landscape and were held in the highest esteem. In the aftermath of the revolt, they could at best defend or decry the cataclysmic events that had unfolded and were often obliged to do so in terms that were cautious and carefully chosen. There was nonetheless a prodigious amount of poetry written in Urdu during and after 1857. The most famous (and controversial) of these commentators was Mirza Asadullah Khan Ghalib, who clear-sightedly perceived the shortcoming of the Mughal rule and regarded the revolt as unjustified. A self-confessed *namak-khwar-e-sarkar-e-angrez* (eater of the salt of the British government, on account of the pension he received), he felt obliged to express his admiration for the British, some of which was undoubtedly sincerely felt, at the same time as he expressed his lament at the cruelty men had inflicted upon each other. Rakshanda Jalil argues, however, that there was no uniformity in the response of the Muslim intelligentsia. Reactions varied from nostalgic lament for a lost age to fixing blame and apportioning responsibility for the terrible misfortunes that had befallen all those who had actively participated in it. Muslims rightly felt that they had been singled out for the terrible retribution that came close on the heels of the British victory, and poets struggled to identify whom they could hold to blame for this terrible outcome. The mutineering soldiers were thus referred to as *mujahid* (martyrs, or those who bear witness) by some and as *balwai* (rioters) by others, and both the *firangi* and the Mughals were held up for criticism and approbation. Above all, the concept of decay is evoked and a muted aspiration is expressed for the recovery of all that had been lost in the destruction of what was once the capital of Mughal art and the centre of patronage for Urdu literature, philosophy and culture.

Expelled by the British following the capture of the city, Delhi's Muslims were only allowed to return in November 1859, some two years later. By then the city had changed beyond recognition. The revolt, Jalil argues, did not merely mark the end of a way of life, it also, in a sense, marked a departure in a way of seeing things. Until then, Urdu prose strove to draw the reader away from the real, often grim, reality and into a magical world of fantasy. After 1857, the rebirth of political consciousness found expression in a far more socially engaged literature. This began a process of modernisation, rehabilitation and recovery, yet it was a process that would take many decades and it is arguably one that is still yet incomplete.

Recovery in the aftermath of the insurrection is also an important facet of Chanda Chatterjee's contribution to this volume, which explores the complicated involvement of the Sikhs in the 1857 insurrection. How was it, she asks, that Sikhs came to be manoeuvred onto the side of the British in suppressing the mutiny in north India? To what extent were their loyalties torn between their paymasters and the victims of British imperialism? And how, in retrospect, was the involvement of the Sikhs to be explained and understood by subsequent generations? She attempts to answer some of these questions by studying a poetic composition *Atha Jang Nama Dilli* (The Story of the War of Delhi) written in 1915 by Khazan Singh, the court poet of Maharaja Bhupinder Singh of Patiala: a hand-written manuscript found by chance in the Moti Bagh Palace Library of Patiala. Chanda Chatterjee provides a close reading of this text to bring out the inner thoughts of the author. Khazan Singh characterises his composition as 'gadar di var' or the poetry of rebellion and tries to explain why the rebellion took place in the ranks of native troops of the British whom he disparagingly describes as 'kaliyan' or blacks. Despite this contempt, he clearly strongly sympathises with their desire to attempt an inversion of the established order in the defence of religion (a cause justified with reference to Hindu mythology), yet he struggles to account for the lack of Sikh support for the uprising and their active connivance with the British. The explanation he offers lies in the intriguing workings of destiny (*honi*), which he illustrates through telling the story of the martyrdom of the Sikh Guru Tegh Bahadur when he visited the court of the Mughal emperor Aurangzeb to request that Brahmins be saved from the emperor's attempts at forcible conversion. Before his death, the guru cursed Aurangzeb and said that the Sikhs will come and despoil his city. It is from this that Khazan Singh derives an explanation for the woeful events that followed in 1857. Poets cannot survive without royal patronage, and Khazan Singh was no exception. His writing was thus necessarily loyalist and eulogist of the role of Maharaja Narinder Singh, the hero of the war of Delhi, which was no doubt the reason the manuscript was preserved. Yet his remorse at the defeat of the kaliyan is obvious, and he feels the need to justify the conduct of the Sikhs by reference to destiny, in the style of a Greek tragedy, and the injustice perpetuated by Aurangzeb. This ambivalence is to be found in the writings of many who survived a war which was anti-colonial, but not nationalist, in which there was not one but many faiths being defended and in which many found reason to respect a foe whom they had until only recently served and whom they would, from necessity, be forced to serve again.

Because of the great diversity of faiths in South Asia, the influence of the Western tradition of post-Enlightenment rationalism (itself a reaction against the undue influence accorded to religious agency) and the determination of most scholars to pursue a secularist agenda in the aftermath of the horrors of Partition, historians have tended to shy away from arguments that situate 'religion' at their centre. This is especially true of 1857. Nonetheless, Kama Maclean argues that it is hard to avoid the importance of religion when discussing the events of 1857 in a major pilgrimage centre such as Allahabad, where the pandas—the Prayagwal Brahmins—joined the civilian uprising after the 6th Native Infantry in the town mutinied against their British officers. The Prayagwals provided religious services to worshippers visiting and bathing at the 'Triveni Sangam', the holy confluence of the Ganges, Jamuna and mythical Saraswati rivers at Allahabad. The arrival of the British in 1901 made a big impact on pilgrimage at the Sangam, not least because their taxes on pilgrims (until 1838) rivalled with the charges being levied by the Prayagwals themselves. According to the demands of protestant missionaries, every attempt was made by the British administration to marginalise the Prayagwals, efforts that were determinedly resisted by various means, including the spreading of rumours concerning the Christianisation efforts of the British. The motivations of the Prayagwals undoubtedly contained a material element. However, Maclean argues that also, their resistance contained a significant devotional element, and it is impossible to separate notions of religion from economy and power, particularly in a society in which religious actors and factors are popularly believed to have agency. To refuse to accept such a position is to ignore an important and potent element of resistance against the British. It was also a position recognised by British contemporaries as General Neill's invading force slaughtered the sepoys, pandits and the citizenry of the city in equal measure and drove the majority of the 1,500 Prayagwal families into exile and a life of beggary.

Marginality as a regional dynamic is explored in the chapter by Veena Naregal, focusing on the case of western India. This was a region in which perfectly ordinary ryots, severely constrained by circumstances, were nonetheless still transformed by the spirit of the times, which allowed them to absorb the language of insurgency, even when they did not actually participate in it. This language she finds echoed in the scattered incidents of activism within rural areas, as well as in the rhetoric of the regions, emerging middle class intelligentsia in the years that followed the insurrection. Examples of local activism are highlighted in Satara and Kolhapur, till only lately under Maratha rule, which became the main sites of mobilisation in Marathi-speaking areas. In Bombay, there were rumours of an imminent uprising on the night of Muharram (30 August) and skirmishes between policemen and soldiers in September. It was said that sepoys had been attending rebel meetings in Bombay for weeks, and a mutiny was only averted when the police broke up one such meeting on 12 October and captured the ring-leaders, who were subsequently publicly executed by being blown from guns before a crowd of hundreds in the Esplanade grounds. Bombay seths were further seriously implicated in money-raising efforts on behalf of Nana Sahib. These and similar instances may have posed little threat to British power, but we should not (as James C. Scott has argued) assume that the absence of armed insurrection meant that there was no resistance or impact at all within localities that were 'marginal' to the great revolt. The mutiny, she argues, and the responses of various social groups within the emerging regional formations to the challenge of 1857 became, in fact, of primary importance to the subsequent distribution of power, both vertically between different social layers and the colonial state and spatially between city and country in subsequent years within each presidency. It would be a mistake therefore to write off any locality as merely 'quiescent'. To understand these effects fully requires a thematic approach and not one merely based upon the adumbration of 'events'.

The multiple meanings of marginality in reality and in colonial discourse are further dissected in Gautam Bhadra's chapter on the insurrection of 1857 in Kolhan in Chotanagpur division. A hilly locality, populated by 'tribes of ignorant and unenlightened savages', it was apparently on the margins of the zone of insurrection but was the locus of exaggerated anxiety for British officials who found it as difficult to 'capture' in a prose of counter-insurgency as they did in terms of men, materials and control on the ground. The meanings of marginality are explored in addition from the perspective of an insurgent chief, the reluctant rebel Arjun Singh, Raja of Porhat, and in terms of the villagers in the interaction with superior local and super-local polities. Marginality here is played out as a product of location and a process of 'othering'. It also, however, denotes a realm within discourse where the boundaries between the spatial and the moral, and between the centre and the margin, are constantly in flux. The centre always assumes the need to exercise control over the margin and in doing so destabilises the very entity it is attempting to grasp. It is this confusion that Bhadra highlights as it is expressed in colonial discourse through the use of metaphors of social Darwinism and disease, which described the 'margins' within Chotanagpur as potentially as great a threat as anything going on in the plains. Such were the motivations of the British. Meanwhile, local Kol chiefs were completely out of sympathy with the mutinous sepoys of the Ramgarh battalion (who had only a few years before helped to crush the rebellion of the Santhals in 1855) and aided in their capture and arrest. However, local politics were paramount, and as British officials began to show favour towards his rivals, Rajah Arjun Singh withdrew his support and subsequently found himself charged with treason upon the evidence of Tal-leaf letters (*Talpatras*), describing the course of the revolt in Delhi. Arjun Singh claimed to have never received or written them, but they perhaps reveal how Arjun Singh (unsuccessfully) sought to serve two masters and thereby preserve the centrality of his authority on the margin. For the ordinary Kols or 'Ho' at Kolhan, details drawn from court cases reveal that common residence and blood relations rather than leadership were the bonds of action in 1857. They were 'brothers', but for the British, used to affixing responsibility on individual leaders, this rendered their attempts at 'pacification' fraught with difficulty. When collective fines were imposed, they had the opposite effect to that intended, appearing to vindicate the violence of which Hos had been accused. The same applied even in village disputes: the local community clearly has its own notion of marginality, which did match that of the imposed judicial regime, by which the so-called delinquents should be judged and punished. What the British desired was a 'civil' order, but its pre-civil behaviour meant that its persona constantly shifted before the searching eyes of the state. Bhadra concludes from these examples that marginality can only be a relational concept, evolving and reconfiguring from time to time. A space may be demarcated as a margin, in need of stabilisation, but the margin has its own expectations that can unexpectedly influence the relationship and course of events. Just as the communities on the margin negotiate the boundaries of marginality within them, so the margin and the centre will tend to stabilise each other through conflict and negotiation. And yet at the end of that negotiation there will still remain a thin line that separates them.

The unpredictable nature of politics within the margins at a time of insurgency is further illustrated in the chapter on the Swat valley in the north-west provinces by Sultan-i-Rome. At one level, the role of Swat was highly significant: not least because it was home to Sayyad Akbar Shah, a follower of the Islamic scholar and revolutionary activist Sayyad Ahmad Shaheed Barelvi, who, in 1849, was made king of Swat as the various factions amongst local Yusufzais united to face the threat posed by the British occupation of the neighbouring Peshawar valley. From his newly established capital of Ghaligay, Sayyad Akbar Shah gave asylum to enemies of the British and constant encouragement and support to neighbouring chiefs and villages. The Pathans were urged to throw off the yoke of British rule, and it is said that Sayyad Akbar Shah was in constant communication with groups who were planning mutiny and rebellion against the British in the months leading up to 1857. However, on 11 May 1857, as the news of the uprising reached the Swat valley, Sayyad Akbar Shah himself died. The events that subsequently unfolded were paradoxical in the extreme. Although there was clearly no lack of local support for the revolt, and mutinous sepoys of the 55th Native Infantry at Nowshera were initially offered refuge, the exigencies of local politics appeared to demand greater priority than the struggle against the British. Although Mir Mubarak Ali Shah, the son of Sayyad Akbar Shah, formally succeeded his father as king, local chiefs, including Akhund of Swat, sought to deny his authority. Within the ensuing power struggle, the mutinous sepoys became a destabilising element. The fact that they were 'high caste Hindoos' and had joined the side of Mubarak Ali Shah caused the Akhund to perceive them as a threat, so he rallied local forces to achieve their expulsion from the Swat valley, along with King Mubarak Ali himself. Thus, unexpectedly, 1857 brought about the collapse of a kingdom that had helped to encourage it, and which had formerly comprised one of the most potent bases of opposition to British rule on the north-west frontier. Tribal rivalry apparently took precedence, but this does not mean that the people of the Swat valley were antithetical to the rebel cause. The events at the 'centre' in the Indo-Gangetic plain were merely perceived through a prism that made them just one factor within the multifaceted politics of the frontier and not the overriding concern they might otherwise have seemed.

The final contribution to this volume by Carol Henderson references Anne Walthall on Pre-Mejii Japanese memorials, Heonik Kwon's investigation of Korean war memorials, and the research of Pierre Nora, Jay Winter and Emmanuel Sivan on European memorialisation in a consideration of memory, landscape and monuments related to ideas of death in north India. A particular example of the memorialisation of 1857 is described in the landscape of memory of the village of Rankhandi, in Saharanpur district in Uttar Pradesh, which found itself at the very heart of the uprising and of subsequent British reprisals. A detailed ethnography of the village undertaken in the 1950s, which included materials on beliefs about death and spirits, is used as part of the background material. Pundir Rajputs are the predominant landowners in the village and Henderson explores the—sometimes conflicting—stories the villagers have to tell about ancestors who experienced the Uprising of 1857 and the legend of a local Muslim saint. This saint, known as the 'Piir', was said to have protected the Rankhandi by appearing in ghostly form, clad in blue and riding on a blue horse, in order to prevent British soldiers from burning down the village. The stories of ancestors are conflicting, since some depict the village as being loyal to the British on account of land grants given to a local zamindar, whilst others faithfully reproduce stories about greased cartridges and forced conversion and insist that the villagers defiantly lent their support to the insurrectionists. One story even told how the villagers attacked a neighbouring village to the east, with the backing of the British. Yet another tells the story of the Piir again intervening to prevent a British cannon that was aimed at the village from going off. Another, in a confused rendering of the events of 1857, tells of ten brothers who take refuge in the village after the Nawab of Awadh was 'killed by the British' following the failure of his attempt to seize the throne in Delhi. As Maurice Halbwachs has argued, human memory can only function within a collective context[10] and collective memory is always selective, Rankhandi is no exception, but Henderson argues that the point is not the veracity or otherwise of the villagers' tales, but what they tell us about social relationships and space within the community and the links that are claimed for Rankhandi to a wider political and geographic universe. Quite clearly the majority of these tales do not relate, in the manner of state-sponsored memorialisation, to a unifying story of the making of the nation state. Nor do they bear any similarity to the imperialist narratives of British monuments that were erected in the aftermath of 1857. Instead, they tell a very intimate tale of the locality, picturing and representing a homeland with links between ancestors, land and kinship that collectively constitute a community.

The chapters in this volume are united in recognition of the fact that although the rhetoric of revolution and imperialism is global, their aims are fulfilled through discrete achievements in the locality. Specific events can sometimes create the opportunities for larger activities and forces to come into play, but that cannot be so easily predicted. History is littered with the casualties of abortive revolutions and tales of great leaders who apparently had no designs on power whatsoever, but were thrown into positions of authority by happenstance. The locality is where the seeds of greater movements in history are sown and where they subsequently wither or flourish, but the purpose of these events and how they are remembered is inevitably the subject of local mediation. This is not to ignore, in Namierite fashion, the importance of ideologies; it is to recognise that ideologies could be multi-vocal and subject to multiple interpretations. This was especially true in 1857 when, with rare exceptions, what Reinhart Koselleck calls the 'horizon of expectation', as well as the spatial and social horizons of the participants on all sides, were comparatively confined and could not so readily cohere into a larger interpretation of the meanings of signs and symbols, of the politics and interpretation of actions leading up the present moment. Instead, people were guided by circumstances within the locality, practical reason and a pragmatic common sense (in the manner described by Obyesekere)[11] in how they responded to actions as they unfolded. This inevitably creates a messier picture than one might wish for, but in recognising this we may be permitted a greater diversity in interpreting what happened in 1857 and its significance for our present and future.

Notes and References

1. Kim A. Wagner, *The Great Fear of 1857: Rumours, Conspiracies and the Making of the Indian Uprising* (Oxford: Peter Lang, 2010).

2. For the online resources resulting from the AHRC 'Mutiny at the Margins' research project, see www.csas.ed.ac.uk/mutiny.

3. John W. Kaye's *History of the Sepoy War in India 1857–58* was published in 1864. Malleson's additional volumes commenced from the second volume of Kaye's History and was first published in 1878. The edited combined work was first published in six volumes in 1888.

4. The 'clash of civilisations' theory was employed (and subsequently discredited by historians) as an explanation for the nineteenth century Opium Wars between Britain and China, and the subsequent fall of Imperial China, long before Samuel P. Huntingdon popularised the idea in *The Clash of Civilizations and the Remaking of World Order* (New York: Simon & Schuster, 1997).

5. William Muir, ed., *Records of the Intelligence Department of the Government of the North-Western Provinces of India during the Mutiny of 1857*, vol. 1 (Edinburgh: T & Clark, 1092), pp. 367–379. See www.csas.ed.ac.uk/mutiny/texts.html (accessed 05 November 2012).

6. See Crispin Bates and Marina Carter, 'Commemorating 1857: A British Dilemma', in *1857: Perception, Narration and Reinvention: The Pedagogy and Historiography of the Indian Uprising*, vol. 6, *Mutiny at the Margins* series (New Delhi: SAGE Publications, Forthcoming).

7. H.P. Chattopadhyaya, *The Sepoy Mutiny, 1857* (Calcutta: Bookland, 1957), p. 202. See also S.B. Chaudhuri, *Civil Rebellion in the Indian Mutinies (1857–59)* (Calcutta: The World Press Ltd, 1957); S.N. Sen, *Eighteen Fifty Seven* (Delhi: GOI Publications Division, 1957) and R.C. Majumdar, *Sepoy Mutiny* (Calcutta: Oriental Press Pvt. Ltd, 1957).

8. Dirk H.A. Kolff, *Naukar, Rajput, and Sepoy: The Ethnohistory of the Military Labour Market of Hindustan, 1450–1850* (Cambridge: Cambridge University Press, 1990).

9. Pramod K. Nayar, *The Trial of Bahadur Shah Zafar* (New Delhi: Orient Longman, 2007).

10. Maurice Halbwachs, *On Collective Memory*, trans. Lewis A. Coser (Chicago: Chicago University Press, 1992).

11. Gananath Obeyesekere, *The Apotheosis of Captain Cook: European Mythmaking in the Pacific*, rev. ed. (Princeton: Princeton University Press, 1997).

BANDITS, BUREAUCRATS AND BAHADUR SHAH ZAFAR
Articulating Sovereignty and Seeing the Modern State Effect in the Margins of Colonial India, c. 1757–1858[*]

Tom Lloyd

Introduction: '1857' Did Not Take Place

IN a common enough historiographical sleight of hand, the chronological signifier '1857' is often used to stand for the totality of 'the events' of the mid-nineteenth century uprisings across northern and central India.[1] In keeping with this reductive metonymy, '1857' acts as a mnemonic black hole, tearing orbiting bodies of historical processes from their contextual moorings, bending them to its own trajectories and smearing them on its singular event horizon.

The historiographical labour of singularising the uprisings of 1857–1859 began at the trial of the last Mughal emperor, Bahadur Shah II, better known by his pen name, Zafar. The trial produced the desired outcome: a verdict of the emperor's guilt and his banishment to Rangoon. Thereafter, Britain's monarch, Queen Victoria, pronounced herself sovereign of India. Semantically, one no longer talked of the Company Raj; rather, one spoke of the Raj. The ramifications of the hugely publicised trial and the simultaneous administrative merry-go-round (coupled with no little intellectual laziness) do much to explain the origins of the historiographical notion that '1857' marked a decisive alteration in India's experience of British colonial rule. In the most simplified reading of this process, the Hanoverian dynasty replaced the Timurid, and a civil administration organised by what started out as a London-based, joint stock trading company was displaced by an alien, state bureaucracy. In London, operations were now

---

[*] I am grateful to Kim A. Wagner and Crispin Bates for their generous assistance in helping me to strengthen the arguments of this chapter.

overseen through a ministerial portfolio, the secretary of state for India, rather than a Board of Control; in the colony, a viceroy presided where previously there had been a succession of governors general. By contrast, this chapter seeks to challenge such a reading of the history of British colonial sovereignty in India.

The first part of the chapter considers the paradoxes of the emperor Zafar's trial. It is argued that the company's claims to legal jurisdiction over Zafar, and the prosecution's particular politicisation of the proceedings, served to further embed British bureaucrats as colonial sovereigns in the Asian subcontinent, rather than constitute them as such for the first time. This re-examination of the argument that the British used Zafar's trial to press hitherto unheard claims to sovereignty in the subcontinent is informed by a slightly wider survey of the landscape of political authority in India from the late eighteenth to the mid-nineteenth century. In pressing claims to sovereignty at the trial of Zafar, it is argued, company administrators and military commissioners were articulating what we may call 'modern' practices of statehood. However, this was not the first occasion on which company employees in India articulated them. Several decades before Zafar's trial, when the notorious campaign to suppress Thuggee (a form of banditry) was prosecuted, the modern colonial state was conceived of, presented and articulated as both a centralised, exclusive and externalised locus of power, and a multifariously embodied actor who would order the socio-economic conditions and civic life of the subcontinent.

An uncritical acceptance of the official, colonial taxonomies of state power has naturalised complacently formulated conceptualisations of modern statehood as a given term of analysis in academic discourse on colonial India. In various incarnations, the imagined entity of the state has been, and continues to be, figured as the agglomeration of bureaucratised institutions allied to governments; as a monopolist of coercive violence; as a bounded, territorial formation (called the 'nation state'), synonymous with large political communities and as an abstracted body, not always acting coherently, dominating the realm of 'politics' or even 'ideology', to facilitate capitalist development.[2]

In the historiography of nineteenth century colonial India, the state, as an entity, finds its way into the discourse on the elaboration of British colonial sovereignty in at least three different arguments. First, that after the mid-nineteenth century uprisings, the administrative structures of the East India Company were straightforwardly replaced by a bureaucratic government that acted upon and intervened in society with more rigor than had hitherto been possible.[3] Second, that after the 1857–1859 uprisings, India was for the first time run by—and as—a modern regime of power, wherein the 'modernity' of the aims of power are measured by their direct coincidence with that supposedly fundamental corollary of 'statehood': the elaboration of a 'national' polity coeval with a fixed geographic territory.[4] Third, using the insights of Michel Foucault, that the abstraction of such a political formation in nineteenth century India heralded the chronological succession of 'governmentalised' strategies for, and technologies of, social control (primarily concerned with the insidious, 'disciplinary' reconstitution of parochial subjectivities) over 'sovereign' forms of rule. In short, that after '1857', the state power was articulated not only by the rough coercion of subjects' bodies, but also by facilitating the conditions for the growth of self-policing minds.[5] Each of these arguments is founded upon the idea of an externalised, institutionalised political entity that stands divorced from the civil society that it more or less successfully orders. In the case of the historiography of the Anti-Thug Campaign, this has meant that the insights into the nature of colonial rule to be yielded from a study of the juridical and bureaucratic practices introduced during the British efforts to suppress Thuggee have persistently escaped critical attention.[6]

The second part of this chapter explores how the Anti-Thug Campaign (ATC) led to the appearance of a particularly modern 'state effect' in early nineteenth century India. A critical advantage of the 'state effect' concept is that it gets beyond the problem of where to locate a material entity called 'the state', imagined as one half of a binary pair (typically, 'civil society', or 'the population') upon which it acts. Instead, we see the dynamic, and therefore changing, ways in which 'the state' is made to appear real. As such, the concept provides the basis for a threefold challenge to the historiographies outlined above. First, that 'sovereignty' refers not to a political system so much as to a type of power. Second, that the articulation of sovereign power is intrinsic to the achievement of a particular kind of state effect that is called modern. Third, that in post-mutiny India, this state effect was neither solely nor straightforwardly a consequence of the political turmoil of the mid-nineteenth century, but may rather be located earlier, in the marginalising practices of teams of colonial officials allied under the company's banner. The year '1857'—the supposedly a decisive moment in the elaboration of colonial claims to sovereignty in India—thus appears as an illusion of historiography.

The Trial of Bahadur Shah II

As rebellion spread across northern and central India over the course of spring and summer 1857, the Mughal Emperor Bahadur Shah II remained trapped in his Delhi palace.[7] For four months, the chosen figurehead for over 100,000 rebelling company sepoys was a hostaged ruler. In September, Emperor Zafar and three of his sons—Mirza Mughal, Khizr Sultan and Abu Bakr (who appear to have directed the rebels with far more vigour than their aged and disinterested father)—fled to the tomb of their ancestor, Emperor Humayun. Several days later, the last Mughals surrendered to the chief of British intelligence, Captain William Hodson. The British summarily executed the three princes. Zafar was spared and a British Military Commission was issued to try him.[8] By making sense of the vagaries surrounding the commission's legal powers, we see how these facilitated both Zafar's conviction and the formulation of an official narrative of the 'mutiny', as well as the production of the subsequent historiographical illusion that a qualitatively different British, colonial sovereignty appeared in India after the mid-nineteenth century uprisings.

On 27 January 1858, the Military Commission assembled in the *Diwan-e-Khas* (Hall of Nobles) of the Red Fort—a spatialised statement of its righteous intent finally to complete the British usurpation of Mughal rule.[9] The commission's primary concern was to establish that Zafar had directed what it called the 'rebellion and mutiny'. There was some evidence for this. The sepoys arriving in May had addressed him thus:

> You are the King of both worlds – terrestrial and spiritual. The whole of India is under your sway and every announcement is preceded by "God is the Master of Creation. Order belongs to the King...". The English have been ruling on your behalf.[10]

The sepoys' formulation of Zafar's relationship to the British accorded to his de jure legal position as the reigning Mughal emperor.[11] It is worth briefly outlining this chronology. In the mid-eighteenth century, at the battles of Plassey (1757) and Buxar (1764) in the eastern subcontinent, the company's armies defeated powerful Mughal tributary rulers (in turn backed by French forces). The Treaty of Allahabad (1765) franchised to the company Emperor Shah Alam II's *diwani* (the administrative rights to collect the taxes and manage the revenues) of the provinces of Bengal, Bihar and Orissa. Lord Clive, leader of the company's armies, now became the first British governor of Bengal. However, an imperial firman (edict), promulgated several days after the signing of the treaty, reaffirmed the emperor's sovereign rights in law. Moreover, despite a major renegotiation of the terms of the treaty in 1803, the legal relationship of the company to the Mughal emperor remained the same in 1858 as it had done since 1765.[12] In law, if not in practice, the company's leading administrators in India were Zafar's tributary vassals.[13]

In 1858, Zafar's most overmighty subjects put their own emperor on trial. Inter alia, his alleged crimes were treason and waging war on the state.[14] Zafar's trial was thus premised on and shot through with contradiction, but it also served as a mouthpiece for British claims to sovereignty in India. By analysing the paradoxes shaping the trial—the legislation, procedures and courtroom rhetoric used by the prosecution—we can see how these political desires speak through the historical record.

On 15 May 1857, the British declared martial law in Meerut—one of the principal centres of the uprisings across northern India.[15] Here, the extant juridical order was directly transferred to military control; elsewhere in company-administered territory, a de facto form of martial law was imposed.[16] Under

Acts XI and XIV military officers were empowered to try any 'persons owing alle-giance to the British Government' in districts proclaimed to be 'in a state of rebellion'. Either a military commission or a court martial could try individuals for a range of offences: generic 'offences against the State'; conspiring, instigating, waging or abetting war or rebellion against 'the Queen or the Government of the East India Company'; exciting 'mutiny and sedition among the Forces of the East India Company'; or 'murder, arson, robbery, or [any] other heinous crime against person or property'. Under Act XI, military commissions could—like courts martial—take place *in camera*. Law officers need not attend. The tribunal's verdict could not be appealed. At Zafar's trial, all three provisions were in force. As such, the five officers who comprised the Military Commission that tried Zafar were temporarily accorded wide-ranging discretionary, summary powers. In the name of the defence of 'the state', these powers abrogated to company officers a form of extra-judicial sovereignty far exceeding the remit of administrators who, in strict legal terms, were subcontracted servants of the Mughal emperor.[17]

Furthermore, the Military Commission vastly overreached the juridical remit specified for such a body by Acts XI and XIV. The prosecuting team was authorised to conduct a criminal trial, not a fact-finding enquiry. Yet, in opening the case against Zafar, the British prosecutor, Advocate-General Major F.J. Harriott, announced that the hearing would unavoidably and deliberately combine both agendas. 'It is deemed that all the circumstances connected with the late rebellion', Harriott argued, 'even though not in direct relation to the indictment [of Zafar], may be here appropriately recorded'.[18]

As Pramod Nayar has shown, during the emperor's trial, Zafar's participation in the uprisings was subsumed into a broader narrative that claimed to have produced an indisputable, rationalised and totalised account of the 'mutiny'. Appealing to stereotypes of timeless Islamic fanaticism, Zafar was located as the mastermind behind a 'Mahommedan conspiracy'. For Harriott, the magnitude of the 'conspiracy' established by the prosecution's account was beyond mortal comprehension: it would not be fully grasped until it had been judged by God— in the fullness of 'time' and 'history'. The prosecution's account, therefore, facilitated Zafar's subsequent conviction in several ways: it appeared to confirm that the British had faced a concerted military insurrection, planned in advance, with the emperor's knowledge; it implicated him in a genocidal plot to eradicate European influence in India and replace the company's franchised government with an Islamic theocracy centred on Delhi; it served to reinforce the claim that it was Zafar who had rebelled.[19]

The commission's insistence upon Zafar's subordinate status was emphasised by repeated references to him as the 'titular majesty' or 'ex-King' of Delhi—a 'possessor of mere nominal royalty'.[20] These euphemisms show how the commission tried to affirm company sovereignty over the emperor. They circumscribed his legal position as the Mughal emperor, reducing it to that of a king—a ruler understood to possess a much smaller territorial jurisdiction and a qualitatively different relationship to the company. Hence, Zafar was described as 'the pensioned subject of the British Government', analogous to the scores of nominally independent princes who, by the mid-nineteenth century, were tied to its administration through treaties of subsidiary alliance. Second, the temporality of the prefixes suggested that Zafar no longer commanded even this vastly restricted territorial authority: this 'possessor of mere nominal royalty' had 'no power beyond the precincts of his own palace', according to Harriott (contradicting the notion that Zafar had directed the uprisings). Third, the retention of generic titles enabled the prosecution to position Zafar as both a recalcitrant petty-sovereign and a prisoner not liable to the same legal process as a 'commoner': he would be the treasonous leader of a vast rebellion but still would be accorded the more 'humane' treatment reserved for nobles and officers.[21] Thus, the language of the courtroom was that of righteous suppression of dissent from company rule; its political corollary was its articulators' claim to sovereignty over their posited subordinate: Zafar.

When the commissioners unanimously decided that Zafar was guilty on 9 March 1858, it would seem that they terminated the only other feasible, alternative imperial, political formation in the subcontinent to the British government. Dismantling Zafar's character seemed like the symbolic removal of the final insignia of the crumbling edifice of Mughal power; it seemed to clear the ground for the emergence of a new level of colonial authority in India. The following section of the chapter argues that a sharper understanding of sovereignty insists that this argument be questioned.

Zafar: *Homo Sacer*?

Nayar argues that the legal marginalisation of Zafar (as a subject lacking legal rights) and the commission's paradoxical identification of him as the leader of the 'mutiny and rebellion' enabled it to claim sovereignty over the emperor. Nayar's understanding of sovereignty is specific and derives from Giorgio Agamben's elucidation of the thought of the German jurist Carl Schmitt. Following Schmitt, Agamben suggests that 'sovereign' is the figure of power that can determine who may be included in society (and therefore its juridical order) by means of exclusion from it; in short, that 'sovereign' is the power which may declare a state of exception. For Nayar, Zafar's trial amounted to the creation of just such a state of exception, in which the emperor became a *homo sacer*—'he who may be killed but not sacrificed'—to use the term made famous by Agamben's recent study of political sovereignty.[22] For Nayar, the exceptionalism of the British Military Commission reduced Zafar to a killable body—one who lives or dies solely at the discretion of sovereign authority.

Nayar's exegesis of the proceedings of Zafar's trial is brilliantly alive to the contradictions and politics of the prosecution's rhetoric and the technical paradoxes of the commission's legal claim over the emperor. He uses Harriott's argument that profane law was not capable of overseeing Zafar's judgement as evidence for his argument that the trial located the emperor as a *homo sacer*. 'There is a yet higher law [than the law of the land]', Harriott suggested, 'which must acquit or condemn him [Zafar]':

> ... the law of conscience and of sense; that law ... which carries with it a verdict more terrible than that which is pronounced in mere conformity to legal codes or military legislation: it is a law that does not depend upon local constitutions, upon human institutes, or religious creeds: it is a law fixed in the heart of man by his Maker: and can it now here be set aside?[23]

According to Nayar, this trapped Zafar in a double bind: abandoned by profane law, he would nevertheless stand trial at the Military Commission's worldly court, pending divine arbitration. Simultaneously, the British prosecutor, Harriott, claimed godlike powers for himself—as the sovereign capable of deciding that human law was inadequate to judge crimes of the enormities perpetrated by Zafar and that an exception must be made.

The argument that the emperor was figured as a *homo sacer* may be seductive, but it is mistaken to argue that Zafar was tried as a subject with no political status and afforded no legal protections. Harriott's invocations of divine law and apocalyptic judgement were certainly hedonistic, but also fairly common in British legal practice at the time; in effect, the leader of the prosecution was asking the commissioners to use their conscience rather than prescriptive law to judge Zafar. Zafar's crimes against 'the state' were posited as extraordinary because they exposed the law's inability to foresee all transgressions of constituent authority.

Moreover, Harriott was conscious of the extent to which such a controversial trial would reverberate around the British Empire and, in particular, of how metropolitan audiences might scrutinise the proceedings.[24] Given their convictions about the causes, nature and intent of the uprisings, the company's administrators did not wish to martyr the figurehead of what they read as a widespread military mutiny and a 'Mahommedan conspiracy'. Furthermore, there was political capital to be gained in India and Britain from an apparent demonstration of clemency towards a noble, and of upholding the military's end of the bargain agreed at Zafar's surrender to Hodson. The decision to spare the emperor may have been arrived at by an extra-legal judicial body, but it was not made because Zafar's life had been stripped of political legitimacy and fully inscribed with that of the power abrogating sovereign authority over him (as is the case for *homo sacer*—and it is this 'stripping' that makes his life 'bare', as Agamben puts it). In fact, it was made precisely in recognition of the political power that Zafar was still believed to possess, as 'the rallying point not only to Mahomedans, but to thousands of others', supposedly 'looked upon by Mohamedan fanaticism as the head and culminating star of its faith'.[25]

Undoubtedly, many aspects of Zafar's trial were remarkable: the brash displacement of the Mughal emperor's ceremonial space and especially his technical relationship to the company in law; the ritualised use of certain tropes of legality (indeed, illegality) deployed by the Military Commission; the calculated grandstanding of the prosecutor. In wider terms, Zafar's excision from the Indian political scene may be, and has been, used to mark a departure in the subcontinent's social, economic, cultural and political history. Certainly, through the reorganisation of the army and civil-service bureaucracies that followed the uprisings' suppression, colonial political economy in India became more rigorously extractive than hitherto, and the British government both seized the vacated ground and cleared new political terrain for social control throughout the subcontinent from the late 1850s.[26]

It would be inaccurate to claim, however, that because it ended Zafar's reign in Delhi, the emperor's trial occasioned the marginalisation of Mughal power in India. Arguably, that process had already been unfolding for one hundred years. Had this not been the case, the trial could not have taken place, and Zafar could not have been successfully figured as the head of a 'mutiny and rebellion' and a 'Mahommedan conspiracy'. Two interconnected and, more significantly, inaccurate conclusions must also be avoided. First, that the extraordinary trial of Zafar—arising out of the turmoil of the mid-century uprisings—was the decisive episode in the establishment of British sovereign power in India. Second, that it heralded the realisation of 'the modern colonial state' in the subcontinent. Such conclusions rely on the application of particular premises about both sovereignty—as a type or level of coercive power associated with a particular set of economic relations—and the modern colonial state—as an epochal and material political entity (indeed, one that is seen to typically succeed the more charismatic rule conventionally associated with sovereign figures).

The second part of this chapter argues that care must be taken over the meaning of 'sovereignty' if historians are to provide informed and nuanced readings of India's nineteenth century colonial experiences. Through an analysis of the British-led campaign to suppress Thuggee—a type of banditry in which travellers were typically waylaid, duped, drugged, strangled and robbed—it is suggested that the effect of a modern colonial state, articulating itself through practices based upon claims to a particular type of sovereignty, is discernable several decades before the mid-nineteenth century uprisings and the trial of the last Mughal.

Practising Modernity: The ATC in the Non-regulation Territories, circa 1829–1841[27]

Timothy Mitchell contends that just as 'the state' names not so much an entity as the effect of a series of practices, 'modernity' similarly names not so much an epoch as a result of practices that reduce life's fluid subtleties into a dualistic worldview. The capacity to make an internally drawn line appear as a fixed, external level of reality is, for Mitchell, the decisively modern characteristic of the state effect, occurring for identifiable historical reasons. Nevertheless, the admittedly elusive phenomenon of the state, and the powerful, if uncertain, distinction between it and the society is popularly believed in, widely disseminated, repetitively inscribed and readily acted upon. In this sense, the effect is empirically real: individuals behave as if the state might come to know their business, compel them to be obedient or law-abiding or shape their financial futures. The challenge is to identify the historical reasons for this effect. I now consider a range of practices adopted by the company's administration during the 1830s to suppress a form of banditry called Thuggee. I argue that the elaborations of sovereignty manifested during the ATC articulated the appearance of a peculiarly modern state effect in British India.[28]

On 23 October 1829, George Swinton, chief secretary to the company's new, recently arrived governor general in India, Lord Bentinck, wrote to the British Resident at the Court of Indore to advise on the prosecution of a gang of seventy-four bandits arrested in the Malwa region of western India. The gang had been betrayed by six of their members, who described their numerous, fatal attacks on travellers throughout western–central India to their captor, one Captain Borthwick. 'These murders having been perpetrated in territories belonging to various Native Chiefs', wrote Swinton,

> ... and the perpetrators being inhabitants of various Districts belonging to different authorities, there is no Chief, in particular, to whom we could deliver them up for punishment, as their Sovereign or as the Prince of the Territory in which the crime had been committed.... The hand of these inhuman monsters being against every one and there being no country within the range of their annual excursions, from Bundelcund [Bundelkhand] to Guzeraut [Gujarat], in which they have not committed murder ... they may be considered like Pirates, to be placed without the pale of social law, and be subjected to condign punishment by whatever authority they may be seized and convicted.[29]

For Swinton, these bandit gangs had transgressed the operative political boundaries—significantly redrawn in north-western and central India following the Anglo-Maratha wars of circa 1802–1818—in two ways. First, their alleged crimes were committed beyond the confines of their native districts, in jurisdictions falling under the rule of several different political authorities. Second, the enormity of the attacks was such that the perpetrators entered a zone of judicial indeterminacy, in the sense that conventional measures could not apply to them: these 'inhuman monsters ... against every one' ought therefore to be 'placed without the pale of social law'. We can see that the world imagined by

Swinton was divided into separate administrative and legal jurisdictions. Thus, districts are said to belong 'to different authorities', with those falling under company administrative jurisdiction and police jurisdiction contrasted to those governed by native rulers (either independently or in alliance with some larger polity). Meanwhile, Swinton alludes to a space beyond the 'social', juridical order—a space in which those (like pirates) transgressing any single sovereign jurisdiction were dealt with. In both cases, the effect is to articulate local practices—the government of a relatively small region of territory in which there were competing and overlapping claims to legal and political authority—into a larger system seemingly external to it. Ultimately, the accused answered to the latter formation. On receipt of Swinton's letter, company officials summarily executed forty leaders of the gang arrested by Borthwick.[30]

The principles laid down in Swinton's letter of late 1829 were immediately adopted by Francis Curven Smith, agent to the governor general in the Sagar and Narmada Territories, adjoining Malwa, who now initiated the trials of seventy-two bandits who had been detained at Sagar jail for the previous seven years. Twenty-six of them were hanged.[31] On the strength of the evidence produced during the interrogations of these suspects, and following a well-timed, anonymously written letter to the *Calcutta Literary Gazette*, Smith's principal assistant, Captain William Sleeman, was given special responsibility to exterminate all Thugs in October 1830.[32] The Anti-Thug Campaign had begun.

More properly, the second Anti-Thug Campaign had begun, colonial investigations into Thuggee having begun in the Ceded and Conquered Provinces some twenty years earlier.[33] The Thuggee phenomenon had to be reinvented before a suppression campaign was launched on the terms advocated from 1830. What drove the ATC in the early 1830s was the expert knowledge about the phenomenon claimed by Smith and, in particular, Sleeman. Sleeman's letter to the *Calcutta Literary Gazette* of October 1830 drew together moralising, scare-mongering and historical analysis with unshakeable conviction:

> ... this pest [Thuggee] is spreading throughout our dominions and becoming in my opinion an evil of greater magnitude than that of the Pindaree system. It is an organised system of religious and civil polity, [prepared] to receive converts from all religions and sects, and to urge them to the murder of their fellow creatures under the assurances of high rewards in this world and the next....[34]

Sleeman's sharp focus on the religious dimensions of Thuggee in this and other writings on the subject seem to have been decisive in gaining the requisite administrative support for (or at least non-interference in) his operations against suspected Thugs. Most obviously, it was the fountainhead for claims that Thuggee was a centuries-old, organised conspiracy operating throughout the subcontinent; that adherents believed that they were sacrificing travellers to the goddess Kali; and that they, therefore, neither felt remorse for their killings, nor hesitated to seek other recruits to their murderous subculture, replete with its peculiar rites and omens. Expertise produced the colonial fear that Thuggee was a pan-subcontinental phenomenon challenging British claims to police 'society'. Indeed, this was the significant difference to the colonial perception of Thuggee in the 1830s compared to that of the 1810s, when—as Kim A. Wagner has ably shown—it was thought of as no more than one among several types of loosely concerted rural banditry.[35]

Throughout the early 1830s, Sleeman augmented his subjective claims to personal expertise on Thuggee with seemingly less contestable evidence to prove his theories. Using information from cross-examinations and so-called conversations with Thuggee suspects, Sleeman set about constructing sprawling genealogies depicting the ancestry of the alleged system. Although he was unable to trace lineages back further than a few generations, and even then in an unconvincing and inconclusive manner, these diagrams seemed to further corroborate the suggestion that Thuggee was a generational or 'caste-like' 'trade' passed on from father to son.[36] In due course, using readings from the skulls of seven individuals executed at Jabalpur, metropolitan phrenologists confirmed that Thugs were biologically predetermined criminals.[37] Similarly, Sleeman's decoding of *ramasee* (his name for the Thugs' alleged argot) was offered as evidence suggesting that they shared a unique subculture that could be objectively recorded. Sleeman was convinced that his investigations had unravelled a grand conspiracy: 'I am satisfied that there is no term, no rite, no ceremony, no opinion, no omen or usage that they [Thugs] have intentionally concealed from me', he announced in the introduction to *Ramaseeana* (1836).[38]

Taken as a whole, the investigations headed by Sleeman produced a textualised body of knowledge that claimed to have totally demystified the arcana of what could now be represented as a discrete practice called Thuggee. As Martine van Woerkens has argued, colonial knowledge about Thuggee seemed scientific: the data appeared to be empirical, the experiments repeatable, the conclusions objective. Both its makers and its audience believed that the corpus of colonial knowledge about Thuggee was not corrupted by political affiliation, not deluded by religious persuasion and not limited by cultural parochialism. Colonial expertise on the phenomenon appeared as an inert, impersonal accumulation of truths.[39] Indeed, *Ramaseeana* was quite consciously presented as just such an exhibition of colonial knowledge: a dictionary of *Ramasee*, an introduction to 'Thuggee', self-consciously written to inform metropolitan audiences about the phenomenon, and a work of reference to be consulted by Sleeman's 'Thug-hunting detachments' as they went about their daily business of searching the rural highways for suspects.[40]

The overwhelming majority of Sleeman's expertise on Thuggee was derived from suspected Thugs who, in the legal parlance of the time, turned approver and offered information on former associates in return for a reduced sentence.

According to the Anglo-Indian administrator Philip Meadows Taylor, 56 of the 3,437 individuals charged for Thuggee between 1826 and 1841 were pardoned and 'made approvers after committed', thereby agreeing to cooperate with British and Indian officials working with and under Sleeman in various ways.[41] Indeed, the first executions of suspected Thugs held under company auspices had been sanctioned on the basis of approvers' evidence. In July 1829, Captain Borthwick explained why he had offered reduced sentences to certain members of the party he had arrested:

> [The suspect's] Deposition … was perhaps alone sufficient to establish the guilt of the prisoners, but as *it was desirable to obtain all the information possible of the acts and proceedings of this band of systematic murderers, that the Government might be the better able to adopt effectual measures for their eventual extirpation*, I held out the promise of a pardon to other individuals of the gang to come forward, on which five of the prisoners, whose Depositions are enclosed, presented themselves as evidence against their associates. [My emphasis.][42]

The ATC was clearly initiated as both a law-and-order challenge and a knowledge-gathering project. To uncover more fully the construction of (what became) the Thuggee Department's (TD's) expert knowledge on the phenomenon, I now examine how it handled the information received from captured suspects-turned-approvers.

Approvers' statements were recorded using a set formula, transcribed in Persian and subsequently translated into English.[43] Depositions began with a statement of the name, age and caste of the person suspected of being a Thug, where they were born and where they were based up to the time of arrest. Thugs then recalled the expeditions they had participated in that featured persons identified to their captors.[44] Testimonies were not rambling recollections of the past, but structured accounts of isolated, specific events and the consequences of them: those details that the prosecution wished to hear. By their sequential relation of separate attacks, which may have occurred years apart, into a temporally continuous 'career of crime', in which the only thing they did is murder and rob people, the depositions gave an artificial coherence to the actions of those accused of Thuggee.[45]

Approvers' depositions were a condensed record of several years of an accused Thug's life, in which details about the precise identities of the victims, the politics of the interactions between different gangs encountered on an expedition or the material and social circumstances of those involved in Thuggee were allowed to fade into the background. By contrast, the foreground of the approvers' testimonies was brilliantly illuminated by empirical facts about each attack: the number of victims killed, the names of the murderers, the amount of loot taken and (roughly) where and when the attack took place. Meanwhile, additional details that may have supplied alternative contexts to an individuals' implication in 'criminality' to that advanced by the bearers of sovereign power—that certain subjects of the colonial polity were inherently, ancestrally and devotionally socialised to a life of crime—were omitted, or even suppressed. The intentions and circumstances that led to a particular suspects' personal 'career of crime' were given no further explanation than the acknowledgement that the suspect was a Thug.

The persistence of the template for recording depositions—physically, a series of forms and tables—as the formalised means of producing 'consistent' (or repetitive) statements meant that the colonial legal archive only retained those details that reinforced the dominant understanding of Thuggee put about from the late 1820s. Thuggee thus appeared as a full-time, hereditary profession and a corporate criminal identity from which there was no escape and for which so-called everyday professions were merely a screen.[46] The accumulation of hundreds of similar statements, taken from different suspects across the subcontinent, throughout the 1830s, served further to authenticate the colonial understanding of Thuggee as a coherent, widespread subculture.[47] In combination, the editing and narrativising of approver testimonies facilitated further arrests by establishing 'Thuggee' as a decontextualised trope of disobedience. If Thuggee was intelligible and condemnable as a practice, the need to establish individual motivations and culpability for specific attacks was obviated.

In the mid-1830s, the company gave institutional and legal formality to the epistemological figuring of 'Thugs' as inherently criminal. By 1836, the year the Anti-Thug Campaign was set on a statutory and institutional footing, well over half of the total Thuggee trials held under British auspices circa 1826–1841 had been completed, and 160 people had been imprisoned, 1,144 transported and 384 executed as convicted Thugs. Of those tried, the conviction rate was 98.9 per cent.[48] The rapid accumulation of guilty verdicts convinced senior company administrators of the significance of Sleeman's and Smith's work. As Radhika Singha points out, the TD was formally convened as an autonomous policing agency in 1835, and its expenses recognised as a '[g]eneral charge being incurred for the welfare of the whole of India'.[49] Sleeman was appointed to the new post of general superintendent of the ATC and his assistants now expanded operations into the Deccan, the Doab, Rajputana, Malwa and Delhi.[50]

The administrative formalisation of Sleeman's growing policing agency was complemented by new legislation. The first paragraph of Act XXX of 1836 read as follows:

… whoever shall be proved to have belonged, either before or after the passing of this Act, to any gang of Thugs, either within or without the Territories of the East India Company, shall be punished with imprisonment for life, with hard labour.[51]

The company's courts were now sanctioned to punish anyone proven to be currently, or at any time previously, associated with 'any gang of Thugs', captured 'within or without' British territory. To resolve the ambiguity of using confessions from guilty Thugs as evidence in the trials of their former associates, Act XIX was passed in 1837, allowing for the use of approvers as star witnesses:

> … no person shall, by reason of any conviction for any offence whatever, be incompetent to be a witness in any stage of any cause, Civil or Criminal, before any Court, in the Territories of the East India Company.[52]

As shown, the architects of the ATC had adopted a range of ad hoc measures in order to generate confessions and convictions. These results—and Sleeman's eye for self-promotion—appear to have been intrinsic in bringing about the administrative support that their predecessors had lacked twenty years earlier. After thousands of arrests, hundreds of confessions and scores of executions, the principles formulated in Swinton's letter of 1829 now stood codified in law.[53]

Practising Modernity: the Anti-Thug Campaign as a 'State of Exception'

As with the subsequent legislation used to prosecute emperor Zafar, the anti-Thuggee laws created a Schmittian 'state of exception'—a form of sovereignty defined by the ability to decide whether or not 'the law' applies to certain individuals. Neither 'Thug' nor 'Thuggee' was defined in the laws passed in 1836 and 1837; the designation of who was a Thug, or what counted as Thuggee, was legally codified as a question of executive discretion. As experts, bureaucrats, policemen, magistrates and even judges, the relevant TD officials were thus empowered to make a cut in 'society'; indeed, to separate the 'extraordinary' criminal from the ordinary. For Agamben, such a cut marks the metaphysical threshold between the political life of the human and the bare life (or mere existence) of *homo sacer*; indeed, the originary structure of politics is, in his view, nothing more or less than a sovereign decision to divide the exceptional from the normal. That said, an analysis of the ATC may also be used to challenge Agamben's normative argument that sovereign dividing practices are ahistorical ('originary', to use his phrase).[54] On the contrary, the ATC shows them to be powerful because they are modern phenomena. An initial clue to this is the ATC's leading architects' biopolitical conceptualisation of Thuggee, which bifurcated the subcontinent's inhabitants into 'inhuman monsters' and everyone else, and spoke of a campaign of 'extermination' that would restore health to the 'Indian' body politic.[55] Indeed, the sovereign exceptionalism elaborated during the ATC was mutually constituting of practices that both tended towards the appearance of a state effect and, simultaneously, its essentially modern referent: the population.

J.R. Lumley's harassment of yogis provides an instructive example of the way in which the vagueness of the anti-Thuggee legislation provided sustenance to the ATC and, by extension, to colonial claims to sovereign authority in the Agambenian sense. In December 1837, Lumley, one of Sleeman's deputies in the TD, wrote to the magistrate at Ahmednuggur to inform him that he had 'the very strongest ground of suspicion for believing all the twelve tribes of Jogees to be in truth Thugs but ostensibly Beggars and Peddlars who traffic in small wares'.[56] 'The Headquarters of the Jogees is [a temple] at Sonaree', he continued, where there are 'some fifteen or twenty Gooroos and three or four Muctiyar Jogee families I wish to seize'. Lumley subsequently arrested '50 or 60' yogis, 'among whom more than a dozen confessed or recorded Thuggee against their accomplices'. Despite admitting that he did not think the 'Gooroos' had 'any connection with Thuggee', he went on to say that he had interned 'a few of them' to try to improve knowledge of 'arcana Jogeeana'.[57] Lumley's ascription of criminality to religious mendicants attests to the reach and robustness of the discretional power at the TD's disposal by the late 1830s. Relocated outside the colonial juridical order as a certain variety of Thug, these individuals were now trapped in a relationship to those attempting to prosecute them, an ontological position fully loaded by the politics of their criminalisation.[58]

Despite Lumley's reservations about the applicability of the noun 'Thuggee' to the activities that he had encountered at Sonaree, Sleeman soon informed his superiors that the TD had 'always had reason to believe that a great part of the Byragees, Gosains and other religious mendicants that infest all parts of India were assassins by profession'.[59] A year later, he argued:

> There is one great evil which afflicts and has afflicted the country, and which no government but a very strong one could attempt to eradicate. This is a mass [around two million people, by Sleeman's estimate] of religious mendicants who infest every part of India, and subsist upon the fruits of all manner of crime.... [They] rob and steal, and a very great portion of them murder their victims before they rob them ... [using] dutoora [*Datura alba*, also spelled 'dathura' in colonial accounts], or some other deleterious drug.[60]

Yogis were now re-figured into a representative portion of a wider section of indigenous society; a portion defined, by Sleeman, by its criminality. 'There are not anywhere worse characters than these Jogies, or greater pests to society', he concluded, 'save the regular Thugs'.[61]

However, Sleeman's suggestion that there were 'regular Thugs' was strikingly at odds with the diversity of people arrested on suspicion of Thuggee throughout the ATC. A striking feature of the approvers' testimonies and their so-called conversations with company officials is the mass of heterogeneous information they contain about their experiences of life on India's roads in the early nineteenth century. More importantly to my argument, it was precisely the lack of 'regular Thugs' that proved a vital source of legitimisation for the ATC's continually expanding sovereign reach. The difficulty of rationalising and categorising Thuggee in the first place—which company officials perceived as a signifier of its extraordinary qualities—had necessitated that it be considered exceptional and, later, underwritten the legislation to interrogate and condemn suspects at the discretion of TD officers.

The consistent justification given for the experimental and, as of 1836, codified extra-legal powers accorded to Sleeman's policing agency was that, for various reasons, Thugs lay outwith or beyond the bounds of humanity itself, as defined by the colonial administration. '[A]bhorrent to human nature, they are the sworn and irreconcilable enemies of mankind', Smith wrote in November 1830, adding, 'they deserve no mercy; mercy to such wretches would be cruelty to mankind'.[62] The parochial use of the term 'mankind'—paradoxically invoked here as a universal signifier, to provide the fundamental justification for the suppression of Thuggee (in that this would protect 'mankind')—shows how, by figuring the Thug as an 'inhuman wretch', the colonial administration elaborated a claim for sovereign power over the lives of all Indians. By locating Thugs as beyond humanity, the TD, of course, simultaneously advanced a definition of what constituted a human. Thugs were the exception that proved the rule, and indeed served to authenticate the sovereign power of the TD, to the degree that institutionalised colonial policing and administrative practices could enforce definitions of Thuggee and humanity.

Following Sleeman's announcement that the organised system of Thuggee had been defeated in 1839, neither the legislation enacted, nor the policing agency especially convened to counteract the perceived threat, was withdrawn. In fact, the sovereign power that vitalised the ATC was extended to a larger proportion of road-users. Invested with discretional powers providing for the definition of suspects, as well as their arrest and detention, TD officers defined several new categories of Thug in the late 1830s. Anti-Thuggee legislation was now deployed against various itinerant groups, such as child-traffickers ('Megapunniastic Thugs'), gamblers ('Tushma-Baz Thugs') and wandering mendicants (classified, variously, as 'Dathura Poisoners', *Tin Naimi*, *Gosain*, *Bairagi*, *Jogi*, *Kan Phuttie*, *Thorie* and *Panda* Brahmin Thugs).[63] During the 1840s, the anti-Thuggee laws of the 1830s were widened, further empowering the police agency to pursue ill-specified groups of alleged criminals. Act XI of 1848 laid down that:

> Whosoever shall be proved to have belonged, either before or after the passing of this Act, to any gang of wandering persons, associated for the purposes of theft or robbery, not being a gang of Thugs or Dacoits, shall be punished with imprisonment, with hard labour, for any term not exceeding seven years.[64]

With this legislation, the colonial administration gave judicial force to the topos of the road as a place of disorder, where 'wandering persons' could escape surveillance, harass travellers, practise unregulated commerce and—worst of all—develop what were perceived to be wild and savage cults, inimical to the envisioned society of 'civilised', taxable cultivators.[65] Indeed, this is unsurprising: it was crucial for the colonial administration not to fully rationalise Thuggee— this would have conceded a modicum of empathy, of identification with what its politics had declared to be 'monstrous', 'wretched' and 'inhuman'. The ATC could never be about erasing Thuggee, so much as policing it, subordinating it; construing an element of 'society' as 'inhuman' and sustaining that construction, or reconstructing it elsewhere. Sovereign power provided the means by which British officials were able to do this: to inscribe and re-inscribe their politics upon the depersonalised bodies of accused Thugs, a fair proportion of whom were ultimately rendered killable.

Conclusions

In general terms, the language and operation of codified, institutionalised and bureaucratised legal practices offer a clear expression of the techniques that produce the effect of the state as a static, external entity. To continue to operate within a legal system based on codified statutes, extant social practices must be radically reimagined; statutory law fixes them in time, removes them from context and objectifies them. Punishments are likewise 'regularised', as is the trial process. In early colonial India, what were previously provisional, negotiable, personal transactions of political authority—which some colonial writers had earlier referred to as the 'arbitrary' nature of the Mughal or 'Oriental despotism'[66]—were now presented as being 'properly' regulated, in an attempt to produce guaranteed, impersonal verdicts attended by predefined and certain punishments. The self-conscious 'bringing' of law to the *mofussil*—the establishment of local magisterial jurisdictions, the regular holding of court-of-circuit sessions and their connectedness to a remote and bureaucratically superior judicial hierarchy—was a highly visible process by which company officials sought to implement abstracted legal power in the Indian countryside during the early nineteenth century. This implementation of 'the law' was consonant with the articulation of localised domains of social control into larger networks of political authority; it achieved the effect of locating company rule as both within and without the prosaic rhythms of daily life.

What is commonly referred to as 'the modern colonial state' was the effect of multifarious appeals to externalised, delocalised, anonymous forms of social control as a new governing rationality. The ATC is a rich example of how certain practices—the imaginative and cartographic construction of political boundaries as frontiers, the delineation of a corpus of expert, scientific knowledge, the bureaucratisation of police recording techniques and the codification of personalised forms of discretionary authority into legal procedure—served to create such an effect in early-nineteenth century India.

Although the company's pursuit of various Thug groups brimmed with assurances of 'due process', the authority of the anti-Thuggee laws came from beyond written rules. It rested instead with officials who believed themselves to be the appropriate arbiters of what was 'criminal' about certain Indian travellers. A generation after the Anti-Thug Campaign was initiated, the last Mughal emperor, Bahadur Shah II, was likewise positioned as criminal by British authorities claiming for themselves the extra-legal right to make a sovereign decision about whom to except from the law. As it happened, Zafar was protected. Although the Military Commission that tried Zafar occupied an exceptional legal space—in its lawful relationship to the very individual it tried for treason, and because it claimed summary powers of sentencing that were not open to challenge—its verdict of the Mughal emperor's guilt brought victory over a recognised political opponent. By contrast, 'Thug' named the inversion of the political community that must come to comprise 'India' in the eyes of the experts who defined it in the 1830s. Thugs were not to be protected, but placed 'beyond the pale of social law'. The 'extermination' of Thuggee was conceived of as a victory over a biopolitical threat to that portion of Indian society under the company's rule.

The novel entity of 'the population' was imagined by the company officials who went on to constitute the TD as the legitimation and binary opposite of another entity: 'the state'—as an abstracted, exclusive, centralised and unitary locus of authority. The institutionalised sovereign decisions adopted by these bureaucrats during the ATC—contingent upon their oscillating, unequal transactions with approvers—cut internal lines into extant social practices that produced the distinctive illusion of an external reality shaping political authority over the Indian life.

As such, sovereignty appears to be neither an epochal, charismatic form of rule, nor a timeless metaphysical arrangement of relations, but a contingently vitalised type of power elaborated in specifically modern contexts. These contexts are amenable to historical explication. In early-nineteenth century India, a set of particular sovereign powers articulated practices that were midwife to the birth of the effects of a modern state. These practices were modern to the extent that they were biopolitical: they served to define, delineate and divide the orderly and the monstrous, the normal and the exceptional. The practices that sustained the ATC—that brought both convictions and knowledge—not only marginalised what was presented as a certain portion of that entity comprising 'the population' as irredeemably criminal, but also made the Thugs' marginality the highly visible business of 'the state', delegating its sovereign political authority to the staff of the TD: a policing agency acting on its behalf as interrogator, examiner and enforcer. Real enough to both the company officials whose careers were made on the back of the ATC, and to more than 450 suspected stranglers themselves strangled on the company's gallows as convicted Thugs between 1829 and 1841, the state effect was precisely what enabled its inventors to sustain the marginalised as marginal. We should not mistake the effects of such a sovereign 'state' formation becoming visible only after 1857 and the last Mughal's paradoxical treason trial.

Notes and References

1. The outstanding episodes in the uprisings occurred between 29 March 1857 (when Mangal Pandey—a sepoy—fired the first, errant shot at his commanding officer in Barrackpore) and 7 April 1859 (when Tantya Tope, the last of the rebel leaders, was captured): Crispin Bates, *Subalterns and Raj: South Asia since 1600* (London: Routledge, 2007), ch. 4, esp. pp. 65–75.

2. See Timothy Mitchell, 'Society, Economy, and the State Effect', in Aradhana Sharma and Akhil Gupta, eds, *The Anthropology of the State: A Reader* (Oxford: Blackwell, 2006), esp. pp. 169–174.

3. See, for example, Sugata Bose and Ayesha Jalal, *Modern South Asia: History, Culture, and Political Economy* (New Delhi: Oxford India Paperbacks, [1998] 2005), chs 7–10.

4. See, for example, Partha Chatterjee, *The Nation and Its Fragments: Colonial and Postcolonial Histories* (Princeton, N.J.: Princeton University Press, 1993), esp. ch. 2.

5. See, for example, David Arnold, 'The Colonial Prison: Power, Knowledge, and Penology in Nineteenth-century India', in Ranajit Guha, ed., *A Subaltern Studies Reader, 1986–1995* (London: University of Minnesota Press, 1997).

6. The foremost historiography on the suppression of Thuggee likewise relies on the dualistic conceptualisations of 'state' and 'society' outlined above. See, in particular: Kim A. Wagner, *Thuggee: Banditry and the British in Early Nineteenth-century India* (Basingstoke: Palgrave Macmillan, 2007); Martine Van Woerkens, *The Strangled Traveler, Colonial Imaginings and the Thugs of India*, trans. Catherine Tihanyi (Chicago: University of Chicago Press, 2002 [first published in French in 1995]); Radhika Singha, '"Providential" Circumstances: The Thuggee Campaign of the 1830s and Legal Innovation', *Modern Asian Studies* vol. 27, no. 1 (1993), pp. 83–146; Sandria B. Freitag, 'Collective Crime and Authority in North India', in Anand A. Yang, ed., *Crime and Criminality in British India* (Tuscon, Ariz.: University of Arizona Press, 1995) and Sandria B. Freitag, 'Crime in the Social Order of Colonial North India', *Modern Asian Studies* vol. 25, no. 2 (1991), pp. 227–261.

7. For a detailed exploration of Delhi under siege, see William Dalrymple, *The Last Mughal: The Fall of a Dynasty, Delhi, 1857* (London: Bloomsbury, 2006), ch. 5.

8. Though there was a considerable dissent from this decision within the company's administration, with such senior figures as Sir John Lawrence favouring an enquiry to a trial. See Lt. E.H. Paske, Offg. Secy. to the Chief Commissioner, Punjab, to C.E. Saunders, Offg. Commissioner, Delhi, 28 January 1858, in Punjab Government Records, *Mutiny Records: Correspondence*, vol. VII, part II (Lahore: Punjab Government Press, 1911), p. 375. I am grateful to Kim A. Wagner for directing me to this reference.

9. See Pramod K. Nayar, 'Introduction', in idem., ed., *The Trial of Bahadur Shah Zafar* (Hyderabad: Orient Longman, 2007), p. xxxiv.

10. Quoted in P.J.O. Taylor, ed., *A Companion to the 'Indian Mutiny' of 1857* (Oxford: Oxford University Press, 1996), p. 33. From the early summer of 1857, rebel proclamations released

from Delhi and elsewhere in northern India exhorted their audiences to transfer allegiance to a re-emergent Mughal *sirkar* (government). Many of them bore Zafar's signature. For further evidence that Zafar's authority remained widely recognised across the northern subcontinent: Rajat Kanta Ray, *The Felt Community: Commonality and Mentality before the Emergence of Indian Nationalism* (New Delhi: Oxford University Press, 2003).

11. If not the self-image depicted in his poetry: 'I am neither the light of anyone's eye/Nor the solace of anyone's heart/Unable to serve anyone's needs/I am no more than a mere speck of dust.' Quoted in Bose and Jalal, *Modern South Asia*, p. 74.

12. At the time of Zafar's trial, the company was a regularised subsidiary of the British Crown, responsible to an unelected executive of six men that periodically met in London and was unaccountable to public scrutiny: the Board of Control. Technically, it was this body to which the Military Commission that tried Zafar was ultimately responsible. See, in particular: 13 Geo. III, c. 63; 24 Geo. III, s. 2, c. 25; 26 Geo. III, c. 16. The Treaty of Allahabad is reproduced in William Bolts, *Considerations on Indian Affairs; Particularly Respecting the Present State of Bengal and Its Dependencies*, 2nd ed. (London: J. Alman, 1772), appendix XVII.

13. For more on the Emperor's legal sovereignty: F.W. Buckler, 'The Political Theory of the India Mutiny', in M.N. Pearson, ed., *Legitimacy and Symbols: The South Asian Writings of F.W. Buckler* (Ann Arbor: University of Michigan Press, [1922]1985), esp. pp. 46–47, 55–61.

14. Zafar faced four charges. First, that he had encouraged company sepoys 'in the crimes of mutiny and rebellion against the State'. Second, that he had encouraged others 'to rebel and wage war against the State'. Third, that he was a 'false traitor against the State', who had proclaimed himself 'the reigning king and sovereign of India', taken 'unlawful possession of Delhi' and raised military forces in the attempt 'to fulfil and perfect his treasonable design of overthrowing and destroying the British Government in India'. Fourth, that on 16 May 1857, he had caused the murder of forty-nine people, 'chiefly women and children of European and mixed European descent', and encouraged others elsewhere to perpetrate similar attacks. See Charges, 28 January 1858, in 'Proceedings on the Trial of Muhammad Bahadur Shah, Titular King of Delhi, before a Military Commission, upon a charge of Rebellion, Treason, and Murder, held at Delhi, on the 27th day of January 1858, and following days' [hereafter, 'Trial of Zafar'], p. 11. Zafar's trial proceedings were forwarded to the House of Commons in June 1859; my references are taken from the version available online at http://www.csas.ed.ac.uk/mutiny/texts.html (accessed 06 November 2012).

15. According to Karl Marx, writing in the *Daily Tribune*, martial law had been declared across all disaffected districts of northern India by mid July: 'The Revolt in the Indian Army', *New York Daily Tribune*, 15 July 1857, available online at http://www.marxists.org/archive/marx/works/1857/07/15.htm (accessed 06 November 2012). For the proclamation of martial law in Meerut: correspondence between the Governor-General of India, Calcutta, and Lieutenant-Governor of the North-Western Provinces, Agra, 15–16 May 1857, in George W. Forrest, ed., *Selections from the Letters Despatches and Other State Papers, Preserved in the Military Department of the Government of India 1857–58*, vol. I (Calcutta: Military Department Press, 1893), pp. 251–252. I am grateful to Kim A. Wagner for directing me to this reference.

16. Indeed, Rudrangshu Mukherjee has argued that the enabling legislation (Acts VIII, XI, XIV and XVI of 1857) in fact, created something more than martial law, since 'Civil Officers' and 'trustworthy persons not connected with the government' were also empowered with the right to judge and take the life of Indians without recourse to the law. See Rudrangshu Mukherjee, 'The Kanpur Massacres in India in the Revolt of 1857: Reply', *Past and Present*, no. 142 (February 1994), pp. 178–189.

17. It should be noted that in this legislation, 'the state' was defined as either the Queen (Victoria) or the East India Company. See Acts VIII, XI, XIV, XV, XVI and XVII of 1857, in *India Acts*, vol. 5, *1854–57*, IOR/V/8/35, Asia, Pacific & Africa Collections [APAC], British Library.

18. Maj. F.J. Harriott, Deputy Judge Advocate General, address to the Court, 28 January 1858, in 'Trial of Zafar', p. 11.

19. See Harriott, address to the court, 9 March 1858, in 'Trial of Zafar', pp. 143–148, 154–156, 160–162. Cf. Nayar, 'Introduction', xxxiv–xxxix.

20. Harriott, address to court, 9 March 1858, in 'Trial of Zafar', pp. 142–143, 163.

21. After he had been found guilty, Zafar was therefore exiled to Rangoon rather than facing execution, the more conventional punishment for a treason felon.

22. Nayar, 'Introduction', lxvi–lxix. See also: Carl Schmitt, *Political Theology: Four Chapters on the Concept of Sovereignty* (Chicago: University of Chicago Press, [1922]2005), esp. pp. 5–15; Giorgio Agamben, *Homo Sacer: Sovereign Power and Bare Life*, trans. Daniel Heller-Roazen (Stanford: Stanford University Press, 1998), esp. pp. 64–65 and Giorgio Agamben, *State of Exception*, trans. Kevin Attell (Chicago: Chicago University Press, 2005), esp. pp. 1, 4.

23. Harriott, address to court, 9 March 1858, in 'Trial of Zafar', pp. 146–167.

24. For further evidence of Harriott's consciousness of metropolitan interest in the trial and Christianisation of the proceedings, see Harriott, address to court, 9 March 1858, in 'Trial of Zafar', esp. pp. 143, 146, 148, 154, 162.

25. Harriott, address to court, 9 March 1858, in 'Trial of Zafar', p. 143.

26. For more, see Bose and Jalal, *Modern South Asia*, ch. 10.

27. The non-regulation tracts of the Bengal Presidency were Delhi (added in 1803), the Sagar and Narmada Territories (1818), and Assam, Arakan and Tenasserim (1824).

28. As Mitchell points out, whenever one tries to find and pin down 'the state' in dualistic terms, it recedes from view, blurring into its supposed mirror-twin: civil society. The idea of frontiers between discrete spheres of action is a fiction. Rather, these frontiers consist of an internally drawn line within those institutional mechanisms that maintain a certain social and political order. See, in particular: Timothy Mitchell, 'Everyday Metaphors of Power', *Theory and Society*, vols. 19, no. 5 (1990), pp. 550–551, 566–574; and Mitchell, 'Society, Economy, and the State Effect', p. 175.

29. G.W. Swinton, Chief Secretary to the Governor General, to Maj. J. Stewart, Officiating Resident at Indore, 23 October 1829, in N.K. Sinha, ed., *Selected Records Collected From the Central Provinces and Berar Secretariat Relating to the Suppression of Thuggee 1829–1832* (Nagpur: Government Printing Central Provinces and Berar, 1939) [hereafter, *SRT*], pp. 12–13. For the Thug-informers' accounts of the attacks, and records of the recovered loot: *SRT*, pp. 15–40.

30. Capt. W. Borthwick, Political Agent Mahidpur, to Stewart, 7 February 1830, Extract Bengal Political Consultations, 5 March 1830, enclosed in no. 46, Board's Collections [hereafter, BC], F/4/1251/50480, no. 1, Asia, Pacific and Africa Collections, British Library, London [hereafter, APAC].

31. H.T. Prinsep, Secy. GG PD, to Swinton, 27 December 1830, BC, F/4/1309/52131, no. 1, APAC.

32. Swinton to Smith, 8 October 1830, in *SRT*, p. 10.

33. The first British-led operations against Thuggee took place circa 1808–1816 in the Ceded and Conquered Provinces (comprising adjacent territories in northern–central India, ceded to the company by the Nawab Vizier of Awadh in 1801, conquered from the Maratha chieftain Daulat Rao Sindia in 1803, and ceded by the Maratha Peshwa of Poona the same year). See, in particular, Wagner, *Thuggee*, esp. pp. 33–99, 167–196.

34. For Swinton's transcription of Sleeman's letter to the editor of the *Calcutta Literary Gazette* of the 3 October 1830: 'Note by the Secretary [Swinton]', 4 October 1830, BC, F/4/1251/50480, no. 2, fos. 669–690, APAC. The quotation cited is from fos. 686–687.

35. *Ramaseeana*, published at the height of the ATC was—inter alia—Sleeman's defence of his thesis that Thuggee was a religious cult as well as a request for a suitable extension of sovereign juridical power. It was also written partly to chastise those colleagues who had queried his earlier methods for generating the evidence that in turn produced convictions and recognition for his

achievements. See William H. Sleeman, 'Introduction', *Ramaseeana* (Calcutta: Military Orphan Press, 1836).

36. For the argument that Thuggee was a hereditary and corporate, even 'caste-like', identity: Sleeman, 'Introduction', esp. pp. 20–21. A sample of ten of the genealogical diagrams can also be found therein. One of them is numbered '88', giving some indication of Sleeman's dedication to the cause of 'extirpating' Thuggee and of how large he imagined the Thug 'conspiracy' to be.

37. For phrenological findings related to Thuggee: R. Cox, 'Remarks on the Skulls and Character of the Thugs', *The Phrenological Journal and Miscellany* (1834); H.H. Spry, 'Some Account of the Gang-murderers of Central India, Commonly called Thugs: Accompanying the Skulls of Several of Them', *The Phrenology Journal and Miscellany*, vol. 8 (1834); W. Turner, *Contributions to the Craniology of the People of the Empire of India. Part III—Natives of the Madras Presidency, Thugs, Veddahs, Tibetans and Seistanis* (Edinburgh: Robert Grant & Son, 1906).

38. Sleeman, 'Introduction', p. 3. Sleeman's dictionary of '*ramasee*' can be found on pages 67–140 of *Ramaseeana*. See also: van Woerkens, *Strangled Traveler*, pp. 295–315. For other examples of Company officials who published vocabularies of the alleged secret languages used by groups similar to Thugs in the early nineteenth century: D. Richardson, 'An Account of the Bazeegurs, a Sect Commonly Denominated Nuts', *Asiatic Researches*, vol. 7 (1803), pp. 475–179; Richard Sherwood, 'Of the Murderers Called Phánsigárs' (Communicated by Colonel McKenzie), *Asiatick Researches*, vol. 13 (1820), pp. 266–268.

39. See in particular van Woerkens, *Strangled Traveler*, esp. pp. 6, 60–84.

40. By contrast, other knowledges—specifically, the 'Indian' ones—were seen as susceptible to these distortions of the truth, as argued in Ronald Inden, *Imagining India* (Oxford: Blackwell, 1990) and Bernard S. Cohn, *Colonialism and Its Forms of Knowledge: The British in India* (Chichester: Princeton University Press, 1996).

41. 'Tabular Statement of the Results of Thug Trials Held in India, 1826–41', in Philip Meadows Taylor, 'State of Thuggee in India', *British and Foreign Review*, vol. 15, no. 29 (1843), p. 293. Shortly after arrest, suspects thought suitable to become approvers were manacled in leg-irons and segregated from other captives. They were interrogated by TD officers and required to produce a testimony (or deposition) in which they admitted to their involvement in Thuggee, recounted the attacks they had participated in and named other Thugs involved. This document formed the centrepiece of evidence used against suspects in trials held throughout the 1830s. Approvers were also required to show TD employees (usually, parties of *nujeebs*—armed militiamen—or sepoys, led by a senior Indian soldier) where their former associates lived and where victims' bodies had been buried; these were then exhumed and, if possible, identified. Associates brought in on the strength of approvers' accusations were identified in face-to-face parades by a succession of informers who had been kept apart to prevent collusion.

42. Borthwick to Stewart, 26 July 1829, in Sleeman, *Ramaseeana*, Appendix X, p. 377.

43. Captain James Paton's papers contain references to the translation process and include a letter sent to all magistrates involved in the ATC of the 1830s, asking them to follow a set list of questions. See Paton Papers, British Library Addl. Mss. 41300, fos 173 (on the translation process), fos. 400–401 (on the letter regarding the formulaic set of questions).

44. For analysis of the way depositions were recorded: van Woerkens, *Strangled Traveler*, pp. 60–67.

45. 'Career of crime' is Sleeman's phrase: see Sleeman, 'Introduction', p. 39.

46. See 'Examination of Thug Approver Rama Jemadar', in *SRT*, p. 127.

47. See 'Examination[s] of [the] Thug approver[s] Rama Jemadar, Moty, Rama, and Mana', in *SRT*, pp. 127, 137, 142, 147.

48. 'Well over half': 1,892 out of 3,437, or 55 per cent, of Thug trials took place between 1826–1835 (inclusive). The acquittal rate is based on the following calculation: a total of 1,892 Thugs were arrested circa 1826–1835; 134 escaped from jail or died before sentencing; of the remaining 1,758 people, 21 were acquitted (1.1 per cent of the total tried), with the rest receiving anything from

the death penalty to conditional release pending the arrival of someone putting up security for them. All percentages are rounded to one decimal place. Calculated from 'Tabular Statement', in Meadows Taylor, 'State of Thuggee in India', p. 293.

49. Quoted in Singha, '"Providential" Circumstances', p. 122, n.159 and n.160. The TD's expenses were accounted to the Sagar and Narmada Territories alone until 1835.

50. A permanent staff of seven assistants, commanding more than 300 *nujeebs*, was further assisted by seventeen British officers: Residents at the courts of Indian rulers based in Indore, Hyderabad and Lucknow, and Agents based in territories under British control. Just as in the trials heard by Smith, those held by Residents were only submitted to the Political Department's secretary, H.T. Prinsep, for review, while Agents tried Thugs at tribunals specially convened by the TD to evade interference from the Judicial Department. See Singha, '"Providential" Circumstances', p. 111 and Sleeman, 'Introduction', p. 56–57. For a selection of the correspondence explaining the expansion of the ATC in the early 1830s: Smith to Swinton, 25 March 1832; Smith to Macnaghten, 24 April and 29 May 1832; Macnaghten to Swinton, 25 June 1832, all in *SRT*, pp. 73–75, 80–81, 90–91, in that order.

51. The third paragraph of the Act sanctioned company courts to punish Thugs without the fatwa (legal opinion) of an Islamic legal officer. For anti-Thug and anti-dacoit legislation passed between 1836 and 1848: W.H. Sleeman, *Report on Budhuk Alias Bagree Decoits* (Calcutta: Military Orphan Press, 1849), pp. 353–362.

52. Sleeman, *Report on Budhuk Decoits*, p. 353. Sleeman had effectively advertised for Act XIX of 1837 in the introduction to *Ramaseeana*, pp. 51–54.

53. As Radhika Singha has observed, the introduction of the anti-Thuggee legislation was partly a political manoeuvre, intended to staunch bureaucratic infighting over the apparent legal contradiction that had arisen within the company's domains. I do not dispute this argument, but only suggest that wider consequences and a deeper logic to the formulation and promulgation of these laws may be seen, with interesting consequences for how one reads the history of 'the modern state' and 'sovereignty' in colonial India. See Singha, '"Providential" Circumstances', esp. pp. 134–137.

54. See Agamben, *Homo Sacer*, esp. pt. 2, ch. 3.

55. 'Extermination': F.C. Smith to Swinton, 20 June 1832, in C.H. Philips, ed., *The Correspondence of Lord William Cavendish Bentinck, Governor-General of India 1828–1835*, vol. II (Oxford: Oxford University Press, 1977), p. 845. See also Smith, 'Plan for the Eventual Destruction of the Associations of Thugs', in *SRT*, pp. 49–55.

56. J.R. Lumley to Magistrate of Ahmednuggur, December 1837, 'Letters from the Assistant General Superintendent at Shorapur to the General Superintendent and Others between October 1836 and December 1837', I1, fo. 261, National Archives of India [hereafter, NAI], quoted in van Woerkens, *Strangled Traveler*, p. 102.

57. Lumley to Magt. Ahmednuggur, December 1837, 'Letters from the Assistant General Superintendent', I1, fos 262–263, NAI, quoted in van Woerkens, *Strangled Traveler*, pp. 101–102.

58. Cf. Agamben, *Homo Sacer*, pp. 183–184.

59. Sleeman to Macnaghten, 3 February 1838, Thagi & Dakaiti, G5, fo. 107, NAI; Sleeman to Lieut. Reynolds, Hyderabad, 6 April 1838, G5, fo. 112, NAI, quoted in van Woerkens, *Strangled Traveler*, p. 102.

60. Sleeman, *Report on Megpunnaism*, p. 9. 'Datura poisoners', as they were widely called, had fallen under colonial suspicion since Perry's encounters with Thuggee circa 1808–1815.

61. Sleeman, *Report on Megpunnaism*, p. 11.

62. Smith to Prinsep, 19 November 1830, in *SRT*, p. 50.

63. See, for example, William H. Sleeman, *Report on the System of Megpunnaism* (n.p.: The Serampore Press, 1839). For the reports of TD officials relating to religious mendicants suspected

of Thuggee: Singha, '"Providential" Circumstances', p. 139, n. 224–227, and p. 142, n. 242. See also van Woerkens, *Strangled Traveler*, pp. 101–104.

64. Sleeman, *Report on Budhuk Decoits*, p. 357.

65. See Neeladri Bhattacharya, 'Predicaments of Mobility: Peddlers and Itinerants in Nineteenth-century Northwestern India', in Claude Markovits, Jaques Pouchepadass and Sanjay Subrahmanyam, eds, *Society and Circulation: Mobile People and Itinerant Cultures in South Asia 1750–1950* (Delhi: Permanent Black, 2003), pp. 163–214 and C.A. Bayly, *Rulers, Townsmen and Bazaars in North Indian Society in the Age of British Expansion 1770–1870* (Cambridge: Cambridge University Press, 1983), p. 219.

66. See, for example, 'Seventh report', 6 May 1773, in *Reports from Committees of the House of Commons*, vol. IV, 1772–1773, esp. p. 324, cited in Radhika Singha, *A Despotism of Law: Crime and Justice in Early Colonial India* (Oxford: Oxford University Press, 1998), p. 3, n. 10.

2

❧❧❧

RUMOURS OF THE COMPANY'S COLLAPSE
The Mood of Dasahra 1824 in the Punjab and Hindustan

Dirk H.A. Kolff

IN India, the calendar is political. The festival of Dasahra, which marks the annual resumption of military activism and the forceful renegotiation of one's alliances and terms of subordination, is fixed for October. In 1857, the mutineers at Merath unseasonably pulled the trigger on 10 May, a case of bad timing and neglect of what makes political sense in Hindustan. It was at the Dasahra of that year, long after the beginning of the sepoys' revolt, when Delhi had already been lost, that it became visible in Hindustan what the impact of their initiative—if postponed for five months and coordinated with the ambitions of the *mufassal*—might have been. A study of the Dasahra campaigns of the pre-mutiny decades could contribute a great deal to the validity of this point of view. This chapter attempts to present such a case study and to show that fairly detailed material for such research is available. The case is that of 1824.

The news of the spectacular defeat of the British troops at Ramu in Burma in May of that year spread quickly, and the further it travelled, the more details were added to the core message, which was one of panic and crisis. In the bazars of Calcutta it was soon speculated that a Burmese force might possibly penetrate through the Sundarbans and attack the great metropolis. The sepoys of the three regiments cantoned at Barrackpur came to consider the Burmese 'as magicians, who had the faculty of rendering themselves invulnerable'. Later, Charles Metcalfe would remember how, during these months, 'the Burma War produced an extraordinary sensation all over India, amounting to an expectation of our immediate downfall'. Frederick Shore, then joint-magistrate of Dehra Dun, however, while admitting that the company's reverses in Burma were the immediate cause of the disturbances, would argue that the protest of 1824 was endemic rather than exceptional. Such upheavals were part of India's political culture. Almost all insurrections had their origin 'in some promise broken, some right withheld, or some injustice practised' towards the people. They were first of all cries for justice. It was only that in 1824, because of the news from Burma, they were a little louder than usual. In that year, there was hardly a district in the Upper Provinces—where Shore served as a joint-magistrate—'in which the spirit of disaffection was not more or less manifested'.[1] Let us give an account of some of the cases of activism of that year and then see in what terms one can try to understand them. We begin with Ranjit Singh's Punjab.

In August, the Delhi *akhbaar*, as received in Lahore, brought intelligence that the raja of the Burmese and other rajas had, for eight days, charged the company's troops and by witchcraft had stayed the English guns, muskets and swords and slain thousands. The British, it was reported, were now strengthening all their main strongholds and drawing a ditch around Delhi. The latter report must be understood in the context of warnings spread by newswriters posted by the company at the Lahore *darbaar* that, in the light of the intelligence received from Burma, a Punjabi invasion of Hindustan was now more than probable. Soon, the entire region buzzed with rumours of Sikh troop concentrations on the Satlej. The reactions to the news were different, both as to place and with respect to different communities and sections of the population. But it was said that the Begam Samru at Sardhana in the Upper Doab, who commanded some redoubtable battalions, was in touch with the Lahore durbar and that Gurkha as well as Maratha envoys had been seen in Lahore. The exiled raja of Nagpur was rumoured to have offered Ranjit Singh large sums of money if he went to war with the company.[2]

This much is certain that Maharaja Ranjit Singh, then at Amritsar, was elated by the intelligence from Burma. The British reverses seemed to increase the number of his military options for the next cold season. He ordered copies of the reports received to be distributed amongst his sardars and his other officers. As always during the end of August, a period of great bustle and activity began at the court of Lahore, the army preparing to take the field at the Dasahra in October. At that stage, it was anybody's guess whether the campaign would be a northward one against the warlike mountaineers in Kashmir, an eastward one to retain the conquests made in that direction and to put pressure on the hill chieftains and the Sikh states across the Satlej protected by the British, or an expedition to the west, i.e., towards Sindh or Kabul. For a while, there was an unusual movement of runners arriving and departing from the maharaja's fort towards the east. This had to do with reports that the British were moving sizable contingents of troops from Hindustan in the direction of Bengal, leaving the field open for the Sikhs in the Punjab. In order to make sure of the best information from Rai Nand Singh, the maharaja's vakil at Delhi, a *sowaar* was dispatched to bring him *parwaanas* with special instructions and a secret dak was laid between Amritsar and Delhi via Ludhiana. *Harkaaras* in disguise were sent to Ludhiana, Ambala, Karnal and Shahjahanpur to enquire into the position of the British cantonments and military depots there. The English, for their part, kept themselves informed about the number of boats available at the several ferries across the Satlej, which served as an indication of any plans the maharaja might have to campaign to the eastward.

Ranjit Singh, of course, kept his cards close to his chest. He issued an order that whoever should be convicted of conveying the intelligence of his durbar beyond the walls of his fort, and more especially to the English newswriters, should be punished with the loss of his nose and ears and with the confiscation of his property. Meanwhile, the secret of the next campaign was made the subject of a special covenant between the maharaja and God himself. It was sealed during a theatrical visit of the former, described by the Lahore *akhbaar*, to the Hari Mandir at Amritsar, now known as Darbar Sahib or Golden Temple. Appearing before the Granth, Ranjit Singh with his own hand wrote two chits in Gurmukhi, each mentioning a plan of campaign. He laid both on the sacred Granth and said, with folded hands, that he would proceed in whatever direction he was ordered. Calling a child, he told him to take one of the chits and bring it to him. This done, the maharaja read the one handed to him, then tore both the pieces of paper and said: 'We shall see how it will turn out.' Ordering ₹725 to be laid before the Granth, he remarked: 'If I shall return in safety and victorious from my campaign and my secret object be accomplished, I will make a more pleasing offering than the present.'

Four weeks later, around 20 September, Ranjit Singh announced that he would march towards the Indus in person and gave orders to his troops to cross the Ravi. The English at Delhi read in the *akhbaar* from Lahore that the maharaja 'in a loud voice' had told his courtiers: 'It is reported, that the English gentlemen entertain doubts and suspicions of me; it is necessary that you go to Captain Claud Wade and Mr Murray and, professing friendship and amity on my part, remove all doubt from their minds.' In a note to Wade at Ludhiana, he warned him against gossip: 'Let the mirror of friendship be clear and polished.' On 3 November, against the advice of his French officers, he crossed the Indus at Attock and fought with the local Yusufzai Pathans, losing many men in both operations.[3]

Ranjit Singh's diplomacy and sophisticated management of news and intelligence on this occasion enabled him to make a fairly accurate judgement of the strength of the British troops in north India. The company, he must have found out, was by no means as weak as the rumours would have it. Yet, because of the British predicament in Burma, it was safe for him to turn his back on the company and move his army across the Indus into Afghan territory. It must have been an expedition he had had in mind, but could now, thanks to the reverses suffered by his British rivals, venture on with more troops and less risk. The same analysis, that old ambitions were now nearer realisation than for many years, was in their own way made by many others in north India.

If Ranjit Singh marched west, that did not mean all was quiet on the eastern marches of Akali influence. Several weeks before the British defeat in Burma, something was already afoot in the territory of Sardar Fatah Singh Ahluwalia, the powerful independent Sikh chief of Kapurthala, north of the Satlej. Amongst the company servants, it was the British officer posted at Ludhiana to keep an eye on 'Sikh and hill affairs' who heard about it first. In the village of Athur, about 50 kilometres to the west, a Jat by name Bahadur Singh—who was a subject of the raja of Bhadaur, a zamindar whom he had served as a shepherd and whose little kingdom was nearby—was inspired to come forward as a prophet. There was at Athur, he announced, a tirth, or holy place, by name Ram Lar, and whosoever bathed in the pool of water there, would obtain salvation and be cured of every disease. Even more spectacularly, he gave out that on 9 Bhadon, i.e., Thursday, 19 August, the reigns of the *firangis*, Ranjit Singh and the other lords of the land would be over and be succeeded by a millennium during which one universal lord, to appear on a grey (white, according to another letter) horse, would govern the country. Sacred political events like this, of course, happened according to divine calculations and did not have to wait for the Dasahra red-letter days. The first report on the movement reached Delhi in June, when thousands 'of the lower class of Hindoos' had repaired to the tirth and Bahadur had collected some armed 'Akalis and Sikhs' around him. He predicted that two forts in the area, in one of which the company had a small party of sepoys, would fall to the ground. He advised the inhabitants to fly, which, from at least one of the forts, they did, whereupon he marched towards it with a multitude of people. A *sowaar* was sent to tell him he had better go home. When one of Bahadur's supporters fired and wounded the horse of the messenger, the local zamindar led his men against the religious crowd and dispersed it, killing two of the Athur devotees.

Captain Murray now arranged for 200 of the irregular Patiala Horse to go to Athur and asked Sardar Fatah Singh Ahluwalia to send a party of sepoys to relieve them. While thousands still continued to bathe peacefully at the tirth, Bahadur Singh seems to have responded by letting it be known that he himself was the man who would appear as the ruler of 'the whole eastern world' and that, in fact, Kalki, the harbinger of a new age and the tenth and last avatar of Vishnu, would become incarnate in him. When Fatah Singh failed to send any of his soldiers, the more cooperative raja of Bhadaur, sent a troop of 200 horses. Subsequently, he succeeded in arresting Bahadur Singh and held him *nazarband* (under surveillance), apparently a kind of house arrest, somewhere in the town of Bhadaur. All seemed under control again. The Patiala Horse were withdrawn and Captain William Murray—the superintendent at Ambala—hoped that once the ninth of Bhadon was over, people would go home, and the troops could be withdrawn. In the end that was what happened, though only after an apocalyptic event of the captain's own making. The concourse of people increased so much that Murray again called on Maharaja Karan Singh of Patiala to send 400 of his horse to strengthen the hand of the Bhadaur raja. The most detailed account of what happened is a letter (*arzi*) addressed by Fatah Jang Khan, the sardar of the Patiala Horse, in response to the maharaja's orders (*parwaana*).

When a large crowd set out from the Athur fair to Bhadaur to liberate their leader, the maharaja wrote to Fatah Jang Khan, to call his *risaaladaar* Rahm Khan from Patiala and the officers Dayal Singh and Ganda Singh from Hariana to assist him and guard the person of 'Bahadur Singh Faqir', to protect the gates of Bhadaur in concert with the sardars of its raja and to prevent the entry of the multitude approaching the town. Early Wednesday morning, the 8th of the month, on the eve of the millennium prophesied, having saddled half the number of his horses and leaving the rest at the pickets, he made the circuit of the walls, and sent a party to check the advance of the crowd. At noon, Rahm Khan and Dayal Singh having arrived meanwhile, news was brought that a party of Akali warriors at the head of a host of armed devotees was advancing on Bhadaur. Fatah Jang Khan ordered all his men to saddle their horses and sent three or four *sowaar*s to bring him intelligence. 'During their absence', his letter reads,

> my party went to water their horses, but before this was done, news arrived that the Akalis and the people of the fair had wounded Run Sing and had captured his horse and were coming on with shouts to the attack. We instantly mounted and, at the distance of half a koss, from Bhudour, the attack commenced. We desired the Akalees not to advance to Bhudour, but they would persist in the attempt and wounded some of my men, when surdar Juwahur Sing and Maun Sing and Sehbey Sing and the Sikhs of surdar Meer Sing's company and Baboo, and moonshi Luchmun Das, Meer Ahshan Ulee and others of Rehm Khan's and Fazil Khan's party drew their swords and slew several of the enemy. About fifty were killed and many wounded, when the remainder who took to flight [*sic*].

On Fatah Jang Khan's own side, twenty men and twelve horses were wounded, while one more horse was missing. He concluded his report stressing that it was a great victory and that the bravery, particularly of five men amongst them Shabaz Khan, his nephew, and one of the Bhadaur raja's sardars had been conspicuous.

Immediately after the fight, the zamindars of the neighbourhood and their men, 'to reimburse themselves for the damage which their crops had sustained', as Charles Elliott at Delhi informed the company's government, plundered the scattered Akalis and the followers of Bahadur Singh. With this, tranquillity was completely restored. The raja did not release the prophet. In Calcutta, the government thought it best to take no further notice of him. His 'influence and repute' were presumably 'destroyed'.[4]

Another instance of the Dasahra excitement of 1824 noticed by Metcalfe and Shore also occurred west of the Yamuna in the Delhi Territory, where the rains of that year had totally failed and the kharif harvest was lost. As it is rather well documented, let us give an account of it. On 24 September, in the Rohtak area to the north-west of Delhi, rumours of the impending collapse of the company's rule and of an expected famine caused by the failure of the monsoon led to the plunder of the half-yearly cattle fair of Beri, a town of about 9,000 inhabitants 70 kilometres west of Delhi. Beri was the centre of the eleven-village territory of the Kadar⁵ clan (*gotra*) of Jats, a territory that the British administrator of the district would report, formed 'a little independent commonwealth'. 'The Jats of Beri', he wrote, 'are at the head of this unit, which is also a military alliance. They are one of the strongest and most formidable factions on this side of Hurreana.' They had heard reports and had received Hindi letters from *sahukaars* that the whole or the greater part of the company's army had left for Calcutta. Some of the Beri Jats may have been present at a conference at Bharatpur, to which I will return, where these and similar reports must have been discussed and a plan for coordinated action seems to have been agreed upon as between Jats and Gujars. Then, for ten or twelve days previous to the fair, looting began on a small scale in the countryside, and the adjacent Charkhi Dadri country towards the west 'was plunged in a state of anarchy'. The Jat zamindars of the region were reportedly busy collecting powder and ball. Various secret meetings were held at different Jat villages in the area, the last of which took place on the eve of 23 September, the day the fair began. It was attended by all the headmen, who on that occasion 'bound themselves by an oath to plunder the fair upon the following morning'.

The cattle fair was held in an open plain close under the town. Every year in April, and again in September, 15,000–20,000 bullocks were brought there. As a commercial project, it was a fairly recent phenomenon and drew fewer people to Beri than the simultaneous mela around the local Devi temple, which represented a much older tradition. No ties of profit and respect bound the Jats either to the cattle dealers, who came to the market all the way from Shekhawati or places as far to the west as Bikaner, or to the purchasers. On the contrary, they despised the 'butchers', as they referred to them, who came to make purchases for the inordinate meat consumption in the Delhi and Merath cantonments of the company. I assume these butchers were Muslims. An anti–cow slaughter and, derived from it, anti-British element is discernible here. It is worth noticing that the latter component seems to be lacking in all the other cases discussed in this chapter.

On the morning of the day fixed as the start of the fair, due to the reports of robberies in the area, only about 10,000 bullocks had arrived. They were, with their owners and prospective buyers, attacked according to plan, by about 120 armed men led by the Jat zamindars of Beri itself. Immediately, the bullocks broke loose and scampered over the plains in all directions. There is no knowing how many were driven off by the Jats, but the number must have been large. Cash and goods to the value of ₹7,500 were also reported as having been plundered. On that and the following days, a series of robberies were committed, eventually affecting twenty-eight villages and at least 299 persons. Three days after the attack at Beri, a caravan of cattle dealers and 550 head of cattle—of which 100 had been bought at the fair on behalf of the company army's stud-farm at Hissar—was, when it took the road to Hansi under the command of the commissariat jamadar Ganga Singh, tackled by fifty or sixty men, all from one particular Jat village. The plunder was renewed the next day. The total value of the stolen property was calculated at ₹36,168. Subsequently, on 11 October, 300 of the company's camels laden with chana (chickpea) and proceeding from Hissar escorted by twenty of Skinner's Horse and fourteen *sowaar*s of Nawab Faiz Muhammad Khan—the Pathan ruler of the nearby principality of Jhajjar—were attacked by no fewer than 600 inhabitants of a town and three villages in the neighbourhood. The attempt was repulsed by another troop of Faiz Muhammad Khan's horses who happened to arrive on the scene during the contest.

Then things settled down, at least as far as the Kadar Jats were concerned. There seems to have been no loss of life. The company authorities restricted themselves to tracing as much of the plundered goods as they could, and the Jats appear to have been content with the results of their lightning campaign. Asked for the cause of the disturbances, they explained that as it was widely reported that 'the authority of the British government was at an end in Hindoostan and all the English gentlemen were proceeding to Calcutta ...', the measures they had taken were nothing less than logical. They were, however, no enemies of the company and, in the event it could re-establish its authority, they would, of course, return all the property carried away. 'If otherwise', however, 'the whole would be theirs, and why should they not plunder at such a time?' Some of the loot—worth ₹6,707, including 280 head of cattle—was then produced; the rest constituted the net profit of the 30 villages that had contributed men to take part in the effort.[6]

In the Delhi Territory as a whole, arms and ammunition continued to be collected everywhere for some time. A certain Suraj Mal, perhaps a Jat and described as a gang robber, returned from his exile to the Hissar area and, on 25 October, at the head of 400 matchlock men and a party of perhaps sixty horses, he stormed and took the fort of Behat, eighteen of his people being killed during the event.[7]

Further to the south, after the dispersion of the Pindari hordes in Malwa and central India in 1818 and 1819, one of the Pindari leaders, Shaikh Dallah, who had formerly been the dread of the northern part of the Nizam's dominions, had continued his annual campaigns in the Khandesh and Nimar area, especially in the *pargana*s there belonging to Shinde. His usual retreat was in the jungles of the Satpura Range near Asirgarh on the border of the Burhanpur district, where he had built a new power base and from where he drew most of his resources. In this district, he was assisted by many connections of his and had partisans who would readily assemble under him for an expedition and as readily scatter themselves among the population when convenient. The *subah*, Shinde's governor of Burhanpur, kept up few local policemen in those wild places and those that were posted there were more Shaikh Dallah's private friends and allies than men to be afraid of. The Shaikh, in short, was a person of greater authority and power than the *subah*, who cooperated with him.

During the monsoon season of 1824, in this part of India as in others, the march of British troops from all quarters to the eastern frontier was widely reported. So, Shaikh Dallah assembled a much larger party than usual consisting, according to reports, of 100 horse and 500 foot, among whom were 200 Arabs, 120 Makranis (men from Sindh or Baluchistan), remnants of the military labour force of eighteenth century western India and eighty 'Karnataki levies'. During previous years, because of the difficult terrain and the small number of his followers, the shaikh had always eluded the company's troops garrisoned in Maharaja Shinde's lands. Now, he had many men and ventured into open country. In October, he swept off the cattle of a British-administered town in the Hoshangabad district and levied contributions in the Sagar district and in Shinde's *pargana*s in the Khandesh and Nimar.

This Dasahra, the Burhanpur *subah* was not the only Maratha leader who supported Shaikh Dallah. Entertaining hopes of a revival of the Peshwa's power, several Maratha leaders—or would-be leaders—joined him or were in contact with him. One of the centres of Maratha diplomacy was a person claiming to be a widow of Madhu Rao Peshwa. With the assistance of another enterprising Brahmin, she secretly recruited 300 or 400 people—horse and foot it was said—and gave out that a relative of hers, on representation of her case, got money from Maharaja Shinde at Gwalior. Whether that was true or not, it appears that she sent some jewels to Gwalior and received in return *hundi*s to the value of ₹2,300. She was in league with at least three or four landholding chiefs of good Maratha families, who visited her daily in Burhanpur, where she seems to have kept something of a court. One of them collected his debts *zabardasti* (with force) and also took on soldiers. However, her plans did not really come to fruition: in the end, she could not pay her people and reduced their number to about a hundred, reportedly at the request of an *aamil*, a revenue collector she could not afford to break with.

More of a sensation amongst the common people was created by Chimnaji Appa, who called himself the brother of the ex-Peshwa Baji Rao and, taking the field with a body of seventy-five horse and 100 or 150 infantry, united forces with Shaikh Dallah. Ten or twelve Rajputs and Marathas, inhabitants of the town of Songaon, who were probably trained sepoys, took employment with the shaikh and Chimnaji. There is a report saying that the shaikh paid them using the funding he had received from 'a *bāi* at Burhanpur', possibly the widow just mentioned. During the short period that their campaign lasted, the area affected by their operations measured hundreds of kilometres from east to west. Some villages were destroyed; from others the cattle was driven off and sold. More often than not, the village heads had no choice but to cooperate. There is an example of a village hiring ten or twenty *sibandi*s, irregular policemen, to defend themselves. The inhabitants of some other villages told the police they would flee if not protected, and some may well have done so. Yet, the campaign was not one of outright and indiscriminate plunder; that would have destroyed the campaigners' logistics as well as friendships. Politics remained important. On one occasion, when the shaikh's followers proposed to carry off the cattle of a particular village, Nagutira, and to employ their cavalry to bring flour from two others, he told them to wait. Then, after a day's march, he sent four men with some money for their expenses to Nagutira to procure intelligence and make ready a quantity of grain for his horses. Such careful management of village contacts and resources must have contributed to the fact that it was impossible that season for anybody British to travel or to send merchandise between Malwa and the Deccan. In large parts of Khandesh, nothing was procurable to feed the military units the British sent after the leaders of the movement, whereas the insurgents in that same area were like 'fishes in the water'.

Assistance came to them from many friends and allies. In Asirgarh, Shaikh Dallah had an adopted son—Shaikh Bhula, or Bulao—a man of influence who had been trusted with the management of three villages by the company. Before the Dasahra, the British colonel at Asirgarh had been in the habit of sending him to see his adopted father, apparently hoping to convince him to keep quiet during the approaching campaigning season. After Shaikh Dallah had left for the jungle, however, the colonel no longer allowed Shaikh Bhula to leave the city and made him show himself daily to prove he was not in communication with his father's camp. Nevertheless, a butcher in Burhanpur by the name of Ilahi Bakhsh, when examined, declared that one day Shaikh Bhula had ordered him to take two sheep to the shaikh's camp, which he had done. When the movement's leaders were in the neighbourhood of Jalgaon, a *sahukaar* of that town sent cash and supplies of grain through the *muqaddam* of a village near their camp. Three grain dealers of Songaon regularly received gold and silver articles from the two leaders in exchange for grain and other supplies. Joining the coalition were what the British called 'the western Bhils', in whose hills the shaikh and Chimnaji had a cantonment. A *harkaara* in the service of the two commanders, and who had been taken prisoner, declared: 'The younger brother of Bander Khan, Bhil of Karibara, and the son of Khair Khan, Bhil of Barkot are in league with the rebels and visit them frequently.' The shaikh's greatest asset, however, was the belief held by many that his campaign was the harbinger of a major political reshuffle. His force may have consisted of no more than 600 men, but, as Major R.T. Seyer, the commander of the Nizam's detachment sent against him, wrote to Charles Metcalfe, the company's resident at Hyderabad, 'the reports of the country assign much larger numbers to him and say that he is supported by money and provisions from Burhanpur and a general impression exists, that some intrigue is on foot of which he is merely an instrument'.

There may have been more truth in these rumours than the British were prepared to admit, but all this support was of no avail when Shaikh Dallah had to face the unproportional military forces that the British unleashed against him. Rather worried about the lack of control the Gwalior government exercised in its possessions in Khandesh and about the unsettling effect of the news from Burma in Central India, the British residents at Indore, Bhopal, Gwalior and Hyderabad called on the company's and the Nizam's commanders posted in the area to quell the disturbance before it became more formidable. As an example of the tone adopted, we may quote Thomas Maddock, the company's political agent at Bhopal. He wrote:

> Anything that would have the appearance of a relaxation in the vigour and promptitude of our measures for preserving the peace of the country, might induce numerous petty leaders whose love of predatory habits is undiminished and whom fear alone has kept honest during our supremacy over Malwa, to venture again on their old courses.

So, no fewer than five or six different detachments, marching at short notice from as many barracks, took part 'in a combined scheme of besetting the marauders' passage on all sides'. A reward of ₹1,000 was held out to anyone who would ensure the capture of death of Shaikh Dallah.

The campaign against the shaikh ended on 12 October 1824 with a stroke of British luck, when Major Seyer located his camp and then surprised a large party that was nearby and under the command of Chimnaji Appa. Of the latter's men, forty or fifty were killed and ten or fifteen taken prisoner; the rest dispersed. Seyer himself had only four wounded. A few days later, Shaikh Dallah had only eighty men, horse and foot, left—a number that was daily diminishing. He was reported to be roaming about not thinking it safe to stay more than four hours at any one place. Stragglers and 'seceders' were continually being picked up by parties under British officers. The spell of the shaikh's name was broken. I have no further information about his fate.

In their analysis of what had happened, the British unanimously pointed to the 'misgoverned state' of the Burhanpur territories of Maharaja Shinde, the 'alarm and apprehension' created by a number of scheming Maratha landholders and the 'impostor' Chimnaji Appa, and the 'system of petty plunder' that was a remnant of the pre-1818 Pindari practices. Together with the *subah*'s collusion with the Pindaris and with Chimnaji, to whom he had given shelter, these were the real causes of the uprising. It was self-evident, the servants of the company assured themselves and their superiors, that something like this would have been impossible in a district under the company's jurisdiction.[8] In this, however, they were mistaken, as the story of the next petty war will show.

The most violent event that took place around the 1824 Dasahra was the storming of the Gujar fort of Kunja Bahadurpur, near Rurki in the Saharanpur district. The Kunja estate was one of the remnants of the *riyaasat*, or little kingdom, of Raja Ram Dayal Singh of Landhaura. Before and after the company's conquest in 1803, the raja had, as chief of the regionally dominant Khubar clan of Gujars, managed large tracts of the north-western Doab: some 900 villages in all, worth an annual sum of at least five lakhs of rupees. The company had, however, decided that many of these villages were not his 'property' and that those that could be considered as such were held at a *muqarrari* (privileged), revenue that was personal and would lapse with his death. Therefore, when, Ram Dayal Singh died in 1813, the government resumed many of his villages and cancelled his farms. A sizable number of villages were nevertheless left in the hands of a widow of his and her infant son, his grandson, and six other *taluqdar*s. Since then, in an administrative climate that favoured settlements with village *muqaddam*s rather than deals with the Gujar aristocracy, the branches of the Landhaura family struggled with little success to perpetuate the power and the dignity of their clan in the region.

In 1817, Chaudhri Bijay Singh, a remote cousin of the Raja Ram Dayal Singh, succeeded to one of these *taluqa*s, that of Kunja Bahadurpur. It consisted of 33 villages, paying a revenue of about ₹22,000. Towards the end of the year, he wrote to Archibald Murray—the newly appointed collector—relating the story of how his family had suffered the hardship of an overrated assessment for some years, and how the recent deaths of first his brother and then his father were the result of the calamitous state of the *taluqa*. His losses ran into many tens of thousands of rupees. Only recently, he had been compelled to dispose of his last elephant, his horses, jewels, etc., to repay a debt he owed to one of his *sahukaar*s, the powerful banker Din Dayal. Even before 1813, when the Landhaura raj was still intact and the revenue of his *taluqa* only a quarter of what the company now demanded, life had been difficult, with all the monthly stipends to be paid to widows and the numerous dependents of his family. He had drastically reduced such allowances, even though such cuts could not be reconciled with a proper management of inherited clienteles and estates. He was a malik, a lord of the land, not just a zamindar, a landlord.[9]

Bijay Singh struggled on for seven more years to make ends meet, his *taluqa* always in debt and in danger of being broken up. Finally, two new phenomena changed the political landscape. First, there was the emergence of Kallu, the sardar, about whom we shall hear more in a moment, then came the exciting news of the expected collapse of the company. In the Upper Provinces, as elsewhere, accounts of the Burmese successes circulated for several months. In the increasingly fluid political atmosphere, a number of opinion makers provided guidance as to what position to take, what potential allies to court. An old Indian officer in one of the corps at Bareilly, an expert in company affairs, analysed the situation as one in which the English attempts to establish their Raj had finally run out of steam. There was, therefore, no need to fight the company or adopt an explicitly anti-British attitude; the English would just pack and go, *aap se*, of their own, as the expression went in Hindi. When, just before the height of the excitement about the Burmese events, 200 volunteer soldiers in the company's barracks at Saharanpur received marching orders to proceed all the way to Calcutta, a rumour gained credence that the company no longer had a single soldier between these two cities. There was a clear sense of a change of regime in the air. Already it was said in the villages of the Upper Doab, that Rivers Grindall, the company's judge and magistrate, had peacefully restored the fort of Saharanpur to Nawab Bambu Khan, a local Afghan nobleman, or amir, whose family had been allies and patrons of the Gujars during much of their rule of the region from 1753 to the Maratha takeover of 1789. The old days were here again. The return of normalcy and the restoration of the familiar pre-company order, many seem to have felt, were imminent.

In Saharanpur, however, as on the other side of the Yamuna, some of the excitement was of a millenarian character. And naturally, there were leaders who felt the need for a measure of violent action. They argued that the strongest parties should now 'seize the sword and possess themselves of the country thus voluntarily relinquished' by the British. Bijay Singh at Kunja was induced to believe that, as the son of the late Raja Ram Dayal Singh of Landhaura was an infant and his grandson Badan Singh an idiot, 'the time had arrived to dispose of them both and set himself up as the head of the Goojurs'. He was said to have indicated that after Dasahra, the annual royal festival that marked the beginning of the season of martial activity, he would make a new start with the revenue collections from the entire Gujar territory once ruled by his 'uncle' Raja Ram Dayal Singh. He even publicly announced his determination, as Grindall quoted him, 'to seat himself upon the throne of Dehly'. Again, we get a glimpse of the mood that prevailed at the time and of the ancien régime attitudes and values that determined the politics of the Doab gentry and peasantry twenty years after the colonial state had imposed its apparatus and promulgated its regulations.[10]

Bijay Singh, I have reason to assume, was dependent on the then 'big man' of the district, Shaikh Kallan, who had, during the preceding years, by a combination of revenue farming, land purchases and the intimidation of rivals, emerged as the most powerful man of the district and seems to have used the Chaudhri's financial embarrassment to further his own ambitions.[11] However, it was Bijay Singh's alliance with minor warlord Kallu that made the company view him as a dangerous enemy. Kallu seems to have been a Gujar freebooter from the Moradabad district, whose gang was recruited from his Gujar clansmen and from the 'more turbulent' Ranghars, a rather loose term used for hillmen converted to Islam. He had been active for years on the bridle paths connecting Nagina with Garhwal and on the banks of the Ganga near Haridwar. In the 1822–1823 season, trade in the area was totally suspended for fear of him. Early in 1823, he shifted across the Ganga to the Saharanpur district. A reward of 1,000 rupees was sanctioned for his apprehension, but without success. For Bijay Singh, an alliance with Kallu, his two fellow-sardars, and their bands or militias presented a tempting, though highly risky, operational horizon of all-Gujar politics.

Kallu, like Shaikh Dallah, was not simply a *daaku*, a dacoit or highway robber, at least not towards the end of his career. During the 1824 monsoon, the slack military season, he travelled 300 kilometres to the south to Bharatpur, the Jat capital, which, at that time, served as a centre of disaffection and a place of refuge for many men hard pressed by the company's police. At Bharatpur, Rao Durjan Sal, the energetic and ambitious nephew of the ailing raja, was busy forging the coalition that would soon assist him in his attempt to seize the throne. Along with Kallu, a number of warriors from Jaipur, 200 kilometres to the west, attended the meeting. The Jats of Beri, as we saw, had also attended, but, encouraged by the news from Burma, there must also have been men from several other places. The talks were part of the 'active negotiations' that went on at the time between Bharatpur, Jaipur and Alwar, the latter a Rajput kingdom that had already been immersed for almost a decade in a struggle between rival factions, but determined to assert its autonomy in the face of the company's interference. Frederick Shore, a man with a good intelligence network in the Upper Doab, would later be told the story that Kallu had been despatched from Bharatpur 'for the express purpose of creating a disturbance in the British provinces, how far true I cannot say'.

From now on, Kallu's attacks became more daring and, assuming the proportions of a rebellion, began to be aimed at the police. In September 1824, he plundered a police post with 40 of his men, wounding the jamadar, the officer in charge, killing the *barqandaaz* and the *sowaars*, and carrying off the horses, arms and accoutrements of the station. The next day, the gang seized a policeman posted at a ghat on the Ganga, pinioned him, and having taken his *chapraas*, or badge, spear and clothes, wounded him with a sword. Four days later, eighty or ninety men sacked the market town of Bhagwanpur, about seven kilometres to the north of Kunja, Chaudhri Bijay Singh's fort. They robbed the houses of several mahajans of property worth 13,000 rupees, and abducted three women, whom they set free after a lapse of four days, having made their families pay for their ransom. Here, they also killed a number of *sowaars*, took away two of their horses and wounded and plundered the pilgrims who were on their way to the Ganga.[12]

Grindall at Saharanpur now received information that the leaders of the gang and some of their men had taken shelter at the fort of Kunja, where they had brought the stolen police horses and other plundered property. A strong police party was sent for them. On their arrival at the fort, Bijay Singh himself, accompanied by Ishq Lal, who was a merchant, a banker and a revenue farmer, two *muqaddam*s loyal to him and a large body of men, came out. Matchlocks were levelled at the police, who retired. Two other attempts to arrest the gang leaders failed. Meanwhile, thousands of men gathered at Kunja and in the surrounding area, in all some 3,000 horse and foot armed with matchlocks.

Many of them must have come from Gujar villages in the region. Kallu, perhaps inspired by his contacts with Jat and Rajput politicians at important centres of power, now assumed the style of a raja. As Raja Kalyan Singh, he 'began in royal fashion to despatch messengers in various directions to exact tribute from the villages within his kingdom'. Zamindars and merchants were told to bring specified sums of money and quantities of grain and other articles to Kunja. As no claim to kingship in India convinces unless supported by the possession of treasure, it was announced that an attack on the English treasury at Saharanpur was imminent. On 1 October, Kallu and other sardars, whose force appears to have been between 1,200 and 2,000 strong, in fact sallied forth from Kunja and attacked a train of bullock carts that, guarded by 150 policemen, was on its way carrying the revenue collected from the tahsil of Jwalapur to Saharanpur. They killed about twenty men, amongst whom were a *thaanadaar* and two jamadars. The treasure captured amounted to 17,613 rupees. As to the time for the sack of Saharanpur, the liberation of the prisoners in the jail there, and the actual takeover of the government, the movement's leaders are said to have settled on the night of Sunday, 3 October 1824.[13]

During those days, Frederick Shore would remember, not one of the leading landholders of the Saharanpur district came forward in support of the company. On the first success of Kallu and the other sardars,

> numbers even of the better sort of inhabitants immediately joined them, and *then* insurrection, and not mere plunder, was the object. The rallying cry all over the country, repeated with the most enthusiastic exultation, was, 'The English reign is over!' - 'Down with the English!' It will not avail to say that it was foreign to the habits of the people to come forward, and that they stood aloof, leaving the business to our police and troops: the history of India abounds with instances in the native states, where, in the event of a disturbance, those of influence called out their retainers and tenants, and boldly stood forth in defence of the Government. But it was very different [in 1824]: they did not merely stand aloof: even those ordinarily in frequent attendance on the different magistrates, separated immediately to their homes, under pretence of exerting their influence to preserve order in their own neighbourhood, and began raising men; but for what purpose? - to be ready, if occasion proved favourable, to turn their whole weight and power against our government.[14]

There may be an element of exaggeration in this, Shore being out to shock his compatriots and make them realise their foolishness in persisting in their lack of interest in Indian public opinion. This colonial inability to communicate was certainly the root cause of the imminent all-Gujar rising of 1824. The participation of the daredevil and talented visionary Kallu in it, however, left the company with little choice. As in the case of Shaikh Dallah, it was suppressed with the most violent means at the company's disposal. With him at Saharanpur, Grindall had 150 Gurkha privates of the Sirmur Battalion. On 1 October, hearing of the large assemblage of armed men at Kunja, he wrote to Dehra Dun for two or three companies more. The next morning, 260 Gurkhas, including officers, set out from their barracks in the Dun under their commander, Captain Frederick Young. On Sunday, 3 October, the two Gurkha detachments united and attacked the fort of Kunja. After unhinging the gate with a young tree, used as a ram, in an action that would become legendary in the Gurkha annals, they shot and bayoneted all who came their way, chasing the Gujars over the flat roofs and in the narrow alleys of the fort. A good number of Kallu's men who fled climbing the walls, were later found out in the moonlit sugarcane fields nearby and were shot. Most of Bijay Singh's Gujars, however, stayed in the fort and fought to the last. The total number killed was 153, about 75 of whom were from Kunja itself. Almost all of the latter were Gujars; they comprised about one-third of the adult male population of the fort. Bijay Singh and Kallu were amongst those killed. Both the fort and the village belonging to it were looted. 'We did not prevent it', Young would write, '[I]t was a lesson that the fellows will recollect.'

The local British district officers were convinced the battle had stopped a major rebellion. 'Had we not stopped the insurgents at Koonju the evening we did, Saharunpore was to be plundered and an attempt made to release the prisoners' from the district jail, wrote Grindall. That appears incontestable.[15]

In his letters on the Kunja affair, Grindall repeatedly assured his corres-pondents of the reluctance with which he passed on news about the 'ridiculous and absurd' Gujar motives, about the 'incredible folly' of even listening to the rumours and the 'extraordinary madness' that had taken hold of the people in the region. He enclosed with his letter 'a paper containing absurdities ... too gross to copy into a public letter. I do it to show the temper of the times more than anything else. Such falsehoods and follies, however, doubtless led to the disturbances in the district'. Indeed, it is clear from his comments on other subjects that it was not his habit to reach out and assess public opinion in Saharanpur. But in this case the excitement around him was real, and he knew that to treat it with silent contempt would not be enough. Though quite disgusted by what he had recently learned on the psychological state of his district, he felt he better pass on what he had heard to his superiors in order to make them understand that the military solution was the only adequate one. There was justification for the panic that had affected the European families of the town of Saharanpur and had made them 'take post in the fort one night'. But he found it impossible to grasp and communicate what exactly had moved the people he administered. And he came very near to admitting as much, when he maintained that in general it did no harm to be out of touch with such absurdities. Anyway, what had happened was madness and it had to be dealt with as such.[16] There were follies in India that an enlightened civil service did best to pass by if it meant to maintain its unity of purpose and its belief in its mission.

In all the little uprisings treated in this chapter, this element of cognitive dissonance is present. Communication did not break down because the initiators of the campaigns, movements and little uprisings behaved 'irrationally' or did not make an attempt to negotiate. On the contrary, one has the impression that it was the arrogance and inability of the British to take their cue from the 'deluded' public and their doctrine unwaveringly to consider themselves the sole judges of what was according to equity and made administrative sense, which was an important element in the genesis of these small wars.[17] Many of them were located not in the core area of colonial rule or in the Purbiyas' home ground, but on the margins of company territory and in princely states where few people would have experience with British idiosyncrasies. One should like to know, therefore, whether it is feasible to write the history of the various ways Indians coped with and adapted to the colonial avoidance strategy we discussed, this extremely non-communicative attitude of a large number of the company's administrators. Studies of the 'Dasahras' of other years may well help to elucidate the issue.

One way of making sense of the series of 'disturbances' like those related in this chapter is to follow Charles Metcalfe's analysis and conclude that during the monsoon of 1824, because of the news from Burma, large parts of India were in a state of unusual political ferment that would culminate in the mutinies at Barrackpur, near Calcutta, and at Jaipur in October and November.[18] In this chapter, on the other hand, we have followed Frederick Shore, pushed the sepoy mutinies to the margins of our attention and suggested that the year we focused on was hardly an exceptional one, but represented a random cross section of, by no means exclusively anti-British, endemic political aspirations in Hindustan. The difference with other years was simply that these aspirations became more than usually visible in 1824 as a result of the sudden feeling of increased insecurity created by the news from Burma. The actual mutinies followed, rather than triggered, as they would in 1857, the more local uprisings, none of which had its base in the sepoy recruiting grounds of Eastern Hindustan.

The study of the 1824 Dasahra—of which, it should be said, this chapter does not give a complete account—can only begin to give an idea of the forms of *mufassal* activism and protest during the pre-mutiny decades. Similarly, detailed studies of other years might gradually reveal the common features of the 53 Dasahra seasons between the company's conquest in 1803 and the events of 1857 and of the forces they unleashed in Hindustan as well as their increasingly anti-colonial ingredients. Our focus on 1857 would decrease in the process, but our understanding of the events of that year might profit.

Notes and References

1. For the panic at Calcutta and Barrackpur and for Metcalfe's opinion, see H.H. Wilson, *The History of British India from 1805 to 1835*, 3 vols (London, 1848), III, pp. 60, 98, 181. I am largely

ignoring here the short-lived mutiny at Barrackpur that began during the last days of October; it followed rather than triggered the movements described in this chapter. Frederick John Shore, *Notes on Indian Affairs*, 2 vols (London, 1837), I, pp. 158–161. Wilson gives short accounts of a series of disturbances and assertions of autonomy in 1824 in western and southern India, several of which are not mentioned in this chapter. For the 1824 Kittur insurgency in the Bombay Presidency, see S.S. Chaudhuri, *Civil Disturbances during the British Rule in India (1765–1857)* (Calcutta: World Press, 1955), pp. 153–154.

2. Translation from the Lahore *akhbaar*, 30 August 1824; Bengal Secret Consultations (Hereafter BSC) 22 October 1824, no. 8. Khushwant Singh, *Ranjit Singh: Maharaja of the Punjab* (London: Allen & Unwin, 1962), p. 154.

3. Charles Elliott, Agent to the Governor General, Delhi, to Govt, 8 September 1824 and 4 October 1824; William Murray, Superint. Ambala, to Ch. Elliott, 5 September 1824; Lt C.M. Wade, Pol. Asst Ludhiana, to W. Murray, 4 September 1824; Govt to C. Elliott, 22 October 1824; all in BSC, 22 October 1824, nos 6–11. Khushwant Singh, *Ranjit Singh*, p. 155. Hari Ram Gupta, *History of the Sikhs* (New Delhi: Munshiram Manoharlal, 1991), V, p. 152.

4. C. Elliott to Govt, 31 July 1824; W. Murray to C. Elliott, 28 June 1824; Bengal Political Consultations (Hereafter BPC), 20 August 1824, nos 37, 38. C. Elliott to Govt, 23 and 31 August 1824; W. Murray to C. Elliott (with translation of Fatah Jang Khan's *arzi*), 20 August 1824; Govt to C. Elliott, 17 September 1824; BPC, 17 September 1824, nos 18–23. Wilson, *History*, III, pp. 166–167.

5. According to the *Rohtak District Gazetteer 1910* (Lahore, 1911), p. 73, the name of the *gotra* was Kadian, but Campbell (see next note) writes 'Kuddar'; the clan's founder's name was Kada.

6. C. Elliot, AAG Delhi, to Major Gen. Reynell, 20 October 1824; BPC, 19 November 1824, no. 19. G.R. Campbell, Ag Princ. Asst, to Bd of Rev. W.P., 29 November 1824, 3 January 1825, 11 January 1825 and 28 February 1825; Bd of Rev. W.P. to Govt, 7 January 1825 and 4 March 1825; Bengal Criminal Judicial Proceedings Western Provinces (BCrJPWP) 24 March 1825, nos 34–39. See also Michael Mann, 'Turbulent Delhi: Religious Strife, Social Tension and Political Conflicts, 1803–1857', *South Asia*, n.s., 28 (2005), p. 27, and his source: Depositions of Inhabitants of *mauza* Mautha, contained in Capt. H.L. Peach to C. Elliot, 28 September 1824; Home Miscellaneous Series (Hereafter HMS) 674, pp. 200ff, AAS, British Library (BL).

7. Henry Graham, Pol. Asst, to W. Fraser, n.d.; BPC, 19 November 1824, no. 21.

8. Th. H. Maddock, Pol. Ag. Bhopal, to Govt, 3 October 1824; Govt to Lt Col. J. Nicol, Adj. Gen. Army, 22 October 1824; both in BPC, 22 October 1824, nos 15–17. G. Wellesley, Resident Indore, to Govt, 14 October 1824; Major Delamain to G. Wellesley, 14 October 1824 (extract); Major R.T. Seyer to Major Delamain, n.d.; Deposition of Narsu, n.d.; Deposition of Ilahi Bakhsh, 14 October 1824; Capt. W. Oliphant to Major R.T. Seyer, 15 October 1824; Lt Col. W. Richards to Major Delamain, 17 October 1824; G. Wellesley to Capt. Stewart, 27 October 1824; Govt to G. Wellesley, 19 November 1824; C.T. Metcalfe, Resident Hyderabad, to Govt, 22 October 1824; Major R.T. Seyer to C.T. Metcalfe, 13 October 1824; Capt. T. Donaldson to Capt. Worsley, 24 October 1824; all in BPC, 19 November 1824, nos 35–46.

9. Substance of the petition of Beja Singh, 25 December 1817, enclosed in A. Murray, Coll. Saharanpur, to Revenue Bd of Commissioners, 2 January 1818; Rev. Bd Comm. Proceedings, 24 April 1818, no. 10.

10. R. Grindall to Govt, 5 November 1824; BCrJPWP, 13 January 1825, no. 51. Wilson, *History*, III, p. 60. Muin ud-din, generally known as Bambu Khan, was the half-brother of the notorious Ghulam Qadir. He lived in the family capital Najibabad in the Moradabad (now Bijnor) district. Their father was Zabita Khan, Najib ud-daula's son. Jos J.L. Gommans, *The Rise of the Indo-Afghan Empire, c. 1710–1780* (Leiden, 1995), pp. 127, 179.

11. See my *Grase in their Mouth: The Upper Soab of India under the Company's Magna Carta, 1793–1830* (Leiden, 2010).

12. Translated *rubkaari* of a proceeding held by R.F. Grindall in the Faujdari Court of Saharanpur, enclosed in W. Ewer to Govt, 16 October 1824; BCrJPWP 13 January 1825, no. 46.

13. F.J. Shore to W. Ewer, 11–13 October 1824, enclosed in BCrJPWP, 13 January 1825, no. 48. Also in Uttaranchal State Archives, Pre-Mutiny Records 35. Wilson, *History*, III, p. 183.

14. F.J. Shore, *Notes*, I, pp. 158–161.

15. Capt. F. Young to Major Gen. T. Reynell, 4 October 1824; HMS, 790, AAS, BL. F.J. Shore to C. Cornish, 5 October 1824; Shore Coll., MSS Eur 307/9, AAS, BL.

16. R. Grindall to Govt, 5 November 1824; see note 10.

17. C. Elliott to Govt, 23 August 1824; see note 4. 'The deluded multitude' was the term used by Elliott.

18. On the Jaipur mutiny, see BPC 12 November 1824, nos 7–35, 19 November 1824, nos 10–12 and 3 December 1824, nos 19–33. Another mutiny took place at Kota in August. Several other minor uprisings and disturbances, not treated here for reasons of space and lack of detailed information, took place in Awadh, Jaisalmer and Shinde's territories.

3

꙳꙳꙳

'THE HAZARDS OF INTERFERENCE'
British Fears of Rebellion and Sati as a Potential Site of Conflict, 1829–1857

Andrea Major

DESPITE revisionist historian Eric Stokes' warning that interpretations of unrest in 1857 must

> touch upon a deeper level than the vague disturbance of the popular mind by fears for religion and caste, springing from British interference with customs like widow burning and widow remarriage or British enforcement of the intermingling of castes through common messing in gaols and the common carriage of passengers by the railway…

these sorts of explanations continue to be influential.[1] Such interpretations reflect an immediately post-1857 agenda concerned with reasserting the ideological basis of colonial rule by representing the uprising as the result of 'irrational' religious fanaticism among 'simple, superstitious, credulous sepoys[2].' They are also embedded in a pre-existing orientalist discourse about Indian religion and the 'hazards of interference' in Indian 'superstition'. Although immediate British reactions to the uprising were fractured and multivalent, after the revolt a consensus began to emerge in imperialist historiography that blamed the uprising on self-interested, reactionary Indian elites who feared the impact that the imposition of 'colonial modernity' would have on their status and authority.[3] In particular, a range of social and religious reforms, from the prohibition of Sati in 1829 onwards, were portrayed as cumulative affronts that provoked Indian fears of religious erosion and even forcible or duplicitous conversion. Such simplified interpretations of the role of religion in 1857 have exhibited surprising longevity.[4] They have also obfuscated the complex matrixes of social, economic, political and religious concerns that prompted the uprising and obscured the varied ways in which specific religious issues acted as sites of contest in the decades before 1857.[5]

Whether depicted as the unfounded paranoia of a superstitious people or the justified consternation of a community under social, religious and cultural siege, the primacy of religious and caste issues in motivating and mobilising dissent has consistently informed popular British accounts of the uprising, from Sir John Kaye to William Dalrymple. Despite, or perhaps because of its widespread acceptance, interpreting the role of religion in 1857 remains problematic. This is not to suggest that religious issues and identities were not significant in uprising, of course, but any attempt to understand the relationship between these and popular unrest must first disentangle varied experiences of religious grievance from a totalising colonial discourse that represents all British interventions in social and religious issues as having a cumulative causal effect, regardless of the paucity of tangible, empirical evidence for their relevance to those involved in the revolt.[6] Despite the popularity of the all-encompassing narratives of colonial reform, encounters between the colonial state and various indigenous groups over religious issues were regionally, socially and culturally specific, and, as a result, their relationship to unrest must be understood as equally diverse. There was no pan-Indian experience of colonial incursions into the sacred—different issues might be sites of contest for different communities at different times. There is little doubt that a general sense of growing religious unease played a role in fomenting revolt in 1857, as it had in many previous outbreaks. Yet uncritical assumptions about the direct causal role of specific high-profile reforms, such as the prohibition of Sati, are destabilised when their relationship to the events of 1857 are seriously interrogated. Such assumptions ignore significant dislocations between event and reaction, submerging the specificities of individual issues in a monolithic orientalist discourse on the role of religion in Indian society. In order to understand the complex nature of socio-religious grievances as sites of contest, we must look critically at the relationship between specific reforms and unrest, questioning both the extent of their impact and the possible agendas behind their incorporation into the colonial discourse on 'the mutiny'.

This chapter will look in detail at the relationship between one specific religious 'grievance', the prohibition of Sati, and popular unrest in 1857. As the first major British intervention in Indian religion, the prohibition of Sati in 1829 is repeatedly cited in British historiography as a precursor of unrest in 1857. The connection is endemic in popular British histories of India: Wolpert, Spiers, Keay and James, among others, all explicitly cite the prohibition of Sati as one of the causes of discontent that led to the insurrection. To give one more, recent[7] but controversial, example, Niall Fergusson, in *Empire: How Britain Made the Modern World*, published in 2003, concludes his discussion of Governor General Bentinck's reform by quoting a stark warning issued by Lt. Col. Playfaire in 1828 that any order of government prohibiting the practice would create a most alarming sensation throughout the native army, they would consider it an interference with their customs and religion amounting to an abandonment of those principles which have hitherto guided government in its conduct towards them. Such a feeling once excited, there is no possibility of predicting what might happen. It might break out in some parts of the army in open rebellion, certainly, in all it would produce distrust and disaffection.[8]

He uses this quotation to move directly into a discussion of 1857, saying 'such concerns were premature … but … far from groundless…. A reaction against the imposition of British culture on India was indeed brewing', implying that the prohibition of Sati was directly causally connected to unrest in 1857.[9] This chapter will explore British fears of rebellion prior to the prohibition of Sati in 1829, their experience of Sati as a site of contest between 1829 and 1857 and role that British assumptions about the dangers of religious interference, crystallised during the Sati debate, played in colonial interpretations of the uprising. It will argue that while Sati was a relatively marginal issue during the revolt itself, its incorporation into later explanations for the uprising reflects both the power of pre-existing orientalist discourses and the discursive expediencies that accompanied the re-establishment of colonial rule.

Sati, the immolation of a Hindu widow on her husband's funeral pyre, was outlawed in British India, after two decades of intense debate, by Lord William Bentinck in December 1829. Although the practice never affected more than a tiny proportion of widows, the rite achieved a disproportionate prominence in the colonial imagination, becoming an icon for Hindu 'otherness'.[10] Its eventual prohibition represented both a formative moment in the construction of the moral terrain of imperialism and a shift in the nature of British power in India. As Lata Mani has shown, the British debate on Sati was about much more than the ethics of burning women. By intervening in what they perceived to be a religious issue, the British were renegotiating the parameters of colonial control, moving away from previous policies of non-intervention in religious issues.[11] Throughout the debate, those who opposed intervention on Sati argued that it would represent an infringement of the avowed colonial policy of religious neutrality and might consequently provoke instability and conflict. This fear effectively stayed the hand of successive governor generals before Bentinck, who thought, as Mountstuart Elphinstone did, that 'if we succeed we save 100 or 1000 victims from voluntary immolation, if we fail we involve sixty millions in all the horrors of war and revolution …'.[12]

Fear of potential rebellion underpinned official policy on Sati throughout the early nineteenth century, reappearing recurrently as an excuse for government inaction. Embedded within the early colonial conviction about the desirability of ruling through Indian structures, arguments about the 'hazards of interference' also drew their power from a wider orientalist discourse that represented Hindus as '... unreflective practitioners of their faith, but nonetheless jealous of it and prone to rebellion at the threat of its infringement'.[13] If a volatile religious fanaticism was characteristic of Muslims, Hindus evinced thraldom to religious injunction that elided rational agency. 'An Hindoo no more thinks of evading the customary rites of religion', commented Rev William Tennent in 1803, 'than an European thinks of evading the unerring stroke of death. Its dictates appear to him the call of invincible necessity, to which he submits without reluctance, because unavoidable; and without choice, because ordered by the Brahmins.'[14] Ostensible colonial adherence to Enlightenment principles of religious toleration was thus reinforced by underlying fears that intervention in even the most heinous religious customs would result in instability and unrest. R.B. Gardiner, the Magistrate for Behar, for example, commented of Sati in 1818 as follows:

> Much as I would wish to see the total abolition of a practice so repugnant to the feelings of humanity, I should consider the prohibition by law of a ceremony which is encouraged by the Shaster, as an infringement of that system of complete toleration in matters of religion, declared to be a fundamental principle of the British government in India, which might tend to shake the confidence at present reposed in it by all classes of its native subjects, and be eventually productive of dangerous consequences.[15]

Similarly, J. Masters, the magistrate for Dacca, believed that

> the government has always stressed its policy of toleration and has tried to ... impress upon their minds how decidedly such an interference was objected to. Here then would be a direct violation of such protestations, and the Hindoo would, with justice, continue distrustful of every future act of the legislature.[16]

Concerns that tackling the Sati issue would lead to 'dangerous consequences' were not universally held, of course; many anti-Sati campaigners and officials believed that the rite could be abolished quite safely. The government, however, remained wary. Even Bentinck was unwilling to act until he had gauged official opinion on the potential impact of prohibition, especially on the army. On arriving in India in 1828, he issued a circular to local magistrates and military officers:

> But the point on which His Lordship is most anxious to consult you, and perhaps it is the most important feature in the whole consideration, is, the effect of any declared intention of the government whether of immediate or gradual abolition might have upon the minds of the native army.... Would debarring the practice of suttee create any sensation among the native officers and sepoys of the Hindu persuasion likely to evince itself in tumult or revolt, or actual opposition to the measures enacted for its abolition? Would they consider the suppression of this particular rite such a hardship, as to cause among them

manifestations of disgust or irritation, or ill will and disaffection to the state? Supposing actual opposition of manifestations of feelings of a serious and unpleasant nature to be in your opinion improbable would interference in the matter of suttee to the extent of a total abolition of the usage, create anxiety and alarm among the sepoys, under the apprehension of other innovations, or excite a dread that this was only the first step towards a more general attack on their customs and religion; or would such an interference be deemed by them an abandonment of our professed desire to abstain from invading their customs? Notwithstanding an apparent passive submission to an edict for the discontinuance of suttee, would the effect of such a measure be to create sullenness amongst the men, or any distrust of our motives; or would it be likely to generate and diffuse among the native soldiers the slightest aversion to our rule and authority?[17]

The language of the circular is significant, foreshadowing as it does explanations for Indian grievance given by the British after 1857. In fact, of the forty-nine responses received from British military officials, the vast majority felt that the prohibition of Sati was entirely safe.[18] The existence of concerns about its impact on the loyalty of the army and the 'prophetic' warnings of military commanders like Lt. Col. Playfair, however, have leant weight to subsequent arguments for a connection between the prohibition of Sati and the unrest in 1857, despite significant dislocations between the social and geographic impact of the reform and the sites of conflict in 1857.

There is little doubt that during the two decades before and for some years after prohibition, Sati represented a site of ideological contest within the colonial polity. There is, however, little evidence to substantiate later assertions that its prohibition caused a major outcry across India. Jorg Fisch, in his comprehensive study of Sati, claims that the prohibition actually amounted to abolition, the success of which surpassed Britain's 'wildest expectations'.[19] Certainly, the British, at the time, believed that the legislation had been successful. The predicted violent backlash did not transpire and William Bentinck himself commented in 1833, 'It is a matter of astonishment to me that it [the question of Sati] should so long have continued to be the bugbear that it was.'[20] Indeed, estimates of both the intensity and social and geographical scope of the controversy may have been inflated post-1857, as the assumptions about Indian opposition to 'benevolent' British reforms that informed mutiny discourses were projected onto earlier events. It is also misleading to characterise the Sati debate as a confrontation between a reforming colonial state and reactionary Indian population. Divisions between reforming and orthodox elements of the Bengali elite and between orientalist/non-interventionist and Anglicist/Utilitarian/Evangelical British groups were as significant as divisions of race in determining the framework of the Sati debate. Indian opposition to Bentinck's regulation against Sati was primarily confined to a small, but highly articulate, orthodox elite in Calcutta. At this level there certainly was discontent. Two petitions against the regulation were presented, with just over 1,000 signatures between them. When these proved unsuccessful, the Dharma Sabha was formed to 'protect Hindu religion' and raise money for an ultimately unsuccessful appeal to the Privy Council in 1832. The orthodox Bengali press waxed lyrical about the infringement of Hinduism; *Samachar Chandrika* warned in 1832 that the Hindus 'are now rebelling in heart because of the injury done to their religion'.[21] As David Kopf points out, while their opposition to the Sati legislation has meant that they have subsequently received a bad press, Dharma Sabha leaders like Radhakant Deb and Ram Camul Sen were also modernisers who were involved, among other things, in the formation of Hindu College, an institution of 'western' education in Calcutta.[22] Their encounter with 'colonial modernity' was, thus, more complex than the reactionary defence of superstition as depicted in later accounts. Kopf suggests that their opposition to the Sati legislation was primarily predicated on a defence of Indian cultural and religious sovereignty, the Dharma Sabha being formed not only to defend the cause of Sati, but also to show how its abolition had compelled Hindus to institutionalise and register their protest against the new colonial policy. As such, he argues, the revivalist Dharma Sabha was the first 'proto-nationalist movement' in India.[23] Such teleological interpretations seem, superficially, to lend weight to suggestions of a connection between opposition to the prohibition of Sati and rebellion in 1857. Such linkages homogenise Indian opposition to the prohibition, however, and obscure both the complex and fractured nature of the Sati issue and the social, political and geographical specificities of the 1857 Uprising. Sati was not a universal custom, affecting only 0.2 per cent of widows even in Bengal, where it was most widely practised,[24] and some sections of the Calcutta elite even signed petitions thanking Bentinck for prohibiting it. Outside Bengal, there is little evidence of protest against the prevention of Sati. Indeed, Foreign Department records from 1830–1857 indicated that in some peripheral areas of British India, the prohibition not only caused no unrest; it had not even been promulgated. In these areas, the local population, not prone to Sati in any case, continued completely ignorant of either the prohibition or the controversy in Calcutta for decades after 1829.[25]

Empirical evidence regarding the existence of Sati between 1829 and 1857 is incomplete. The Government of India, who meticulously recorded all Sati cases in British India between 1815 and 1829, stopped keeping records on it once it was outlawed. Moreover, many of the judicial files relating to illegal Satis post 1829, listed in the original Board's Collection's indexes, have not been preserved. We, therefore, have only piecemeal information about the existence of Sati in British India after prohibition, based on sporadic government records, press reports and anecdotal evidence in personal memoirs and correspondence. For the purpose of this chapter, it will suffice to say that there does not seem to be any evidence to suggest that intervention to prevent and prosecute Sati caused ongoing violent resistance or aggressive protest. This is not to argue, of course, that Sati did not survive undetected in parts of British India, or that the ban on it was entirely successful. If police and judicial records from late colonial India (1860 onwards) can give an indication, Sati, though always exceptional and after prohibition extremely rare, represented a site of contest between colonial authorities and local communities throughout the colonial period, with some neighbourhoods closing ranks in order to keep an immolation secret or hamper later state investigations. In other cases, it seems that Indian police may themselves have been complicit in allowing Sati to take place. H. Newnham, in 1833, recorded a conversation with a Bengali zamindar, in which his informant told him:

> If it be his (alluding to the Deity) pleasure, all is right, if not the act of man is a presumption. As for myself, I know that women will continue as before to burn and should a sati appear amongst women of my family, I shall try the effects of secrecy and bribery. If such fail I will have recourse to intimidation of witnesses taking care that no one shall whom I consider likely to tell the tale, and thirdly shall be prepared to oppose with the sword the thana or police station if driven to necessity.[26]

Examples of open resistance or outright violence resulting from state intervention in Sati were rare, however. In August 1830 a policeman was fatally wounded and two more injured trying to prevent a Sati in Moradabad district. A more serious confrontation took place in the princely state of Ahmadnagar in 1835. As an 'independent' state, the British prohibition of Sati did not apply in Ahmadnagar, and armed British intervention to prevent the burning of five wives of the deceased Raja Kurn Singh, however humanely intentioned, was a direct violation of the state's sovereignty and British treaty obligations. Perhaps more significantly, the region was extremely unstable at the time and the reaction of Ahmadnagar mercenaries in firing at British troops who sought to prevent the Sati must be understood in the context of endemic violence in the region.[27] These examples aside, accounts of violent clashes or simmering resentments over the prohibition of Sati in British India are conspicuous in their absence, and, as Jorg Fisch points out, such isolated incidents as did occur, did not crystallise into general dissatisfaction.[28] Rather, as the Bengali zamindar's statement suggests, confrontations were primarily responsive, provoked by a specific Sati event, not ongoing ideological opposition to the legislation itself.

Always exceptional, the 'true' Sati in the Hindu idiom was not only voluntary, but miraculous and divine. This interpretation is, of course, deeply problematic; the supernatural narration of Sati is embedded in community strategies to circumvent criminal responsibility for Sati, provide ideological sanction for acts of violence against women and blur the boundary between coercion, compulsion, indoctrination and agency.[29] That said, belief in the possibility of 'authentic' Sati certainly existed among some communities, and the perception that a 'true' Sati had emerged, whatever the reality of the situation, could be enough to create confrontation in usually law-abiding communities. This was not, however, a generalised conflict over the hypothetical 'right' of the colonial state to prohibit Sati, but the immediate strategies of a local community in the grip of a specific event. Moreover, there are many examples of successful state intervention to avert Satis, and even of families and communities taking it upon themselves to prevent immolations. The Bentinck Manuscripts contain references to Satis prevented in the year immediately after 1829, and include one incident where a local British judge was dismissed for taking a bribe to allow a Sati to proceed.[30] Newspapers and journals from the time also occasionally carried articles adverting to the successful prevention of Satis, or to the prosecution of individuals involved in illegal immolations.[31] Pre-1857, the British, at least, believed that the measure had passed off successfully and uneventfully.

The absence of a continuous history of protest against the prohibition of Sati does not automatically imply that it was not a cause of resentment in 1857, of course. There is, however, very little evidence that the localised opposition in 1829–1833, or the sporadic confrontations that occurred subsequently, were directly linked to the rebellion in 1857. Geographically, the two events do not fit. Although the British conspiracy theories abound, there is no evidence that the Calcutta elite that had been so vocal in their opposition to the Sati legislation had any role in fomenting unrest in 1857. Indeed, it is widely accepted that this section of the Indian society was hostile to the revolt; they certainly did not use the opportunity to exact revenge for the prohibition of Sati, or any other grievance, real or imagined. Moreover, the vast majority of recorded Sati cases occurred in the Lower Provinces, Bengal and Bihar, from which very few army recruits came and which remained relatively quiet during 1857. The main centres of the uprising were in central India, around Delhi, the United Provinces and Awadh, where few Sati cases occurred. Between 1815 and 1823, for example, there were on average 375 Satis annually in the Calcutta division, compared to only 45 in Dacca, 22 in Murshidabad, 97 in Benares, 47 in Patna and only 16 in the all-important Bareilly division, which included key centres of the uprising like Meerut, Kanpur and Saharanpur.[32] Furthermore, the Muslim rulers of Awadh had been among the first Indian rulers to prohibit Sati, and had done so voluntarily as early as 1833.

The other main centre of Sati was in the Rajput states. In the years between 1830 and 1857, and especially after 1844, the British brought indirect pressure to bear on the Indian rulers to prohibit the practice, with varying degree of success. The majority of princely states quickly followed the example of Jaipur, which outlawed the custom in 1845, although some Rajput rulers, like those of Jodhpur, Udaipur, Kota and Bikaner, held out longer. Initially, British policy on Sati in princely states was cautious, due to the fear that authoritative intervention would provoke violent opposition—a concern partly predicated on the assumption that Rajputs were both particularly warlike and volatile and exceptionally devoted to

Sati. More importantly, however, any direct British intervention in a 'domestic' issue like Sati would be a direct violation of British treaty obligations, creating the potential for Sati to become a site for political conflict over the integrity of Indian sovereignty.[33] Despite this, the British had, by 1857, been able to bully and cajole all the princely states except Udaipur into prohibiting the rite. In many cases, Indian acquiescence on this issue was effectively coerced, but discontent over British interference in Sati does not seem to correlate with unrest in 1857. Indeed, many of the Rajput states remained either 'loyal' or neutral during the uprising, and some of the states that had been subject to the greatest British pressure to prohibit Sati, such as Udaipur and Bikaner, were not only loyal but even offered shelter to British fugitives.

There is little evidence from the Indian side that the prohibition of Sati was a direct cause of the revolt. The famous Azamgarh proclamation lists a number of grievances, mostly economic and/or political, but while there is a general call to religious sentiment, there is a conspicuous lack of religious grievances cited, and certainly no mention of Sati.[34] Khan Bahadur Khan, in one of his proclamations, does advert to the prohibition of Sati as an example of the indignities and injustices to which the people of India were subject, but these proclamations, made once the rebellion was under way, can be read as attempts by Muslim rebels to galvanise Hindu support, rather than a declaration of the motivations for revolt. Moreover, as Jalal and Bose point out, when religious themes do inform the uprising, they usually appear in the guise of Islamic millenarianism in districts like Muzaffurnagar and Saharanpur. Hindu religious millenarianism does not seem to have figured significantly in the revolt.[35] Even to the extent that infringements of Hindu religion were influential for 1857, other measures, as Ainslee Embree points out, such as the 1850 Act that made it possible for converts to Christianity to retain their inheritance and inherit ancestral property, were likely to have caused more immediate and widespread resentment than the prohibition of Sati nearly thirty years previously.[36]

The above-mentioned discontinuities suggest that while it may have contributed to a general sense of unease, the prohibition of Sati was a less significant factor in the uprising than subsequent British accounts imply. Certainly, any relationship between the prohibition of Sati and the outbreak of unrest in 1857 is far more complicated and fractured than the simplistic, teleological linkages suggested in so much traditional British historiography, leaving us to question why the connection has been so often and so uncritically invoked. I would argue that the appropriation of the Sati issue in later British discourses on 1857 works at two levels. Preconceived orientalist ideas about the nature of the Indian society that solidified during the Sati debate had a significant influence on the ideological framework through which the uprising was processed and represented, a trend reinforced by the discursive utility that the Sati issue offered in discourses designed to delegitimise the uprising and reassert the moral basis of colonial rule.

Whether from the perspective of Tory criticisms of the insensitive imposition of liberal reforms and Christianising policies that had 'amazingly disturbed the religious mind of Hindoostan',[37] or a providentialist evangelical perspective that saw it as a Brahminical struggle to maintain the oppressive structures of 'paganism' against benevolent British reform and evangelisation,[38] interpretations of the uprising drew heavily on ideas that had crystallised during the Sati debate. Disraeli's indictment of East India Company legal and administrative reforms as 'nibbling at the religious systems of the natives'[39] did not mention Sati directly, but it drew on precisely the same assumptions about the hazards of interference that had informed the non-interventionist side of the Sati debate. The evangelical community, on the other hand, represented the prohibition of Sati as a proof that laws which affected to 'improve' Indian society could and should be implemented. 'We have observed too, in our own time', Reverend George Salmon remarked, 'distinct marks of decay in the force of Hindu superstition, and have seen the government put down without a struggle, superstitions such as widow-burning, once deemed too powerful to grapple with'.[40] In their focus on the mutiny as the death throes of Brahminism,[41] they too were reproducing pre-existing tropes about the nature of the Indian society and religion that resonated strongly with those found during the Sati debate.

The cruel, scheming and rapacious Brahmin was a stock figure in nineteenth century British accounts of India, for while in the eighteenth century he might be portrayed as noble and learned, by the early nineteenth century his religious teachings were considered self-interested subterfuges. Nowhere was this more obvious than in relation to Sati, where conniving Brahmins were represented as exerting their religious influence to beguile the innocent widow, coaxing her onto the funeral pyre with specious promises of felicity in the next life, while they filled their pockets with payments for presiding over the ceremony and offerings from the pious, and even scrabbled in the ashes to retrieve their victim's jewels.[42] Francois Bernier, whose seventeenth century accounts of Sati were hugely influential in the early nineteenth century, wrote:

> I have seen some of these unhappy widows shrink at the sight of the piled wood; so as to leave no doubt on my mind that they would willingly have recanted, if recantation had been permitted by the merciless Brahmens; but those demons excite or astound the affrighted victims, and even thrust them into the fire. I was present when a poor young woman, who had fallen back five or six paces from the pit, was thus driven forward; and I saw another of these wretched beings struggling to leave the funeral pile when the fire increased around her person, but she was prevented from escaping by the long poles of the diabolical executioners.[43]

As the atrocities of the uprising began to filter back to Britain, very similar imagery was used to demonise the perpetrators of acts of violence against British men, women and children.[44] Although in the early days of the uprising, the revolt was thought to be a Muslim conspiracy,[45] by Autumn 1857, news of events at Kanpur and the actions of Nana Sahib had reached Britain, implicating high-caste Hindus in the violence. The fast day sermons of 7 October 1857, together with the national press, worked to 'demonise Indian culture and Indian colonial subjects'[46] and 'vilify Indian religions, focussing attention most typically and most intensely, on the piquant barbarities of Hindooism'.[47] From this point on, although Muslims were not absolved, attention was focused on disgruntled Brahmins as well as duplicitous mullahs. Reverend Benjamin Rice of Bangalore put it as follows:

Although the Mohammedans have taken the lead in the revolt, yet it has to a large extent been a high caste Hindoo rebellion. No one ever expected Brahminism to descend from the position which it had held for ages without a struggle, and the present conflict may be the beginning of the end. That end, the utter downfall of Brahminical power and of Hindoo superstition, must come, and the sooner the better for this benighted, priest ridden, wretched country.[48]

Similarly, Reverend James Kennedy of Benares wrote:

The Brahmins, even when illiterate, have first-rate talents for plotting … They are also intensely superstitious. They are not high-principled, or even as a body, orderly in their lives, but their immorality is quite consistent with superstitious zeal. They are superstitious from policy as well as from education and habit, being well aware that the downfall of Hindooism would be the downfall of that fancied greatness to which they attach so high a value.[49]

Attacks on Hinduism, 'that combination of cruelty, falsehood and lust, which has ever been and must ever be the direst curse of India'[50] were, of course, embedded in a pre-existing evangelical/Anglicist discourse that utilised sensational customs such as Sati and infanticide to vilify the whole edifice of 'idolatry' and its Brahmin guardians, and prove the need for both British rule and Christian evangelisation.[51]

Suggestions that the uprising was a plot fomented by the Brahmin elite[52] were reinforced by a providentialist evangelical portrayal of the uprising as the bloody realisation of the metaphorical struggle between 'darkness and light', between those who would burn women and those who would redeem them. The Brahmin conspiracy theories also appeared in non-evangelical accounts, reproducing more secular perspectives on the Brahmin capacity to make trouble. Captain Benson, for example, in answering Bentinck's circular about the safety of abolishing Sati in November 1829, had warned as follows:

In reply I beg leave to observe that although I certainly should not apprehend any immediate ill consequences from the promulgation of such an order, yet I am in my own mind convinced that it could be ere long seized upon by the priesthood and be by them converted into a desire on our part of upsetting their religious customs and usages, and which they would take every opportunity of instilling into the mind of the sepoys on meeting them at their homes on furlough who I fear, blind to the justice and humanity of our motives, would be but too proud to listen to, and be guided by, a class who in all other matters so arbitrarily lead them; imbibing such an opinion could not but tend to gradually lessen the attachments which at present hold them to their duty.[53]

Nearly thirty years later, Lt. William R. Aikman, in a letter to Lord Palmerston written on 26 September 1857, reproduced very similar imagery, arguing that the uprising was the result of a deliberate conspiracy fostered by elite Hindus in Calcutta. He remarked:

It is well known that families of the highest caste among the Baboos of Calcutta have been scandalised and openly put to shame through the adoption of Christianity by certain of their members ... these families are wealthy and, in the way of secret intrigue, powerful ... There is no doubt that of late years extreme exasperation has prevailed among this class generally ... combined with an irrepressible foreboding that if British supremacy were to last their religion would be a thing doomed.[54]

Although the sepoys had not been directly touched by religious grievances, he argued, they had been influenced by discontent emanating from Brahmin families in Bengal.

The scale of chaos and carnage that accompanied the Uprising of 1857 might have been unprecedented, but unrest and conflict were endemic in early-nineteenth century India, being the natural corollary of British expansion and state formation. Despite British attempts to instil colonial order, fears of the potential for rebellion and disorder were ever present beneath the surface of the colonial discourse. Glimpses of the potential for violence can be gleaned in British accounts of Satis, in which the Hindu population is repeatedly depicted as a bloodthirsty mob. Such images reappeared, magnified many times, in accounts of atrocities during 1857, suggesting that the British preoccupation with real and imagined atrocity stories was partly a gruesome manifestation of their ongoing concern with the potentially dangerous and uncontrolled side of the Indian population. The Baptist missionary Joshua Marshman commented as follows in his depiction of a Sati:

The most shocking indifference and levity appeared among those who were present. I think I never saw any more shockingly brutal than their behaviour. The dreadful scene had not even the least appearance of being a religious ceremony. The rabble, for such it literally was, presented the appearance of an abandoned rabble of boys in England collected for the purpose of worrying to death a cat or dog. Such was the confusion, the levity, the bursts of brutal merriment while this poor creature was burning alive before their eyes ...[55]

The above-quoted comment makes an interesting comparison with Amelia Horne's account of the massacre at Kanpur:

> While we were endeavouring to embark the shore was lined with spectators, who were looking on and exalting like so many demons, as they undoubtedly were, over our distressing condition, taunting and jeering at us for having at last fallen into their hands. The black devils grinned like so many apes, keeping up an incessant chatter in their monkey language ... the sepoys laughed and cheered, inciting each other to even greater acts of brutality.[56]

Both the accounts situate the acts of violence within an almost inhuman, alien landscape that dominated colonial fears of indigenous spaces and the dark underside of Indian life. Radhika Singha has argued that one of the key reasons for the vilification of Sati in the early nineteenth century was that the rite, with all its associated sights, sounds, smells and unruly crowds, was often performed in 'British' public space, bringing into sharp juxtaposition the British desire for colonial order and the 'disorderly' behaviour of the Indian 'mob'. Furthermore, she suggests that Sati was a public demonstration of the possibility for Indian control over people's bodies and lives, at a time when the colonial state was attempting to reserve for itself 'the privilege of taking life'.[57] If Sati represented a site on which the colonial hierarchy could catch discomforting glimpses of the potential violence and disorder that could exist outside the carefully disciplined colonial structures, the anarchy that ensued in 1857 represented for many of its victims the complete loss of colonial control, leaving them submerged in an unpredictable and brutal indigenous milieu.

Gayatri Spivak has famously characterised the colonial reaction to Sati as 'White men saving brown women from brown men'.[58] Such idioms were central to a justificatory discourse of empire that positioned British men as the protectors of oppressed Indian women, affirming both a 'muscular Christian' identity and the moral basis of imperialism. In the context of the uprising, it was white women who needed protection from 'brown men'. The emphasis on (largely imaginary) accounts of rape and mutilation of British women in popular discourses on 1857 acted both to rally public sentiment against the metaphorical violation of the nation, and to mask the vicious acts of retributive justice with which the uprising was suppressed.[59] Jenny Sharpe tells us:

> The British army subsequently preserved the Bibighar ... with its dried blood and rotting remains, as a kind of museum for passing troops to visit.... Thus began the mythic invention of the dying women's torments, as soldiers covered the walls with bloody inscriptions in the hands of the 'ladies' directing their men to avenge their horrible deaths.[60]

The supposed outrages perpetrated against Hindu women through Sati and against British women during 1857 both serve a common function in allowing the British male to position himself as the protector, rescuer and avenger, and are embedded in a wider colonial discourse that saw the treatment of women as an index of civilisation. The famous *Punch* cartoon 'Justice' captures the continuities between these two events, showing British justice (in female form) avenging the violation of British womanhood, while in the background sepoys are blown from the British guns. A similar motif is employed in the cartoon 'Sir Colin Campbell to the Rescue!' from *Harpers Weekly* for 17 October 1857 (see Figure 3.1). In both cartoons, Indian women and children are seen taking shelter and protection behind the vengeful sword-yielding figures of 'Justice' and Campbell, who are busily slaying rebellious sepoys. The implication is that the re-establishment of British power in India was as much for the protection of Indian women as British ones.

If implicit images of the Sati debate haunted the early interpretations of the uprising, as the rebellion was suppressed and British commentators sought more cohesive explanations for events, Sati entered the discourse explicitly. In 1864 Sir John Kaye's influential *A History of the Sepoy War in India, 1857–1858* explained the uprising as a plot by disgruntled Brahmins, who saw the imposition of British authority as a threat to their own social and religious superiority. For Kaye these fears were not unfounded, but nor were they an indictment of colonial rule;

SIR COLIN CAMPBELL TO THE RESCUE!

Figure 3.1: Sir Colin Campbell to the Rescue!

Source: CORBIS.

the British were the harbingers of necessary progress and enlightenment in India. He writes:

> Every monstrous lie exploded, every abominable practice suppressed, was a blow struck at the Priesthood; for all these monstrosities and abominations had their root in Hindooism and could not be eradicated without sore disturbance and confusion of the soil. The murder of women on the funeral pyre, the murder of little children in the Zenana, the murder of the sick and aged on the banks of the river … were all religious institutions from which the priesthood derived either power, or profit, or both.… Now all these cruel rites had been suppressed, and, what was still worse in the eyes of the Brahmins, the foul superstitions which nurtured them were fast disappearing.

Although the majority of Kaye's argument would not now be taken at face value, the idea that the prohibition of Sati was the first, and perhaps the most significant, of a series of colonial interventions in religious issues that fostered hostility by destabilising the authority of reactionary elites has had surprising longevity. I would argue that the popularity of this interpretation reflects the ease with which Sati could be slotted into a discourse on 1857 that drew many of its stock images and assumptions from the same ideological heritage. Sati also had an explicit discursive utility for the British as they rebuilt their empire. Incorporating the prohibition of Sati into the discourse on 'the mutiny' helped to legitimise British actions in India in 1857 and more generally. Propagating the idea that 1857 was a reactionary defence of superstitious customs like widow burning allowed the British to present the uprising as grounded not in a complex matrix of 'real' economic, social, political and religious grievances, but in the 'irrational' and purely religious fervour of 'the native'. As the extract from Kaye makes clear, there were a number of institutions and practices reformed by the British that might be used to support this argument. Sati was particularly useful because, unlike some other British infringements of Indian religion, which might be deemed ill-advised or insensitive, it represented a relatively unproblematic example of the 'civilising mission' in action. Discursively it was not difficult to imply that those who rebelled against a reform that prevented burning women alive were both backward and barbaric, allowing the British to retain the moral high ground. Such a position enabled the British to shift blame for the uprising away from their own actions and on to the Indians, who reacted so unreasonably to eminently humane and beneficial reforms. Edward Thompson, in his 1928 study *Suttee*, even went as far as to comment that it was the humanitarianism of Dalhousie 'reinforced and sharpened by his experience of the unwillingness of the native states to set their houses in order in matters of elementary decency' that was responsible for his desire to annexe whenever possible. 'I believe there was no "earth-hunger" behind his doctrine of "lapse"', Thompson asserted, 'and while criticising him we should remember the exasperating refusal of many states to abolish suttee and female infanticide'.[61] More importantly, invoking Sati also allowed the British to legitimise their own response in putting down the uprising and reinstating British rule. As Reverend William Butler put it in a volume published in America: '[L]et us bless God for that wonderful victory of civilisation in 1857–1858 over Brahminical rebels, who, had they triumphed, would most surely have rekindled the fires … and the daughters of Hindustan would again have had to mount their chariots of flame….'[62] The desirability of positioning the prohibition of Sati as a cause of 1857 is thus fairly self-evident in the context of a colonial discourse concerned with reasserting the ideological basis of justifiable imperial rule. That such explanations have survived in more recent accounts, however, is indicative of the hold that late Victorian interpretations of the uprising still have on British historiography and underline the urgent need for more revisionist analysis of this seminal event.

Notes and References

1. Eric Stokes, *The Peasant Armed: Indian Revolt of 1857* (New Delhi: Oxford University Press, 1986). Stokes himself commented that the principal obstacle he had faced was 'folk memory' of the 'mutiny', suggesting that a responsible rewriting of 1857 must struggle constantly against these deeply traced 'lines of interpretation'.
2. Sir William Lee Warner, cited in Haraprasad Chattopadhyaya, *The Sepoy Mutiny 1857. A Social Study and Analysis* (Calcutta: the author, 1957), p. 32.
3. See Ainslie Thomas Embree, ed., *1857 in India: Mutiny or War of Independence* (Boston: Heath, 1963).
4. In 1958, Hugh Tinker complained that the many British works on 1857, whether commemorative or apologetic, had produced few significant reassessments of the 'mutiny', instead reiterating, slightly modified, the judgements of Victorian writers. Hugh Tinker, '1857 and 1957: The Mutiny and Modern India', in *International Affairs*, vol. 34, no.1 (1958), p. 58. More recently, Eric Stokes, *The Peasant Armed* (published posthumously in 1986). See note 1.
5. See Stokes, *The Peasant Armed*; Gautam Bhadra, 'Four Rebels of 1857', in Ranajit Guha and Gayatri Spivak, eds, *Selected Subaltern Studies* (Oxford: Oxford University Press, 1988).
6. See, for example, Sir William Lee-Warner, *Life of the Marquis of Dalhousie* (Macmillan, 1904):

   > The abolition of sati, the abolition of infanticide, the introduction of vaccination, the law to legalise the remarriage of Hindu widows … were pressed upon the attention of the army and the masses as so many deliberate attacks on the outworks of both Mahommedanism and Hinduism. And the simple, superstitious, credulous sepoys were told that the time was rapidly approaching when by some piece of jadu (magic) the Christians would … uncaste the whole Hindu population and outrage all their traditions and feelings.

   Cited in Chattopadhyaya, *The Sepoy Mutiny 1857* (Calcutta: Bookland, 1957), p. 32. More recently, Lawrence James, *Raj. The Making and Unmaking of British India* (London: Softback Preview, 1998), p. 235.
7. There are numerous other examples: see Richard Hilton, *The Indian Mutiny. A Centenary History* (London: Hollis and Carter, 1957), p. 20. James, *Raj*, p. 226.
8. Niall Fergusson, *Empire: How Britain Made the Modern World* (London: Penguin, 2004), pp. 143–144.

9. Fergusson, *Empire*, p. 144.

10. For more on the various contours of the Sati debate, see Andrea Major, *Pious Flames. European Encounters with Sati 1500–1830* (New Delhi: Oxford University Press, 2006).

11. See Lata Mani, *Contentious Traditions: The Debate on Sati in Colonial India, 1780–1833* (Berkeley: University of California Press, 1998).

12. Cited in Thomas R. Metcalfe, *The Aftermath of Revolt* (Princeton: Princeton University Press, 1965), p. 6.

13. Mani, *Contentious Traditions*, p. 20.

14. William Tennent, *Indian Recreations: Consisting of Thoughts on the Effects of British Government on India* (Edinburgh: Edinburgh University Press, 1808), p. 191.

15. Parliamentary Papers 18, R.B. Gardiner, Behar, to W. Ewer, Lower Provinces, 30 Dec. 1818, p. 240.

16. Parliamentary Papers 18, J. Masters, Dacca, to W. Ewer, Lower Provinces, 12 Dec. 1818, p. 240.

17. Government Circular on Sati (Addressed To Military Officers), 10 November 1828, in C.H. Philips, ed., *The Correspondence of Sir William Cavendish Bentinck: Governor General of India 1828–1835* (Oxford: Oxford University Press, 1977).

18. Of the forty-nine experienced British officers approached on the issue, five advised no action at all; twelve favoured abolition, but not by direct prohibition by government regulation; eight supported suppression by direct intervention of magistrates and twenty-four urged complete, immediate and public suppression by the government. Philips, *Correspondence*, p. xxvii.

19. Jorg Fisch, *Burning Women: A Global History of Widow Sacrifice from Ancient Times to the Present* (New Delhi: Orient Longman, 2005), p. 432. While I would not go that far, my own findings from the incomplete archive that exists suggest that the level of outcry and conflict caused have been significantly inflated post 1857.

20. Cited in V.N. Datta, *Sati: A Historical, Social and Philosophical Enquiry into the Hindu Right of Widow Burning* (New Delhi: Manohar, 1987), p. 136.

21. Ibid., p. 146.

22. David Kopf, *Orientalism and the Bengal Renaissance: The Dynamics of Indian Modernization, 1773–1835* (Berkeley: University of California Press, 1969), p. 266.

23. Kopf, *Orientalism and the Bengal Renaissance*, p. 271.

24. Anand A. Yang, 'Whose Sati? Widow Burning in Early 19th Century India', in *Journal of Women's History*, vol. 1, no. 2 (1989), p. 22.

25. See, for example, Board's Collections, vol. 2308, Collection 119265, Lt. Col. W. Sleeman, A.G.G. Saugor And Nerbudda Territories, to Government, 7th February 1848.

26. Cited in Datta, *Sati*, p. 145.

27. Board's Collections, vol. 1540, Collection 61224, various letters.

28. Fisch, *Burning Women*.

29. See Sudesh Vaid and Kumkum Sangari, 'Institutions, Beliefs, Ideologies: Widow Immolation in Contemporary Rajasthan', in *Economic and Political Weekly*, vol. 26, no. 17 (27 April 1991), pp. WS2–WS18 for an excellent exposition of these issues in the context of contemporary India.

30. The Judge, J.W. Sage of the 24 Pergunnahs was found to have received ₹800 to ₹900 as a bribe to allow the sacrifice to take place. Datta, *Sati*.

31. See, for example, *The Times*, London, 12 April 1831.

32. Figures cited in Chattopadhyaya, *The Sepoy Mutiny*, p 32.

33. Fisch, *Burning Women*.

34. Embree, *1857 in India*.

35. Ayesha Jalal and Sugata Bose, *Modern South Asia: History, Culture, Political Economy* (New Delhi: Oxford University Press, 1998), p. 93.

36. Embree, *1857 in India*.

37. Cited in Embree, *1857 in India*, p. 18.

38. See, for example, various accounts in the London Missionary Society (LMS), *Missionary Magazine*, 1857–1858.

39. Cited in Embree, *1857 in India*, p. 17. It should be noted, of course, that Disraeli and the Tories were opposed to liberal reforms both at home and overseas, so their position on the causes of the Indian Uprising is consistent with their general ideological stance.

40. *The Indian Mutiny and Missions*, a sermon by Rev. George Salmon, given on 5 September 1857 (London: Wertham and Macintosh, 1857), p. 16.

41. See Andrea Major, 'Spritiual Battlefields Evangelical Discourse on 1857 and the Writings of the London Missionary Society', in Andrea Major and Crispin Bates, eds, *Britain and the Indian Uprising of 1857: Fractured Narratives and Marginal Experiences* (Delhi: SAGE Publications, 2013).

42. For more on British images of Sati, see Major, *Pious Flames*.

43. Francois Bernier. *Travels in the Mogul Empire, AD 1656–1668*, trans. Archibald Constable and ed. Vincent A. Smith (London: Oxford University Press, 1913), p. 313

44. A century later, M.M. Kaye's 'mutiny' novel *Shadow of the Moon*, published in 1957, contained a scene where a positively fiendish Brahmin priest murders an infant English boy in a pseudo-religious sacrifice designed to bind the plotters of rebellion together in secrecy. The hellish imagery of this scene resonated strongly with Bernier's portrayals of Sati and reflected the longevity of these tropes and stereotypes.

45. A perception that, as E.I. Brodkin points out, informed the actions of the British forces in India, who often characterised Hindu factions as loyal and Muslim ones as rebel. E.I. Brodkin, 'The Struggle for Succession: Rebels and Loyalists in the Indian Mutiny of 1857', in *Modern Asian Studies*, vol. 6, no. 3 (1972), pp. 277–290.

46. D. Randall, 'Autumn 1857: The Making of the Indian Mutiny', in *Victorian Literature and Culture*, vol. 3, no. 17 (2003), p. 9.

47. Ibid.

48. Rev. Benjamin Rice, 'Extract of a letter from Bangalore', *Missionary Magazine*, 23 September 1857, p. 267.

49. Rev. James Kennedy (Benares), *The Great Indian Mutiny of 1857. Its Causes, Features and Result* (London: Ward and Co, 1858).

50. *Missionary Magazine*, 'India', *Missionary Magazine*, June 1858, p. 140.

51. There were equally strong pre-existing discourses on the nature of Muslims that underpinned ideas about 1857 as a Muslim conspiracy. These are beyond the remit of this study, but see Alex Padamsee, *Representations of Indian Muslims in British Colonial Discourse* (Houndmills, Hampshire: Palgrave Macmillan, 2005) for a study of British attitudes to Muslims before, during and after the revolt.

52. William R. Aikman, *The Bengal Mutiny: Popular Opinions Concerning the origin of the Mutiny Refuted, the Real Causes Considered, with Suggestions for the Future* (London: Richardson Brothers, 1857), pp. 14–15.

53. Transcripts of documents omitted from J. Phillips, ed., *The Correspondence of Lord William Cavendish Bentinck* (Oriental and India Office, British Library, c.1977).

54. Aikman, *The Bengal Mutiny*, pp. 14–15.

55. Joshua Marshman to J. Ryland, 29 January 1807, Baptist Missionary Society Archives (BMSA).

56. Cited in Rudrangshu Mukherjee, '"Satan Let Loose upon Earth": The Kanpur Massacres in India in the Revolt of 1857' in *Past and Present*, no. 128 (August 1990), p. 109.

57. Radhika Singha, *A Despotism of Law: Crime and Justice in Early Colonial India* (Oxford: Oxford University Press, 2000).

58. Gayatri Spivak, 'Can the Subaltern Speak? Speculations on Widow Sacrifice', in *Colonial Discourse and Post-colonial Theory* (Hemel Hemstead: Harvester Wheatsheaf, 1994).

59. Jenny Sharpe, 'The Unspeakable Limits of Rape', in Williams and Chrisman, eds, *Colonial Discourse and Post-colonial Theory* (Hemel Hempstead: Harvester Wheatsheaf, 1993), p. 228.

60. Ibid.

61. Edward Thompson, *Suttee: A Historical and Philosophical Inquiry into the Rite of Widow Burning* (London: Unwin and Allen, 1928).

62. Rev. W. Butler, *The Land of the Vedas: Personal Reminiscences of India* (New York: Eaton Mains, 1906).

4

✄

PROSTITUTING THE MUTINY
Sex-Slavery and Crime in the Making of 1857*

William R. Pinch

Meerut on the Margins

WHY did '1857' happen? The big explanations are well known: anxieties over religion and caste, embodied most dramatically in the greased cartridge question; resentment due to the annexation of Awadh, the home province of many soldiers in the Bengal army, and the consequent decline of privilege that that entailed; high-handed company seizures of Indian 'princely' territory over questions of inheritance and legitimacy; the increase, and increasing inflexibility, of state revenue demands; and a widening cultural and racial divide between the Britons and the Indians, especially in (but not restricted to) the military. Also well known is the chronological fact that the local military uprising at Meerut on 10 May was a key factor in sparking off the wider rebellion that soon followed, and that the military mutiny and civil rebellion fed off each other as the weeks and months passed. Indeed, without the initial bloodbath at Meerut, it may be counterfactually argued that '1857' might not have happened at all. This is because a crucial ingredient of all subsequent garrison mutinies was the arrival of the news of the Meerut Uprising and the forty-mile dash of the mutinous 3rd Light Cavalry and 20th Native Infantry to the 'puppet' Mughal emperor at Delhi. More than simply emboldening infantry and cavalry malcontents, the

---

* The research for this chapter was made possible by 'The Colonel Return Jonathan Meigs First (1740–1823) Fund' (Department of History) as well as the Office of Academic Affairs, Wesleyan University, and by the National Endowment for the Humanities, Washington DC. Thanks are due as well to the following persons who read or heard the chapter and offered suggestions: Seema Alavi, Clare Anderson, Indrani Chatterjee, Michael Fisher, Sumit Guha, Philip McEldowney, Thomas Metcalf, Radhika Singha and Claire Natalie Snell-Rood. The seed for this chapter, and for the larger book project in which prostitutes play a part, was planted in an undergraduate Wesleyan seminar in the spring of 2006 on the mutiny/rebellion; I am especially grateful to Ian Renner and Matt Lesser for their early reactions to my arguments.

arrival of the news of Meerut at each cantonment in north India served to cement the growing distrust between the Britons and the Indians. The subtle and sometimes not-so-subtle precautions that the British took in the wake of Meerut lent to the unfolding of 'the mutiny' a kind of preordained, inexorable quality, which, I would argue, served to further inscribe the year 1857 as an 'event' in imperial and, later, national memory. Thus, no 'Meerut', no '1857'. In historical hindsight, without Meerut the British would not have experienced, as William Dalrymple recently phrased it, 'the single most serious armed challenge any Western empire would face, anywhere in the world, in the entire course of the nineteenth century'.[1]

Given the importance of Meerut to the fate of the British Empire, it might well be asked why the 3rd Light Cavalry and the 20th Native Infantry mutinied there on 10 May in the first place. The question is especially relevant given that by mid-April, soldiers in the Bengal army were not being asked to bite the offending cartridges—rather, a new drill had been introduced that involved simply tearing the cartridge with the fingers.[2] Nevertheless, when the question is posed, the answer almost always centres on the greased cartridges. J. Cracroft Wilson, special commissioner in nearby Moradabad District during the suppression of the rebellion, offered an interesting variation on this theme in a set of recollections published in 1871. Yes, Wilson acknowledged, the fateful arrest of the 85 'skirmishers' of the 3rd Light Cavalry on 24 April was due to their open refusal to obey a direct order to load their weapons with the offending cartridges while on drill. But the ill-considered decision to hold the 'firing parade' in the first place was perceived (and, indeed, intended) as a direct challenge to the men in the regiment. And responsibility for that decision belonged solely to their commanding officer, Lt. Col. George Monro Carmichael-Smyth. Regardless, according to Wilson, the decisive event occurred during the hours that followed the court martial and 'ironing parade' of those eighty-five 'skirmishers' on Saturday, 9 May, before their subsequent liberation from jail by their comrades in the late afternoon of 10 May. During the evening and night of 9 May, according to Wilson, the cavalrymen who had not been jailed but had stood by while their brother soldiers were put in irons and marched off to jail were the subject of merciless ridicule by the prostitutes —the 'frail ones'—of the Sadar Bazar:

> [T]he frail ones' taunts were heard far and wide, and the rest of the regiment was assailed with words like these:—'Your brethren have been ornamented with these anklets and incarcerated; and for what? Because they would not swerve from their creed; and you, cowards as you are, sit still indifferent to their fate. If you had an atom of manhood in you, go and release them.'[3]

Wilson's account may be apocryphal, but there is additional evidence that points to prostitute involvement in the Meerut Uprising. In one of his several encyclopaedic volumes on the mutiny, the late P.J.O. Taylor cited an August 1857 letter from Captain Henry Norman, acting adjutant general of the Delhi Field Force, reporting that one 'Mees Dolly' of Meerut had recently been captured and 'was hung [*sic*] at Meerut, being implicated in the arrangements for the first outbreak'.[4] According to Taylor's research, Mees Dolly was a 'pure-bred' European woman, the widow of a sergeant in the British army who had 'turned sour' and pursued a living by running a 'house of refreshment of sorts' in the Meerut bazaar. Taylor explains:

> [I]n those days if such a widow did not re-marry, she had a hard time of it to survive. Mees Dolly had declined all offers of marriage, had got into trouble, probably for theft, and drifted to the bazar.... It seems certain that Mees Dolly was no better, as the saying is, than she should be, ran an establishment in which there were girls working for her and, enraged by the cold shoulder shown to her on all sides, was ripe for mischief and the fermentation of any kind of trouble that would let her get back at those she felt had left her friendless and deserted.

According to the letter from Norman that Taylor cites, a fortnight after the uprising in Meerut,

> Mees Dolly fled from the Sadar Bazar and hid herself in a near-derelict bungalow at the government stud-farm at Hapur not far outside the city. There she was apprehended by a patrol of European cavalry, in the act of driving off in haste. She was brought into Meerut under escort. She was wanted for helping in the murder of two Eurasian girls and, significantly, for 'egging on the mutineers'.

On the Margins at Meerut

The attraction of Wilson in the nineteenth century and Taylor in the twentieth to the idea of prostitute responsibility for the Meerut Mutiny, and thus '1857' in general, should be understood in the context of another theory that circulated widely in both imperial and nationalist circles, namely, that Meerut, crucial bloodbath though it may have been, was nonetheless a premature uprising that doomed the larger mutiny to failure. According to this logic, the actual mutiny was supposed to occur across the cantonments of northern India in a coordinated fashion, thus destroying British power in one fell swoop. Meerut, coming too early, gave the British a chance to regroup. In Wilson's words, 'The mine had been prepared and the train had been laid, but it was not intended to light the slow-match for another three weeks. The spark which fell from female lips ignited it at once'. Over a century later, Taylor was prompted to ask his readers: 'What if the "female lips" were those of Mees Dolly? Then she may be said to have saved, quite inadvertently, the British Raj in India: with hindsight perhaps the authorities might not have hanged her!'

The image of the British Empire condemned and saved, in the same moment, as a consequence of the fury of a fallen woman wronged is so powerfully iconic, not to mention ironic, that one might be tempted to conclude that 'Mees Dolly' and the 'frail ones of the bazaar' were the inventions of a discourse of gender and sexuality that sustained British imperialism in the nineteenth century and popular historical interest in it in the twentieth.[5] But were we to go that route and simply dismiss the accounts—and especially that of Mees Dolly—as products of overheated imperial imaginations, we might miss an interesting detail: the murder of the two Eurasian girls. Taylor's evidence offers no clue as to who these girls were or how Mees Dolly might have been entangled in the crime of their murder. However, it seems plausible that they too were prostitutes (hence Mees Dolly's involvement), and had somehow fallen afoul of the mutinous sepoys and *sawar*s during the initial outbreak of violence. These suppositions are given further credence by a series of depositions taken by George W. Williams later in 1857 and 1858.[6] According to Williams, one of the early targets of the mob violence that erupted following the outbreak of mutiny was the surgeon of the Veteran Establishment, one Dr Smith. Smith was killed in his bungalow, situated opposite the Sadar Bazar. He had been warned of the impending violence earlier in the day by Golab Jaun, described in the depositions as a 'Cashmerian' or Kashmiri. According to her deposition, Golab Jaun resided with Smith and had received the news from her mother, who had learned it from a 'Cashmerian girl, named Sophie', who had heard it from a sepoy at about 2 p.m. Smith's misfortune was that he dismissed the news as just another bazaar report, 'void of foundation'. Golab Jaun's mother Zeenut, who resided in the Sadar Bazar, was also deposed. She gave a slightly different version: Sophie had told her own mother, Mehonee, of the impending massacre. Mehonee had passed this information on to Zeenut, who 'did not believe it', but mentioned it to her daughter Golab Jaun anyway. Finally, Golab Jaun reported that the mob turned Sophie out of the bazaar and knocked down her house. Sophie, however, told a different story in her deposition: she denied any prior knowledge of the outbreak, and denied as well that any sepoys and *sawar*s visited her house in the Sadar Bazar. She also reported that at about 4 p.m., she was visited by one Pundit Dhurm Narain, formerly in the office of the Meerut Cantonment Joint Magistrate. He left when the shooting and tumult started, at which point she closed her doors. Finally, she asserted that her mother was named Mehree, not Mehonee, and that she had departed for Ludhiana two months prior to the outbreak, and that she had reported her departure to the kotwali at the time. Given the discrepancy in these reports, Williams ordered Bukhtawur Singh, the kotwal (head police official) of the Sadar Bazar to make enquiries. Sophie's neighbours reported that contrary to her protestations, *sawar*s were in the habit of visiting her house; he confirmed, however, that her mother had departed well prior to the outbreak.

Obviously, none of these 'Cashmerian' women can be taken to be identical with either of the two Eurasian girls in whose murder Mees Dolly was said to be implicated. This is not because the depositions refer to them as 'Cashmerian', which by the nineteenth century had evolved into a generic term for 'nautch girls' and 'loose women' and did not necessarily preclude Eurasianness. Rather it is because Sophie and Golab Jaun were deposed by Williams long after the uprising and its immediate aftermath, including the said murders of the Eurasian girls. Nevertheless, the details of the accounts of the 'Cashmerian girls' and the discrepancies between them offer compelling clues as to why Mees Dolly might have been implicated in the murder of two Eurasian girls. Let us examine the statements again: *according to Golab Jaun*, a sepoy told Sophie about the impending revolt; Sophie told her mother Mehonee who told Zeenut who 'did not believe it', but passed the information along to her daughter Golab Jaun; Golab Jaun told Dr Smith who, to his misfortune, treated the report as bazaar rumour and dismissed it. As she paraphrased his response: 'I always brought him bazar reports void of foundation, and [he] took no notice of it'. Golab Jaun adds that after the uprising the mob turned Sophie out of the bazaar and knocked down her house. *Sophie*, for her part, denied everything: she denied that sepoys were in the habit of visiting her house; she denied that she told her mother anything; she denied that her mother was in Meerut; she even denied that her mother was named Mehonee. The Sadar Bazar kotwal, Bukhtawur Singh, learned that while Sophie may not have entertained sepoys, she did entertain cavalrymen.

Clearly, Sophie had something to hide, and it seems likely that she was apprehensive about having been identified as an originating link in the information chain that resulted in Golab Jaun's warning to Dr Smith. Sophie had been turned out of the bazaar and her house destroyed by the mob; though Golab Jaun does not tell us why these summary punishments were inflicted upon her, we can speculate that it may have something to do with where her sympathies were seen to lie on 10 May. Perhaps, word had gotten about that Sophie was warning other women of the bazaar, especially those who were known to be close to Europeans. As for Golab Jaun, her sympathies were clear and unambiguous: she lived with Dr Smith, and she openly admitted to having warned him. She even begged him to flee with her, but he refused. For a while they stood together by the garden hedge, until a 'dooly' (or covered chair) arrived to fetch her, sent by her mother Zeenut. Smith's house was destroyed soon after by the mob.

The depositions of the 'Cashmerian girls' Golab Jaun and Sophie allow us to see one possible motive for Mees Dolly to have involved herself in the murder of two Eurasian girls. If those girls were, like Sophie and Zeenut, passing sensitive information to Europeans during the mutiny and its aftermath, they quite naturally would have incurred the wrath of the mutineers and their partisans. The bigger and more complex picture that the 'Cashmerian girls' depositions afford tends to undercut the dramatic irony of Taylor's account, whereby the Empire was condemned and saved—in the same breath and from the same lips, namely, 'the lips of the frail ones' of the bazaar. However, this new picture, at the same time, raises intriguing questions about the place of those 'frail ones of the bazaar'—call them what we will—in the mid-nineteenth century, certainly about their own conflicted politics in the spring and summer of 1857, but also what they tell us about the nature of company rule and Indian society.[7]

Oddly, we know precious little about such women, so little that it seems inadequate to simply refer to them as 'prostitutes', even though it is clear that the sale of their bodies for sex was a central component of their lives. Most work that has been done on prostitutes in British India focuses on the period after about 1860. The bulk of this arises from documents detailing official anxieties over venereal diseases and the felt need for increased surveillance over, and control of, prostitutes' bodies, especially those that came into contact with the rank-and-file British and Indian soldiers who formed the backbone of the British Empire in Asia.[8] Much less has been done on prostitution in the period prior to 1860, and that which has, tends to focus more on concubinage, courtesanship and family politics.[9] The impression that we are left with is that the late Mughal courtesan-cum-concubine somehow evolved during the course of the late eighteenth and early nineteenth centuries into the cantonment prostitute of the regimental *lal bazaar*. There may well be some truth to this, even if we should bear in mind that a version of *lal bazaari* prostitution seemed to exist well prior to 1757, while the gharanas of the cultured courtesan continued to exist (if not thrive) well into the late twentieth century.[10] While this essay cannot delve too deeply into this complex question, it is hoped that the discussion that follows will shed light on some key structural dynamics that allowed for the expanded recruitment of young women and girls for work in the sex trade in the increasingly fraught moral climate of early-nineteenth century British India.

Sixteen Prostitutes of the North-west Provinces

But how to go about finding prostitutes? Philippa Levine, who has worked on prostitution, race and disease in the later nineteenth century, observes that prostitutes only begin to appear in large numbers in the official records after legislation concerning sexually transmitted maladies and the emergence of a felt need for 'Lock Hospitals' in which to enforce treatment. Then there is the wider problem of the language of respectability that tends to permeate certain nineteenth century records, what might be termed 'the prose of counter-sexuality'. P.J.O. Taylor, for example, notes that while 'comfort women' were a common enough feature of pre-mutiny regiments, propriety required that they remained unmentioned in official dispatches. 'Had it been known generally in England that such women existed', he writes, 'there would have been an outcry, and Queen Victoria would certainly have been most displeased. As a result, there is little reference to such persons, particularly in official correspondence....' Taylor, however, did find one private letter from the Punjab that 'lets the cat out of the bag'. Though the unnamed author of the letter did not make clear the precise nature of the role the women played in this particular regiment, referring to them simply as 'dusky beauties' and 'ladies', the tone is such that makes it quite clear that their position in the regiment was not only secure but of considerable importance to the men.[11]

Taylor's archival reflections notwithstanding, prostitutes do appear in official records connected to the company army—just not in the official records Taylor consulted.[12] Kenneth Ballhatchet encountered occasional references to prostitutes prior to 1860 in the Military proceedings, mostly consumed, however, with the question of disease and varying methods of maintaining health in the *lal bazaar*. These have been explored in greater detail by Douglas Peers.[13] Likewise, if one trolls through the Criminal Judicial Proceedings, prostitutes crop up—not in droves, but with sufficient regularity and occasionally in strikingly sharp detail.[14] Before we examine the contours of their existence in these latter records, however, it bears asking why prostitutes were showing up in the Criminal Judicial Proceedings in the first place. It is not, as one might assume, due to the fact of their being engaged in an illegal profession. This is because prostitution was not illegal. Prostitution did not come under any formal legal restriction in India until the passage of the Contagious Diseases Act of 1864 which sought, as noted above, to control the spread of venereal diseases by controlling prostitutes' bodies.[15] Nor was it necessarily due to a proclivity on the part of prostitutes for crime: indeed, more often than not, based on the available records, prostitutes tended to not be the ones engaging in criminal activity; rather, they were usually the ones being preyed upon by criminals. In other words, based on a survey of the Criminal Judicial Proceedings from the North-western Provinces held in the India Office Records of the British Library, prostitutes usually appeared because they were *victims* in cases of murder, wounding and theft. On occasion they are seen to be the ones doing the thieving and (very rarely) murdering, but this was the exception rather than the rule.

An important caveat is in order here regarding the nature of the evidence afforded by the Criminal Judicial Proceedings. Not all crimes were described in sufficient detail in these records to enable the reader to discern the identities of those involved. Usually, the only crimes that merited sustained prose descriptions were those of a 'heinous' nature. Sometimes these crimes were included in an annual police report, which was a summary of the crimes that occurred during the previous calendar year; sometimes a particular crime, due to its unusual features, was deemed important or interesting enough to merit its own dedicated correspondence between a district magistrate and divisional commissioner. Petty crimes, though they were included in final tabulations, did not merit mention in the official proceedings unless they erupted into serious violence. The salient point, then, is that what follows should not be taken as an exhaustive analysis of *all* crimes and disputes involving prostitutes in the North-western Provinces; rather, it is a reflection on crimes that both involved prostitutes and rose to a level of significance to merit inclusion in the official record being sent to the lieutenant governor of the province sitting in Agra, and thence to Calcutta and London.

That said, the numbers are still suggestive.[16] For example, if we take the nineteen-month period beginning on 1 January 1855 and ending on 31 July 1856, there were sixteen discrete cases involving prostitutes in the North-western

Provinces that were serious enough to warrant mention in the criminal judicial correspondence sent to the lieutenant governor at Agra.[17] One or two of these cases involved more than one prostitute, though most involved only one. The regional breakdown is as follows: five cases in the Meerut Division; four in the Agra Division; two in the Benares Division; two in the Saugor Division; two in the Delhi Division and one in the Allahabad Division. Of these sixteen cases, only two involved prostitutes as criminals; and in one of these, a prostitute (in Delhi) was implicated in a crime simply because stolen property was found in her house. In the remaining fourteen cases, prostitutes were the victims of crime. In half of these, the prostitute in question was murdered. There was an additional case of attempted murder of a prostitute by a spurned sepoy named Madaree, in which the intended victim, named Bilaso, appeared, in the words of W.G. Probyn, the officiating magistrate, 'to have had a most wonderful escape'—though her mother and sister were severely wounded and a man asleep in her doorway killed.[18] In only one case was a prostitute implicated in a murder: a Rajput brought a 'mistress' from Awadh to his house in Jaunpur District; she was accompanied by a man named Bhani Singh who called himself her brother. In the night, Bhani Singh murdered the Rajput and decamped with the woman.[19] Four of the cases resulted in the wounding of a prostitute, two of which involved either theft or attempted theft. In only two cases were prostitutes the victims of theft where they did not also suffer some form of bodily harm.

To put these numbers and crimes in perspective, consider that the annual police report in 1855 for the district of Meerut (not to be confused with the entire Meerut Division, which comprised several districts) stated that there were a total of 2,640 crimes reported.[20] Most of these cases appeared to stem from various kinds of agrarian conflicts, such as boundary disputes, grass-cutting rights, cattle theft, etc., and were usually not described in detail in the proceedings. The sixteen cases involving prostitutes for the entire province will seem, in this light, like a very small drop in a very large bucket. On the other hand, given that only serious crimes—such as murder, homicide, highway robbery, violent theft and burglary, child stealing and 'affray' attended by wounding or homicide—merited prose descriptions in the annual police reports, the fact that prostitutes were appearing in the records bears some social significance.

The Meerut District cases that merited prose description in 1855 were arranged as follows:[21]

No.	Category	No. of Cases
1.	Murder	5
2.	Attempt at murder	1
3.	Wounding with intent to kill	3
4.	Culpable homicide	2

(Continued)

(Continued)

No.	Category	No. of Cases
5.	Highway robbery with homicide	1
6.	Highway robbery with wounding	1
7.	Highway robbery without violence	1
8.	Burglary with murder	1
9.	Burglary with wounding	5
10.	Burglary with theft (simple burglary)	8
11.	Theft of property attended with murder	3
12.	Attempt at theft of property with wounding	5
13.	Theft of children	1
14.	Theft of property valued at ₹500 and upward	5
15.	Cattle theft	1
16.	Cattle theft attended with wounding	4
17.	Affray attended with homicide	3
18.	Affray attended with severe wounding	10
19.	Perjury	3
20.	Theft of property after administering deleterious drugs	1
21.	Cases in which from ₹100 to ₹300 value of property has been stolen	9

Interestingly, a large proportion of the cases that ended in death or serious wounding stemmed from illicit sexual-emotional relationships, whether in the context of marriage or extramarital relations. And in Meerut in 1855, the victims of the violent crimes emanating from such illicit relations were almost always women. For example, of the five murders described in Meerut District for 1855, two were wives murdered by their husbands for alleged infidelity; a third case involved a rich widow who had been poisoned by family members. Likewise, of the three woundings with intent to kill, one involved a man who inflicted a sword wound on a woman who refused to live with him, before killing himself; the other involved a husband who wounded his wife because she refused to come home with him. Of the two culpable homicide cases in Meerut District in 1855, one involved the killing of a mother by two sons who were enraged because she had arranged the marriage of their sister without their consent. Finally, the burglary with murder case (under Category 8) turned out, upon investigation, to be not a case of burglary at all, but a premeditated murder made to look as though it was the result of a property-owner defending his home from a burglar; the primary victim in this case was not a woman, but rather a local chowkidar 'who had for some time been engaged in an intrigue with one of the females' of the house in question. (One can imagine, however, that the woman with whom the chowkidar was carrying on the intrigue did not fare well at the hands of her relatives.) A similar pattern can be seen in Agra District in 1855.[22] Of the twelve cases of murder or wounding with intent to murder, seven stemmed from illicit sexual-emotional relationships. Six of these clearly involved a 'love-triangle' or 'quadrangle' in which a man became enraged at the infidelity of either his wife or paramour. In four of these cases, the wounded or murdered victims were the rival male lovers; in two cases, the women were the victims. A seventh case involved the murder of a prostitute; the motive for the murder was unknown, but the features of the crime suggested a jealous rage.

We might conclude, then, that based on the above glimpse of crime in Agra and Meerut districts, violence against prostitutes across the North-western Provinces was a function of violence against women generally—particularly given the apparently high incidence of violent crimes resulting from illicit sexual-emotional relations. But of the fourteen cases noted above in which prostitutes were victims, only three can be said to have stemmed from jealousy (interestingly, of these three cases, two of the culprits were sepoys). In eight cases the motive for the crime was theft (in only one was the culprit a sepoy; however, in several cases the culprits escaped and their identities were concealed). In two cases the motive was unknown. And the final case was the murder of a prostitute who had the bad luck to visit the house of a client embroiled in a land dispute on the very night he was attacked by his enemies.

Whether or not prostitutes were over-represented as victims of serious crime—and there seems to be good reason to think they were—there can be no question that the profession of sex for money made them particularly attractive targets. This is because prostitutes were more likely than most to find themselves inhabiting two dangerous worlds: the world of illicit sexual–emotional relations, and the world of property.[23] Of course, the picture of the prostitute as a two-dimensional victim is partly a product of the source material: it will be recalled that the nature of the records is such that petty crime did not merit sustained discussion. That prostitutes did dabble in petty crime is suggested by the case of Jowala Devee, a murdered prostitute of Delhi, whose fate was said to have 'excited little sympathy, as she had repeatedly plundered her customers in the most shamefaced manner'.[24] We know from other records, moreover, that prostitutes in Meerut were also known to trade in kidnapped girls (more on which later), and they were involved in the illicit sale of liquor.[25]

Another way of probing the significance of the sixteen cases involving prostitutes is to ask how those cases were dealt with by the authorities. Of the fourteen cases in the proceedings for 1855 and 1856 in which prostitutes were victimised, nine ended in the capture of the suspected parties. Of these nine cases, seven ended in conviction and punishment. The punishments ranged from execution in three cases of murder to various terms of imprisonment (six months to life) for wounding. In the one case of simple theft in which a suspect was captured, the prisoner was released 'for want of proof'. These figures would seem to suggest that the authorities tended to regard crime against prostitutes as a serious matter, and this impression is generally supported by the prose commentary. For example, F.W. Pinckney, the deputy commissioner of Jabalpur, reported that his investigation of the case of the severe wounding of the prostitute Bussuntee began in the predawn hours of 8 October 1855 at the hospital, where the victim had been taken by the police and her relatives. Bussuntee had been badly cut up by her companion the previous evening while returning from a local *urs* mela at the Rani Talab. Pinckney arrived at the hospital with the civil surgeon, who tended to her wounds (including the amputation of her right hand). Despite her wounds, Bussuntee was able to describe her assailant to Pinckney: she told him that though she did not know his name, she could recognise him and his mother, and also knew where they lived. Pinckney ordered Bussuntee to be put upon a charpoy and rode by her side while she directed her bearers to the house in question. Pinckney and the kotwal entered the house and seized the residents along with corroborating evidence. The alleged assailant, Wazir Khan, was tried, convicted and sentenced to life imprisonment.[26]

A more extensive report was provided in the case of the murder by poisoning of Hydree, a prostitute of Kydgunge in Allahabad, which occurred on 4 February 1855. The lead official on the case, Deputy Magistrate P. Carnegy, learned of the crime from Hydree's sister, Sahebjan, also a prostitute. Sahebjan had also been poisoned, but had regained consciousness within a few hours and had managed to make her way to the police post in the neighbourhood. Carnegy soon received from Sahebjan 'such a description of the murderers as enabled me to take active measure for their pursuit'. They were arrested within twenty hours, on the road to Banda. The principal assailant turned out to be a notorious poisoner named Khanazad Khan of Patna, who had been preying on prostitutes throughout Bihar and the North-west Provinces in recent years. According to his confession, he and his accomplice, a boy named Munee, had spent two nights with Sahebjan and Hydree in the former's house, during which time they had given money to the women to procure 'bazaar spirits', overpaying on each occasion to gain their confidence. On the third night, Khanazad Khan slipped some drops of poison into the women's drinks; when they 'became insensible', he began removing their ornaments and robbing them of their cash. Carnegy may have found this case particularly interesting because it emerged during the course of the investigation that the accused was a member of a gang of 'reclaimed thugs' who'd been many years earlier granted some land in Patna district so as to '[betake] themselves to honest pursuits'.[27]

Of course, it is in the nature of government statistics to cast a generally positive light on the performance of government. Still, if we look more closely, it is possible to see some cracks in the evidence that suggest a more conflicted picture of the prostitute's relationship to the world of officialdom. Most of the murdered and wounded prostitutes whose cases appear in the Criminal Judicial Proceedings were assaulted in or near their own houses, like Hydree and Sahebjan of Allahabad.[28] These houses were usually located in the city or cantonment bazaar with easy proximity to a police post, which should have meant prompt investigation by the authorities, as in the case of the Allahabad poisoners and the Jubbulporee attack. An additional example of such prompt investigation was, indeed, the 1853 murder of Nuseebun, a prostitute who lived in the Sadar Bazar adjoining the Meerut Cantonment. Ameerun Dhye, who lived with Nuseebun, deposed that she was roused in the night by the 'moans and groans' of Nuseebun who was being murdered by a sepoy whom she recognised as Ram Singh of the Sappers and Miners. She bolted her door in 'great terror' until daybreak, when she 'gave intimation at the Kotwalee'. The suspect was immediately seized; but despite damning evidence in the form of additional eyewitness testimony and a bloody footprint that matched his oddly shaped foot, he was eventually acquitted on the testimony of his fellow soldiers that he was not only in the lines during the night in question, but on duty.[29] An aggressive police response did not always result in a conviction, even if the culprit was captured.

On other occasions, the proximity of the police post did not even translate into rapid action. For example, in the case of another Meerut prostitute murder, in late December 1855, the Cantonment Magistrate R. Cookson complained that even though 'women carrying on in the same trade lived on either side and below' the victim, they would not give 'the slightest clue nor disclose the name or description of a single person who visited her, with some of whom they must be acquainted'.[30] Cookson attributed the silence of the victim's neighbours to 'the usual apathy of natives of this country' and gave the crime little additional thought. One of those reasons may indeed have been a form of apathy, or the sense that the prostitute victim was receiving her due. Such seemed to have been the case with the murder of Jowala Devee of Delhi, noted earlier, who was reputed to rob her customers.[31] Ironically, however, one sepoy of the 70th Regiment, Native Infantry, did provide a hint to the identities of the culprits in her case, one of whom was as a result speedily captured on the road to Aligarh with a wagonload of incriminating evidence in the form of stolen goods. This individual implicated three other sepoys. However, only the sepoy caught red-handed with the evidence was hanged for the crime.[32]

Another reason prostitutes living near a police post might not report a crime is that they had little faith in the police on the spot, because those members of the police were either thought to be incompetent or known to be complicit. Local official complicity was the suspicion in the March 1855 murder of Beeba Jan, a prostitute of Agra city, who had her throat slit in addition to being strangled—an odd detail that suggests a kind of warning to others, namely, to avoid talking to the police. The murder was not discovered for two whole days even though someone had reported to the chowkidar on the day after that something was amiss. A suspect was identified, and though it was learned that he had fled towards Gwalior and Tonk, he was not apprehended. Meanwhile, the magistrate who visited the scene of the crime 'immediately on its being reported' noted the 'great neglect on the part of the chowkeedars' for failing to immediately break open the lock; he even harboured 'some suspicions of accessoryship though not sufficient for conviction'. In the end the chowkidar was dismissed.[33]

Suspicions of a different kind of malfeasance, percolating higher up the official and unofficial chains of command, distinguished the murder of another prostitute, 'Bujjo of Furruckabad', in September of 1855. Bujjo, who lived alone in a house in the city, only 'a few hundred yards from the Kotwalee', had been stabbed repeatedly in her house on or about the 25th of September. On 30 September, by which time the stench from her decomposing body was overwhelming, the police finally broke open the lock. After some prodding, Ajooba, a nine-year-old daughter of a neighbouring prostitute named Hooseinee, identified some men whom she had seen enter the house five nights earlier; these individuals were immediately arrested but eventually released for lack of evidence. However, the reporting magistrate, W.G. Probyn, was convinced of their guilt and stated that he 'never released any prisoners in the whole course of my experience with greater regret than I do these'. Probyn added that he suspected that the kotwal, who was 'intimately connected with one of the principal personages in Furruckabad', had purposefully neglected to register the official report of the crime because he did not wish to delay his own departure to a better posting in Mirzapur District under one Mr Lushington, Probyn's predecessor in Furruckabad. This allegation made its way across the province and led to several subsequent follow-up correspondences between himself, the commissioner of the Agra Division, the secretary to the lieutenant governor of the Province and Lushington himself; Probyn chose to stand his ground, however, and refused to retract his original opinion of the case that had the kotwal 'exerted himself directly the matter came to his ears, the whole case would have come to light, and the perpetrators of the murder brought to justice'.[34]

The vague involvement of Magistrate Lushington of Mirzapur in corrupting the expeditious investigation of Bujjo's murder raises a related question, namely, the absence of cases in the NWP Criminal Judicial Proceedings from the 1850s involving Europeans directly victimising prostitutes. Does this mean Europeans—particularly British soldiers—did not murder, wound, rob or otherwise harm cantonment or regimental prostitutes? This seems unlikely in the extreme, given what we know about crime against prostitutes in Europe in the same period. More likely, rather, is that soldiers did commit such crimes, but the cases were dealt with outside the normal magisterial channels—that is, by the regimental authorities in courts of enquiry and courts martial. Though one might suspect that the outcome of such cases were less than satisfactory from the plaintiff's point of view, a systematic investigation would need to be undertaken to arrive at any certain conclusions on this score.[35] The impression one is left with is that the views of the occasional upright officer notwithstanding, the soldiers welcomed the opportunity to leave the cantonment for the local 'fleshpots' of the city. If so, there would be an incentive for the regiment to punish any soldier who harmed a prostitute, since the frequency of such crimes could result in government proscriptions against regimental access to bazaar sex. What we do know is that British regiments regularly availed themselves of the services of Indian prostitutes in the cantonment and even city bazaars, often in very large numbers. On more than one occasion well into the 1860s, the military and civil authorities found themselves at loggerheads on this issue—with the former insisting that diseased prostitutes be locked up or otherwise kept off limits to British soldiers, and the latter stating in no uncertain terms that enacting such prohibitions would not only be impracticable but illegal. The Allahabad magistrate in 1863 put it best: confronted with a demand by the brigade major of Her Majesty's 77th Regiment that some particularly infectious women be arrested, he coolly declined, observing not only that prostitution was not an offence but that the women had done nothing to render themselves 'amenable to the Law'.[36]

The Prostitute and the Raj

One may conclude, based on the foregoing, that company officials in the mid-nineteenth century deemed prostitutes to be worthy of legal and police protection, even if the bureaucratic machinery and a sometimes questionable level of official integrity—not to mention the imperial double standard of race—rendered this a task difficult of accomplishment. Indeed, in some cases, like those of the severe woundings or murders of Beeba Jan of Agra, Bussuntee of Jubbulpore, Hydree and Sahebjan of Allahabad and Bujjo of Furruckabad, the officials on the spot even seem to have made the successful investigation and prosecution a point of personal pride. There are many possible bases for such official 'benevolent paternalism' towards prostitutes. One possibility that cannot be discounted is that such self-representation on the part of officials in the reports was a function of the desire to inflate the official record and, thus, gain the notice of superiors in the divisional and provincial headquarters; but even this assumes that prostitutes were deemed to be deserving of legal protections. Another possibility is that British officials recognised the implicit importance of the work that prostitutes did to the social and sexual contentment of soldiers in both Indian and British regiments, and they sought to protect them accordingly—especially when those soldiers abused the privilege of ready access to these women. A third possibility is that the commercial nature of prostitution inadvertently endowed it with a special status under company rule, and thus violence against prostitutes was seen to bear a family resemblance to other crimes that threatened the peaceful conduct of commerce.

Whatever the cause, an official 'benevolent paternalism' towards prostitutes is consistent with the tenor of British Indian legal reform in the first half of the nineteenth century. According to Radhika Singha, magistrates in the Bengal Presidency (which included most of North India in this period) were increasingly concerned with 'wives, children and the female relations of [poor] families being seduced away from them for the purposes of prostitution', so much so that Regulation 7 of 1819 gave magistrates specific provisions to

> punish any person who enticed and took away a married woman from her husband, or an unmarried female under the age of fifteen living with her parents or legal guardians, 'for the purpose of rendering [her] ... a prostitute or concubine, or otherwise disposing of her in an unlawful manner ...'[37]

This legal reform, aimed at protecting the inviolability of the family, was constructed, as Singha argues, around the increased rights and responsibilities of the male head of household. As such, it made 'the domestic more domestic'.[38] It also had the perverse effect, however, of drawing attention to the prostitute as an object deserving of state consideration, even pity.

Despite a host of legal interventions, the traffic in women and girls continued to be a familiar phenomenon in the North-western Provinces, especially the further west one travelled. As the Muzaffarnagar District magistrate, H.G. Astell, observed in 1849:

> their [Banjara slavers'] jurisdiction extends I believe to the whole of the Upper Provinces, from one end of which to the other this trade of Kidnapping appears to thrive.... Of the existence of this nefarious trade I believe all Magistrates are aware but from the above circumstances [the jurisdictional boundaries] find themselves unable to do much for its suppression.... The populous district of the Doab lying between Ally Ghur and Cawnpore appears to furnish the Chief supplies whilst in this neighbourhood [near Muzaffarnagar] and in that of Lahore, seem to be the principal marts at which the Females are sold.[39]

William Sleeman even delineated a distinct brand of 'thuggee' devoted to a version of this species of crime throughout northern India, termed *Megpunnaism*, the murder of indigent parents for their children, in which *Banjaras* and other mobile communities were often implicated.[40] S. Fraser, the commissioner of Delhi, reported a rash of complaints in 1855 that thieves had carried off young girls in the Rohtuck District and had, with the connivance of the Jhujjur Nawab and other chieftains of the region, sold them to the 'dancing women of the Jhujjur Ilaqua'. One of the women even showed one of the girls to her parents, apparently with the idea of selling her back—to no avail.[41] In the same year, the Agra authorities were sent two individuals who had been arrested by the Political Agent at Gwalior for child theft in Mathura District.[42] By far the most detailed case, however, comes from the Meerut Division, and involved the capture of a gang of *Banjaras* red-handed by an intrepid kotwal in 1849. The arrest occurred in a village near Muzaffarnagar where the *Banjaras* were putting up in the house of a local zamindar while they conducted sales in the vicinity. A total of fourteen women and girls were recovered, six of whom had already been sold and taken to prostitute establishments in Meerut and Sardhana. The women had been kidnapped from the districts of Aligarh, Etawah and Mainpuri, all located well to the south of Muzaffarnagar by between 200 and 300 miles. The authorities attempted to reunite the victims with their families, but were only able to do so in the case of three of the fourteen—the three that were young girls. The remaining eleven, said to be 'women of full age', were disowned by their friends because they were presumed to have become prostitutes. 'They were allowed to go their own ways when the case was finally disposed of.'[43]

It is difficult to know which way that was. Like stocked trout in season, they were probably too dazed to do more than swim in plain view against the current, ready to be caught again. Many surely ended up returning to the prostitute establishments from which they had been rescued, though this would have been complicated to some degree in the particular case cited above by the fact that the women that ran those establishments had been arrested and convicted.[44] Whatever their fate, the apparently docile behaviour of these young women presented what Astell described as 'the most curious circumstances elicited from the investigation', namely, the apparent ease with which the females were 'captured' and conveyed about the province. Even though most of the victims were 'women of full age', which Astell later specified as between fifteen and twenty years, and though they 'appear[ed] to have been brought ... against their will', they nevertheless allowed themselves to be transported all the way from the *Banjara* slave 'depot' in Aligarh District 'without making the slightest attempt to make their situation known to the Travellers on the road, or at the Halting places'. Even more astonishing for Astell, these women allowed themselves to be 'tempted to go a little way from their village with the promise of sweetmeat', evincing a degree of gullible simplicity 'one would think only applicable to that of a child of 4 or 5 years of age'. Two gut responses seem to be competing for primacy of place in Astell's mind: the alarming suspicion that these young women wanted to run away from home, versus the conviction that the docility of these women was a mark of their race, not unrelated to 'the usual apathy of natives of this country' invoked by Cookson of Meerut a few years later. The first response imagines the women as subjects, the latter as objects, in the grammar of enslavement and prostitution. Astell may have been programmed to favour the latter conviction, given the racialist paradigms that increasingly structured British thought in the nineteenth century. We in the twenty-first century, on the other hand, are more likely to favour the suspicion that they were willing runaways, to interpret their flight as a bid for freedom—even as an embrace of prostitution as sex work, free of the modern moral stigma that much of the nineteenth and twentieth centuries placed upon it. In any case, it is possible to imagine that the docility and childlike simplicity that Astell saw in these young women was in fact a series of defensive masks that they put on after being rescued, the first steps towards a feigned innocence as they sought to navigate the unfamiliar moral shoals of company law.

Assuming that a postmodern injection of agency into the action of mid-nineteenth century women is not entirely off the mark, we might ask what could prompt a young woman to let herself be taken from her home, or (more likely) the home of her husband. In later depositions, some of the women stated that 'they were beguiled under false pretences'.[45] Perhaps, what some of these young women sought, not unlike already enslaved women in western India who fled their masters' homes,[46] was a new home and new kin—and that this is what the *Banjaras* offered them as a way of luring them into their net. Not all north Indian homes were happy ones, as we know not only from common sense but from the illicit sexual–emotional relations in Agra and Meerut glimpsed earlier. New marriages could be arranged, but they would have to be far enough away to evade the existing kinship webs in which the women were already enmeshed. Hence, the willingness to travel long distances with the *Banjaras* with relatively little complaint or calls for help. Another motivating factor may have been more basic: simple destitution.[47] Astell suggested as much when he explained that the women could not return to their homes because the presumption of their having become prostitutes 'made their *friends* disown them' (emphasis added). That he spoke of 'friends' and not 'family' suggests that these women had no family to turn to, perhaps due to death—though it is also possible that the presumption that they had fallen into prostitution prompted their families to sever ties.

It is also difficult to know how much prostitution in northern India began with a moment of enslavement. Yet the slave dimension does offer an additional insight as to the nature and evolution of a 'benevolent paternalism' on the part of the company. Perceiving this, however, requires rethinking slavery not in terms of the conjoined discourses of property and freedom that have dominated the historiography of Atlantic plantation slavery (not to mention the philosophy of British and British Indian law), but in terms of the social death and rebirth, or marginal kinship, which slavery in fact constituted in practice.[48] What did this mean for girls enslaved into prostitution? As the Civil Surgeon of Rangpur (in Bengal) noted in the early 1870s, 'girls sold to elderly prostitutes "generally look up to the woman who brings them up as their own mother"'.[49] This was because, as the Deputy Magistrate of Tippera (also in Bengal) noted in the same year, the 'old prostitutes' would 'obtain children too young to know their parents' who were then 'taught to call them [the old prostitutes] mamma'.[50] As Indrani Chatterjee has argued, not only was marginal kinship central to slavery in south Asia, thinking about slavery in this way helps us see continuities and ruptures between the 'pre-colonial' and the 'colonial' in new ways. Sumit Guha, Ramya Sreenivasan, Richard Eaton and Dadu Ali have elaborated on this key point, describing the centuries prior to 1800, by highlighting the fact that often the claimant kin of the slave was the corporate body of the king—in other words, the state.[51] Sometimes these royal slaves were soldiers, and sometimes they were concubines. The Nagpur state in the early nineteenth century even claimed low-caste widows at risk of falling into prostitution, deeming them *rajbetis*, 'daughters of the state', and selling them off to the highest bidder, often at a considerable profit.[52] The company obviously chose a different tack, especially as the abolitionist movement gained steam. Instead of claiming destitute women at risk of prostitution and selling them, usually to wealthy men, nineteenth century officials did the reverse—they sought to 'rescue' women and girls sold into prostitution. But while the girls could usually be reunited with their families, the women were left, as we have seen, 'to go their own ways'. The company was willing to be a 'benevolent paternalist', but it would only allow the recipients of that 'benevolent paternalism' to be free agents. Thus was the discourse of slavery reconfigured from kinship to freedom during the course of the nineteenth century.

Were increasing numbers of prostitutes free agents in the nineteenth century? This is flip side of the problem posed above, about the degree to which prostitution in northern India began with a moment of enslavement. Perhaps, the cantonment and regimental bazaars were attractive to some women—especially those captured in their teens whom the magistrates did not manage to rescue, and for whom the elderly prostitutes who purchased them could never be maternal figures—precisely because it was thought to be an arena where they could establish a degree of free agency and engage with company officials as 'benevolent paternalists'. In other words, perhaps such women looked to the corporate military body of John Company as an owner–patriarch–parent, not unlike the way royal slaves in earlier regimes conceived of their kings. This is, of course, speculation, but it does present the beginnings of a logic whereby 'common' prostitutes might look one way on 10 May 1857, while the wealthy elite who owned establishments, such as Mees Dolly, might look another. What we do know is that the conditions were ripe for an expansion of prostitution throughout northern India in the early nineteenth century. The cantonments of the Bengal Army, the single most potent embodiment of imperial legitimacy in the early nineteenth century,[53] grew exponentially after the company's capture of Delhi in 1803.[54] The decisive military component of this new standing army was the infantry, which required large numbers of disciplined men willing to work for long periods of time away from home. That *Banjaras* and other slavers could undertake the outright kidnapping and sale of women and girls with relative ease and on such a large scale suggests that there was a growing demand for prostitutes. Perhaps it was being met by 'free' women as well.

Whether or not we can perceive a transformational logic based on enslavement, kinship and freedom to understand the choices prostitutes made in Meerut on 10 May, what is interesting about all this is the degree to which prostitutes come out of the shadows prior to 1857. They appear as surprisingly visible figures in early British India, both at the level of ideology (as the strong shadow cast by a rising domesticity) and practice (as the resilient victims of crime). Prostitutes seemed to matter in different ways to different people. And because they mattered, it should not surprise us that they might have operated decisively on both sides of the political fence on the 10th of May. Whether or not they caused '1857' the event, they were very much part of the world that gave rise to it, and gave it meaning.

Appendix 4.1:   Prostitutes in Criminal Judicial Proceedings, OIOC, London

Prostitute Victims

Date	Place	District	Division	Name of Victim	Murder	Wounding	Theft	Sentence	Motive and Comments
n.d. 1855	Delhi	Delhi	Delhi	Jowala Devee, prostitute	X		X	executed	motive theft: sepoy hanged, 3 other sepoys implicated but released
n.d. 1855	Tarpoora village	Jhansi	Saugor	Musstt. Raheemun		X		imprisoned 5 years labor	motive jealous rage; sepoy was spurned lover, he bit off her nose and upper lip
14 Mar 1855	Meerut Kotwalee	Meerut	Meerut	Musstt. Hyat Buksh, prostitute		X		6 months with ₹200 fine	motive unknown; quarrel, Mussee Ollah broke Hyat Buksh's arm
17 Mar 1855	Agra Kotwalee	Agra	Agra	Musst. Beeba Jan, prostitute	X			not captured	motive unknown; chowkidar dismissed
17 Mar 1855	Meerut Cant.	Meerut	Meerut	prostitute			X	released for want of proof	motive theft; culprits not named
16 Jun 1855	Sirdhana	Meerut	Meerut	prostitute		X	attempted	not captured	motive theft; culprits unknown
8 Jul 1855	Goruckpoor Kotwalee	Goruckpoor	Benares	prostitute	X		X	1 hanged, another transported	motive theft; two men not sepoys the culprits
22 Aug 1855	Russulgunge, Coel	Allyghur	Meerut	Musstt. Motee, Tuwaif			X	not captured	motive theft, culprits 'thieves' not ID'd

(Continued)

(Continued)

Date	Place	District	Division	Name of Criminal	Murder	Wounding	Theft	Sentence	Motive and Comments
25 Sep 1855	Furruckabad city	Furruckabad	Agra	Musstt. Bujjo, prostitute	X			captured but unpunished	motive probably theft; culprits local men, not sepoys; magstr. very upset by outcome, Kotwal implicated. Detailed follow-up
7 Oct 1855	Jubbulpore city	Jubbulpore	Saugor	Mussumat Bussuntee, prostitute		X	X	imprisoned for life	motive theft; local miscreant the culprit. Magstr. very concerned; hand amputated
31 Dec 1855	Meerut Cant.	Meerut	Meerut	prostitute	X			not captured	motive apparent case of jealousy; culprit unknown
4 Feb 1856	Kydgunge, Allahabad	Allahabad	Allahabad	Mussumat Hydree, prostitute	X		X	sentenced to be hanged	motive theft; culprit notorious poisoner; escaped in 1857, recaptured
6 Jul 1856	Bhoropoor	Etawah	Agra	Mussumat Chutteeree, prostitute	X			caught, punished?	motive enmity between client and third part; prostitute killed with him over land dispute
11 Jul 1856	Furruckabad	Furruckabad	Agra	Bilaso, prostitute	attempted			absconded, reward offered	motive jealousy; Madaree sepoy was spurned suitor

Prostitute Criminals

Date	Place	District	Division	Name of Criminal	Murder	Wounding	Theft	Sentence	Motive and Comments
n.d. 1855	unknown village/town	Jounpore	Benares	Mistress from Oudh	X			escaped with brother	so-called 'brother' of mistress murdered the client; reward offered, ₹200
n.d. 1855	Delhi	Delhi	Delhi	prostitute			X	unknown	stolen property recovered in her house

Notes and References

1. William Dalrymple, *The Last Mughal: The Fall of a Dynasty, Delhi, 1857* (London: Penguin Viking, 2007), p. 192. Given the importance of Meerut, it is odd that with the exception of Kim A. Wagner's recent book, *The Great Fear of 1857* (London: Peter Lang, 2010), it has received almost no sustained attention from historians. The main exceptions are George W. Williams in 1858, whom I discuss below (and who, though a police superintendent, was an early proponent of detective work and historical forensics), and J.A.B. Palmer, author of *The Mutiny Outbreak of Meerut in 1857* (Cambridge: Cambridge University Press, 1966). Both were concerned with the 'why' of the mutiny, and whether there was a conspiracy behind the event. Williams argued that there was not: that the uprising was the result of bazaar rumour in which the figure of a 'cook's boy' loomed especially large. Palmer argued that while there may have been a broader conspiracy, there is little evidence that supports that conclusion; however, as for a conspiracy specific to Meerut in early May after the arrest of eighty-five skirmishers of the Third Light Cavalry for disobedience over the cartridge issue, he inclined towards the positive and felt that the peculiar sequence of events did point to some local premeditation. Both Palmer and Williams' accounts make clear the importance of local 'rabble' to the contingent nature of the unfolding mutiny on 10 May in Meerut. Gujars, butchers, servants, cooks boys, and other 'creatures of the bazaar' played a leading role in the initial violence that shattered the calm of Meerut on 10 May.

2. Palmer, *Mutiny Outbreak*, Chapter 2 on the greased cartridge issue, esp. pp. 17–19.

3. John Cracroft Wilson, *Narrative of Events Attending the Outbreak of Disturbances and the Restoration of Authority in the District of Moradabad, in 1857–1858* (London: Anglo-American Times Press, 1871), p. 2. This passage is quoted in P.J.O. Taylor's account of 'Mees Dolly', details of which are given in the following note.

4. P.J.O. Taylor, *Companion to the Mutiny of 1857* (Delhi: Oxford University Press, 1996), pp. 217–218. A slightly less detailed version appears in P.J.O. Taylor, *Chronicles of the Mutiny and Other Historical Sketches* (New Delhi: Indus, 1992) and, before that, in his column for *The Statesman* (New Delhi), 6 October 1989. Unfortunately, Taylor was less than forthcoming about the whereabouts of this source, beyond a cryptic remark about wanting to visit 'a certain regimental museum'—presumably the one to which Norman belonged. I am grateful to Clare Anderson for bringing Mees Dolly to my attention.

5. On the degree to which such matters reflected deep imperial anxieties, see Nancy L. Paxton, *Writing Under the Raj: Gender, Race, and Rape in British Colonial Imagination, 1830–1947* (New Brunswick: Rutgers University Press, 1999), and the review by Indira Karamcheti, 'Writing Rape and the Difference it Makes', *NOVEL: A Forum on Fiction*, vol. 33, no. 1 (Autumn 1999), pp. 125–128.

6. George W. Williams, ed., *Depositions Taken at Meerut under the Direction of Lt. Col. G.W.W.* (Allahabad: Government Press, 1858), pp. 23–24.

7. Their vulnerable position and conflicted politics in 1857 may be perceived just as well in the oppressions and opportunities that confronted 'dancers' and 'courtesans' in Delhi during the summer of 1857; see Dalrymple, *Last Mughal*, esp. pp. 12–13, 208, 326–327.

8. Kenneth Ballhatchet, *Race, Sex and Class under the Raj: Imperial Attitudes and Policies and their Critics, 1793–1905* (London: Weidenfeld and Nicolson, 1980); and Philippa Levine, *Prostitution, Race, and Politics: Policing Venereal Disease in the British Empire* (New York: Routledge, 2003). I am grateful to Philippa Levine for suggestions on these source issues. For an examination of the early-nineteenth century evidence, see Douglas Peers, 'Soldiers, Surgeons and the Campaigns to Combat Sexually Transmitted Diseases in Colonial India', *Medical History*, vol. 42, no. 2 (1998), pp. 137–160; and 'Privates off Parade: Regulating Sexuality in the Nineteenth-century Indian Empire', *International History Review*, vol. 20, no. 4 (1998), pp. 823–854, in which Peers

complicates the general argument about increasing regulation of sexuality by British authorities in the nineteenth century.

9. Indrani Chatterjee and Sumit Guha, 'Slave-Queen, Waif-Prince: Slavery and Social Capital in Eighteenth-century India', *Indian Economic and Social History Review*, vol. 36, no. 2 (1999), pp. 165–186; Indrani Chatterjee, *Gender, Slavery and Law in British India* (Delhi: Oxford University Press, 1999); Durba Ghosh, *Sex and the Family in Colonial India: The Making of Empire* (Cambridge: Cambridge University Press, 2006); Vijay Pinch, 'Gosain Tawaif: Sex, Slaves, and Ascetics in Rasdhan, 1800–1857; *Modern Asian Studies*, vol. 38, no. 3 (July 2004), pp. 559–597; and Ramya Sreenivasan, 'Drudges, Dancing Girls, and Concubines: Female Slaves in the Rajput Polity, 1500–1850', in Indrani Chatterjee and Richard Eaton, eds, *Slavery & Society in South Asian History* (Bloomington: University of Indiana Press, 2006), pp. 136–161.

10. On the latter, see Veena Talwar Oldenburg, 'Lifestyle as Resistance: The Case of the Courtesans of Lucknow', in V. Graff, ed., *Lucknow: Memories of a City* (Delhi: Oxford University Press, 1997), pp. 136–154. On the former, Badauni's is the most famous passage:

> 'the prostitutes of the imperial dominions, who had gathered together in the Capital in such swarms as to defy counting or numbering', Akbar 'made to live outside the city, and called the place *Shaitanpura*. And he appointed a keeper, and a deputy, and a secretary for this quarter, so that any one who wished to associate with these people, or take them to his house, provided he first had his name and condition written down, might with the connivance of the imperial officers have connection with any of them that he pleased. But he did not permit any man to take dancing-girls to his house at night, without conforming to these conditions, in order that he might keep the matter under proper control'.

Muntakhabu-t-tawarikh, vol. II, trans. George S.A. Ranking (Calcutta: Asiatic Society of Bengal, 1898; New Delhi: Atlantic, 1990), pp. 311–312.

11. Taylor does not provide the source for the passage, which is on page 188 of his *Companion to the Mutiny of 1857*:

> On July 26th (1857) we had to cross the Beas River. Engineers reported the bridge of boats fairly safe.... Just then there appeared the conveyances bearing the native ladies attached to the regiment. Tommy Atkins was much agitated: would they or would they not get over? Ladies seated in ekkas, carts had tops and curtains descended hiding the dusky beauties ... just as the line of ekkhas had passed the centre of the bridge a cry was heard. It is gone! Too true the boats which had held together during the passage of HM's soldiers, the camels and the baggage, gave way under the immense responsibility now entrusted to them, and amid despairing cries boats and ekkhas were borne away by the current of the swollen river ... which way would they be taken? ... watched by anxious eyes the boats bearing their precious burdens gradually but surely neared the shore, and as they touched, many willing hands caught and secured the wandering boats, the ekkhas were brought safely to land, and the ladies restored to their position with the regiment.

12. The probable reason Taylor did not encounter such records is, first, that official correspondence dealing with political and military events after 10 May 1857 tended to focus on deployment of troops, combatants and punishment of soldiers who rebelled, deserted or simply failed to report for duty promptly in the summer of 1857 (a charge which, until September of 1858, was usually treated as desertion and punished by death); and second, that the official records that

Taylor consulted tended to be concentrated in the Foreign Political, Foreign Secret and Military Department Proceedings, or in the various 'Mutiny Papers' held in the National Archives of India and Allahabad Archives. By contrast, as is made clear below, the Judicial Department proceedings for the 1850s do include reference to prostitutes, and they are far less likely to employ polite or ironic euphemisms.

13. See note 9 above.

14. See, for example, Indrani Chatterjee, 'Colouring Subalternity: Slaves, Concubines and Social Orphans in Early Colonial India', in Gautam Bhadra, Gyan Prakash, and Susie Tharu, eds, *Subaltern Studies X: Writings on South Asian History and Society* (Delhi: Oxford University Press), esp. pp. 62–68.

15. There were abortive attempts to institute Lock Hospitals in the early nineteenth century, but these were abandoned when it appeared that they served, inadvertently, to increase the rate of contagion. See Ballhatchet, *Race, Sex and Class under the Raj*, Chapter 1. Post-1864 legislation, such as the various provincial 'Prevention of Prostitution Acts' and the wider 'Suppression of Immoral Traffic Act', began describing prostitution as a species of deplorable behaviour, verging on the criminal; these eventually evolved into the 'Immoral Trafficking Prevention Act' of 1956. Significantly, drafters of legislation were careful not to criminalise the actual women engaged in prostitution, who were seen to be the main victims of the practice. The goal was to punish the sin, not the sinner, but the effect was usually the same in that it marginalised prostitutes and made their profession increasingly dangerous.

16. See Appendix 4.1 for a tabular statement of these cases and the records from which they are drawn.

17. I have not included cases involving women identified as 'concubines', of which there were three instances; nor have I included cases involving women said to be entertaining multiple lovers. All the women in the cases I have included here were identified explicitly as prostitutes—save for one case, in Russulgunge Kotwali, Aligarh, in the Meerut Division, where the woman was identified as 'Tuwaif'. There were several additional cases where women were engaged in long-standing extramarital relationships that may have had a contractual nature, but because the term 'prostitute' was not used to describe these women, their cases were not included in the tabulations. An additional case was recorded for Mirzapoor in the Benares Division (see North-west Provinces Civil Judicial [NWP-CJ], 118 of 8 July 1856), but it dated from 1837 and was included due to the release of the prisoner over uncertainty as to his actual identity; hence it is also not included in the tabulation.

18. NWP-CJ, 363 of 22 August 1856: W.G. Probyn, Offtg. Mag. Furruckabad, to G.F. Harvey, Commr. Agra Dv., 11 July 1856.

19. NWP-CJ, 98 of 8 July 1856: H.C. Tucker, Commr. of Benares Dv., to Secy. Govt. NWP, 15 March 1856. This case may have been an incidence of a slightly different species of crime that appeared to be fairly widespread across northern and central India, in which gangs of 'Beriahs' used their women as sexual bait to lure men whom the Beriahs would then rob and kill. See, for example, NWP-CJ, 18 of 1 March 1856: 'Translation of the Confessions of Phoolwaree Shah', who was active for about ten years before being captured (originally deposed in 1853), and 'Translation of the Confession of Buddyan'. This particular gang operating in a belt that extended across northern Bundelkhand. Capturing such criminals was difficult due to their high mobility; hence, they fell under the purview of the Department of Thuggee and Dakoiti.

20. NWP-CJ, 533 of 22 Sep 1856: 'Triennial statement of crimes and offences, and statement of convictions for the year 1855 in Zillah Meerut', by E.M. Wylly, 9 February 1856. In addition to the figures given in the table, the district report noted for the record 247 additional burglaries 'unattended with aggravating circumstances', 522 'other cases' of theft, 649 cases of cattle

stealing 'unattended with aggravating circumstances', and 910 cases of 'crimes and offences not specified above'.

21. NWP-CJ, 530 of 22 September 1856: 'Narrative of Crimes Committed in 1855' [Meerut District], probably by R.H. Dunlop, Officiating Magistrate. It is not immediately clear what distinguishes burglary and theft, given the descriptions of the individual cases.

22. NWP-CJ, 189 of 10 July 1856: 'Extract Cases no. 1 to 18 from the Agra Magistrate's Narrative of Crimes in Connection with Police Report for 1855'.

23. Sometimes that property was considerable. Thieves broke into the house of one prostitute, 'Motee a Tuwaif', and 'stole property amounting to 820 Rs'. NWP-CJ, 541E of 22 September 1856: 'Abstract of Heinous Offences for the year 1855' (Allyghur), G.P. Money, Magistrate, 13 March 1856. The fact that she is referred to by Money as 'Tuwaif' is, I think, an indication that she was perceived to be of an altogether different class than the 'common' bazaar prostitute.

24. NWP-CJ, 108 of 6 August 1856: S. Fraser, Commr. Delhi, to Sec. to Govt. in Agra, 19 May 1856.

25. On the involvement of prostitutes in the liquor trade, see NWP-CJ, 309 of 22 April 1853: Captn. G.R. Cookson, Cantt. Jt. Mag., Meerut, to Lt. Col. Steel, Sup. Cantt. Police. For the sale of kidnapped girls to prostitutes in Meerut, see NWP-CJ, 61 of 10 June 1850: G. H. France, Sessions Judge Saharanpoor, to M.R. Gubbins, Offg. Regr. to the Court of the Niz. Adt. NWP, Agra, 6 February 1850. I am grateful to Clare Anderson for directing me to this latter reference. These girls came mostly from the region around Coel, Etawah and Mathura. I discuss this case in greater detail below. Similar trafficking in girls was occurring in what is now Haryana; see 108 of 6 August 1856: S. Fraser, Commr., Delhi, to Sec. to Govt., Agra, 19 May 1856, para. 91.

26. NWP-CJ, 361 of 13 September 1856: 'Abstract of cases of the 1st and 2nd class, during the past year' [Jabalpur], signed F.W. Pinckney, Dep. Commsr., Jabalpur, 8 April 1856.

27. NWP-CJ, 59 of 4 March 1856: P. Carnegy, Dy Magstr., Allahabad Dt., to G. Chester, Officiating Commsr., Allahabad Dv., 9 Feb 1856.

28. See, e.g., the three cases listed for Meerut District in 1855. The first two occur in NWP-CJ, 530 of 22 September 1856: 'Narrative of Crimes Committed in 1855' [Meerut District], probably by R.H. Dunlop, Officiating Magistrate; the third case is from NWP-CJ, 541E of 22 September 1856: 'Abstract of Heinous Offences for the Year 1855' [Allyghur], signed G.P. Money, Magistrate, 13 March 1856.

29. NWP-CJ, 58 of 5 June 1854: Capt. G.R. Cookson, Cantt. Jt Mag, Meerut, to Lieutt. Col. J. Steel, Supdt. Cantt. Police, 1 January 1854. This was the only murder in the Meerut cantonment during 1853; there were no murders in the previous two years.

30. NWP-CJ, 10 of 2 April 1856: R. Cookson, Cantt. Jt. Magstr., Meerut, to J. Steel, Suptd. Cantt. Police, 1 January 1856. Cookson concluded that because a box of clothes and some jewels were left untouched among the ruins of the house, which had been burned to the ground, the motive was not theft but jealousy.

31. NWP-CJ, 108 of 6 August 1856: S. Fraser, Commssr, Delhi, to Sec. to Govt., Agra, 19 May 1856.

32. NWP-CJ, 126 of 6 August 1856: R. Robertson, Suptdt., Delhi, to S. Fraser, Commr., Delhi, 21 February 1856. The other three men involved were acquitted on a technicality.

33. NWP-CJ, 189 of 10 July 1856: 'Extract Cases no. 1 to 18 from the Agra Magistrate's Narrative of Crimes in Connection with the Police Report for 1855', signed R. Drummond, Magistrate, 4 February 1856.

34. NWP-CJ, 201 of 10 July 1856: 'Extract Entries 1 to 3 Theft with Murder from the Abstract Statement of Heinous Crimes for the Year 1855' [Furruckabad], signed W.G. Probyn. See also 232 of 10 July: C.B. Thornhill, Sec. to Govt., to G.F. Harvey, Commissioner of Agra Dvn (which identifies Lushington as the former magistrate in Furruckabad); and 318 of 13 Sep 1856, Probyn to Harvey, 30 August, Furruckabad (in which the influential personage is identified as the uncle of the kotwal, the 'naib' of the 'nawab rais' of Farrukhabad). Lushington's views on the allegation were solicited by the Lieutenant Governor, but if he provided them they are among

the records that are missing due to the rebellion. Probyn is the same official who reported in the case of the attempted murder of the prostitute Bilaso, noted earlier, that though her mother and sister were wounded and a doorman killed, she seemed 'to have had a most wonderful escape'. See 363 of 22 August 1856: W.G. Probyn, Offtg. Mag. Furruckabad, to G.F. Harvey, Commr. Agra Dv., 11 July 1856.

35. An example of such a case, not involving a prostitute however, is the 3 July 1856 killing in cold blood of one Mahomed Khan of Sopheepoor, near Meerut, by a British artilleryman. According to R.H. Dunlop, the magistrate of Meerut, two British artillerymen had gone out shooting and had bagged a pigeon that happened to belong to an individual named Ramdhun of Sopheepoor. Ramdhun and his friend, Mahomed Khan, demanded the pigeon and threatened to complain to the quartermaster of the regiment about the shooting, at which point one of the two artillerymen, who had quietly been reloading, suddenly lifted his weapon and killed Mahomed Khan. The men then fled to their regimental barracks, where their fellow soldiers barred entry to the crowd of the villagers that followed them. The body of Mahomed Khan was eventually brought to the sergeant, who instituted a court of inquiry. The plaintiffs were unable to identify the guilty parties in a line up however. The two artillerymen later confessed to the sergeant in private, but they alleged that the 'affray' was the result of a scuffle in which the victim was accidentally shot. A court martial was ordered; however, its verdict is unknown, the records probably having been lost during the 1857 uprising. NWP-CJ, 144 of 6 August 1856: R.H. Dunlop, Magistrate Meerut, to Greathead, Commr., 10 July 1856.

36. Ballhatchet, *Race, Sex and Class under the Raj*, p. 36–38 (pp. 37 for the quote), citing India Military Proceedings in the India Office Records. When the magistrate suggested that the brigadier simply restrict his men from going to the haunts of these women, the brigadier became apoplectic and called the proposal 'absurd', noting that the regimental 'Lines are surrounded in every direction by Bazars that are in the civil jurisdiction'. The brigadier was reprimanded for his intemperate tone, and no action was taken—until the passage of the Indian Contagious Diseases Act of 1868. A similar scenario occurred when the Agra magistrate was asked by the regimental brigadier to have some 'diseased women "turned out" of their villages, and the local *zamindars* ... heavily fined for harbouring them'.

37. Radhika Singha, *A Despotism of Law: Crime and Justice in Early Colonial India* (Delhi: Oxford University Press, 1998), p. 147; Singha cites Bengal Criminal Judicial Proceedings, 31 of 9 [or 10?] July 1819: J. Eliot to Regr. Nizamat Adawlut, West Bengal State Archives, as well as the Regulation 7 of 1819.

38. Radhika Singha, 'Making the Domestic more Domestic: Criminal Law and the Head of the Household, 1772–1843', *Indian Economic and Social History Review*, vol. 33, no. 3 (1996), pp. 309–343.

39. NWP-CJ, 261 of 30 September 1850: H.G. Astell, Magstr. Moozuffernuggur, to D.B. Morrison, Commr. Meerut Dv., 12 June 1850. I am grateful to Clare Anderson for alerting me to this file. For Bengal, see Chatterjee, *Gender, Slavery and Law*.

40. Sleeman, *A Report on the System of Megpunnaism or, The Murder of Indigent Parents for Their Young Children (Who Are Sold as Slaves) as It Prevails in the Delhi Territories, and the Native States of Rajpootana, Ulwar, and Bhurtpore* (Serampore: Serampore Press, 1839); Singha, *Despotism of Law*, 161–162, cautions against discounting Sleeman as simply a sensationaliser. Though his work was clearly possessed of an 'Orientalizing' dimension, one claim that he made, that many ascetics were involved in the enslavement of children, would seem to be borne out by the evidence: on *gosains*, see William R. Pinch, *Warrior Ascetics and Indian Empires* (Cambridge: Cambridge University Press, 2006), Chapter 4, and on *bairagis*, see Indrani Chatterjee, *Gender, Slavery and Law*, 222–223, 246; in both, however, women procurers were explicitly involved as well.

41. NWP-CJ, 108 of 6 August 1856: S. Fraser, Commssr, Delhi, to Sec. to Govt, Agra, 19 May, paras 91–94.

42. One of them was described as a 46-year-old Gosain named Golab, and the other, a 28-year-old Brahmin named Bhowany. NWP-CJ, 220 of 14 February 1856: Cover Letter from G.F. Harvey, Offg. Commissioner Agra, to Sec. to Govt, 31 Jan 1856. See also 271–272 of 19 January 1856, describing a 60-year old 'Goshein' woman named Ghanee arrested for kidnapping a female in Jaipur and trying to sell her in Patiala.

43. NWP-CJ, 261 of 30 September 1850: H.G. Astell, Magstr. Moozuffernuggur, to D.B. Morrison, Commr. Meerut Dv., 12 June 1850.

44. On the procuring of girls for regimental and Sadar Bazar, see Chatterjee, 'Colouring Subalternity', 62–68. The close connection between female enslavement, female procurers, prostitution as sex-slavery, and the cantonments in British India is now widely accepted; see Ketan Mehta's film, *Mangal Pandey: The Rising* (2005), which features an early scene of a slave mart near the cantonment in which the local brothel owner is implicated (Indrani Chatterjee, personal communication, 27 March 2007).

45. According to a later report of the actual trial by the Sessions Judge at Saharanpur, some of the women later deposed that 'they were forcibly taken away by threats, and others that they were beguiled under false pretences'. See NWP-CJ, 61 of 10 June 1850: G.H. France, Sessions Judge Saharanpoor, 6 February 1850, to M.R. Gubbins, Offg. Regr. to the Court of Niz. Adt., Agrah.

46. Sumit Guha, 'Slavery, Society, and the State in Western India, 1700–1800', in Chatterjee and Eaton, eds, *Slavery & Society in South Asian History*, p. 179.

47. Singha, *Despotism of Law*, p. 160; Pinch, *Warrior Ascetics*, pp. 80–81; Chatterjee, *Gender, Slavery and Law*.

48. See the discussion in Chatterjee, *Gender, Slavery and Law*, esp. pp. 26–28; Guha, 'Slavery, Society, and the State in Western India, pp. 162–165; Miers and Kopytoff, eds, *Slavery in Africa: Historical and Anthropological Perspectives* (Madison: University of Wisconsin Press, 1977); and Patterson, *Slavery and Social Death: A Comparative Study* (Cambridge: Harvard University Press, 1982).

49. Judicial Proceedings, West Bengal State Archives (WBSA), no. B269 of October 1872: Civil Surgeon Rangpur to Commr. Rajshahi Divn, 27 May 1872, cited in Chatterjee, *Gender, Slavery and Law*, p. 222.

50. Judicial Proceedings, WBSA, no. B271 of October 1872: Dy. Magt. Brahmanberia to Magt. Tipperah, 25 May 1872, cited in Chatterjee, *Gender, Slavery and Law*, p. 222.

51. Daud Ali, 'War, Servitude, and the Imperial Household: A Study of Palace Women in the Chola Empire'; Richard Eaton, 'The Rise and Fall of Military Slavery in the Deccan, 1450–1650'; Ramya Sreenivasan, 'Drudges, Dancing Girls, and Concubines: Female Slaves in the Rajput Polity, 1500–1850'; and Sumit Guha, 'Slavery, Society, and the State in Western India, 1700–1800'— all in Chatterjee and Eaton, eds, *Slavery & Society in South Asian History*.

52. Guha, 'Slavery, Society, and the State in Western India', p. 167.

53. Seema Alavi, *The Sepoys and the Company: Tradition and Transition in Northern India, 1770–1830* (Delhi: Oxford University Press, 1995).

54. Douglas M. Peers, *Between Mars and Mammon: Colonial Armies and the Garrison State in India, 1819–1835* (New York: Tauris, 1995).

5

THE ROOTS OF PEASANT TURBULENCE
Tenure Structures and 1857

Amaresh Misra

A rarely answered query in 1857 studies concerns the uneven graph of turbulence across rural India. This, it will be argued here, is related to different peasant-tenure structures and their complex association with pre-British class/caste/clan and sub-clan (*gotra*) patterns of landownership in nineteenth century British India. Turbulence here is defined primarily as a cognitive category, representing instances of specifically anti-British peasant upheaval. Caste is seen mainly as a lingering social manifestation of Asiatic modes of economic production. Thus, caste is not just a social superstructural reality, but has structural roots as well. Similarly, sub-castes, clans and sub-clans are seen here in their relationship with the land and their productive role in the economy, and thus as institutions of pivotal importance.

This chapter is dedicated to Eric Stokes, whose path-breaking but unfinished *The Peasant Armed*[1] remains an underrated work of 1857 history. Stokes' hard-nosed analysis of peasant structures in western Uttar Pradesh (UP) inspired me to extend his methodology to central and east UP, as well as to other areas of the great North Indian Plain. Unfortunately, C.A. Bayly, who tried to conclude *The Peasant Armed*, misread Stokes completely. Bayly's strong point was nineteenth century north Indian bazaars and urban towns, not rural structures. Stokes was moving towards a rational explanation of the extremely complex 1857 Indian peasant rural behaviour. A true empiricist in the great British tradition, and a student of Karl Marx as well, Stokes focused more on ruptures and radical breaks in structures and how they led to rebellion, or 'revolution'. Bayly, on the other hand, remained focused on continuities: his book *Rulers, Townsmen and Bazaars* is similarly more concerned with establishing the continuity between the precolonial and the colonial elites than with noticing disjunctures. Bayly somehow held that British rule was relatively non-destructive and that the British found a base within the existing precolonial society, which remained to a great extent unchanged. Stokes' genius lay in his unsentimental recognition of the radical destruction wrought by the British, particularly regarding rural social structures. Stokes was also the first to recognise the dynamism of India as lying in its communitarian peasant associations. The (ultimately unsuccessful) attempt of the British to destroy this communitarian *pattidari* system not only created the conditions for 1857 but sustained the twentieth century Indian national movement, allowed the revival of India as an economic powerhouse in the twenty-first century, and now propels a new Asiatic capitalism. Stokes was thus more than a genius—he was a visionary with an instinctive grasp of the subterranean currents of society.

Contrary to conventional thinking, I intend to begin by assuming that on the eve of the British conquest, India was a relatively flourishing centre of Asiatic modernity, progress and capitalism. This premise is also the starting point of my book *War of Civilisations: India 1857 AD*,[2] a two-volume history of the 'mutiny', which endeavours to revive, albeit from an opposing Indian point of view, the long histories written by nineteenth century British historians like Kaye and Malleson. Thus, rather than assuming the enduring superiority of all that is European, we begin by remembering that India, along with China, dominated world trade and economy until 1750. Based on finished luxury goods and exotic items like spices and pepper, India's manufacturing base was vital and strong. Factory-stage rudiments were present especially in the workshops of cotton and silk textiles. Agriculture had already entered the petty commodity production stage, and the Mughals practised a form of moral, territorial and economic nationalism. Mughal writers on economics, such as Muhammad Baquir, consequently wrote: 'property can be acquired stock both for this world and the next. A man who has nothing can enjoy nothing and achieve nothing'. Baquir's *Maniz-a-Jehangiri* was a major work. Another, *Tehzeeb-ul-axlaq*, written during Aurangzeb's time, recognised the possession of money 'as an agent of social mobility'. But Indian capitalism sang a different tune to its 'Western' counterpart. Unlike in Europe, there were no burghers forcing change from above. The Asiatic sense of property did not have a rigid character. It could be communal and private depending on circumstances; theoretically, the entire land could belong to the King; it could otherwise belong to the village or a small principality with the King enjoying tributary rights. *Pattidars*—or proprietary brotherhoods—could control large parcels for their family, or *gotras*. A *gotra bhai* could leave his portion for his son, and thus that land would become private property in practice, although theoretically the *gotra* or sub-sect held moral and material authority. Religion could also be factored into the economy: the land was God's, and proprietors were mere shareholders.

Altering Indian tenure structures constituted a major part of the British policy of colonial control. The Permanent Settlement in Bengal literally invented not only Indian landlordism but Indian feudalism as well. Before that, under the Bengali nawabs, despite pockets of concentration of land control, there were no hereditary zamindars. The Bengal village economy had an artisanal sector as well; in fact, the town existed in the countryside and the countryside in the town. This aspect was similarly visible in a concrete manner, in the Hindi–Urdu belt. Here, in the present-day north and central Indian states of UP, Bihar, Madhya Pradesh, Delhi and Haryana, peasant brotherhoods held land in a sort of joint stock ownership. This was the *pattidari–bhaichara–hissedari–biswedari* system, which Charles Metcalfe described famously as constituting the basis of 'mini Asiatic republics'. Far from being stagnant pools, these village republics were as dynamic as the joint family or *gotra* section which held lands; had one brother who tilled the land; another who worked as a trader between, say, Central Asia and the Middle East; a third who was a soldier; a fourth who was a courtier or a poet; a fifth who was a wanderer or an ascetic; a sixth who was a portfolio capitalist/entrepreneur, establishing *ganjs* and *qasbahs*; and a seventh who looked after *jajmani* affairs.

The *jajmani* system is much misunderstood. It was not simply a form of barter. On the contrary, it was a form of dynamic exchange and division of labour. The artisan families supplied clothes to *pattidars* who supplied grain to artisans. Yet *pattidars* only did so after paying land revenue in cash and selling the surplus in the market. If it was a case of barter, it was a uniquely post-cash scenario of barter. Artisans, too, exchanged clothes in the village after selling off their wares in the market. *Jajmani* pressures involved both peasants and artisans in an unending cycle of production, exchange and consumption, where self-sufficiency itself demanded market relations and vice versa. This is the crucial dialectic of the relationship that is missed by traditional Marxist scholars.

The British Permanent Settlement broke the former unity of agriculture and manufacture, peasant and artisan, and trader and tiller. In the name of creating an 'energetic', competitive sense of private property, the Permanent Settlement actually atomised the peasant. It created the depressed tenant and the slothful, sloppy landlord with no cultural–ideological ties to production and exchange. This was a major rupture, as Indian capitalism was never individualistic or landlord-driven. It was communitarian, state- and peasant-driven. The Talukedari system in Awadh, which survived in its indigenous form until 1856, is a case in point. Awadhi Talukedars were not holders of big estates. Most of the land the British attributed to them was actually possessed by their *pattidar* brothers. A Talukedar in Awadh was mainly titular: he was the descendant of the bravest *pattidar* family who had the right to build a *garhi* or fort, own weapons and raise a small army. But he seldom paid taxes on behalf of the *pattidars*. Nor were his village-level 'crown' lands a permanent fixture. This is seen in the sixteenth-century records of the administration of the Ain-i-Akbari, the Emperor Akbar. In the Awadh district of Unnao, not a single revenue settlement is recorded as present in a landlord's name:

> [The] *mahal* of Unam (Unnao) was held by the Saiyyads ... contained a brick
> fort ... and a garrison of 50 horse and 4,000 foot ... Sarusi ... was owned by

Chandel Rajputs who maintained 20 horse and 1,000 foot ... Harha was held by Bais Rajputs who supplied 100 horse and 1,500 foot and possessed a brick fort ... Bangarmau was owned by Chandel Rajputs who supplied 40 horse and 1,000 foot....Fatehpur Chaurasi, also a Chandel *mahal* was assigned a force of 10 horse and 500 foot ... Mohan, owned by Bais Rajputs, had a brick fort and contingent consisting of 30 horse and 2,000 foot ... Parsandan, *held by Rajputs and Kurmis* supplied 200 infantry ... the proprieters of *mahal* Jhalotar were Chandel Rajputs who supplied a force of 20 horsemen and 2,000 foot soldiers ... *mahal* Asiyun ... was divided between Chandels and the Bais who together supplied 10 horse and 500 foot to the government ... the mahals of Unchagaon and Sidhupur were both owned by Bais Rajputs, the contingent assigned to the former being 1,000 cavalry and 2,000 infantry and to the latter 150 horse and 1500 foot ... Moraon ... also possessed a brick fort, was held by the Bias Rajputs and furnished 150 horse and 2,000 foot ... Saron, owned by Rajputs, supplied only 100 foot soldiers, and Konbhi, also held by Rajputs, only 400 foot soldiers ... Makraed was in the hands of the Bais Rajputs and furnished 1,000 foot ... so was Panhan with an assignment of 300 foot ... *the proprieters of Ghatampur were Brahmins and those of Asoha, Ahirs,* the former supplying 5,00 and the latter 4,00 soldiers....[3]

This absence of landlordism is astonishing. The pattern is repeated in every district from Hardoi to Pratapgarh and the mention of Ahirs and Kurmis as clans shows that the *pattidari* system was not limited to the upper castes. In fact, it was only after 1856 and the British annexation that 'true' landlords emerged in Awadh.

In West UP, Doab and Bundelkhand the story is the same. Here the British had ruled since 1801, 1803 and 1818, respectively. They tried a number of experiments in land administration, but ultimately they settled on the *mahalwari* system, which could be described as a modified form of *pattidari*, or a modified form of zamindari with certain Permanent Settlement features. There was also a third form: under several Mahalwari areas, the *lambardar*, or the *malguzar*, was accorded the status of a rent collector. He enjoyed certain privileges, but before 1857 he was not a landlord and was socially closer to the *pattidars*. Lambardari and Malguzari extended all the way to the Sagar and Narmada region in present-day Madhya Pradesh. As we shall see, it directly affected the peasant turbulence of this area.

Central India or modern Madhya Pradesh was quite similar to the Deccan, an area where the British implemented the Ryotwari system. Ryotwari has been heralded as the great antidote to the ills of Permanent Settlement—a system in which the British made a direct settlement with the peasantry. Hitherto, criticism of Ryotwari has been limited to how it failed to uproot zamindari in west India and the south. But this is not the main point. In the Indian context, Ryotwari was itself reactionary and anti-peasant, as it ruptured peasant brotherhood and peasant–artisan unity from 'below', just as the Permanent Settlement ruptured the same from 'above'.

On the eve of 1857, in both Permanent Settlement and Ryotwari areas, the peasantry were economically and politically depressed as a consequence of the destructive effects of British land policies. The Bengali pre-1857, anti–Permanent Settlement Faraizi movement illustrated that, in Bengal, it was no longer possible to mobilise peasants on the basis of Asiatic brotherhood. A new ideology was needed. In the Faraizi case, Islam supplied that ideology. But the Faraizi impulse had dissipated by 1857. Most Bengal army sepoys and *sowars* came from *pattidar–bhaichara* areas of present-day UP and Bihar. Yet there were differences. In the Doab, for example, a quasi-landlord-type settlement, of absentee bania landlords, had emerged, but, and this is crucial—the clan-*pattidar* landholders had not been eliminated. In Etawah district, for example, out of 4,282 mahals, 2,030 were held as zamindari and 1,252 as *pattidari*. This was in contrast to lower Doab areas like Allahabad or Poorvanchal (East UP). In Etawah, where zamindari outstripped *pattidari*, the zamindari–*pattidari* relationship was highly important: Khattris, Banias and Rajputs dominated the ranks of zamindars; Brahmins and Rajputs held *pattidari*s (over one-third in proprietary rights); critically, Rajputs, Brahmins and Ahirs served overwhelmingly as tenants. In Bengal, the peasants as tenants were economically and socially oppressed, but unlike Bengal, in Etawah, the upper-caste tenantry were actively antagonistic. This was because in UP the Banias and Khattris were held in low esteem: caste thus played a critical economic and political revolutionary role.

At Etawah, the Awadh condition of powerful Rajput–Brahmin–Muslim Talukedaris succumbing to overwhelming *pattidari* pressure from below was absent. The caste–culture continuity gap between peasants and landlords, which in other places led to the suppression of turbulence, here contributed heavily to tumult. Thus, amongst the districts of the middle and upper Doab, Etawah district was the 'most disturbed'. A comparison with Etah and Mainpuri, the neighbouring Doab districts, is revealing; in Etawah, zamindari mahals comprised less than 50 per cent;[4] at Etah, zamindari mahals exceeded the 50 per cent mark.[5] In 1857, Etah and Mainpuri districts were turbulent, but less so than Etawah.

In the eastern districts of UP, the crucial clan-*pattidari* interface was as much evident as in the west. In Azamgarh, amongst all the Rajput clans, the Pulwars were the most turbulent. With an 86 per cent Hindu and 14 per cent Muslim population, Azamgarh was typical of the eastern districts—Chamars (257,000), Ahirs (219,000) and Brahmins (108,000) were the most numerous amongst the population. With a total of nearly 100,000, the Rajput population was also large. The 56,000 Bhumihars were far behind numerically, yet as zamindars, Bhumihars owned more than 16 per cent of the land, Brahmins owned 10 per cent, while the Rajputs held the largest share (33 per cent).[6]

Despite constituting a large element of the Azamgarhi Rajput population, the Pulwars did not feature at all amongst the ranks of the larger zamindars; Rajkumars and Bachgotis held that privilege. Among the Bhumihars, only 10 per cent of a 56,000-strong community held zamindari rights; amongst Brahmins, the zamindari numbers were even smaller. The bulk of Brahmins, Rajputs and Bhumihars existed as cultivators, tilling only 14 per cent of the land. Most Pulwars survived on *pattidari*-type small plots. In Azamgarh the mahals or revenue units were 'complex ... extending over a number of *mauza*s or villages';[7] proprietary rights were very minutely subdivided and inferior proprietors called *mushakhasidar*s were also found. The picture here is of a large number of high-caste, quasi-free but small peasants distributed across the length and breadth of the district, rubbing shoulders with Kurmi, Ahir and Kori tenants. Crucially, the bulk of Azamgarh fighters thus hailed from the ranks of the middle and small peasantry.

Once again, Pulwars were not to be found amongst the big landholders in Sultanpur and Faizabad. In Sultanpur, the Rajputs, although only 8 per cent of the population, held 90 per cent of the land. Rajkumars, Bandhalgotis and Bachgotis dominated the 'big men' club. The numerous Pulwars were not recorded as land controllers at all, while the Brahmin population (17 per cent), also very turbulent, held less than 5 per cent of the land.[8] Sultanpur was an Awadhi Talukedari area, more than 80 per cent of the land was under the Talukedars, but Awadh's distinctiveness rested on the fact that even the Talukedari areas possessed substantial inferior, or under, proprietors. Sultanpur was witness to a situation where, despite the huge Talukedari share, sub-settlement and *pattidari*-type tenures comprised, as in Azamgarh, a high 60 per cent share of rights on the land.

Situated in eastern UP and south of Azamgarh, Benaras also had a complex rural structure. Brahmins stood ahead of Chamars, Kurmis and Ahirs in terms of numbers. Rajputs and Bhumihars were not very far behind the Kurmis and Ahirs in a district noted for its relatively low population density. Along with Jaunpur (a neighbouring east UP district), Benaras had experienced the Permanent Settlement for several decades in the late eighteenth century. As a result, the *pattidari* tenure in Benaras was the weakest of all eastern districts. The heartland of the Benaras Bhumihar Raja's estates was located here and the Benaras Raja was merciless in reducing Rajput and Bhumihar *pattidar*s to the status of tenants or inferior cultivators. Outside the Benaras Raja's estate

> zamindari mahals numbered 2,688, and pattidari 1,972 ... some of the mahals are of the variety known as complex, which comprise portions of a number of separate villages ... there are also tenants at fixed rates, who have a transferable as well as a heritable right, and under-proprietors called mukararidars....who hold permanent leases ...[9]

Benaras, thus, did not enjoy the Sultanpur–Azamgarh quasi-free rural structure, and its response to the Uprising of 1857 was similarly skewed. Yet the Benaras Rajkumars of Dobhi enjoyed a compact *pattidari*-type structure, and they were the most turbulent of all the Benaras Rajput clans.

At Jaunpur, the Brahmins came behind the Chamars and Ahirs numerically. Rajputs made up around 10 per cent of the population and owned more than a third of the land and, as in Benaras, Banias and some Muslim families also owned huge tracts of land. Yet what distinguished Jaunpur was the absence of Benaras-style zamindari mahals. In fact, there were even fewer *pattidari* tenures here than in Benaras. Another factor in the rural social and political economy, found here and nowhere else in the eastern districts, was high castes holding land 'as tenants a rather greater proportion than the low castes...'.[10] This was mainly an effect of the eighteenth century Permanent Settlement. At one point, the entire Jaunpur district was held by Benaras Raja and freebooting agents like Raja Sheoram Dubey. It may be assumed that those days must have reduced the high castes from quasi-free status to that of tenants. The high-caste status of tenants, however, was no guarantee that the district was ripe for a peasant jacquerie. On the contrary, the upper-caste tenants were isolated as a result of the mixing of several clans in their localities. This was a major reason why Jaunpur sent relatively fewer upper-caste soldiers to the Bengal army. Ahirs, settled after the Permanent Settlement disturbances, and enjoying more socially cohesive *patttidari*-type tenures, sent more soldiers to the army. Several Ahir sepoy leaders in the 1857 Uprising hailed from Jaunpur.

Despite constraints, Jaunpur Rajputs did play a significant role in 1857. Most of those actively involved were from the rural areas of Jaunpur, particularly Shahganj and Machlishahr, where a stunted Permanent Settlement had led, not to the erasure, but to the transformation of *pattidar* proprietors into small landlords. The result was the emergence of substantial families, especially of the Bais sub-caste, holding tenures somewhere between the large Talukedaris and the extremely small (relatively) zamindari mahals. This was an exclusively Jaunpuri situation and was reflected in the way social forces, Rajputs and Brahmins reacted to 1857 when small landlord pressure forced several big Rajput zamindars to join in the fight against the British. Yet Jaunpur was still less turbulent than Azamgarh or Sultanpur.

In central India, especially in the Sagar and Narmada territories, the nature of the mixed *malguzari–lambardari–ryotwari* tenure system seemed to determine the rural response. In Sagar, Brahmins (upper castes), Kurmis and Dangis (backward castes) constituted the chief Ryotwari tenure peasants and their response to revolutionary overtures was decidedly lukewarm. Lodhis were the predominant *malguzari* section, and they participated most in the risings. Being Bundelas, the Sagar Rajputs were considered the highest amongst all Central Indian Rajputs. They represented the explosive combination of a self-aware high social status coupled with recent economic degradation. Thus, 'the Bundela Rajputs were a renowned freebooting tribe ... proud and penurious to the last degree, and quick to resent the smallest slight ... [N]o Bania dare go past a Bundela's house without getting down from his pony and folding up his umbrella....'[11] Interestingly, such restrictions were not imposed on Lodhis and other backward castes. The banias were reviled because of their neo-rich status. By contrast, the Sagar Gond population, 41 per cent of the total, were largely labourers and small tenants. Their old power entirely gone, they formed no significant threat to either the Bundela Rajputs or the British.

In consequence of the proprietary structure in Sagar, the Lodhis (mostly of North Indian origin) and the Bundelas participated passionately in 1857, whilst other sections of society apparently lacked their zeal. The predominant form of proprietary right was a modified form of the Malguzari system, involving the creation of smaller mahals or estates. Multiple small landlords resulted, almost on the Jaunpur pattern, but at Sagar the small landlords also had much smaller plots of land approximating sometimes to the size of plot that might be held by a tenant in UP. Thus, as small landholders with a quasi-zamindari status, Sagar Lodhi proprietors occupied a privileged position. They were masters of their destiny and yet not 'too big for their boots'. In effect, they approximated to the position occupied by UP *pattidars*. The only problem was their small number: in Sagar, Lodhis comprised just over 6 per cent of the population.

At Jabalpur, Lodhis were again less than 9 per cent strong, but the Jabalpur rural socio-economic structure was more even. Brahmins, mostly from Awadh, held small plots on revenue-free grants. Lodhis had 'several fine estates frequently held on quit-rent tenure and locally called jagir'.[12] Comprising more than 10 per cent of the population each, the Gonds and Kols held no land and were mere labourers. The Jabalpur Bundela Rajputs were relatively few in number. The Bharias, existing as a watchmen-cum-'thieving' caste, symbolised old-world turbulence. However, in neighbouring Damoh district, Lodhi participation in the 1857 wars was the highest. At 13 per cent of the total, their population exceeded that in Sagar and in Jabalpur, and some of the most influential proprietors in the district were included in their number: 'Lodhis ... as a class they were openly disaffected in the Mutiny....'[13]

Spread in significant numbers over small, free—or quasi-free—plots, Damoh Lodhis actually came closest to the Unnao-Hardoi-type Kanyakubja, or Gonda–Sultanpur Saryupari, or Ballia–Ghazipur Bhumihar *pattidars*. They also appeared closer here, more than anywhere else, to a minimised version of the 'turbulent' Jaunpur small landlord. Culturally, Damoh Lodhis combined a 'hard-work' ethic—well-known in north India as characteristic of Kurmi cultivators—with the turbulence and belligerence associated normally with Bhumihars and Rajputs. Their unique cultural–economic position thus made Damoh Lodhis the revolutionary vanguard of the Sagar–Narmada belt. By contrast, the large Damoh Gond population seemed too poor and depressed for action. The same was the case with Chamars, though compared to Jabalpur and Sagar, Damoh Chamars were both better off and more numerous, and their participation in the revolution was occasionally conspicuous.

To sum up, the pattern of turbulence seems to be thus: *pattidars*, irrespective of caste, the most turbulent; upper-caste tenants, turbulent mainly when clan continuity in place; backward and lower-caste tenants, largely depressed and less turbulent; backward and lower-caste *malguzars* and *lambardars*, turbulent; upper-caste *malguzars* and *lambardars*, less so in comparison. Small landlords amongst upper and backward castes were turbulent or semi-turbulent; big landlords, amongst upper castes, were very susceptible to clan pressure, and could be inclined to join the revolt but were conservative and pro–status quo if that pressure was absent; big landlords amongst Muslims were generally turbulent; big landlords amongst backward castes, generally pro–status quo. This all bears some familiarity to students of V.I. Lenin and Eric Wolf who theorised that peasant insurgency most commonly arises from the ranks of the independent, 'middle' or rich peasantry, with leadership being offered by small landed elites. Above all, however, it leads us to conclude that the destructive effects of the resettlement of proprietary titles to the land by the East India Company played a major factor in determining levels of rural participation in the Uprising of 1857. Both the Permanent Settlement with large landlords and Ryotwari settlements in favour of cultivating peasants served to weaken the structure of local society and the potentialities for organised dissent. But where big zamindars had their power otherwise usurped in favour of a class of largely indigenous, precolonial medium-sized landholders, both local leadership and the bonds of clan and sub-clan communities survived and were able to provide an important focus for a militant and determined resistance to colonial control. In Ryotwari or semi-Ryotwari areas, survival of *pattidari*, communitarian or indigenous small landlord tenures thus provided the basis for the most intense forms of anti-colonial resistance.

Notes and References

1. Eric Stokes, *The Peasant Armed* (Oxford: Oxford University Press, 1986).
2. Amaresh Misra, *War of Civilisations: India 1857 AD* (Delhi: Rupa, 2008).
3. Amar Singh Baghel, *Uttar Pradesh District Gazetteers: Unnao* (Allahabad: Government of Uttar Pradesh, Department of District Gazetteers, 1979), pp. 27–28. Emphasis added by the author.
4. 'Etawah District', *Imperial Gazetteer of India Vol. 12*, Digital South Asia Library (Oxford: Clarendon Press, 1908), pp. 38–43.
5. 'Etah District', *Imperial Gazetteer of India Vol. 12*, Digital South Asia Library (Oxford: Clarendon Press, 1908), pp. 29–33.
6. 'Azamgarh District', *Imperial Gazetteer of India Vol. 6*, Digital South Asia Library (Oxford: Clarendon Press, 1908), pp. 158–159.
7. Ibid.
8. 'Sultanpur District', *Imperial Gazetteer of India Vol. 23*, Digital South Asia Library (Oxford: Clarendon Press, 1908), p. 133.
9. 'Benaras District', *Imperial Gazetteer of India Vol. 7*, Digital South Asia Library (Oxford: Clarendon Press, 1908), p. 183.

10. N.L. Gupta, *Uttar Pradesh District Gazetteers: Jaunpur* (Lucknow: Government of Uttar Pradesh, Department of District Gazetteers, 1986), p. 49.

11. 'Saugor District', *Imperial Gazetteer of India Vol. 22*, Digital South Asia Library (Oxford: Clarendon Press, 1908), p. 140.

12. 'Jubbulpore District', *Imperial Gazetteer of India Vol. 14*, Digital South Asia Library, Vol. 14 (Oxford: Clarendon Press, 1908), p. 209–210.

13. 'Damoh District', *Imperial Gazetteer of India Vol. 11*, Digital South Asia Library (Oxford: Clarendon Press, 1908), p. 138.

6

❧❧❧

THE POLICE IN DELHI IN 1857*

Mahmood Farooqui

The handful of Europeans occupy four times the space of the city which contains tens of thousands of Hindus and Musalmans. The sole mark of the rule of the former which exists in the latter, is apparently a large native house, from the top of which floats a flag, and in front of which is a group of natives in blue cotton tunics, with red piping and tulwars by their sides. They are the police and the house is the Kotwalee or residence and office of the native mayor or Kotwal.

—W.H. Russell[1]

THIS chapter endeavours to examine the role of the police in the administration set up by the rebels in Delhi in 1857. The soldiers arrived in Delhi on 11 May and the British reconquered the city in mid-September. During those four months, an estimated 100,000 professional soldiers and other volunteers thronged the city. Where did these soldiers stay? How was their food arranged? Who provided for their upkeep and their needs? In addition to staying there, they were also fighting a daily, incessant battle against the English forces stationed on the ridge. How were arrangements for the battle being made? Who supplied the army with rations, provisions, war materials, tents, flaps, sulphur and gunpowder?

Orders were implemented, the paperwork required for conveying and effecting orders was thorough and copious, and the paraphernalia required for sustaining this massive correspondence—the writers, the paper and the carriers, or runners—remained in place right till the very end. I argue that it is only by studying the situation on the ground that we can actually study what the uprising meant in terms of the organisation and management of people. Very often, as seen in these documents, the uprising meant being able to arrange for a few carts or coolies or tents or grain as the case may have been. The conscription

* I wish to thank William Dalrymple, Narayani Gupta, Shahid Amin and Radhika Singha for their comments and suggestions.

All selections of *Mutiny Papers* from the National Archives of India.

of labour, the expropriation of goods and their distribution to the theatre of war—these were the three principal axes of the 1857 Uprising in Delhi.

When the city fell to the rebels, after an initial period of confusion and pandemonium which lasted a couple of weeks, a measure of order began to be restored. Documents from the early period of the uprising represent attempts by the Royal government to assert its authority. In an attempt to take control, the king wrote to the officers, or *thanadars*, of all the thanas or police stations in the city, in the second week of the uprising. It was in the same period that Moinuddin Hasan Khan was appointed kotwal, or city police chief, for a brief period, replacing Qazi Faizullah.[2] Shortly afterwards Syed Mubarak Shah was appointed kotwal and he continued in this post till the end. The remarkable thing, once the confusion had settled down, was the ease with which the old administrative machinery began to service the cause of the rebels. The daily reports of the thanas show that almost all *thanadars* and their subordinates remained in place and, in fact, there were new recruitments. By the end of May, some degree of order had clearly been fully established as was noted by the *Dehli Urdu Akhbar* when it praised the new kotwal for bringing things under control.[3] It was the same with other administrative mechanisms. The magistracy and its secretariat were taken over by Mirza Mughal, and although some of the old functionaries abstained from work,[4] there was enough staff to allow the courts to function as before, and the commander-in-chief (CiC) brought in his own men. Henceforward, the court was rechristened after his name, but its mode of functioning and its methods of dispensing justice were modelled on the English system. The Court of Mutineers, too, functioned parallel with—and sometimes in tandem with—this court.

From the very beginning, the soldiers, as well as ordinary people, began to look to the government established by the royal court to provide for them. While the soldiers had reached Delhi on their own initiative, it was as if they were fighting not their own war but someone else's. This is evident from scores of petitions and complaints by soldiers expecting the court and its functionaries to look after them. They evidently saw the police as a representative of the royal establishment, or of the government that had been established, because they could go to the police and demand rations, provisions and shelter. The ordinary citizens too recognised the police as the representative of the new government that had come into being, because they complained to the police about the soldiers' excesses and expected to find redress. Inter alia, it is noticeable that the relations between the CiC and the soldiers were not as hostile as is made out, as the documents contain any number of commands, edicts and orders to regiments which, it appears, were executed promptly. But in the symbiotic relationship between the government, the soldiers and the ordinary people, the police acted as the major interface and the intermediary.

The police were petitioned when people's houses were plundered by soldiers, when women ran away or children went missing, when shops and grains were required for soldiers' camps, when affrays occurred between citizens and when the administration had to implement orders and commandeer resources. Police duties could range from notifying all people living in dilapidated houses to vacate them before the big gun was supposed to go off,[5] to arranging for a charpoy and fuel for the purpose of cremating the dead body of a *subedar*,[6] to figuring out the details for anyone standing bail as to whether they had the property they claimed,[7] to paying the expenses for and arranging the funeral of indigent women,[8] to getting the refuse cleared from the city,[9] to making sure that dead bodies were allowed through by the guards at the city gates,[10] to issuing general proclamations and informing the citizenry of the orders of the commissariat and the court[11] and issuing notice of a general levy[12] and to awarding and maintaining contracts to different contractors for shops.[13] Their indispensability to the administrative set-up of the rebels makes a study of the police establishment an exploration into the nature of the rebellion. It emerges that the administration kept itself going by the force it could exert on the subalterns: both those who serviced this rebellion in the form of skilled and unskilled labour, as well as the subalterns within the police force, the *barqandaze*s, who did the major leg work. On occasion when the subalterns revolted, as cases listed below show, it produced a crisis of authority. If the subalterns begin to rebel, then what will happen to the wider rebellion itself?

It remains unclear how and why the police continued to fulfil their duties when other systems, the revenue machinery and the postal system—to take analogous examples—completely broke down. As far as can be made out, the police in Delhi, prior to the uprising, were under the control of the magistracy. Why the police service moulded itself to serve the rebel cause is something that still needs investigation. Perhaps, it was the prestige of the court, and the fact that the kotwal in the older dispensation functioned directly under the king, which played a role in this easy switching of loyalties. On several occasions, the king corresponded directly with the policemen, and on the occasion of the festival of Baqrid, all the *thanadar*s appeared before him and paid him *nuzzur*s, but beyond the call of the duty the motivation that impelled them to exert themselves in such an evidently arduous manner remains ambiguous.

The records on which this paper relies are a set of papers stored in the National Archives in India called the *Mutiny Papers*. The *Mutiny Papers* are a particular set of documents that were extricated and extracted from various sources in Delhi by the occupying English army—from the kotwali, the secretariat, homes, spies—each one diligently marked and copied, sometimes in triplicate, stored as a monument for posterity, one of the great founding moments of the colonial archive. There are thousands of these, indexed in a published catalogue called the 'Mutiny Papers'.[14] Most of them are in *Shikastah* Urdu, some in Persian and a handful in English translations. Most of these documents have never, ever been seen by anyone. The papers were brought together for the trial of Bahadur Shah, the last king of Delhi. However, for all the colonial intentionality motivating this extensive, meticulous and arduous classification, these papers provide one of the densest descriptions of a city at war and at work, of administration and anarchy, of deceit and desperation.

Talmiz Khaldun, writing for the collection on 1857 brought out by P.C. Joshi,[15] first looked at these papers as a clue to the administrative order of the city. Khaldun, however, concentrated exclusively upon the Court of Administration formed by the mutineers, and even there he looked rather more at the legalistic norms set by the court than at actual practice. Khaldun claimed that the Court of Administration was 'the highest judicial authority and regulated the judicial procedures for civil and criminal matters and appointed police officers and civil servants'.[16] The documents, however, stipulate, as will be obvious later, that the bulk of the correspondence of the police officers was with the CiC Mirza Mughal, and most criminal matters too went to his court. Iqbal Husain's study of the rebel administration[17] takes a top-down view and follows the well-trodden line of castigating the princes and finding a general run of disorder and administrative chaos right through. In fact, the princes, at least two of them—Mirza Khizr Sultan and Mirza Zaheeruddin alias Mirza Mughal the CiC—manifest themselves in a very good light in these documents. The soldiers, on occasion could even be arrested on the orders of the CiC.[18] Following conventional wisdom, Husain makes much of the arrival of Bakht Khan, but the documents do not substantiate such primacy for him. However, whether it was Bakht Khan or the CiC or the Court of Mutineers issuing the orders, their implementation was the handiwork of the police.

There certainly was a lot of chaos, there is no doubt that prices were rising, goods and vegetables were scarce, and the people were sandwiched between the army, the native war effort and the English. But this was an intense theatre of war. In those circumstances, if an order could be successfully implemented, it was a marvel, and the fact that dozens of such orders were implemented everyday is far more worthy of note than the fact that there was general disorder and chaos. Moreover, the immense outpourings of petitions from ordinary people as well as the soldiery also indicate a certain amount of faith in the ability of the administration to deliver. Plus, the fact that people chose to express their grievances in the conventional mode, via a formalised petition, also indicates a continuity of the practice of governmentality.

The main police station of the city, headed by an officer called the kotwal was the kotwali. Under the kotwal there were twelve police stations, or thanas, each of which was headed by a *thanadar*, also called a Darogha. Other than these, jamadars and Mohurrirs, or clerks, were the other members of the Officer class. Following them were the *barqandaz*, semi-armed, the ordinary policemen who did most of the leg work. We do not have the exact figures for the number of policemen employed in Delhi, but the daily diary of the kotwali shows that on 27 July there were in all forty-two people employed there. There was a kotwal and two deputy Kotwals, eight Mohurrirs or clerks, one jamadar and twenty-five *barqandaz*es, the equivalent of ordinary constables of a later date. Of the 42 people employed at the kotwali, ten were Hindus, thirty were Muslims while the religion of two cannot be determined. We do not know exactly how many of these had been employed from before the mutiny, but the numbers had certainly increased since the uprising.[19] This is evident from the daily diary of the Dariba thana of 24 May which lists, apart from the *thanadar*, one jamadar, two Mohurrirs and eight *barqandazes* as the old employees of the thana and nine new employees, most of them *barqandazes*.[20] During the uprising, the *thanadar* was paid ₹4 a month, the old *barqandazes* were getting ₹2 and the new ones fifty paise each.[21] Extrapolating from that, taking twenty men for each thana, and considering that there were twelve thanas in the city, one can arrive at a rough figure of 400 for the total police strength in the city. In addition to the regular policemen, every *thanadar* also had some sweepers, drum-beaters and chowkidars—the last paid by local dues—who functioned under him.

Provisions

The police establishment was the mainstay of the rebel administration that came into being in Delhi after 11 May. Police were in the forefront not merely of policing duties, detecting and preventing crime, but became, as in any war effort, the main force for collecting supplies, provisions and labour that was essential to waging a war. Monetary contributions were raised through the police, it was the force which arrested, detained, browbeat and assisted in the transportation of, bankers and merchants. The supply of provisions to different regiments was also the responsibility of the police, so the police force had to make sure that enough shops were open and running wherever the regiments were stationed.

In addition to supplying the regiments with food and with delicacies like puri-kachori and *sheerini* as the occasion demanded,[22] they had to provide resources for the war effort. This included not just materials of war, for example, sulphur for gunpowder, but the raw manpower required to fight the war. Coolies, labourers, bakers, water-carriers, farriers, masons, anything and anyone who was required was asked of the police. A very large section of the *Mutiny Papers* consists of documents between different *thanadars*. At a frantic pace, handling upwards of sometimes a hundred documents a day, the thanas provided for, or managed hundreds of things, or people. A list of objects and persons they were providing makes for staggering reading: oxen, cobblers, coolies, water-carriers, cattle, rations, doolie-bearers, conveyances, grocers, gunny bags, daggers, spades, axes, flour, ghee, baskets, pulses, sulphur, saddle makers, molasses, wood, husk sellers, carpenters, shoe-smiths, ekkas, mares, carts, sweepers, butchers, blacksmiths, corn, curds, flour, milk, sugar and doctors—and this is only a selection.

The *thanadar* of Turkman Gate sent in a distiller to the kotwal on 22 June, three water carriers, six coolies and two carpenters on 21 June, and four tailors on 18 June, to take further random examples from that particular thana, sent doolie-bearers, carpenters and milk on 3 July while stating, for the last date, that due to the non-payment of wages doolie-bearers, coolies, labourers and water-carriers were difficult to find, and when found, they confronted the *barqandaze*s. He requested that 'they be paid their wages and told not to stand up to *Barqandazes*'.[23] The *thanadar* of Turkman Gate stated, in another letter, that two grain shops had been provided for near the Nasirabad camp and a *barqandaz* posted at each.[24] Money was a constant problem, as was the issue of, getting the subalterns to work. The potters of the city wrote a petition to the CiC complaining about the *thanadar* of the Turkman Gate, saying, '[H]e compels us to do the work of the coolies, many of our men have run away, if we are conscripted for the work of coolies who will make pots and pans for the army.'[25] Apparently, this petition had no effect for they sent in another one on 21 August repeating their grievances and adding that they had been sent to the trenches, and they did not know what to do and had no work there to do.[26]

Even as the police conscripted and requisitioned labour, it could, on occasion, also speak up for them as the kotwal did, by raising the question of the wages of 40 doolie-bearers who had been sent to the platoon of the 48th Regiment.[27] Likewise, the *thanadar* of Turkman Gate wrote to say, in the second week of the rebellion, that twenty-three cobblers were being sent in, but that the diggers who used to reside in that area had all left town and the cobblers too 'have emerged from their houses with great difficulty and if they are not paid their wages, they would also leave the city in a day or two'.[28] On 29 August, the deputy kotwal wrote in to say that coolies had been sent to the Teliwara trenches from the kotwali and that they had not been paid their daily wages for two days. He, therefore, requested that their wages be paid 'because if wages are not paid to coolies how will they do the work of government … as it is scores of coolies have run away from the city'.[29] Whatever it supplied, however, the police expected to be paid—as the kotwal said, while supplying fifty sacks and three maunds of rope, which had been 'bought from the market and sent to his Lordship. We hope their price would be repaid as quickly as possible by the government'.[30]

Despite their best efforts, the kotwal came unstuck when asked to supply animals of carriage: 'it is known to your Lordship', he wrote to the CiC,

> that it is difficult to provide for animals of carriage in such numbers and on such a short notice. For *it is possible for the obedient one to arrange to supply those things, through the Thanadars, which are available in the city but things which are not to be found in the city are highly difficult to procure.*[31] (Emphasis added.)

Compliance, thus, depended on feasibility and an explanation resting on that ground was, it appears, acceptable. The police could only deliver what was in the realm of the possible.

Instead of the demand being routed through the commissariat or the court, soldiers could go directly to the concerned thana and ask for supplies, as Imam

Bakhsh, a rider of the Nimach brigade, did by reporting to the kotwali on 27 July. The kotwal sent in a requisition to the different thanas to supply him with various kinds of grains, and the order was complied with.[32] Soldiers could also write directly to the police concerning other requirements, as did the *subedar* of the 30th Regiment when he wrote to the kotwal demanding six thatchers who were needed at the hospital for making fences. As the bureaucratic norm demanded, the kotwal responded by inscribing on the margins that a note had been sent to the *thanadar* of Turkman Gate demanding thatchers.[33]

Apart from trying, ineffectually, to protect the citizens from the excesses of the soldiers, the police faced fundamental problems in making arrangements for their supplies. Grain merchants posted to serve the encampments at Delhi gate protested to the kotwali that the men of the platoon rarely paid up for the wares they bought and showed cruelty to the shopkeepers. In this case, the king inscribed on the margins an instruction for the secretary of the commissariat to deduct the dues from their salaries.[34] A similar case was that of the shopkeepers billeted at the lunatic asylum who complained that soldiers forcibly took their goods and beat them up in the bargain, and that if things continued in the same way, they would go on a strike.[35] The relations between the soldiers and the citizens were always fraught with tension, and the police had to constantly negotiate their way through this logjam of dire necessity, lack of money and the refusal of the soldiers to abide by the compulsions of the administration.

The dependence of the rebel army on the police for provision could sometimes take dangerous forms. The kotwal wrote in one urgent missive to the CiC that, upon going through the daily diary of the thana Chandni Chowk, he had learnt that one Ramzan Khan, the *hawaldar* of the regiment arrived from Gwalior, had issued an open threat. Ramzan Khan came to the thana and said that they had hitherto been subsisting on their own, somehow, but 'now they have been hungry for three days and if they do not get anything to eat they are going to plunder the mohalla of Teliwara and he is giving advance notice of that'. This was on 4 September, and the administration was faced with a real poverty of options, so the king could do little more than write that they should be admonished and told that they would get their salaries soon.[36]

Bankers

Dealing with bankers and raising money presented a double bind for the police. On the one hand, they were constantly commanded to arrest and detain recalcitrant bankers and merchants who refused to make contributions, and on the other, they were constantly restrained by orders urging them to avoid offending the public.

The *thanadar* of Chandni Chowk wrote to the kotwal reporting on the bankers of the famous and rich Katra Neel where 'some people disappear inside their houses and do not give any response while most of them make one excuse or another to keep this servant at bay and are forever on the lookout for creating trouble or making complaints'. Accordingly, he was sending some bankers hoping that 'a strong rebuke will be administered to them for unless that happens the money will not come forth'.[37] On 17 August, Nazar Ali again wrote about the refractory nature of the bankers of Katra Neel, complaining that 'they do not come out of their houses or simply vanish', and that as their houses could not be searched without permission, he was unable to do much in the matter.[38]

The kotwali records are replete with efforts to summon the leading bankers and traders of each area. Writing sometime in August, the kotwal circulated a list of names to all thanas saying that these bankers should be brought to the kotwali, and that if any resisted, a contingent should be sent to arrest them. The following merchants were called in from Chandni Chowk on another day: Kanhaiyya Lal Saligram, Thakur Das Chunnumal, Jagannath Bansi Lal and Nanak Chand. Merchants were also called in from Dharampura, Maliwara and Dareeba Kalan—the first two areas lying outside the city proper.[39] In an undated communiqué, the CiC wrote to the kotwal to ask him to raise contributions from the respectable Muslims of the city.[40] Sometimes it could work in reverse, with the police forwarding petitions from the people requesting to be exempted from making money contributions, as the deputy kotwal indicated to the CiC in the case of the poor people of the Faiz Bazar area.[41]

Excessive zeal, though, could earn censure. The same file contains an admonition from the kotwal to the *thanadar* of Kashmiri Darwaza, scolding him for raiding the shop of Bahauddin without permission from the kotwali. He is instructed specifically that nobody is to be raided without permission from the kotwali: 'when and if you intend to raid somebody's house you should immediately inform the Kotwali. Until permission is granted by the Kotwali no raids should be conducted.'[42] In a similar vein, an order was sent to the kotwal on 18 August by the CiC, advising him to refrain from collecting money as the matter had been taken over by the court. 'Except for the members of the court nobody is authorised to arrest any banker and if you receive an order to this effect you should immediately inform the court.'[43]

Regulating Morals

The police were called upon, and sometimes its personnel volunteered, to act as the moral guardian of the people at a time when all consensus about right and wrong had broken down. Sometimes the duties given to them required an impossible degree of resourcefulness, at the same time putting enormous powers into the hands of the police. The kotwal was asked, in one communiqué from the CiC, to 'make sure that no one buys or sells plundered or looted articles to any one. And if anyone is caught doing so they were to be strongly punished'.[44] Whether the police acted any more urgently on this order than by simply issuing a proclamation is not clear, but it did create enormous room for suspicion and for potentially oppressive action by the police. A similar occasion was when Bakht Khan went to the kotwali and asked the authorities there to issue a general proclamation and 'send notice to all the *thanadars* that anybody found flying kites, discharging fireworks, raising a weapon or flying pigeons' was liable for punishment.[45] The need for regulating personal conduct was potentially limitless, but the coercive structure needed to ensure compliance with these orders would never have been possible without the presence of soldiers on a mass scale.

Sometimes the police, already overburdened, could display zeal for taking on more work. On 24 July, one and a half months into the uprising, it struck the kotwal that 'clandestine gambling continues again in the areas commanded by *thanadars* posted in the city'. He, therefore, wrote directly to the king to say that 'since there are no standing orders on the matter therefore I humbly inquire whether we should end it by arresting all the gamblers'. Fortunately, the king showed some restraint and asked the kotwal to first issue a general proclamation banning gambling before proceeding to arrest people.[46] Gambling was presumably banned because a later document shows a Prince Mirza Mohammed Hasan summoning some arrested gamblers to his court.[47] Then, as now, gambling came accompanied by other vices. On 3 August, Mir Akbar Ali, a resident of Faiz Bazar, lodged a complaint stating that a gambling house existed near his house and that the gamblers used abusive language and stared at the females of his house.[48] Some gamblers, apprehended by the *thanadar* of Turkman Gate, resisted arrest and attacked a couple of *barqandaze*s; the zealous *thanadar* reached the spot and had three of them arrested. They were all sent to the kotwali to be fined.[49] Gamblers were certainly having a hard time because they could be arrested by ordinary soldiers as well, as the case of the sepoy Tehdil Khan, noted below, makes clear.

The dilemmas and problems faced by the police in acting at once as the preventive arm as well as the chief executive wing of the government were exemplified on the occasion of Baqrid, when a general order banning cow slaughter was passed in the city. The police were not only urged to make sure that the ban was implemented, but were also persuaded to take preventive steps. On 30 July, the CiC wrote to the kotwal asking him to issue a general proclamation to

> arrest anyone who so much as even thinks of [committing cow slaughter]. It has been heard that some mujahideen (volunteers) intend to perform this act, so go to the Maulvi Saheb and ask him to talk to them.... This year nobody should think of doing so otherwise unnecessarily there would be a riot and the enemy's hands would be strengthened.[50]

Apart from circulating the order to all the *thanadars* and issuing a general proclamation everywhere, the kotwal wrote to all the *thanadars* asking them to send him a list of all the cow-owning Muslims in their respective areas.[51] The *thanadars* acted accordingly. The problem occurred when the king issued an order instructing the kotwal to assemble all the cows owned by the Muslims and keep them in the kotwali. As the kotwal explained to the king, there was insufficient room in the kotwali to assemble all the cows owned by the Muslims in the city there. In turn, he suggested that *thanadars* may be directed to have bonds executed by the Muslims to the effect that they would not sacrifice cows.[52] Accordingly, the *thanadar* of Turkman Gate wrote to say that undertakings had been taken from all the cow-owning Muslims of his area.[53]

But was this enough to make sure that the orders would be implemented and there would be no cow slaughter in the city? In order to further ensure that no slaughter happened surreptitiously, the CiC wrote to the kotwal to count all the skins of dead animals and the amount of grease available with the butchers—an order that was sent to all the leading butchers as well.[54] One can only wonder what this would have meant for the citizenry at large, for the police could arrest anybody on any of the following charges: sacrificing cows, owning cows and not giving an undertaking, possessing skins or showing an intention of killing cows. Three weeks earlier, there was the case of a kebab-seller who had been arrested on the charge of cow slaughter. Hafiz Abdur Rahman stated in a petition to the king that he had been arrested by some soldiers while selling kebabs, a profession he had been forced to take up 'in the present when all jobs of Shahjehanabad are at an end'.[55] When the king wrote to the kotwal asking him why Abdur Rahman had been arrested, he replied that they had been reported by Debi Prashad *Hawaldar* of the First Company, appointed at the Lahori Gate, 'on the charges of cow-slaughter with the notice that he had taken five hundred rupees from the English to commit cow slaughter in front of our barracks with the intention of creating a riot between Hindus and Muslims'.[56] Vigilantism, evidently, was not an exclusive preserve of the police.

Tilangas[57]

The biggest stumbling block for the police was the presence of an enormous body of armed soldiers who would make demands of them, but not allow them to function without hindrance. Not only would soldiers interfere in their work but they would also lean on the police to do their bidding when simple force was not enough. They would arrest people and bring them to the kotwali or to a particular thana, or assault the thana and free a particular accused as they saw fit. On 22 June, some *barqandazes* of thana Bhojla Pahari were making their customary rounds near the Lahore Gate when they noticed two sacks. Feeling suspicious, they enquired about them, whereupon the soldiers appointed there gathered together and proceeded to give a solid thrashing to the two hapless *barqandaze*s.[58] At the Farrashkhana, the guards appointed to man it were regularly charging bribes. The *thanadar* of Guzar Qasim Jan wrote to the kotwal saying that when challenged by the *barqandaze*s of the *thana*, they threatened to beat them up and explicitly told the *thanadar* to mind his own business, who would have let it pass but for the fact that they were 'now even demanding money to allow documents to pass'.[59]

Sometimes soldiers would interfere with the police when they were busy raising supplies or commandeering labour.[60] Then there was interference in its investigative agency, well illustrated by the case of the prostitute Waziran. A soldier Ram Prashad brought a charge of theft against her, and on inspecting her house, the kotwal recovered the stolen goods. But when he brought her to the kotwali, just before she recorded her statement, a large group of soldiers arrived there and forcibly took her away. An exasperated kotwal wrote to the CiC complaining of the soldiers and saying that the said prostitute had been accused in several cases before and was about to admit her guilt when the Tilangas took her away. 'The situation is this', he wrote, '*that the soldiers interfere in everything* ... and this prostitute has been brought to the *thana* in several cases earlier [emphasis added]'.[61]

The plunder of Gopi's house, a resident of Guzar Dariba, presented a similar set of dilemmas. The plundered goods were lying in the house of Banne, of Bazar Urdughar, and at the house of Daya Kaur, but, wrote the kotwal, 'at the houses of these accused soldiers are staying', and so it was difficult to appoint guards there. If their houses were to be searched, it would be better that they do it, 'since it is the provenance of war [soldiers] therefore the matter is outside the purview of normal criminal affairs'. The soldiers had also forcibly taken away Banne and Daya Kaur after they had been brought to the kotwali.[62]

The case of Jangyaar Khan further illustrates the difficulties the police had in dealing with the soldiers. In this case, Sheikh Gulzar claimed to have recovered some of his stolen goods from the quarters of one Jungyaar Khan. When he woke up one night, he found his *huqqa* missing and when he stepped out to search for it, he found his colleague beating up a thief. Together, they went to the latter's quarters, found other stolen goods and arrested the five men loitering there.[63] The accused Jungyaar Khan, on the other hand, claimed he was arrested

> while he was carrying some flour and the soldiers looted a gun, rifle, a dagger, a sword and some cash which was in my possession, along with a dupatta, a handkerchief and a pagri and accusing me of stealing goods they took me to the thana. I am a volunteer, one brother of mine has been killed, I have never been arrested on any charge and now I have been looted.

Another accused, Budhoo, claimed that he was arrested not from the address pointed out by the soldiers, but from atop a shop where he was sitting when the soldiers were passing it. Another rider sitting with him seized his sword and 'said to the Tilanagas that this man here is not in the employ of anyone, arrest him too'.[64]

Sepoys could, thus, arrest people simply for loitering or for carrying flour, which, in the highly strained nature of supply of provisions was not such an insignificant thing. This posed a problem for the kotwali authorities. Since the accused had been brought by soldiers, they were bound, under the circumstances, to treat the complaint seriously. On the other hand, as the deputy kotwal said in his report, 'the case was weak and the evidence weaker'. But since the case concerned 'soldiers of war therefore the accused have for the moment been kept in custody and the details of the case are beings sent to the commander in chief for him to take the necessary action'.[65] The soldiers' power of detention, however, only acquired legal force once the police had been involved. Jiwan Singh, a sepoy of Sixty First Platoon, Seventh Company, who arrested Basanti on charges of theft because he had seen a boy entering his house with stolen goods, immediately brought him to the nearest thana.[66] After gambling had been banned in the city, a sepoy Thedil Khan of Bailey Platoon, Fourth Company, arrested some people for gambling, but he had to call out to the *barqandaz* of the thana before he did so, and, even then, it did not become a bona fide case until he brought the *thanadar* to the spot to confirm their arrest.[67]

In a collection from 1 July, the CiC wrote to the kotwal asking him to stop forced searches of houses by soldiers by saying, 'without the order of the government and the presence of the informer no [forced] searches will be conducted at any respectable person's house'.[68] Accordingly, when the soldiers were hell-bent on searching the house of a rich magnate, Ajudhia Parshad, the kotwal instructed the *thanadar* to

> tell the soldiers that they should first go to the General Bahadur with the informant and submit an application there, when an order is passed from there a search will be conducted. Without the application of the spy/informant no searches will be conducted at respectable people's houses.[69]

Discipline

Discipline within the force was at a premium. All *thanadars* were urged to maintain a regular daily diary, a practice of the past, and send it punctually to the kotwali. The king himself wrote to all the *thanadars* in the second week of assuming command, warning them that they would be punished if they neglected their duties.

It has been heard through the Kotwal that the reports and diaries of different *thana*s do not reach the Kotwali and the *thanadar*s are not present in the *thana* day and night. Therefore they are being commanded to be present and prompt day and night in administering the city and should present reports of each case to the Kotwal everyday. If they act contrary to this they will be punished.[70]

On 24 July, the CiC wrote to all the *thanadar*s and the kotwal to make sure that all *thanadar*s send in their diaries by eight in the morning.[71] Every circular, whether from the kotwal or other *thanadar*s or *parwana*s, or orders from higher up, was supposed to be copied in hand and a receipt signed on the document itself. When circulars returned unsigned, it indicated absenteeism—something which, even in spite of the turbulence of the times, did not go unnoticed. The deputy kotwal, therefore, complained that there was no officer in the Dariba thana to receive petitions except for two illiterate *barqandaze*s.[72]

There could sometimes be graver problems. In one of the rare documents which allows the *barqandaz*—the subaltern employee of the thana who actually implemented all the orders and did the rounds—to speak, Ghazi Khan of the Turkman Darwaza thana refused point-blank to carry out an order in the middle of the night saying 'such urgent orders come everyday, we are not going out just now we will only go in the morning'. The matter involved the requisitioning of four water carriers, an order for which arrived at the Turkman Gate thana at twelve o'clock at night. When the *barqandaze*s were called out, Ghazi Khan, leading four others, refused to comply. Only in the morning, after the jamadar had given them a written order, did they go. Whereupon, a panicked kotwal wrote to the CiC saying that

> if this goes on and the barqandazes do not obey the command of the officers then how will the work of government be done. Earlier too a complaint about the barqandazes had been sent in by the said thanadar… If every barqandaz makes bold to rebel [to do ghadar] and at a time of urgency begins to make excuses then that will be the end of it. Therefore [I hope] that Ghazi Khan and the four barqandazes will be dismissed and then they will learn their lesson otherwise they will not obey anyone.[73]

We do not know whether the *barqandaze*s were actually dismissed, but it is interesting to note that neither the *thanadar* nor the kotwal had the power to dismiss or appoint anyone in his command. Other documents outlining requests from kotwals or *thanadar*s seeking dismissal of blind, infirm or old *barqandaze*s, or even their transfer to another post, had to be routed to the CiC. On 22 June, the kotwal wrote to all *thanadar*s, asking them to report if any posts of *barqandaz* or jamadar or Mohurrir were vacant in their respective thanas[74] or 'if any *Barqandaz* was inefficient or negligent in carrying out the orders of the government'. Even as small a matter as the room rent that should be paid to accommodate a *barqandaz* had to be cleared by the CiC. The *thanadar* of Bhojla

Pahari, Mirza Amani Beg wrote to the CiC on 30 July saying that 'since the time the royal government took over, the number of *barqandaz*es have increased and there is not enough room for charpoys for all to fit in'; therefore, he requested the sanction of two rupees a month for renting a room for them.[75] The *thanadar* of Guzar Itiqad Khan, Faiz Talab Khan, wrote on 27 May stating that 'the older employees of the *Thana* have not been paid their salaries of two months, let alone the newer ones'.[76] The police was functioning as the strongest arm of the revolution, but it was not an arm which was free to move on its own.

The zealousness shown towards following orders and being on duty seems to have been there from the beginning. This is evident from the case of Faiz Mohammed Khan, resident of Turkman Gate, a merchant artisan who made a complaint that on the night of Id, his house was broken into, but when he went into the thana to lodge a complaint, he could not find anyone there.[77] Upon this, the *thanadar* sent in an indignant reply refuting the fact that he was not on duty and impugning the motive behind the complaint in the boot. He said that he had gone to offer Id prayers while the clerk was in the toilet, and when asked to wait, this fellow had chosen to go home. He went on to add that Faiz Mohammed Khan had concocted the report of the break in order to take over the goods by stealth, and that in such situations, the complainant never desired a search or registered claims against anyone. 'As far as being absent or present is concerned, the situation is this: that this devoted one never absents himself from duty even for a minute and the clerk of this thana is an outsider and he never goes anywhere.'[78] What is remarkable here is the eagerness shown by the *thanadar* to deny the charge of dereliction of duty; whether he was doing this out of fear of censure or out of a lure for reward remains unclear.

But it was not just the top officials who were at times dissatisfied with the functioning of the police. Ordinary citizens too had their share of complaints. On 24 June, barely a month into the uprising, the residents of Chandni Chowk sent in a petition to the CiC complaining about the oppression of Hafiz Aminuddin Khan, the *thanadar* of Chandni Chowk, saying that he was a badmash who spent all his time loitering around with bad characters and that he had proved so cruel that if he continued, 'the subjects are sure to be ruined'.[79] If the *thanadar* was warned or reprimanded, we do not have the evidence to be sure, but he was replaced sometime in July. Before that, however, he himself had problems implementing orders. On 3 July, he wrote to the kotwal complaining about a certain Punjabi tailor who refused to obey orders from the thana. The Punjabi tailor, he said, was a rogue who had abused the *barqandaz*es and 'has made many tailors run away and unless he is properly punished he will not obey the orders given out'.[80]

Sometimes one thana could interfere with the work of another. When a *barqandaz* of Chandni Chowk was sent to collect carts in the area of the Allahabad Road, he faced an unexpected problem. The jamadar and Mohurrir of the said thana forcibly took it away from him and handed it over to some soldiers. So

Nazar Ali, the *thanadar*, wrote to the kotwal requesting him to 'issue a circular to the *thanadar* of Guzar Allahabad inquiring into why they acted thus'.[81]

Interference could come from other quarters too. A *thanadar* wrote to complain about a ruffian Afzal who had assaulted some *barqandazes* while they were trying to conscript labour, and said that 'I too rule this place, if you take people away by force we will confront you ... if you have arms, we too are armed, you cannot take them away like this'. He freed all the coolies and labourers who had been assembled.[82]

Not only were the work and responsibilities of the *thanadar* carefully monitored, their jurisdiction, too, was closely watched. Although they were being asked to perform all sorts of extra-policing duties, in the performance of them they were not allowed to step beyond their exact imprimatur. On 19 August, when the kotwal, replying to an order of the CiC, wrote that the particular case being enquired into had already been compromised; he earned a sharp rebuke from General Tale Yaar Khan, member secretary of the Court of Mutineers.

> That the plaintiff had first made a claim and then you write they have compromised with each other, it is not clear whether the complainant's case was true or false. Therefore it is being written to you that you should not, for any case, make a decision and send it to our court. Send both parties to our court now.[83]

If the jurisdiction of the kotwals was closely guarded, the police too, on occasion, could refuse to undertake a chore by saying it was not a part of their duties, as did the kotwal when he was asked to remove the carcasses of dead camels lying in Daryaganj. He clarified, to the king, no less, that it was the duty of Mir Ami Ali and that he should be made to do it.[84]

Women

Along with many other demands made upon them, the police had to deal with an inordinate number of cases of missing women. Women were eloping with soldiers, soldiers' wives were deserting them, courtesans and prostitutes were colluding with soldiers, and all this was happening at a rate that ensured that at any moment during the uprising, at least one thana in the city was dealing with the case of a disappeared woman. In the circumstances then prevailing in the city, when the population of the city had doubled, it was no mean task to try and locate a missing woman. Unsurprisingly, there were few instances of reports being made of the recovery of any of these women. And even the police functionaries were not immune to this misfortune. The missing wife of Gopal *barqandaz* of thana Paharganj was spotted with Jiwan Khan and Nawab

Khan, *hawaldar*s of Third Company Sappers and Miners, who were said to be looking after her. In case of arrest, wrote the kotwal, it was highly likely that there would be a riot since '*his Lordship is well aware of the situation of the soldiers of war* [emphasis added]'.[85] He appeared to advise, therefore, against any haste in effecting her recovery.

On 24 July, the deputy kotwal wrote to a *thanadar* about the case of the woman kept by sepoy Hira Singh who had run away with all his belongings and was now staying with Baluchar grenadier arrived from Agra. He instructed the *thanadar* to find the woman and leave the arrest to the sepoy himself. The *thanadar* wrote back to say that the accused sepoy was not staying in his jurisdiction.[86] There were similar communiqués from the *thanadar* of Bhojla Pahari, on 16 August, reporting the missing wife and property of Haider Ali, a rider of the Sixth Cavalry, Regiment 14, arrived from Datiya Jhansi;[87] from the *thanadar* of Faiz Bazar regarding the case of the groom of a Risaldar Ghulam Mohiuddin of 18th Cavalry running away with Dilpasand Kaur;[88] from the kotwal to all *thanadar*s regarding the wife of Pir Bakhsh who had run away with his goods and valuables; and scores of others. In the case of these missing women, often a physical description of the woman accompanies the report. Pir Bakhsh's wife was described as being 25 years old, of wheatish complexion, average height, slim body; wearing a pajama choli; with close-knit eyebrows.

There was the extended case of Bilasia, daughter of Basti, formerly married to Suraj Bali, son of Chhote, of Merath. Suraj Bali left her and in fact sold her to a sweeper, and she came to Delhi. Her father Basti then came to Delhi and paid off the due of ₹10, buying her back from the sweeper. He then wrote a letter to Suraj Bali asking him to take Bilasia back, but was refused. A case was then filed in the court of one Mr Cook at Merath and Bilasia was handed over to Basti. When the uprising took place, for some reason, Suraj Bali decided to reclaim Bilasia. So he came to Delhi, reached the camp of the Merath soldiers and, with the help of his caste fellows (vegetable sellers), found her whereabouts and wrote a petition to the CiC. He then solicited help from some of the Merath soldiers, and together they went to the Nigambodh ghat area, located Basti and forcibly took her away. In the process, they assaulted her father and mother and injured Bilasia with a knife on her neck. The whole proceedings were recorded at the kotwali where it transpired that Bilasia was now seven months pregnant by another man, Bhikhari. Detailed statements from all the principals, including several witnesses, were taken at the kotwali and at the court of the CiC.[89] Eventually, all were allowed free on bail, but not before Bilasia gave birth to a stillborn child in the lock-up.[90]

In some cases, missing or eloped wives were found, but they refuted the versions given out by their spouses. Pir Bakhsh, tinman, complained that the wife of his deceased brother, whom he treated with great consideration, had recently run away with a soldier, Jabar, of the volunteer platoon, and when he located her and urged her to return the ₹100 that she had made away with, she refused to return and, in fact, threatened him by saying, 'I will get you beaten up by soldiers'.[91] An order was then sent to Kalwant Singh, commander of the Fourth Platoon, Regiment 38, asking him to produce the woman along with the soldier, Jabar.[92] The soldier was duly arrested and the woman was produced in the court. Her version of the events was that Pir Bakhsh assaulted her and threw her out of the house, because of which she had gone away.[93] In cases like these, it was impossible to determine who was lying and who was telling the truth. Eventually, it was decided that no charge could be proven against the woman, and she was therefore allowed to go free, but the case was not finally decided until 11 September, three days before Delhi fell. Thus, until almost the very moment that the city fell to the British, the administrative order remained in place pretty much as it had been.

Other cases involving women included disturbances created by prostitutes. Kunwar Lal, the *thanadar* of Dariba, wrote to the kotwal at the end of June, reporting the case of the dispute between a prostitute Sundar and her tenant Abdur Razzaq about the payment of rent. Three soldiers then present in her quarters had apparently fired upon Abdur Razzaq. After the *thanadar* had brought both of them to the thana, a further set of soldiers dropped in, this time claiming to speak for Abdur Razzaq: 'He is our brother, we will take him and this prostitute to the court of the Commander in chief.' The *thanadar* managed to stay his ground and send the disputed parties to the kotwali for the case to be decided as the kotwal saw fit.[94] Sundar Kasbi (the prostitute) apparently managed to make a name for herself, since in another undated communication, the clerk of the Dariba thana wrote to the kotwal, requesting him to reprimand a bad character called Gopal who frequents her place. He advised that his visits can cause an 'untoward incident and that if he continues he will be punished'.[95] Sundar Kasbi, thus, seems to have enjoyed the close protection of her local thana.

Conclusion

In conclusion, it can be said that the police did the 'dirty work' for the revolution in Delhi. In many ways, which have very contemporary echoes, the police were called upon to conscript, commandeer and procure, even as they were urged not to offend the public or to alienate the population. What is remarkable is both that the police did this work and that they got things done. Yet, the documents do not show any particular partisanship of the police towards the rebels. If they had sympathy or feeling for the rebel side, it is not reflected in the documentary evidence. Hence, it is intriguing to note that when all other government departments collapsed, the police continued to function as well as before, and even better in some ways. Perhaps this is due to the fact that it was a largely Muslim force and, therefore, instinctively sympathised with the fate of the Emperor Bahadur Shah. Or, perhaps, simply because it was a hierarchically organised body, and by setting in motion the chain of command, the machinery was kept going. What does come through is the fact that most police officers were functioning as salaried bureaucrats and doing their jobs. A much more demanding kind of a job, no doubt, but it was still just a job for most of them. The official nature of the correspondence, conducted and composed by professional scribes in all cases, never betrays any emotional attachments. It is order and impersonality everywhere.

The effectiveness of the police is all the more remarkable, given the fact that its coercive authority was undermined by the presence of such a large body of armed soldiery within the city. Further, given the way in which the police were acting, and the presence of such a mass of soldiery, one would expect the citizens to be coerced into silence. However, the presence with the records of a huge body of complaints by the citizenry shows that, rather than abandoning faith in the administration, the people were looking to it for salvation. This was true regarding complaints against the police itself as much as in complaints concerning the wider affairs of the city. The people could speak out against injustices and expect the government to respond to them. Furthermore, the police could not always bend everyone to their will. Intransigence was encountered not merely among the subalterns it was pressing into service, but also amongst other citizens such as the Punjabi tailor who quarrelled with *barqandaze*s; Afzal, the ruffian, who freed conscripted labourers; or the citizens of Chandni Chowk who complained against their bullying *thanadar*.

By and large, the force held its discipline. There are plenty of documents stating the inability of a particular *thanadar* to fulfil the task required of him for reasons of unavailability, but there is not a single document where a *thanadar* could be said to have displayed insubordination of any kind. There may have been other instances of a *barqandaz* refusing work, but examples of outright rejection are rare for the subordinates and officers alike. Considering that the *thanadar* could neither appoint nor dismiss a *barqandaz* of his free will, the lack of reports on instances of insubordination from them is extremely remarkable. The noticeable thing, therefore, was the degree of order that could still be maintained. The bureaucratic norms that had been established for the mode of receiving grievances, as well as for the way in which they were addressed, remained in force. As the inordinate amount of paperwork indicates, orders and commands issued by the commissariat could reach a particular thana within the day itself. The *thanadar*s, with the help of their clerical staff, could produce or reply to dozens of missives every day, and obviously the carriers were in place to allow this correspondence to happen. Every order sent by the CiC to the kotwal or to the *thanadar*s was to be copied by hand and recorded in the register of the thana or the kotwali. It is amazing that *thanadar*s who conscripted coolies, to take one instance, to send them to the CiC should insist on getting a receipt for it and should insist that they be paid. Receipts for all goods and persons sent at all times—that was the motto for each *thanadar*. The receipts do not necessarily add up to any particular reward for any of them; in fact, some of them remain unpaid, but they are an indication of the relatively healthy nature of the administrative order that had taken charge of the city, in which all transactions had to be recorded, however unusual they may be. Not only were documents zealously produced, they were also supposed to be sealed and covered properly. Syed Nazar Ali, the *thanadar* of Chandni Chowk, wrote an apologetic note to the CiC on 14 August stating that the documents 'in future will be sealed properly and that the incorrect sealing which has been pointed out was done not by he himself but by the Mohurrir of the thana, Durga Prashad'.[96]

The reason the police became so indispensable to the administration and to the war effort in Delhi was because it was the only organised body available to the government. It helped that it was a coercive body and was semi-armed. This was the first time that the ancien régime was called upon to perform tasks and functions that befit a modern government. In order to successfully wage the war effort, the administrative order in Delhi perforce needed a mechanism to implement and act upon its orders which were, oftentimes, coercive in nature. At the same time, the administration was relying quite intensively on public morale and support. All the while, therefore, the police had to walk a tightrope between getting the job done and not stepping on too many toes. Apart from the soldiers, the superior officers were not in favour of granting the police too many summary powers. The police, therefore, had to tax the public without offending them—an impossible task at all times, but made even more difficult by the lack of money.

The soldiers come off badly in the documents found amongst the *Mutiny Papers*, but then everybody comes off badly in police records. Most of them were ill-fed and ill-cared for; most of them were fighting bravely too. Delhi was peculiar compared to other centres of the uprising in so far as it did not have a hinterland to feed off. There was no body of *taluqdars* sending in supplies and men to service the cause and for this reason the inhabitants of the city were increasingly discomfited and querulous. The citizens of the city were disparaged not just by the soldiers but also by the editor of the *Delhi Urdu Akhbar*, who found their lack of fervour quite alarming.[97] But the picture that emerges here of the soldiers has to be offset against other documents in the *Mutiny Papers*, where preparations for and the practice of war gain more attention. They were, after all, fighting a voluntary war, without resources.

It was the events of 1857 that ultimately lent urgency to the cause of Police Reform which was enacted in 1861. The organisation of that force was heavily coloured by the experiences of the uprising and the force that emerged was, perforce, a semi-military one. Discussions about Police Reform from the 1830s centred fundamentally on the autonomy of power enjoyed by the Darogha, on the manner in which he could influence the outcome of the case by his powers of detention and by the case report that he prepared.[98] Interestingly, this was something the authorities of the rebel administration tried to keep in check by a constant inspection of the police diaries. The other essential question facing Police Reform was the question of the separation of judicial and revenue duties. The main issue was, however, the unauthorised judicial power exercised by the police Darogha and the lack of supervision over the clerk who recorded statements.[99] As we saw in the case of Delhi, even during the uprising, the police were chastised for making decisions on their own when statements were supposed to be recorded in the court run by the CiC. When the reforms were finally enacted, the code writers were 'careful to provide a complete system of supervision by European Officers, the want of which … has been one of the greatest disadvantages of the Civil Police system heretofore existing in India'.[100] Lacking it may have been, but there is little evidence from the Mutiny Papers that this was a cause of inefficiency. Yet, perhaps the demands of a different master may have caused that zealousness to be tempered.

Notes and References

1. W.H. Russell, *My Diary in India* (London: Routledge, Warne and Routledge, 1859).
2. Charles Metcalfe, *Two Native Narratives: The Narrative of Mainodin Hasan Khan* (Westminster: A, Constable, 1898), p. 50.
3. *Dehli Urdu Akhbar*, 31 May 1857.
4. Notably Munshi Jiwan Lal, see 'The Narrative of Munshi Jiwan Lal', *Two Native Narratives*.
5. Collection 111a, Number 148, 22 June 1857.
6. Collection 111c, Number 127, 7 August 1857.
7. Collection 111c, Number 159, 10 August 1857; see also Collection 111c, Number 160.
8. Collection 124, Number 115, 20 June 1857.
9. Collection 128, Number 64, 16 June 1857.
10. Collection 128, Number 34, 10 June 1857.
11. Collection 57, Number 543, n.d.
12. Collection 120, Number 129, n.d.
13. Collection 45, 26 July–3 September 1857.
14. A scanned copy of the *Mutiny Papers* index volume has been made available to download from the 'Mutiny at the Margins' project website at http://www.csas.ed.ac.uk/mutiny/texts.html.
15. Talmiz Khaldun, 'The Great Rebellion', in P.C. Joshi, ed., *Rebellion—1857. A Symposium* (Delhi: People's Publishing House, 1957 and 1986), pp. 1–72.
16. Ibid., p. 40.
17. Iqbal Husain, 'The Rebel Administration of Delhi', *Social Scientist*, vol. 29, nos 1–4, 1998, pp. 25–39.
18. See, for example, Collection 103, Number 218, 30 July 1857.
19. Collection 103, Number 213, 25 July 1857.
20. Collection 104, Numbers 2 and 3, 24 May 1857.
21. Collection 123, Number 6, 27 May 1857.
22. Collection 103, Number 220, 1 August 1857.

23. Collection 61, Numbers 84, 22 June 1857, 82, 21 June 1857, 66, 18 June 1857 and 111, 3 July 1857.
24. Collection 61, Number 86, 22 June 1857.
25. Collection 67, Number 152, n.d.
26. Collection 67, Numbers 111, 21 August 1857.
27. Collection 45, 26 July–3 September 1857.
28. Collection 61, Number 1, 23 May 1857.
29. Collection 129, Number 80, 29 August 1857.
30. Collection 111c, Number 34, 28 July 1857.
31. Collection 45, 26 July–3 September 1857.
32. Collection 103, Number 215, 27 July 1857.
33. Collection 111c, Number 49, 29 July 1857.
34. Collection 125, Number 12, 11 June 1857.
35. Collection 124, Number 306, 23 August 1857.
36. Collection 103, Number 362, 4 September 1857.
37. Collection 61, Number 547, n.d.
38. Collection 61, Number 396, 17 August 1857.
39. Collection 53, 19 May–10 August 1857.
40. Collection 63, Number 98, n.d.
41. Collection 63, Number 46, 16 August 1857.
42. Collection 53, 19 May–10 August 1857.
43. Collection 129, Number 61, 18 August 1857.
44. Collection 101, Number 26, 13 August 1857.
45. Collection 120, Number 190, 31 August 1857.
46. Collection 111c Number 11, 24 July 1857.
47. Collection 111c, Number 222, August 18 1857.
48. Collection 62, Number 80, 3 August 1857.
49. Collection 45, 26 July–3 September 1857.
50. Collection 111c, Number 64, 30 July 1857.
51. Collection 45, 26 July–3 September 1857.
52. Collection 111c, Number 44, 29 July 1857.
53. Collection 61, Number 265, 30 July 1857.
54. Collection 111c, Number 45, 29 July 1857.
55. Collection 103, Number 132, 10 July 1857.
56. Collection 103, Number 134, 11 July 1857.
57. A common word for soldiers employed by the East India Company—probably originating in Telengana where they were first recruited—particularly popular in Delhi and in these documents where it stands for sepoys.
58. Collection 103, Number 24, 22 June 1857.
59. Collection 110, Number 293, n.d.
60. Collection 45, 26 July–3 September 1857.
61. Ibid.
62. Ibid.
63. Ibid. Copies of reports from the kotwali.
64. Ibid.
65. Ibid.
66. Collection 71, Number 165, 15 August 1857.
67. Collection 103, Number 412, n.d.
68. Collection 60, Number 253, 1 July 1857.
69. Ibid.
70. Collection 120, Number 1, 20 May 1857.

71. Collection 120, Number 134, 24 July 1857.
72. Collection 45, 26 July–3 September 1857. Copies of reports from the kotwali.
73. Collection 45, 26 July–3 September 1857. Copies of reports from the kotwali.
74. Collection 120, Number 16, 22 June 1857.
75. Collection 122, Number 22, 30 July 1857.
76. Collection 123, Number 6, 27 May 1857.
77. Collection 61, Number 3, 25 May 1857.
78. Collection 61, Number 4, 25 May 1857.
79. Collection 61, Number 95, 24 June 1857.
80. Collection 61, Number 117, 3 July 1857.
81. Collection 61, Number 256, 29 July 1857.
82. Collection 124, Number 327, n.d.
83. Collection 103–303, 19 August 1857.
84. Collection 111b, Number 14, 3 July 1857.
85. Collection 45, 26 July–3 September 1857.
86. Collection 123, Number 143, 24 July 1857.
87. Collection 121, Number 105, 16 August 1857.
88. Collection 120, Number 137, 25 July 1857.
89. Collection 60, Numbers 349–359, 20–21 July 1857.
90. Collection 60, Number 361 22 July 1857.
91. Collection 60, Number 686, 7 September 1857.
92. Collection 75, Number 22, 7 September 1857.
93. Collection 60, Number 688, 11 September 1857.
94. Collection 106, Number 31, 30 June 1857.
95. Collection 104, Number 67, n.d.
96. Collection 61, Number 367, 14 August 1857.
97. *Dehli Urdu Akhbar,*14 June 1857.
98. Ibid., p. 305.
99. Radhika Singha, *A Despotism of Law-Crime and Justice in Colonial India* (Delhi: Oxford University Press, 2000), p. 304.
100. From the Police Commission to the Secretary of to the Government of India, Home Department, Calcutta, September 1860, p. 3, clause 14.

7

REFLECTIONS OF 1857 IN CONTEMPORARY URDU LITERATURE

Rakshanda Jalil

'POLITICS and history are interwoven, but not commensurate', wrote Lord Acton.[1] So also politics and poetry. In the Delhi of the nineteenth century, everybody—from the king down to the beggar—was smitten by poetry. Before 1857, poets dominated the city's cultural and intellectual landscape; they were held in greater esteem than the Mughal emperors whose 'rule' did not extend beyond the shabby grandeur of the Quila-e-Moalla, or the Exalted Fort, as the Red Fort was then called. After 1857, especially in its immediate violent aftermath, the political climate became far too volatile for poets and writers to chart the course of the city's fortunes. They could, at best, defend or decry—depending upon their lot after the cataclysmic events of the revolt—the causes and effects of the year that was to change their lives irrevocably. And this they did in prodigious amounts of poetry written in Urdu during and after 1857.

However, just as there is no generalised or undifferentiated response to the Revolt of 1857 among the Muslim intelligentsia of the late nineteenth century, there is no uniform, un-variegated, one-dimensional reflection in contemporary Urdu poetry of what would later be dubbed the First War of Independence. It reflects a bewildering and often contradictory array of opinions. Reactions vary from nostalgic lament for a lost age, to fixing blame and apportioning responsibility for the terrible misfortunes that had befallen them. Heroes become villains and vice versa: the mutineering soldiers, referred to as *mujahid* (martyrs, or 'those who bear witness') by some, become *balwai* (rioters) for others. So also the firangi and the Mughals, both of whom invite varying degrees of criticism and approbation. Two worlds—the decaying and the emergent—fuse and merge. Pathos, confusion and conflict reign supreme. It would take several decades for the clouds of uncertainty to part and the debate on the Old Light versus the New to usher in the Lamp of New Learning. But for that to happen, Delhi—the focus of the 'Dilli Chalo' movement, victim of its worst excesses and also the *markaz,* or centre, of the finest Urdu poetry of its time—had to first rise, phoenix-like, from the ashes of its siege and slaughter.

Given the close relationship between social reality and literary texts, it is important to revisit and re-examine the literature produced during times of great social upheaval. Often, it gives a far more nuanced understanding of historical events than official records and documents. In Urdu, there exists a body of poetry known as *shehr ashob,* literally meaning 'city in mourning' to express political and social decline.[2] While admittedly much of this genre of poetry is melodramatic, self-pitying and exaggerated, with a great deal of rhetoric and play upon words in the best traditions of elegiac poetry such as *nauha, marsiya* and *soz, shehr ashob* also affords ample opportunities for the poet to paint graphic word pictures of what he sees and experiences first hand. Using the conventional imagery of Persian–Arabic tradition, *shehr ashob* allows the poet to speak of his personal sorrows and losses while, ostensibly, bemoaning a crumbling social order. When Sirajuddaullah was killed by the British in the Battle of Plassey (1757), his friend Raja Ram Narain Maozoon expresses his anguish:

Oh! where have the mad lovers who once roamed the desert gone
And where have those days of love vanished

Over the years, events conspired to give plenty of fodder to the Urdu elegist's mill. There was the decline and dismantling of the Mughal Empire, the sack of Delhi by Nadir Shah, the establishment of British control over the city in 1803, and the most cruel blow of all—the annexation of Awadh in 1856—which turned even loyal Muslim supporters of the British into discontented suspicious malcontents, if not ardent jehadis. With each fresh catastrophe, the Urdu poet evolved a vocabulary to express his angst, clothing his sorrow in a time-honoured repertoire of images and metaphors. Some favourite synonyms for the British were *sitamgar, but, kafir, yar* or *yaaron,* expressions interchangeably used for the beloved in conventional Urdu poetry, but now used with an often sly twist for the *gora.*

The revolt divided the Urdu poets into two camps: those for it and those against. Some were for Zafar, but against the *ghaddar* (the traitors in the British army); others gave vent to their ire against the emperor too. Interestingly, these poets not only contradict each other, often they contradict themselves too; against the British before and during the siege of Delhi, they turn into fervent admirers of British rule in Hindustan shortly after the fall of Delhi. A great many, however, refuse to take sides preferring instead to chronicle the end of an age and a way of life.

A staunch 'royalist' like Dagh writes:

Calamity has seized the populace, misfortune befallen the city
The coming of the Purabiyas has spelt God's doom for the city

Muhammad Sadruddun Khan Azurdah, a poet, scholar and magistrate, however, directly attacks the people of the Fort and holds them responsible for the calamity:

> Misfortune befell the city because of the fort
> Due to their evil deeds retribution came upon Delhi
> Calamity arrived with the black men from Meerut

Azurdah goes on to catalogue the woes of Delhi after the *kale* are defeated by the *gore*: the massacres of innocents, men pulled out of their homes on the flimsiest of pretexts (often their being Muslim being reason enough), but his real concern is with people like himself, the aristocracy of Delhi. He mourns the loss of his friends, in particular Sehbai, the teacher, poet and scholar, the leading light of the 'Dilli Callege' (Delhi College), who was shot dead by the British troops. Azurdah writes:

> Why shouldn't Azurdah go crazy and run to the wilderness
> When Sahbai is killed so brutally, though he was guiltless

The notion of 'guilt' itself is interpreted differently by different Urdu poets of this period. On the one hand, you have poets accusing the Indians of being guilty ('You have destroyed your garden, despite being the gardener'), others such as Maulvi Fazle Haq Khairabadi and Munir Shikohabadi hold the British guilty of unleashing terror upon hapless Muslims. Writing in his island prison, an unrepentant Fazle Haq says:

> I did not commit any crime except this
> I did not like them (the British), nor was I friendly with them

Munir Shikohabadi, a poet who was actively involved in the uprising, was employed by the Nawab of Banda. Like Fazle Haq, he too was arrested and sent to the Andamans, where he wrote prolifically during his imprisonment. Munir Shikohabadi saw himself as a follower of the legacy of Shah Walliullah and exhorted the Muslims to rise in a holy war against the British.

A similarly militant sentiment is found in a quatrain written on the occasion of Id-uz-Zuha (which fell on 2 August 1857), rather surprisingly written by the emperor Zafar himself:

> O Allah, may the enemy troops be all killed
> May the Gurkhas, Whites, Gujars and Englishmen be all killed
> We shall recognize this day as the Festival of Sacrifice only when
> O Zafar, your murderer be put to the sword today!

In one sher, Zafar even urges the rebellious soldiers to ply their swords against the British, and 'reach London' if necessary! Depressed by the state of his desolate Delhi and the state he has been reduced to, he holds the *hakim-e-waqt* (the ruler of the time) responsible:

> Has anyone heard of such cruelty
> That the innocent should be hanged
> From the rows of the devout arise
> Clouds from discontented hearts

After the fall of Delhi, Qazi Fazal Husain Afsurdah holds the soldiers and spies guilty for the madness that spirals out of control and catches both the 'guilty' and the 'innocent':

> Calamity came with the coming of the soldiers
> The spies added fire to the fury
> Both the guilty and the innocent were arrested

Several felt that Muslims were singled out for the reprisals. Shah Ayatollah Johri rues the desecration of mosques and holy places, claiming that the Brahmins prosper while the Muslims suffer, and the masjids remain desolate while in the temples, the conches can now be heard:

> The House of God lies in darkness whereas the lamps are lit in the temples
> The traditions of the infidels thrive whereas the light of faith flickers

The mystically inclined Syed Ali Tashnah, a much-loved poet of Delhi, blames the outsiders who robbed and pillaged:

> The Tilangas came and looted the entire city
> As the saying goes, the naked came to rob the hungry

Several poets such as Zaheer Dehlvi, Hakim Agha Jaan Aish, Nawab Mirza Dagh, Qurban Ali Beg Saalik, Mohsin and Kaukab speak of the weeping, of the homeless men and women, carrying bundles of precious belongings on their heads, who flee Delhi only to be robbed or murdered on the way. Some speak of unemployment and acute poverty. Dagh writes that 'the only job left for Muslim men is to fill up the prisons' and Sehr says that 'it has been an age since one has seen the face of a rupaiya'. Ruing the slaughter of an age (*ek jahan qatl hua*), Zaheer Dehlvi writes:

> People have been pulled out of their homes
> Corpses line the road, layers upon layers
> Neither grave, nor shroud, nor mourners are left

Many of these poets belonged to the privileged classes who were the worst hit. So there is an element of personal sorrow and loss mingled with the general lament and mourning. A collection of forty poems called *Fughan-e-Dehli* (The Lament of Delhi) presents a graphic picture of the havoc and destruction making the city out to be as much a victim of changed circumstances as its people.

However, the most useful firsthand account of the Revolt of 1857 and its aftermath is provided by Mirza Asadullah Khan Ghalib (1796–1869), the pre-eminent poet of Delhi and an important eyewitness. From the coming of the mutineers from Meerut on 11 May 1857 to the siege and fall of Delhi on 14 September, and all through the two terrible years that followed when the city was voided of its Muslim citizens, Ghalib stayed put—a bit like the boy who stood on the burning deck whence all but he had fled. While some of his verses written after 1857 refer, though obliquely, to the shock and trauma of those months, the events of that annus horribilis are recorded in a memoir he wrote in Persian, called *Dastambu*, meaning 'A Posy of Flowers', an incongruous name for a document so grim.

✳✳✳

Covering a period of 15 months, from 11 May 1857 till 1 August 1858, let us first look at the *Dastambu*³ which was published from Agra in 1858 under the personal supervision of Ghalib's friend and disciple Munshi Shiv Narayan Aram. Its first print of 500 copies was sold out in months, prompting two subsequent editions in 1865 and 1871. In the words of Khwaja Ahmad Faruqi, who translated it from its Persian original into English in 1954, it is

> the story of the planned revolt, the ebb and flow of changing fortunes, of alternating hope and gloom as it affected a Delhi citizen—the throbbings of a sensitive soul and the reactions of a poet to an important historical situation—a story hitherto untold.

Ghalib makes one thing amply clear at the very outset: his indebtedness to the British and his unequivocal admiration for them. 'Readers of this book should know that I who, through the strokes of my pen scatter pearls on paper, have eaten the bread and salt of the British and, from my earliest childhood, have been fed from the table of these world conquerors.' He then begins his tale proper:

> We have a chronogram for this year, which is expressed in the phrase *rast khezi bija*, which means unwarranted revolt ... suddenly, at noon on Monday, the 11th of May 1857, the walls and ramparts of the Red Fort shook ... (as) rebellious soldiers from Meerut, faithless to the salt, entered Delhi, thirsty for the blood of the British.... Swarming through the opened gates, the intoxicated horsemen and rough foot soldiers ravished the city like madmen. They did not leave their bloody work until they had killed officers and Englishmen, wherever they found them, and had destroyed their houses.

These *sowars* from Meerut, uninvited guests for some such as Ghalib, are initially welcomed by the unsuspecting people of Delhi who have no inkling of what they have brought upon themselves. Mistrustful from the beginning of these creatures of ill-intent, Ghalib can only watch helplessly as the mayhem and murder unspool; he makes it very clear that he is one of those 'poor, reclusive men, who received their bread and salt by the grace of the British', one who does not know 'an arrow from an axe' and who cannot, therefore, put this genie back in the bottle, much though he would like to.

In a reaction typical of an urbane city dweller, he goes on to heap abuse on the rebellious hordes, calling them 'lawless multitude', 'black-hearted cruel killers', 'cowardly robbers' who not only turned upon their masters but also turned 'their shameful lust' upon the innocent citizens of Delhi. Sword in hand, they looted and plundered, seized guns from the royal armory, stabled their horses in the fabled Red Fort, took the Royal Chambers for their sleeping rooms and set all prisoners free. 'Some of the soldiers', Ghalib writes,

> although they had no leaders, prepared themselves for battle by seizing guns, gunpowder and gunshot from the British. All the tactics they had learnt they employed against their former teachers … The city of Delhi was emptied of its rulers and peopled instead with creatures of the Lord who acknowledge no lord—as if it were a garden without a gardener, and full of fruitless trees.

With no one at the helm, there is chaos and confusion—the merchants stop paying taxes, houses are abandoned, looting becomes the order of the day. Conscious of his own high birth and fine breeding, Ghalib is appalled by the crassness of the country hicks who have overtaken his beloved city. He considers 'these newly-rich, vile-natured' rabble 'not men but whirlwinds puffed up with conceit'.

After brief digressions on the virtual breakdown of the postal system and little homilies on the state of anarchy when 'brave men are afraid of their own shadows and soldiers rule over dervish and king alike', Ghalib continues his narrative of real, historical events:

> When these wayward, hostile rebels first entered Delhi, they brought treasure with them. This they deposited with the royal treasury and they bowed their head on the royal threshold. Rebellious armies from various directions converged on Delhi and assembled here. When the emperor could no longer contain this army, the army itself took control into its own hands and the king was rendered helpless.

Once in Delhi, all sorts of riff-raff seek and are granted an audience with Bahadurshah, where they kneel in obeisance and, in return, demand governorships and the grant of fertile lands. That they should be allowed to meet the emperor so freely by the emperor's minders is, for one such as Ghalib used to stringent royal protocol and court etiquette, 'part of the strangeness of the times'.

All through the hot months of May and June, the city of Delhi becomes a vast encampment. By Ghalib's reckoning, there are '50,000 cavalry and infantry' inside and outside Delhi, whereas the British 'control no ground except for a ridge at the western edge of the city' which they have turned, rather skilfully, into a fortress by arranging their batteries and fixing 'their fire-breathing, lightning-striking cannons' on all four sides 'and, in this manner, through their perseverance, they have made a haven of peace in a land of adversity'. All this while, the rebel armies are converging upon Delhi from different parts of the country. Bowing to popular pressure, the rulers of Farrukhabad, Bareilly, and Lucknow send expensive gifts to the emperor as tokens of support and solidarity—a gesture seen as misguided by Ghalib; the Nawab of Rampur (his patron and benefactor in later years) sends only a verbal message to the rebels in view of his strong ties with the British, and this is recorded with some satisfaction by Ghalib. But this display of homage to an ageing monarch, Ghalib observes dourly, is the last flicker of the lamp of Mughal splendour. Hurrying through this section, the writer of *Dastambu* chooses instead to wax eloquent on the successful siege and fall of Delhi at the hands of the British.

On 14 September, the British mount a successful attack on Kashmiri Gate. A jubilant Ghalib writes: 'In the month of May justice was taken from Delhi; in September the days of atrocity drew to an end and justice again prevailed.' Calling the British 'possessors of knowledge and wisdom', he is pleased when Delhi is 'divested of its madmen and conquered by the brave and wise' after a lapse of four months and four days. His joy will prove to be short-lived when he discovers that the fury unleashed by the vengeful British troops outdid the drunken excesses of the native soldiers—but this we shall see only in the letters and the occasional verse. In *Dastambu*, Ghalib is reticent to the point of being blinkered. He repeats his professions of loyalty to the alien masters and tells his readers of the panegyric in praise of 'the just and exalted Queen Victoria' he had written two years earlier, and the courteous letter from Lord Ellenborough, 'that Cyprus of the garden of sovereignty', acknowledging receipt of the said panegyric. In these dark days, Ghalib writes, he has nothing but these 'letters of good omen, which are a talisman on the arm of wisdom and remind me of my deep longings'. Why such desperate need to establish his bona fides as a faithful servant of the British? Why this scrupulous distancing from the rebels and the Mughal court alike? Why these constant professions of admiration for British rule? We shall come to his reasons later.

Meanwhile, to return to the *Dastambu* and its story: while many of the rebels escaped, some stayed back to fight the conquerors. Fierce battle raged on all the roads from Kashmiri Gate to Chandni Chowk, but the three main gates to the city—Ajmeri, Turkman and Dehli Darwaza—remained in the hands of the rebels, thus allowing large numbers to escape the wrath of the vengeful

British. They fled to the countryside, taking what they could of their belongings and seeking shelter in the tombs and ruins that dotted the neighbourhood of Shahjahanabad. Once again, Ghalib makes his own position very clear: those who have stayed back and are fighting the British are 'destroying the honour and prestige of Delhi', whereas the British are to be forgiven their excesses. 'When the angry lions entered the town, they killed the helpless and the weak and they burned their houses. *It may be that such atrocities always occur after conquest*' (emphasis mine). For his own part, he says that he feared no reprisal, 'for I am not a wrong-doer and the English do not kill the innocent'. Partly because he loved his city so much and partly because he wished to prove his blameless existence and his unquestioning loyalty to the British, he chose to stay on. By 8 September, the city had fallen:

> The misguided rebels fled like swine, and the victors captured the city and the Fort. The horror of mass arrests, assassinations and slaughter now reached our lane and the people shook with fear.

Ghalib and his neighbours shut the door of their lane, piling stones against the entrance and remained barricaded for almost a year. The ruler of Patiala sent guards who kept the worst of the looters at bay, but no one could help with the shortages—of food, water and service providers. Again, Ghalib chooses to go lightly over the extent of British vengeance, saying discreetly: 'It is believed that those who were killed were ones who did not show obedience (to the British) and it is widely known that although looting was common, killing was generally abjured.' This, incidentally, is not borne out by other chronicles and is certainly contradicted by Ghalib himself in his letters.

In the *Dastambu*, Ghalib mentions several important landmarks in passing: on 5 October he is summoned by the military governor of Delhi for questioning; on 7 October he hears the twenty-one-gun salute from the Fort when Delhi formally passed into the hands of the British; on 19 October he receives news of the death of his brother Mirza Yusuf who had been declared insane several years before; and then with almost telegraphic brevity, he records the arrest and execution of the rulers of Jhajjar, Farrukhnagar and Ballabhgarh. The cataclysmic event that marked the end of an epoch is summarily dismissed thus: 'Nothing more can be said of the fate of the Mughal princes than that some were shot ... and some were hung by their necks ...; and the aged and fragile Mughal emperor is under trial by the court'.

It pains Ghalib, however, to record that two sets of rules apply to the Hindu and Muslim citizens of Delhi. While the Hindus are allowed to return by February 1858, no such respite is visible for the Muslims: 'The houses of the dispossessed Muslims had long remained empty and were so covered with vegetation that the walls seemed to be made of grass—and every blade of grass tells that the house of the Muslim is still empty.' And elsewhere, he talks with heartfelt anguish of the Muslims, men and women from some of the best Delhi families, who live outside the city limits, sleeping in ditches and mud huts, whose sole occupation seems to be to keep up a ceaseless barrage of petitions: asking the British to release their near ones from prison; allowing them to return to Delhi; or, in many cases such as Ghalib's own, renew their pensions. 'In the entire city of Delhi it is impossible to find more than one thousand Muslims; and I am one of these.'

Having made this significant entry, he digresses on several seemingly unrelated events: the successful British invasions of Bareilly, Muradabad and Gwalior; the fall of Lucknow; the sky-high price of English wine to which he admits he is habituated; and his several Hindu friends without whom he could not have coped—Mahesh Das, Hira Singh, Shivji Ram Brahman, Bal Mukand, and his disciple Hargopal Tafta. Ghalib talks with no trace of self-consciousness of his utter and complete poverty: 'I live by selling my clothes and bedding. While others eat bread, I eat clothes. I am afraid that when I have sold all my clothes I shall die, naked, of starvation.' And with this, he lays down his pen on the first of August 1858 and the *Dastambu* comes to an end.

A self-confessed *namak-khwar-e-sarkar-e-angrez* (an 'eater of the salt of the British government', on account of his pension, which incidentally stopped after May 1857 and was restored after much trouble only upon the intervention of Sir Syed Ahmad Khan in May 1860), Ghalib may have initially written *Dastambu* as a memoir to while away the period of confinement; however, it was published, with several significant alterations, after the British were installed as the undisputed masters of Hindustan. The *Dastambu* makes Ghalib a mute spectator cloistered in his house inside a shuttered lane, fighting shy of being associated either with the rebels or the King. Ghalib is noncommittal about the role of Bahadurshah Zafar as the messiah of the rebels and highly critical of the resistance movement.

Keen to establish his own credentials as one faithful to the British, he must necessarily walk a tightrope. He cannot afford to be seen as being close to the last Mughal emperor, whose ustad he was and whose verses he corrected during the siege of Delhi and with whose court he continued to maintain outwardly friendly relations—as is borne out by his letters.[4] Of Zafar, he says in the *Dastambu*, 'As the moon is eclipsed, so the army overshadowed the king. An eclipse cannot obscure the crescent moon, but only the full moon of the fourteenth night. The king was a waning moon, yet his light was eclipsed.' And elsewhere, rather snidely commenting on the king's rising stock among the rebels and ascending star as a unifying force for the armies that had gathered from different parts of the country, he says: 'The emperor's star reached such lofty heights that it went quite out of sight of the world's eyes.'

One can only conclude that grinding poverty and the exigencies of the times coupled with his deep-seated admiration for British rule in India and his clear-sighted assessment of the shortcomings of the Mughal rule[5] made Ghalib alter *Dastambu* for publication. Desperate to save his skin, at a time when

Muhammadan meant rebel, Ghalib had to do all he could to impress the British: underline his being only 'half-Muslim' since he drank wine (but did not eat pork, as narrated in a famous incident), list his many Hindu friends and keep stressing his unswerving loyalty to the British. If, apart from keeping him safe, it could also reinstate his pension and the honours that went with it, then it was worth a shot. Russel and Islam, while admitting that Ghalib may have

> omitted or toned down passages which could give serious offence to the British … and added emphasis to his horror at the acts of the rebel sepoys, there is no reason to believe that the book in any way misrepresents his essential attitudes, and it remains the clearest connected account we possess of his personal experiences during these months.[6]

* * *

Ghalib survived the *ghadar* and lived for another twelve years. His letters, from 1857 onwards, bear ample testimony to the hardships of everyday life and the many humiliations heaped upon the Muslims of Delhi. Soon after the fall of Delhi on 20 September 1857, British soldiers entered the Jama Masjid, desecrated it and set about unleashing the most terrible atrocities. Thousands were killed, the rebels and their sympathisers summarily executed, 160,000 inhabitants driven out of the city limits and forced to camp in the open countryside. Every citizen wanting to return had to pay a fine: Muslims—25 per cent of the value of their property; Hindus—10 per cent.[7] Writing to Tufta on 5 December 1857, Ghalib describes the desolation of Delhi under martial law, his continuing fears for his safety and his acute sense of isolation:

> House after house lies deserted, and the punishment of offenders goes on… By God, you may search for a Muslim in this city and not find one—rich, poor, artisans alike are gone. Such as are here are not Delhi people.

Lonely, ailing, grieving over dead friends and relatives, chafing at the enforced isolation, he tells Hakim Ghulam Najaf Khan on 19 January 1858, 'So far we are still alive—I and my wife and the children—but no one knows what may happen from one hour to the next.' Continuing to lie low and keep out of sight till the troubles blow over, on 30 January 1858, he tells Tufta, that the authorities know he is in Delhi, but he has not been sent for. And to Majruh, on 7 February 1858, he repeats: 'I am not in hiding or living here secretly. The authorities know I am here; but I have neither been interrogated nor arrested.' Finally, giving up waiting to be summoned, he decides to write a petition seeking the re-issuance of his pension. 'I am a slave to my belly; I need to eat.' The pension is important also because it would clear him, finally and unequivocally, of any suspicion. From August to early November 1858, his letters are full of plans to publish the *Dastambu* because he sees it as a means of recovering his pension.

Where the *Dastambu* does not allow Ghalib to bare his soul, his letters do. They show his keen awareness of political events on the national arena while also serving to provide a valuable record of small, everyday sorrows and tragedies. Sometime in June or July 1858, Ghalib began his letter to Tufta thus:

Rakhiyo Ghalib mujhe is talq nawai pe maaf
Aaj kuch dard mere dil mein siwa hota hai
[If Ghalib sings in a bitter strain, forgive him
Today pain stabs more keenly at his heart]

The most direct reference to the events of 1857, by far, is found in a ghazal appended, without comment to a letter written in 1858:

Now every English soldier that bears arms
Is sovereign, and free to work his will

Men dare not venture out into the street
And terror chills their heart within them still

Their homes enclose them as in prison walls
And in the Chauk the victors hang and kill

The city is athirst for Muslim blood
And every grain of dust must drink its fill ...[8]

The Muslims are allowed to return by November 1859, over two years after their expulsion. But the city has changed: large parts of historic Shahjahanabad are demolished, making way for clear spaces and wider roads, shops and houses pulled down in a radius of 25 feet around the Jama Masjid, libraries burnt, mosques desecrated, lands confiscated. A 'Town Duty' tax is levied on all commodities entering the city (except rice and cow dung) and the levying of the tax given to three local merchants—Salig Ram, Chunna Mal and Mahesh Das. On 1 November 1858, an order is issued: 'All well wishers of the British are to illuminate their houses, and there are to be illuminations in the bazaars and on the Deputy Commissioner sahib's bungalow. Your humble servant', writes Ghalib somewhat plaintively, 'even in this state of penury, not having received his appointed pension for the last eighteen months, will illuminate his house, and has sent a poem of fifteen couplets to the Commissioner of the city.'

The revolt did not merely mark the end of a way of life; it also, in a sense, marked a departure in a way of seeing things. Till then, Urdu prose was either didactic or educational. It did not always draw from society; instead it strove to draw the reader away from the real, often grim reality, into a magical world of fantasy. The burst of political consciousness released by 1857 found expression in socially engaged literature. This is exemplified in the writings of both poets and novelists of the late nineteenth and early twentieth centuries. Faced with the challenge of living in a colonised world and making good, Nazir Ahmed, Maulvi Zakaullah and others tried to find a modus vivendi with the colonial government. In the process, they dealt with wide-ranging themes which had been overlooked in the pre-1857 decades and, thus, began a new phase of politically and socially charged literature.

Notes and References

1. Lord Acton (1834–1902) in his inaugural lecture 'The Study of History' as Regius Professor at Cambridge in 1895, quoted in Mushirul Hasan, *A Moral Reckoning* (New Delhi: Oxford University Press, 2005), p. 191.
2. The first proper *shehr ashob* is said to have been written by Mir Jafar Zatalli, during Farrukhsiyar's reign. It initially had elements of satire and humour, but with time these leached out and what was left was poignant, pathos-laden protest poetry.
3. All references to *Dastambu* (also written as *Dastambuy*) are taken from the translation by Khwaja Ahmad Faruqi (Delhi: 1954, reprinted New York: Asia Publishing House, 1970). This translation from Persian into English was based on the first edition, published in 1858, and contained an introduction, glossary, notes, chronology and index.
4. In a letter to the Nawab of Rampur, written on 14 January 1858, he says, 'In those turbulent days, I held myself aloof [from the Court]. But I feared that if I completely severed all connection with it my house might be destroyed and my very life perhaps endangered. Thus I continued inwardly estranged, but outwardly friendly.' Ralph Russell and Khurshidul Islam, trans and eds, *Ghalib: Life and Letters* (New Delhi: Oxford University Press, 1969), p. 132.
5. Lest we forget, when Sir Syed asked Ghalib to write a foreword to the new edition of *Ain i Akbari* being prepared by the Syed, the latter wrote such a scathing critique of the old order that it could not be appended to the work.
6. Russell and Islam, *Ghalib: Life and Letters*, pp. 132–133.
7. Hasan, *Moral Reckoning*, p. 284.
8. Russell and Islam, *Ghalib: Life and Letters*, p. 149.

8

CONTEXTUALISING TRUTH
Deconstructing the Poet Khazan Singh's Account of the War of Delhi, 1857*

Chhanda Chatterjee

LITERATURE, especially good literature, mirrors life. The author's insight into his life and times is woven into the text of such literature, and the truth of a literary text can sometimes be considered of more value than mere historical narration, because literary imagination can be a reliable subjective representation of a community's sentiments and aspirations. A critical reading and 'deconstruction' of a text can lead to the discovery of certain new sets of truth, quite different from what the author had explicitly been trying to say. The political limits of the times might sometimes restrict the conscious aim of the author to the statement of certain facts in the text, but the very act of narration might contain elements of subjectivity which, when deconstructed, reveal other truths that open up a completely new horizon of thinking. The poet Khazan Singh's manuscript, 'Atha Jang Nama Dilli' (The Story of the War of Delhi), composed during Vikrama era 1915 (corresponding to the year AD 1858), in the reign of Maharaja Narinder Singh of Patiala, had the professed aim of winning accolades for his patron's participation in the British war effort against the Rising of 1857. However, the

* I am grateful to Professor Parambakshish Singh Siddhu, former registrar, Punjabi University, Patiala, for having helped me locate the poem by Khazan Singh in Shamsher Singh Ashok, ed., *Prachin Jangname* (Amritsar: Shiromani Gurdwara Parbandhak Committee, 1950), available in the Bhai Kahan Singh Nabha Library, Punjabi University, Patiala. Mr Awtar Singh of the Sikh Cultural Centre, Calcutta, helped me in translating and understanding the poem. My thanks are due to him. Professor Kirpal Singh read my chapter in full and gave his valuable comments. I also thank Professor Sudhir Chandra, Dr Amaresh Mishra, Professor Azizuddin Hussain and Professor Suranjan Das for their comments and suggestions at Jamia Millia Islamia where the chapter was presented.

text transcends its immediate purpose and goes into an 'overrun' (débordement) to become an authentic record of many strands of contemporary thinking that are not contained within the margins of a precise text.

Plato would have no place for poets in his ideal republic. The reason was his dislike for untruth. According to Plato, poetry was often prone to untruthfulness because of its use of figurative expressions. This Platonic observation triggered a series of debates in the fields of linguistics, philosophy, literature and history, emphasising the problem of establishing a direct link between the signifier and the object that is to be signified. An attempt is made to get as close to reality as possible through a resort to metaphors, metonyms and euphemisms. And in spite of all these efforts, reality remains as elusive as ever, defying all orders of significations.[1] Michel Foucault, in his 'What Is An Author?', noticed the penchant of the signifier for 'testing the limits of its regularity transgressing and reversing an order that it manipulates'.[2] True to this propensity of the author to indulge in a game 'that inevitably moves beyond its own rules and finally leaves them behind',[3] the poet Khazan Singh began his writing in the vein of a loyalist to the British cause, but in the course of his narration, strayed into the pent-up sorrow of the people of Punjab at having to fight a lone battle against the slow penetration of the English into the province following the death of Maharaja Ranjit Singh in 1839. In 1845–1846 the Khalsa army tried to stop this silent infiltration by taking the field against the English, but their efforts came to grief through the treachery of two leaders of non-Sikh origin—Raja Lall Singh and Raja Tej Singh.[4] The last heroic resistance of the Sikhs to the British— orchestrated by the leadership of Diwan Mulraj of Multan, Chutter Singh Attariwala, Raja Sher Singh and Bhai Maharaj Singh during the Second Sikh War of 1848–1849—had broken on the bayonets of the collaborating Hindustani armies allied with the British.[5] Punjab's struggle for independence came twelve years too soon when people in other parts of India had yet to wake up to the aggressive character of British imperialism.[6] They came to their senses only when Punjab's fate was shared by Satara, Jhansi and Nagpur in 1854 and Awadh in 1856. The dawning of consciousness in different parts of India at different times did not allow the spontaneous resistance of the Khalsa army to be synchronised with the uprising in the 'heartland'[7] of India. The forces of 'localism' and 'territoriality',[8] thus, played into the hands of the British who could employ the forces of Punjab against the people of the rest of India, just as they had won Punjab with armies from the eastern parts of their empire a few years earlier. However, such issues only enter the text of 'Atha Jang Nama Dilli' in an auxiliary capacity. Khazan Singh's poem is primarily concerned with eulogising Maharaja Narinder Singh's role in the task of encountering the rising of the British.

sal chaupahe jeth di panchami nu
khat vich Patiale de aiya si
hukm doriya vich malum hoiya

> *megazin sare vartaiya si*
> *Maharaja Narendra Singh kuch karke*
> *Dera au Thanesur aiya si*
> *Kavi Singh sari fauj sath leke*
> *Thau thai da aur hatayiya si*
>
> *Maharaj Narendra Singha ap charuke*
> *Kile kot ke taraf nigaha layi*
> *sare sahir da kot parvasat hove*
> *Bina takht te top na rahe koi* (p. 2)[9]

When, on 11 May, the telegraph lines in the Punjab flashed the news of the mutiny at Meerut the day before and the advance of the rebellious regiments of the Bengal army to Delhi, Sir John Lawrence, chief commissioner of Punjab (then convalescing from an illness at Rawalpindi), immediately understood that the task of recovering Delhi for the British would devolve on the forces that Punjab would be able to mobilise.[10] The passage to Delhi, however, lay through the cis-Sutlej states of Patiala, Jind, Nabha and Faridkot, a long chain of Jat Sikh states that had entered into a treaty of alliance with the British as far back as April 1809 to escape incorporation into the kingdom of their illustrious and much more powerful neighbour, 'the lion of Punjab' Maharaja Ranjit Singh. Since 1806, Ranjit Singh had regularly visited these states, sometimes at their invitation (Raja Bhag Singh, who claimed an agnate kinship with the King of Lahore, had invited him in 1806 to settle territorial disputes among chiefs across the Sutlej). He conferred new estates upon them, took them away from others and settled his own men in quite a few.[11] These encounters convinced the cis-Sutlej Rajas of their feebleness vis-à-vis the Maharaja of Lahore, and they saw their only means of self-preservation in buying protection from the English. The English Resident of Delhi was approached by Jind, Kythal and Patiala in March 1808. However, the sort of terms the English would be able to secure from Ranjit Singh for the protection of the cis-Sutlej states did not become clear until the conclusion of the treaty of Amritsar between the British government and the Raja of Lahore on 25 April 1809. In the event, the presence of British troops under Lt. Col. David Ochterlony made it clear that Ranjit Singh could no longer dictate terms to the Metcalfe mission. He therefore accepted the Sutlej as the southernmost limit of his kingdom, agreeing to withdraw from Kythal and some recent conquests while ensuring that older conquests would not be interfered with. But he had to promise that he would not ask for the allegiance of the cis-Sutlej states even when he had helped them acquire new estates.[12]

The cis-Sutlej states had all sprung up on the remains of the tottering Mughal Empire by taking advantage of the contentions between the Mughal wardens of the marches, the invading armies of the Maratha General Jaswant Rao Holkar from the south and those of Ahmad Shah Durrani from across the north-west frontier. The territories between the Jumna and the Sutlej were being ravaged by marauding bands or *misls*[13] of Sikhs, who often fought with each other for the control of a well, and then clustered there along with their supporters and built their strongholds or towers surrounded by mud walls. They added new territories to their settlements through hunting expeditions, visiting repeatedly at harvests and establishing a claim for *bakee* (something comparable to the Maratha *chauth* or a proportion of the crop lying on the ground). Their claims to these territories were recognised as their *shikargah* (hunting ground).[14] Originally these Sikhs had come from the *manjha* country, but later they began to be called Malwa Sikhs, probably because of the resemblance of these territories to the Malwa country.

The Sikh settlers in the cis-Sutlej were partly pastoral and partly agricultural, lying somewhere on the borders of sedentarisation.[15] Their earliest remembered personality was Phool, who built the town Garhi Phool. Phool came from the tribe of Sidhu Jats who could trace their links to the Bhatti Rajputs of Jaisalmer. Because of their relationship to Phool, the *misls* in the cis-Sutlej territories were called the Phoolkean *misls*.[16] The Rajas of Patiala, Nabha, Jind, Faridkot and the sardars of Bhadour, Malod and Badrukhan, the Bhais of Kythal and Arnowli and many other chiefs of no less note—all traced their origins to the Sidhu Jat clan. They rose to the position of independent princes from mere cultivators of the land in the course of only a century and a half.[17] Of these, Patiala was the most prominent consisting of 2,450 villages yielding a revenue of 22 lakh rupees in 1844, according to an estimate by Sir Henry Lawrence.[18] Patiala got its name from 'Pat-i-Ala' or the abode of Ala, the illustrious direct descendant of Phool. Ala Jat, a disciple of Guru Govind Singh, had helped the Marathas during the battle of Panipat in 1761 and had fought Nadir Shah, Abdali and the Mughals. He suppressed Bhatti raiders and founded the fort of Barnala; his conflicts with the Mughals and Rohillas continued until the death of Mir Mannu, the Mughal governor of Sirhind, in 1753. Ala Singh escaped the shaving of his hair by Ahmad Shah Abdali in 1762 by paying ₹125,000 during the *Ghallughara* when 15,000 Sikhs were killed near Barnala. In 1765 he had to buy off Abdali once again through *hundi*s exciting the ire of the Dal Khalsa.[19]

Ala Singh's able grandson Umer Singh laid the foundation of the future Raj by adding important places like Bhatinda, Fettehabad, Sirsa, Runeea, Lolpore and Rohtak and some *manjha* Sikh colonies on the southern banks of the Sutlej to his list of conquests. During his last invasion of Hindustan, Ahmad Shah Abdali made him the military commander of Sirhind and bestowed on him the title of 'Maharajah'. The services of Sahib Singh, Umer Singh's successor, to Ochterlony, during his Nepal campaign in 1814, made him a favourite of the British, and the following year, the British used their good offices to procure the title of 'Maharajah' from the 'puppet king' Akbar Shah II of Delhi.[20] The Jind Raj owed its rise to prominence to the bounty of Ranjit Singh, who helped his cousin Bhag Singh acquire Ludhiana, Morinda, Bussein and Jandiala. But in

1809 Bhag Singh responded to Metcalfe's call for an alliance to save himself from subservience to his mighty cousin. The British added Khurkhowda, Bursat, and Boana to his possessions, and his son Futteh Singh was given a further accretion of territory in Moodkee, Phugwarah and Talwandi. The death of Futteh Singh's successor without an heir in 1834 would have ended in the lapse of Jind to the British, but the British thought it more politic to confer this kingdom on Sarup Singh, a scion of the Phulkean *misl*, who had put in his claim.[21] The Nabha sardar was recognised as a Rajah on the recommendations of Ochterlony in 1810. Deo Inder Singh, who was on the *gadi* in 1845, lent his support to the Khalsa sardars, inviting the wrath of the British, but his son, Bherpoor Singh, was restored to power on his death.[22] Thus the cis-Sutlej states were established.

While elsewhere in India the East India Company was adding to its possessions by pushing through subsidiary alliances or insisting on the principle of lapse upon the failure of heirs, in these Sikh states at least, it was not possible to accuse them of 'grasping propensities'.[23] Even if there was a failure in succession, the *gadi* was offered to distant kinsmen, as in the case of Raja Sarup Singh of Jind, and even recusant rajas were given a reprieve, as in the case of Nabha in 1846. The continued existence of these petty states with conflicting interests served as a breakwater against the much more formidable Sikh Raj across the Sutlej and also to weaken the force of nascent Sikh nationalism. This was important, as the British were well aware that 'if there be any feeling of nationality in India whatever, it may be most fairly looked for among the Sikhs'.[24] The surge of Sikh nationalism under Banda Bahadur was not far from memory, and the strength of Ranjit Singh's political will was a living danger beyond the Sutlej. The British, therefore, decided to maintain a strict policy of discreet restraint with regard to their allies of 1809.

The wisdom of British policy was borne out during the crisis of 1857, when the petty Sikh rajas mobilised the entire resources of their country to help the smooth flow of military traffic from the Punjab to Delhi. The roads were kept safe, carriage and provisions were taken care of. A small contingent of 500 horse and foot, under the command of Sardar Pratab Singh, was even sent by the Maharaja of Patiala to assist in the assault on Delhi. It was with the forces from these states that order could be maintained at Delhi, Karnal, Thanesur and Ambala, and anti-British forces were kept at bay in Sirsa, Rohtak and Hissar. A detachment with General Van Cortlandt was actually employed in Saharanpur and Jagadhri, and the rising of the 10th Cavalry at Ferozepur was put down with the help of this detachment.[25]

Far more significant than the Maharaja of Patiala's military involvement was the moral impact of his interventions on behalf of the British. The British were at this time at pains to establish their non-partisan, secular credentials before the people of India and to counter the rumour that plans were afoot to take away the caste of Indian people by forcing sepoys to bite rifle cartridges lubricated with cow and pig fat. Henry Lawrence employed all his eloquence in his address to the soldiers on the lawns of Lucknow Residency on 12 May 1857. To emphasise the non-partisan attitude of the British compared to the bigotry of earlier regimes:

> Alumgeer in former times and Hyder Ali in later days forcibly converted thousands and thousands of Hindoos, desecrated their fanes, demolished their temples and carried ruthless devastation among the household gods. Come to our times. Many here present well know that Runjeet Singh never permitted his Mahomedan subjects to call the pious to prayer—never allowed the muezzin to sound from the lofty minarets which adorn Lahore and remain to this day a monument of their magnificent founders. The year before last a Hindoo could not have dared to build a temple in Lucknow.[26]

The espousal of the British cause by the Maharaja of Patiala served to undermine, at least in the Punjab, the rumours about greased cartridges, about the mixing of the powder of cow bones with flour and such other 'subtle designs to destroy their caste'. 'The Maharaja was an orthodox Hindoo, whose position and career alike commanded respect', wrote Lepel Griffin, and '[h]is support at such a crisis was worth a brigade of English troops to us, and served more to tranquilise the people than a hundred official disclaimers would have done.'[27]

Khazan Singh's composition was intended as a loyalist tract focusing on the Maharaja Narinder Singh's service to the British Raj in the fateful year of 1857, as is obvious from the careful preservation of the manuscript in the palace library of the Patiala Raj. He does not hide his disapproval of the acts of the native troops by characterising them as *kaliyan* or 'blackies' after the fashion of the British. And yet his straightforward narration of the facts provides clues as to the contemporary consciousness, and thereby deviates from his initial purpose of eulogising Maharaja Narinder Singh's role in the recovery of Delhi for the British. Thus, there is a clear divergence between the immediate narration and its ultimate implications, making Khazan Singh's narrative 'a text that is no longer a finished corpus of writing, but a differential network, a fabric of traces referring to something other than itself'.[28]

It is not uncommon for texts to branch out from their original starting point into different kinds of narration and the boundaries between history, philosophy, critical reason and poetry can become blurred. Thus, we come to learn from Khazan Singh that whatever the political calculations behind his master Narinder Singh's strict support for the British might have been, the common people of Punjab were well aware of the justness of the uprising. The ethnic make-up of the south-eastern districts of Punjab, lying between the Sutlej and the Jumna, was not so very different from the country lying further east, and the culture and beliefs of the people of this region straddled across the Jumna to the regions beyond.[29] Thus, apprehensions about a threat from Christianity were not incomprehensible to men such as Khazan Singh.

The Church Missionary Society had been active in northern India for a long time, with 1,263 missionaries and teachers in their retinue. Their crowning success was the conversion of the deposed heir of the late Maharaja Ranjit Singh in March 1853. Lord Dalhousie had, of course, made sure from his guardian John Login 'that no improper influence had been, in their estimation made use of to make him change his belief in the religion of his people'.[30] But the accomplishment of this object ensured that the Sikh people were deprived of the probability of an upsurge in Sikh nationalism centring on the last legitimate heir of the Great Maharaja Ranjit Singh, whose name still worked wonders in the Sikh mind.

The introduction of *pahul* and *Guru ka langar* (the Sikh rite of Baptism, which involved a sharing of water, and communal dining at the gurdwara) must have eliminated all prejudice about commensality from among the adherents of Sikhism. They could well understand that what was at stake was more than a few inscrutable rituals. *Dharm* (faith) in this context meant an entire way of life and culture—the freedom to pursue one's ancestral practice and to stick to the traditional mores of the country. Hence, Khazan Singh's 'Gadar di var' (Verses of War) could not avoid making a reference to this threat of the invasion of Christianity while trying to contextualise Maharaja Narinder Singh's role in the war of Delhi.

Nandan company sahib salahi kiti
Eka mai da panth chalayiye ji
Pahila apni fauj kastan karke
Man bhanv de amal kamayiye ji
Musalman, Hindu, Gore ik piyale
Khana tina nu baith khilayiye ji
Kavi Singh akhe Hindustan andar
Dohan dhiran da dharam pratiaye ji …
Eka bhai da panth chalabhna hai
Jahar kholke akh sunayiyu yi
Kabi Singha akhe raj kardiya nu
Mar hauni na akal bhulaiyu yi …
dharam dohan do din da khovne nu
kartus kalattayun aiyu yi
sanu saddake lat ne hukm ditan
Chahe tusan kailo katvaiyu yi (p. 9)[31]

The spectre of loss of caste through contact with the offensive cartridges had been haunting the army recruits from Calcutta to Peshawar for quite some time, and secret associations or panchayats had been formed to deal with the threat. The matter came to the notice of the authorities as early as March in Ambala cantonment, where training was being conducted in the Depot for Instruction in Musketry. Two trainees in this depot, one Kasee Ram Tewaree, a *hawaldar*, and Jeeolall Doobe, a *naik*, reported on 19 March to E.M. Martineau, the instructor, that the *subedar* of their original corps (the 36th Native Infantry) who had been visiting Ambala as an escort of General Anson, the commander-in-chief, had jeered at them for having become Christians and had refused to touch their lota (water pot) and hookah (smoking pipe). 'The rumour has been industriously propagated (how it first originated no native knows) that the rifle cartridges were purposely smeared with the mixture of cows' and pigs' fat, with the express object of destroying caste', wrote E.M. Martineau to Captain S. Becher, the Assistant Adjutant General, on 20 March; 'in fact, the weapon itself is nothing more nor less than a Government missionary to convert the whole army to Christianity.'[32]

The revolt had not yet taken place. But the sepoys let their resentment be known through frequent outbreaks of fire in buildings connected with the musketry depot. On 17 April the sepoys were forced to use the cartridges and, the same night, some ₹30,000 worth of government property caught fire. A personal address from the commander-in-chief was not enough to allay the suspicions of army personnel, and orders to use the cartridges continued to foster disaffection. In a report of 23 March 1857, Martineau blamed the innate anxiety of the natives for the mischief: 'The Asiatic mind is periodically prone to fits of religious panic; their imagination runs riot on preconceived views, and often the more absurd they are, the more tenaciously do they cling to them.'[33] But he also knew that once the belief had taken root, it would be difficult to oppose it. It had already spread to the recruits' homes and villages, and the possibility of becoming an outcaste was too great a risk for most sepoys to take. The cartridge had, thus, posed a great challenge to the troops, pitting loyalty to the army against their beliefs, society, families and homes.

Martineau, however, had had an inkling that the cartridge should be regarded 'more as the medium than the original cause of this widespread feeling of distrust that is spreading dissatisfaction to our rule'.[34] The greased cartridges concealed more fundamental grievances against British rule, not only among the sepoys but in the villages where sepoys were recruited. As the most articulate and effective section of the Indian populace and having been persuaded that 'their loyalty was of supreme importance to the government who held dominion in India on their sufferance alone',[35] they were best placed to raise their voice against foreign domination. The greased cartridges had provided an opportunity—a rallying cry, 'serving for Hindus and Mahomedans alike'.[36] The pressure of foreign oppression had given birth to a new consciousness of a 'political community couched in terms of two combined religions'.[37] However, as the sepoys had no conception of an alternative political order, they merely replaced the rule of the 'Company Bahadur' with that of the Mughal Badshah, although the levers of control were exercised by the sepoy council, and an attempt was made to impose *Hukum-i-sipah*[38] (sepoy rule) in an inversion of the old order. While the projection of the Mughal Badshah at the forefront made the movement appear a 'traditional resistance movement',[39] as Eric Stokes would characterise it, Rajat Ray has emphasised the novelty of this development, describing it as a 'movement unrecognisable to tradition',[40] given the extent of control exercised by the sepoys over the Mughal Badshah. Even the simple pen of Khazan Singh did not fail to notice this unusual state of affairs:

> Sari desh ne baith salah karke
> Badshah ne takht bithaiyu yi
> Badshahan de vakht da hukm sara
> Dilli sahir da vich chalaiyu yi
> Asin karange mulkh abad tera
> Badshah nu akh sunaiyu yi
> Honi hon na deyi Khazan Singh
> Jeda kaliyan sata sataiyu yi (p. 11)[41]

Khazan Singh's enthusiasm could not be contained when it came to the question of war for the sake of one's religion, *Khatar dharam di*, and it is difficult to believe here that he was representing the royal court of the state of Patiala, which had gone out of its way to help restore British rule in Delhi. Although the logic of the situation would have demanded an economy of words in talking about sepoy intentions, Khazan Singh could not disguise his sympathy for the 'war for religion' and his language became quite effusive while dwelling on this aspect of events:

> Khatar dharam di fauj ne shor payiya
> Asi karange jang lalkar ke ji
> Dharm jo hi na cheez hai har koi
> Tusi dekh le bat vichar ke ji
> Sonu naukri di nahi laur koi
> Asin marange usnu marke ji
> Dharam chhroriyan jinhan Khazan Singha ...
> Gaye es jahan te harke ji
> Dharam rakhna kam hai suriyan da
> Es dharam de bharne jayiye ji
> Koi divas da jivna jagat ute
> Ki waste dharam gavayiye ji
> Dharam apne bhul na horu koi ...
> Dhari dharam nu vist mai jayiye ji
> Kavi Singha je hor na vas chale
> Dharam karne sis gavayiye ji. (p. 11)[42]

Khazan Singh could not have shown a greater awareness of the general mood, Indian culture and the Indian way of life had he been writing from within the sepoy camp. The emotions contained in the language of this peasant-poet were those of a true patriot asserting the identity of the people of the entire subcontinent from Peshawar to Calcutta. Khazan Singh speaks of the Indian mythological hero, the Raja Dadhichi, who had given up his life so the Gods could use his bones to make weapons with which to fight the demons; he mentions Raja Harishchandra, who left his kingdom with his loyal wife and children just to keep his word; he is eloquent in his praise of Bhartrihari, the King who gave up all his riches in pursuit of the ultimate truth; he reminds his countrymen of Bhai Taru Singh who preferred death with honour to renouncing his religion; and above all, he focuses on the unparalleled sacrifice of Guru Tegh Bahadur who thought it more important to defend the faith of his countrymen rather than protect his own life.[43] Khazan Singh thereby establishes a close affinity with the general sympathies of the inhabitants of India: the Brahmins of Kashmir, whose *janau* (sacred thread displaying their Hindu Bramhin identity) Guru Tegh Bahadur had defended at the cost of his life, down to Raja Harishchandra and Raja Bhartrihari who hailed from central India. Khazan Singh's linking of these different episodes from Indian history and mythology shows his awareness of the common origins and shared cultural identity of the subcontinent. Furthermore, Khazan Singh was clear about the duty of his countrymen in this national war and his pen did not hesitate to describe it:

Asi marange teg di tab age
Jang karange morche laike ji
Asi bhajjake kite na javna hai
Tainu Farange sindh tapaike ji.(p. 12)[44]

In the struggles in defence of the country and its religion, Punjab had always taken the leading role. Lying to the extreme north-west, it had invariably experienced the main brunt of foreign onslaughts. And yet, when it came to the question of throwing the *firangis* (the foreigners) out into the sea, why did Punjab lag behind? Why did this region, which witnessed the selfless martyrdom of Bhai Taru or Guru Tegh Bahadur, suddenly appear to sound a discordant note with the anti-foreign uprising? Khazan Singh's allegories and metaphors ultimately attempt to provide an explanation, and labyrinthian twists of logic lead to several reasons as to why the Sikhs rejected the Hindustanis, or, as Khazan Singh referred to them, the 'blackies' (*kaliyan*).

The first explanation, as previously mentioned, lies in the conduct of the Hindustanis themselves during the conquest of Punjab by the British. Punjab would never have tasted defeat if the British had not secured the assistance of Hindustani soldiers in subjugating the province. When the *Gadar* of 1857 started, strategic outposts of Punjab were still being held by Hindustani recruits of the Bengal army. The Sikhs were understandably slow to react to the call for action from the members of this army of occupation, albeit in another part of the country.

Unhan dina nu tusin bisar baithe
Jande jang Lahor de nal kita
Fauj dhaubi ke jang nu kaliyan di
Tusa mar Panjab nu ranj kita
Kavi Singha akhe unhan kaliyan nu
Tusan ant nu ehu inam dita
Asan jitian des Parozpur da
Ludhiana de chhauni paiye ji
Sabhe rajiya ne mulakat kita
Sathe kaliyan the kaunf khaike ji
Sabhi fauj de zor Lahor mari
Jang vich maidan machaike ji
Sare desh de vich malum hoyi
Liya Singha te raj chhuraike ji
Jaibu walia nu taden chhoriyan si
Jande ayi mile age dhaite ji
Asi mar Multan nu ranj kita
Thana vich Pashaur bithayiye ji
Jinhan Singha de jor tun tapda hai
Sathen naththa gaye kaunf khaike ji
Yehe jehi tun fauj gahavana haihese
Hathi apni ilm sikhaike ji. (p. 14)[45]

The British were aware of these Punjabi grievances and, adept at the game of *divide et impera*, they were not slow to rub salt into these wounds and discourage the entry of Punjab into the general combination against the company's rule.

The greatest strength of the British was the subsidiary alliances with the Indian princes. The stationing of British troops in these kingdoms made palace revolutions impossible and perpetuated an enfeebled form of government by the princes. The huge cost of maintaining European troops put a heavy burden on the exchequer and compelled the subsidiary ally to impose ever-increasing demands for revenue. The people of these states were, therefore, often ripe for rebellion. This had been the case in Gwalior, where the people rose in spontaneous revolt while the Sindhia ruler sought refuge with the British.[46] In Punjab, things went a different way, probably because of the success of the administrators in maintaining the rift between the Hindustanis and the Sikhs.

The masterstroke of the British was the timely employment of Sikhs in the British army. This immediately provided a release for the pent-up energy of the able-bodied Sikh youth who had been left largely underemployed in the overcrowded agricultural plots of the *manjha* districts since the disarmament of the Khalsa army in 1849–1850. The return of the Khalsa army to their village homes not only imposed a heavy burden on the minutely divided agricultural holdings in the central Punjab districts, it also stopped additional sources of capital investments arising from military earnings and war booty. Deprived of this long-standing avenue of employment, the Punjab villages could easily have become potential sources of sedition. Khazan Singh's pen provides a lively picture of the impact on the countryside resulting from this decision of the Chief Commissioner Sir John Lawrence to recruit in the villages:

Eho jehi jan jang di khabar hoyi
Lat vich Lahor lachar hoiya
Majhe desh de rakhne naukran
Dilli jang de waste tiar hoiya
Maharaj de wakht di talab kiti
Sor pind te sahar bazar hoiya....
Kavi Singh dekhe tej goriya da
Kaththa auke kai hazar hoiya
Singh saheb de wakht de naukar di
Majhe desh de vich talas hoi
Talab pandra di use wakht leve
Jerha javanda lat de pas koi
Jithan jam ke na kade kamm kita
Bhane tina de band khalas hoi
Kavi Singh akhe fauj goriyan di
Jang Dilli de Kalam taras hoi (p. 15)[47]

The prospect of military recruitment with the British and the return of prosperity to the villages took the wind out of the sails of sedition for quite some time. Having been offered a renewed chance to retrieve their lost fortunes, the large body of valiant warriors was only too grateful to avoid the horrors of silent extinction. But the lure of plundering Delhi appears too selfish an explanation for the motivation of a people who had been heirs to the tradition of Bhai Taru Singh or Guru Tegh Bahadur. Khazan Singh, therefore, had to attribute the isolation of the 'blackies' to the workings of destiny (*honi*). At this point he introduces the reader to the story of the martyrdom of Guru Tegh Bahadur who had visited the court of the Mughal Emperor Aurangzeb following the entreaties of the Brahmins to save them from the Emperor's forcible attempts at conversion (*dharam rakhne waste Hinduan da*). He reminds his readers of Tegh Bahadur's curse on the Emperor Aurangzeb—*singha nal mel karke tere sahar nu an turavanige* (the Sikhs will come and despoil your city). This teleological explanation resolves Khazan Singh's problem of explaining Sikh collusion with the British during the Rebellion of 1857, and in one couplet Khazan Singh is able to provide the solution to this otherwise puzzling question of history:

Ese waste rajiya mukh mode
Sare mulkh ne ghatia an ghara...
Sare mulkh di mat parer hoyi
Kita sant-saraf ne an phera (p. 16)[48]

It is not known exactly when the story of the Guru Tegh Bahadur's prophecy gained currency. Khazan Singh's poetic composition was dated on the second day of Jeth, sammat (Vikrama Era) 1915, corresponding to AD 1858. It is not certain whether the story had existed earlier or if it was a later concoction to justify or explain away Sikh opposition to the uprising against the British. But the fact that such a story had to be invented points to the deep sympathy running amongst all sections of society for the cause of the insurgents. Poets cannot flourish without royal patronage and Khazan Singh seems to have been no exception. His literary efforts must have received the encouragement of Maharaja Narinder Singh, the hero of the war of Delhi. The eulogistic and loyalist content of the writing undoubtedly explains the careful preservation of the manuscript in the palace library. And yet Khazan Singh is unable to mask his remorse at the defeat of the 'blackies' (kaliyan), his own dark-skinned countrymen. The instrumentality of the Singhas (Sikhs or lions) in bringing this about is attributed to a predetermined plot of destiny or honi. He rambles on about the role of 'destiny' with the inevitability of a Greek tragedy. The Tegh Bahadur prophecy about the ravage of Delhi is hypostatised as a nemesis resulting from Aurangzeb's injustice to the Sikh Guru. What is at issue here is not the truth of the prophecy, but the use that has been made of it, bearing out Ludwig Wittgenstein's famous dictum: 'Do not ask for the meaning, look at the use.'[49] Hair-splitting debates about the objective truth or otherwise of this adage are redundant here as there is always a difference between cognitive truth and poetic truth. The latter does not rely on an eye witness testimony, but is intertwined with emotional convictions which enjoy much greater acceptability than any 'verification-transcendent'[50] truth. The truth of the prophecy does not lie in the triumphant avenging of the death of the Guru, the purpose of the prophecy is to explain the mésalliance of the Sikhs in a national uprising against the firangi, otherwise fit to be thrown across the sea.

Notes and References

1. Christopher Norris, preface to *The Deconstructive Turn: Essays in the Rhetoric of Philosophy* (London: Methuen, 1983).
2. Michel Foucault, 'What Is an Author?', in Donald F. Bouchard, ed., *Language, Counter-Memory, Practice: Selected Essays and Interviews*, translated from the French by Donald F. Bouchard and Sherry Simons (Oxford: Basil Blackwell, 1977).
3. Ibid., p. 116.
4. Ganda Singh, *The British Occupation of the Punjab* (Patiala: Sikh History Society, 1955); John Malcolm Ludlow, *British India: Its Races and Its History* (London: Macmillan, 1858), pp. 142–146.
5. Kirpal Singh and M.L. Ahluwalia, *The Punjab's Pioneer Freedom Fighters* (New Delhi: Orient Longman, 1963).

6. The theme of how the panchayats of the Khalsa army anticipated the later organisation of sepoy councils of action during the Uprising of 1857, and the reason why the Sikh Revolt of 1845–1846 and 1848–1849 should be regarded as the first spontaneous uprising of the people of India, foreshadowing the Uprising of 1857 and spreading over a wider territory, deserves to be treated in a separate publication on which I am presently working.

7. For the concept of a Hindustani 'heartland', see Gyanesh Kudasiya, *Nation and 'Heartland': Uttar Pradesh in India's Body Politic* (New Delhi: SAGE, 2006).

8. Ranajit Guha, *Elementary Aspects of Peasant Insurgency in Colonial India* (New Delhi: Oxford University Press, 1983), pp. 278–332.

9. Translation:

> On the fifth day of the month of June in the year fourteen
> The letter had come to Patiala
> The orders became known in the area
> All the magazines had been appropriated
> Maharaj Narendra Singh had marched
> To the outpost at Thanesur
> Kavi Singh says that he took all his forces with him
> And raised a hue and cry in various places....
>
> Maharaj Narendra Singh himself rode to Kila Kot
> To look after the arrangements himself
> The entire city came to look after the fort of Kot
> As everyone knows that without forts and cannons thrones cannot be kept.

10. R. Bosworth Smith *Life of Lord Lawrence*, vol. 1 (London: Smith, Elder & Co., 1883).

11. Lepel Griffin, *The Rajas of the Punjab: The History of the Principal States in the Punjab and their Political Relations with the British Government* (1870; repr., Patiala: Languages Department, 1970). Ranjit Singh robbed the Musalman Rajputs of Rajkot to reward his allies. The widow of Rai Aliyas Khan was deprived of Ludhiana, Jhandala, Kot, Jagraon and Basia, including fifty-four villages of an annual rent of ₹23,260. In 1807 Ranjit Singh came once again on the invitation of the monarchs of Nabha, Patiala, and Jind to settle their differences. Rani Aus Kaur of Patiala was presented with an estate of ₹50,000 when she presented Ranjit with a brass gun 'Khuri Khan' along with money and diamonds. This was followed by the conferment of Wadni on Sada Kour, Ranjit Singh's mother-in-law. Wadni had been conquered by Diwan Mokham Chand in 1808.

12. Ibid.

13. According to one interpretation, the word *misl* was derived from the Arabic word *musluhat* which means armed men or warlike people. *Misl* also meant equal in Arabic. The word was also used in another sense to signify people ranked serially. Together, they would mean armed bands where all members were treated alike. See Reverend J. Cave-Browne, Appendix of *The Punjab and Delhi in 1857: Being a Narrative of the Measures by which the Punjab Was Saved and Delhi Recovered during the Mutiny* (London: William Blackwood and Sons, 1861).

14. Sir Henry Lawrence, 'The Seikhs and Their Country', in *Selections from Calcutta Review*, vol. II, (October 1844), p. 154.

15. Chetan Singh, *Region and Empire: Panjab in the Seventeenth Century* (New Delhi: Oxford University Press, 1991), pp. 258–270.

16. Cave-Browne, *The Punjab and Delhi in 1857*, p. 369.

17. Griffin, *The Rajas of the Punjab*.

18. Lawrence, 'The Seikhs and Their Country'.

19. Kirpal Singh, *Baba Ala Singh* (Amritsar: Guru Nanak Dev University, 2006).

20. Cave-Browne, *The Punjab and Delhi in 1857*, p. 371.

21. Ibid.

22. Ibid.

23. Lawrence, 'The Seikhs and Their Country', p. 195.

24. Griffin, *The Rajas of the Punjab*, Preface, p. ix.

25. Griffin, *The Rajas of the Punjab*, pp. 213–214; Cave-Browne, *The Punjab and Delhi in 1857*, p. 221.

26. Cave-Browne, *The Punjab and Delhi in 1857*, pp. 32–33.

27. L. Griffin, *The Rajas of the Punjab*, p. 214.

28. Jacques Derrida, 'Living on: Border Lines', in *Deconstruction and Criticism* (New York: Seaburg Press, 1979), pp. 83–84, quoted in David Carroll, 'Institutional Authority vs. Critical Power, or the Uneasy Relations of Psychoanalysis and Literature', in Joseph H. Smith and William Kerrigan, eds, *Taking Chances: Derrida, Psychoanalysis and Literature* (Baltimore: John Hopkins University Press, 1984), pp. 107–134.

29. Robert Needham Cust, *Linguistic and Oriental Essays. Written from the Year 1846–1878* (London: Trübner & Co., 1880).

30. E. Dalhousie Login, *Lady Login's Recollections: Court and Camp Life 1820–1904*, (London: Smith, Elder, 1916), p. 31.

31. Translation:

> The sahibs of London Company had decided
> That they would have only one religion
> First they turned their own army into Christians
> Then they had a fine idea
> They thought they would make Muslims, Hindus and Europeans
> All drink from one cup sitting close together
> The poet Singh would tell you what was happening in Hindustan
> How the religion of both the major sects became threatened...
> There should be only one religion
> I am telling you the story very openly
> The poet says that having come to rule
> They tried to carry out their wishes forcibly...
>
> For destroying the religion of both
> The cartridges had come from Calcutta
> The orders were made known to everyone
> The blackies had to bite the cartridges.

32. Cave-Browne, vol. i, pp. 41–42.

33. Ibid. pp. 45–46.

34. Ibid.

35. Login, *Lady Login's Recollections*, p. 14.

36. Ibid.

37. Rajat Kanta Ray, *The Felt Community: Commonality and Mentality before the Emergence of Indian Nationalism* (New Delhi: Oxford University Press, 2003), p. 358.

38. Ibid. p. 421.

39. Eric Stokes, *The Peasant and the Raj: Studies in Agrarian Society and Peasant Rebellion in Colonial India* (Cambridge: Cambridge University Press, 1978), p. 120.

40. Ray, *The Felt Community*, p. 359.

41. Translation:

> The entire country sat together and conferred
> They put the Mughal Emperor on the throne
> They enforced the rule of the Emperor
> In the entire city of Delhi

'We will make your reign prosperous'
Thus they spoke to the Badshah
But Khazan Singh says that fortune did not allow it to happen
What the blackies had decided upon.

42. Translation:

They created trouble for the sake of their religion
We will challenge the orders and go to war
There is no such thing as a person's religion
You can easily see it for yourself
We don't have any use for such a job
We would rather kill them and die ourselves
Khazan Singh says that those who did not care about religion
They always left this world with repentance
It is the duty of the Gods to keep up religion
Try not to lose your religion sir
How many days are we to live in this world?
Why should we lose our religion
One's religion is the most valuable thing
You can go to heaven if you are loyal to your religion
Kavi Singh says that one should go to the extent
Of giving up one's head for the sake of religion.

43.   *Dharam rakhiya si Hari Chand raje*
        Gallan vich jahan de tauriyan ni
        Dharam rakhiya si Taru Singh dekho
        Khalan puthiya lar nachoriyan ni
        Dharam rakhiya dekho dadhich raje
        Sura chadiyan ang na maudiyan ni...
        [The King Harishchandra had kept up his religion
        He did not break his promise
        Look how Taru Singh kept up his religion
        Tearing his skin and wringing out his blood
        The King Dadhichi had for the sake of religion
        Given up his body for the use of the Gods]
        Also see, Dr Trilochan Singh, *Guru Tegh Bahadur: Prophet and Martyr (A Biography)* (New Delhi:
        Gurdwara Prabandhak Committee, Sis Ganj, Chandni Chowk, 1967).

44. Translation:

We would die fighting with swords and weapons
We would combine with each other and fight
We won't go away anywhere
We would drive them out to the sea.

45. Translation:

You have forgotten all those days
When you had fought the war in Lahore
Armies composed of blackies
Had come and beaten Punjab red with blood
You had won the battle of Ferozepur
And had encamped in Ludhiana
All the kings had conferred together

> Having been sadly beaten by the blackies
> The entire forces had overran Lahore
> The war was going on in full force
> In the entire country it became known
> That the rule of the Singhs had fallen
> The forces from Jammu had come
> As they received the orders
> Multan was beaten red with blood
> In Peshawar they established their camps
> The Sikhs who were overrun
> Were forced to flee with heaviness in their hearts
> These are the forces you had defeated
> And you taught them a lesson with your own hands

46. Karl Marx, 'Chronological Excerpts on East India in the Years 1854–1858' (Photostat copy in the Institute for Marxism Leninism, Berlin) 'Scindia Loyal to the "English Dogs" Nicht so his "Troopers"; Rajah of Patiala for Shame— Sends Large Bodies of Soldiers in Aid of the English.' in P.C. Joshi, '1857 in Our History', in P.C. Joshi, ed., *Rebellion:1857* (New Delhi: National Book Trust: 2007), p.189.

47. Translation:

> When such was the news of the war
> John, the Lord of Lahore became desperate
> He decided to recruit people from the *manjha*
> He started preparing them for the war in Delhi
> The forces of the time of the Maharaja were called
> The cry was raised in the villages, towns and cities
> Kavi Singh says look at the strength of the white people
> They brought together thousands of men
> The fighters of the days of Ranjit Singh
> Were looked for in the middle country
> They would immediately get a salary of Ruppees fifteen
> Whoever goes to the commander
> Those who had never fought in their life
> Even they came out of the enclosures
> Kavi Singh says that the forces of the white people
> Were being recruited for the war in Delhi

48. Translation:

> That is why the kings are turning away their faces
> In the whole country the time has come …
> The whole country will have to suffer for it
> The curse will now be realised.

49. Ludwig Wittgenstein, *Philosophical Investigations*, trans. G.E.M. Anscombe (Oxford: Blackwell, 1958).

50. Christopher Norris, preface to *Truth Matters: Realism, Anti-realism and Response-dependence* (Edinburgh: Edinburgh University Press, 2002).

9

❧❧

SITUATING THE ROLE OF RELIGION IN THE REBELLION
The Case of the Prayagwals in the Allahabad Uprising

Kama Maclean

THE role that religion played in firing the vehemence of the rebellion which ignited key regions in north India in the summer of 1857, and burned for a year afterwards, has long been debated. Largely unheeded voices of caution in the years leading up to 1857 frequently referred to religious grievances and transgressions on the religious lives of Indians by the East India Company. Accounts written by Europeans in the heat of the conflict frequently cited religious motives, as did rebel proclamations. The mutiny chronicler, Sir John Kaye, counted offences committed by proselytising missionaries as being an important catalyst for the outbreak. However, later scholarship tended to eschew religious grievances, attributing the rebellion to a range of non-religious grievances of groups as diverse as traditional elites and peasant castes, over issues from company maladministration to disputes over land tenure, being held as important factors. The prevalence of Marxism in the analysis of Indian history meant that, too often, religious forces tend to be reduced to the political and economic.[1] This was compounded by scholarly concerns with orientalism in Western readings of the past, which made scholars even more cautious of emphasising the role of religion in the non-Western world. In addition to this, the prevalence of secularisation theory—the presumption that with the march of modernity, religion would lose its relevance—has also encouraged a certain level of religious illiteracy, and a failure to adequately recognise 'the profound role that religion plays in human social, cultural, and political life in both contemporary and historical contexts'.[2]

The trend towards de-emphasising religion in the rebellion somewhat abruptly reversed recently, with William Dalrymple's account, *The Last Mughal*, which focused predominantly on events in the Mughal capital of Delhi. Drawing on largely untapped documents, Dalrymple emphasises rebel discourses on the defence of dharma (righteousness, but also translatable as religion), kafirs (infidels), *nasrani* (Christians) and jihad (religious struggle) in his analysis. 'In the aftermath of 9/11 and 7/7, they are phrases we understand all too well, and words like jihad scream out from the dusty pages of the source manuscripts, demanding attention.'[3] Explicitly alluding to jihadi forces and recent terrorist attacks in the attempt to explain the events of 1857 may resonate with readers faced with media coverage of a 'clash of civilisations' (and we might take issue with the contention that these contemporary forces are well understood), but this recourse to presentism is not particularly helpful. Nor does it adequately account for the ongoing opposition to colonial rule which was represented by several uprisings and rebellions, among which the Great Indian Mutiny is the best example.[4]

The role of religion as an agent in history always sat uncomfortably in historiography. The Western tradition of post-Enlightenment rationalism, itself a reaction against undue influence accorded to religious agency, has informed a school of history-writing which is sceptical of arguments that situate 'religion' at their centre. At one level, religion's capacity to act in history has always been conceded; generally, it is simply shorthand for acknowledging that religious bodies and institutions can be influential players in the making of the past. Being able to control and deploy 'the sacred' brings with it undeniable advantage, particularly where religion finds itself in alliance with (or in popular resistance to) the state. As arbiters of moral and social conduct, religious bodies are frequently established in an enviable position of power and able to deploy incredible resources to influence history; recognising and detailing this aspect of religious power is one of the tasks of Religious History. Another manifestation of religion in history, and the one most often challenged by the Marxist tradition in particular, is the supposition that when agents *claim* they are acting in the cause of their religion, this is in fact a guise, and what really underpins their actions are material interests.[5] As such, the claim that religion is a motivating factor is seen as a regrettable 'false consciousness', or even as deliberately disingenuous, and rational analysts have therefore been able to dismiss the grievance as misplaced.[6] How, after all, are we to establish verity in such a situation, given that material evidence of religious agency is difficult to furnish within the framework of conventional historiography? The very claim that one had been moved by a religious motive could be seen as evidence of irrationalism, and therefore in itself, a justification for the Raj.

Below, I contribute to the ongoing attempt to position religion within the rebellion by focusing on the role of religious actors, Prayagwals, in the rebellion in Allahabad. An examination of the roles played by Prayagwals confirms several existing, if dated, theories on the rebellion, including the argument that elites sought to protect their economic interests by rebelling against the British, and that concerns of 'religion in danger' were also central to the concerns of rebels. Indeed, in the case of the Prayagwals, the two were deeply intertwined and inseparable—pilgrimage was their livelihood. In addition to this, I look at ways in which Prayagwals, as religious elites, played an important role in spreading dissent and advancing their grievances, which, following Chris Bayly's work on the 'information order' that prevailed in the subcontinent, further emphasises the role of pilgrimage networks as active communication hubs in a modernising society. Finally, I draw attention to the immediate post-mutiny era, as the political landscape of north India was redrawn, and the rhetorical role that 'religion' took in shaping the post-rebellion polity.

Allahabad is frequently characterised as a sacred centre, revered by Hindus as 'Tirtharaj Prayag' (Prayag: the king of all pilgrimage places) for its famed melas or festivals held at the *triveni sangam* (the confluence of three rivers: the Ganga, Yamuna and the mythical Saraswati), but Allahabad is much more besides. A former Mughal capital, where Akbar had established a fort at the confluence of the holy rivers, in 1857 Allahabad was also home to the remnants of Mughal culture, evidenced by shrines such as Khusru Bagh, active Sufi groups, madrasas and a Muslim literati that nurtured the likes of the poet Akbar Allahabadi (1846–1921). It was the riverine fort, however, and the town's strategic location, which attracted the East India Company (EIC) in the late seventeenth century. In 1801, Allahabad was ceded to the British, and by 1860 it was a major administrative hub of the North-western Provinces (NWP); the site of a legal college and later university, and the high court. Allahabad's pivotal role in crushing the rebellion in the region—it proved itself to be one of the most defensible positions in the Doab—expedited the town's growth as a cosmopolitan centre, as it became capital of the province in 1858. These were developments that Prayagwals had resisted for some time.

Who Are the Prayagwals?

Prayagwals are the caste of Brahmin priests, or *panda*s, that service pilgrims visiting Allahabad; their primary function is to guide pilgrims through the rituals associated with a visit to the holy city of Prayag.[7] Prayagwals attest that their exclusive right to minister to pilgrims was given to them by the Emperor Akbar, who made Allahabad his capital and began construction of the fort at the sangam in 1574. Oral histories claim that when Akbar's attempts to sink foundations into the sands of the sangam for the new fort repeatedly failed, a seer advised the emperor that construction could not proceed without a human sacrifice.[8] A local Brahmin offered himself as a sacrifice, in return for the granting of exclusive perpetual rights to his descendants to minister to pilgrims at the sangam. Akbar is said to have granted this to the Brahmin's descendants, the Prayagwals; the sacrifice was made, and the fort was built without further complication. As a caste, Prayagwals are related to other priestly jatis, broadly known as *tirthapurohits*, who perform similar services at holy places, such as the Gayawals of Gaya, the

Chaubes of Mathura and the Gangaputras of Varanasi. The Prayagwals occupy a somewhat marginal status within the Brahmin community, ostensibly because they accept money and gifts for performing religious duties for pilgrims in the holy city of Prayag, contravening a directive in the *Matsya Purana* that a Brahmin should 'avoid, as far as possible, the accepting of any gift at sacred places'.[9]

In the early nineteenth century, the Prayagwals had a somewhat tighter control over the pilgrimage industry in Allahabad than they do today, where the massive scale of festivals such as the Kumbh Mela demands strict government control. Robert Minturn, a traveller who visited Allahabad just before the 1857 rebellion, declared with an air of dissatisfaction that the Prayagwals had 'entire control of the bathing ghat', including over other service providers, such as barbers, who performed *mundan* (tonsure) for pilgrims.[10] Minturn's observation, however, was the cursory one of a tourist. Prayagwals had in fact been forced to considerably alter and adapt their modes of work in the previous decades, to accommodate the broader social and economic developments associated with the consolidation of the power of the company in the NWP (modern Uttar Pradesh). Prior to the nineteenth century, the nature of pilgrimage was quite different, occupying months of travel under perilous conditions. The dangers involved in such peregrinations necessitated large armed retinues to travel together, and such requirements favoured India's princes and those under their patronage; thus, the pilgrimage as an institution was dominated by nobles and notables.

In the early nineteenth century, *panda*s in pilgrimage towns began to feel the brunt of changes in pilgrimage patterns and patrons acutely, as social and economic changes became felt with the consolidation of British imperial power.[11] Princely pilgrimage was heavily impacted by policies such as the 'measures adopted in consequence of numerous applications from persons of rank for exemption from the tax on pilgrims'. The company had, prior to 1814, waived pilgrim taxes for 'friendly chiefs' as a matter of diplomacy. However, after multiple applications for massive pilgrimage retinues, company hospitality became exhausted and residents were directed to limit princely applications to more 'sensible' proportions.[12] This restriction was not palatable to many princes, for whom ritual bathing had always been attended by full regalia, including attendants, *sowar*s, sepoys, elephants and camels. Princes ceased to patronise pilgrimage centres in the numbers that they had previously. In Haridwar, this translated into concerns about the future of Hinduism, with *panda*s overheard lamenting that without the protection of princely patrons, 'nothing would be able to withstand the British power, and nothing [would] prevent men from embracing the Christian faith'.[13]

While the pilgrimage industry was hit hard by the decline of a princely clientele, to proclaim a win for Christianity at large was premature. For pilgrimage did not decline as a social activity; in fact, it rose in response to other changing social forces. A growing number of prosperous peasants embarked upon pilgrimages to complete vows, make marriage contracts and establish family lineages with pilgrimage registers, held by *tirthapurohit*s such as Prayagwals. For newly prosperous villagers, attending pilgrimage centres still carried the aura of elite activity and was a means of expressing their status as well as a meaningful devotional expression. Such an enterprise was not as dangerous as it had been a century before, since the British policing of roads and territories offered a degree of security to pilgrimage parties that previously could only be supplied by a princely retinue. Further, establishing ties with a priest at a major pilgrimage centre gave the enterprising peasant the opportunity to document their family and property. Lineages could be claimed and inscribed into Prayagwal registers, as well as claims to land ownership, which might be used as evidence in court cases should any dispute arise.[14]

Thus, the loss of the patronage of princely parties was somewhat compensated for by the rise of peasant pilgrimage. Prayagwals adapted their services to suit their changing clientele, and they began to provide pilgrims with accommodation in Allahabad and extend credit to pilgrims for services rendered. Prayagwals travelled widely to advertise forthcoming melas—dividing subcontinental territory amongst themselves—or sent 'pilgrim hunters' to advertise the sanctity of the sangam. Increasing numbers of pilgrims attended Allahabad's biggest social and ritual event, the annual Magh Mela, a month-long fair of bathing, fasting and praying, in which an important attraction for pilgrims was darshan (viewing) of the attendant congregation *akhara*s of *sadhu*s (groups of holy men).

The Pilgrimage Economy

The presence of the EIC in Allahabad dates to 1765, when Lord Clive contrived to install a garrison in the Fort, as part of the Treaty of Allahabad. The company later succeeded in having the fort ceded to them, along with the town of Allahabad, in 1801. Situated in an ideal strategic position (see Figure 9.1), in 1803 Allahabad Fort was made a major military post for the company: a repository for military stores, its grand Mughal palaces demolished to make it conform to British notions of a secure cantonment.[15] With the cession of Allahabad, the British also inherited an established custom of collecting a pilgrim tax at the sangam.[16] 'Every man, even the veriest beggar, is obliged to give one rupee for the liberty to bathe at the holy spot', wrote Fanny Parkes in the 1820s, 'and if you consider that one rupee is sufficient to keep that man in comfort for one month, the tax is severe'.[17] The tax was levied until 1838, when the cries of missionaries accusing the government of 'complicity in idolatry' forced its abolition.[18]

Figure 9.1:   Map of Allahabad, from *The Imperial Guide to India,
Including Kashmir, Burma and Ceylon* (London: John Murray, 1904) p. 98,
demonstrating the sangam (conjunction of the Ganga and Yamuna rivers),
fort and bridge of boats (which the Prayagwals took control of during the
rebellion), and the key rebel suburbs of Kydganj (to the left of the fort)
and Daraganj (to the north of the fort).

Source: K. Maclean.

Even after the withdrawal of the pilgrim tax, the British continued to profit
from melas by levying a range of tolls and taxes on traders and service providers,
such as barbers, flower and sweet sellers, who plied their wares at the sangam. In

the immediate period before the cession of the region to the company, the *pandas* had enjoyed some freedom from state intrusion,[19] and they did not welcome the turn of events which saw Allahabad morph into a major cog in the British imperial apparatus. Allahabad's rising economic, military and administrative importance frequently put it at odds with the pilgrimage trade, and the local administration would, until independence, regard pilgrimage with suspicion, viewing it as a source of disease epidemics and subversion that threatened to undermine British dominance in the region.

The British recognised that the Prayagwals were the chief instigators and, in their view, the sole benefactors, of the pilgrimage trade. Protestant missionaries, who established a proselytising presence at the mela grounds in the 1820s, predicted that 'in a few years this great folly [ie. pilgrimage to Allahabad] will get out of fashion, especially if the crowds of brahmins lose their interest in keeping it up'.[20] Prayagwals had no intention of allowing this to happen, and they resisted all machinations aimed at marginalising them. Relations between the British and the Prayagwals were consequently strained, as both parties imposed charges on the users of the holy sangam; each regarded the other's levies as illegitimate.

Prayagwal subversion of company policy extended to abetting the evasion of the pilgrim tax by their clients, by 'determining places along the banks of the river which may be equally holy', but were outside the reach of tax collectors.[21] After the abolition of the pilgrim tax in Allahabad, at the Magh Mela in 1839, a missionary complained that the Prayagwals had been 'very busy' telling pilgrims that the company had not dropped the tax, rather, it had been covered for three years by a 'wealthy and philanthropic Hindu at Calcutta'.[22] This cannot have pleased the company, whose motive in withdrawing the tax was not only to counter missionary accusations, but to 'augment the popularity of Government … in these disaffected times',[23] and it also alerted them to the possibility that Prayagwals might attempt to revive the tax themselves, three years hence. Even missionaries reduced the Prayagwals' dislike of them to economic factors, as David Batavia wrote:

> The Puyrag [sic] Brahmins … get their livelihood by imposing on the ignorant Hindoos; when they see the people are crowding to hear, they endeavour to get them away from us: sometimes when they see our books in the hands of any Hindoo, they make them throw them into the river, or snatch them from his hands by force, and tear them to pieces.[24]

However, the Prayagwals' resistance to British authority cannot be reduced to economics, as that would be to interpret these spiritual specialists as mere cash registers, dispensing holy goods and services according to demand. To accept such a position would be to uncritically accept the discourses of those colonialists and missionaries who were keen to emphasise the material over the religious in Hindu praxes.[25] A good deal of Prayagwal resistance was in response to the challenge to their hegemony at the sangam, and this power had ramifications for ritual practices.

Prayagwals had, in the past, negotiated an understanding of sorts with the Mughals and later Nawabi residents of the fort. The oral history mentioned above, regarding the original Prayagwal's suicide, makes it clear that for those who circulated the story, it was the complicit sacrifice of a Prayagwal that enabled the fort's construction on the sangam in the first place. This story may be 'folklore', but it nonetheless functions to rationalise the absolute agency of the Prayagwals at the sangam. It is therefore an important indication that whatever the actual historical processes involved in the construction of the fort above the sangam,[26] the Prayagwals have their own interpretations of the event that emphasises their prestige and power at the sangam.

The challenge presented by the British presence in the fort, however, threatened to reach beyond any accommodations that were made for the Great Mughal. The Prayagwals were closely impacted by the company's restrictions on social and religious practices at the sangam. The British had, thus, upon gaining tenancy in the fort in the final decades of the eighteenth century, managed to relocate the famed underground Patalapuri shrine to the fort's outer edge.[27] This shrine had housed the Akshaybat tree, a major destination for pilgrims to Prayag, and relocating it partially solved the problem of allowing open access to the heart of the fort, which had troubled the fort's commandant as undermining the fort's security. The keepers of the shrine cannot have been pleased with this transition, and public revelations of it in the 1950s led to a public controversy which served to undermine the shrine's claim to authenticity. Another religious intervention by the British had taken place in 1798, when Colonel Kyd had removed an Ashokan column—which pilgrims revered as the *gada* (club) of the Pandava hero of the Mahabharata—Bhima, and had it placed in storage in order to put a stop to worship of it, and thereby demand for access to the fort.[28] Denying access to objects of reverence such as these mattered to Hindus, as the heated nature of the debate about the *nakli* (fake) shrine in the 1950s shows.[29]

While Prayagwals were undoubtedly motivated by an element of the economic, their resistance to the British presence must also be interpreted in devotional terms; indeed for religious specialists such as the Prayagwals, economy and religion are inseparable. Ritual is thought to be 'less efficacious when on land where another is sovereign',[30] and it is clear that British policies, aimed at securing the fort from threats of sedition and epidemics, had an impact on religious and social practices. British medical and sanitary regulations frequently clashed with devotees' understandings of purity and cleanliness, as debates about the containment of disease, sanitation, pilgrim accommodation and diet demonstrate. British administrators frequently found themselves at cross-purposes with ailing pilgrims who travelled long distances specifically to die at the sangam in a form of palliative care that the British styled as 'ghat murder' (the dying were instead whisked away by officious administrators to a 'native hospital' established at the site for such occurrences). Even the manner of tax collection had to be carried out with sensitivity after a pilgrim complained that he had been touched in the process of paying an entrance fee, by a polluting British solider at the shrine in the fort.[31] The presence of this solider alone surely counteracted the entire purpose of pilgrimage, which was purification.

Prayagwals were thus aggrieved by the company's presence in Allahabad, and unfortunately for the British, as hosts and arbiters of ritual at one of north India's most popular pilgrimage centres, the pandits were well placed to spread their politics. Pilgrims from all over India converged on Allahabad, bathed in the sangam, and spent a few days in the mela taking darshan of holy men, before dispersing to their homes, where they were welcomed and their stories and experiences eagerly heard by those who had stayed behind. As such, pilgrimage constituted a vital role in the 'information order' that flowed throughout the subcontinent.[32] One witness to the events of 1857 alleged that the Prayagwals' mobility had intensified their propaganda against the British: 'the Pragwal brahmans spread over the villages, abusing their supposed sanctity and their personal influence to mislead the simple credulous villagers'.[33] In 1857, in the lead up to the events of June, they were noted to have been 'playing upon the passions of people and making propaganda that the aim of the British government was to convert people to Christianity', and it was this rumour in particular that many found so unsettling.[34] Several conversion rumours were reported in Allahabad; one claimed that the company had devised a terrible new punishment: 'to cause a sweeper to spit into the mouth of every native pronounced guilty of forgery … and that these prisoners be then handed over to the padries that they may set them right in dress and religious faith'.[35] Another alleged that the government had planned to deprive Hindus and Muslims of their brass eating vessels, forcing them to eat off earthenware plates and dishes: 'of course they think that such a process will at once change them into Christians'.[36] An Indian aide accompanying the 7th Madras Native Infantry refused to enter Allahabad; 'they had an idea that whoever once got into Allahabad, did not get out again, except as a Christian'.[37]

While the Prayagwals clearly had an important role in shaping opinion, it is important to note that they were a small part of the indigenous information mechanism, and that pilgrims were not simply pawns manipulated by scheming Brahmins, as the accounts quoted above would have it. Melas acted as an effective conduit for rumours and news that did not necessarily involve the agency of Prayagwals. In the presence of a large crowd of pilgrims at an Allahabad mela in 1845, an American missionary, James Warren, decided to test a *naga* (naked) *sadhu*'s claim to have 'overcome all natural feelings' by pelting him with small stones, to which the *naga* reacted indignantly.[38] We cannot know for certain how such a sight was interpreted and reported by the watching crowd, but it is no great leap of historical imagination to presume that it helped to confirm notions that India's rulers did not respect its religions, and that the fact of Warren's Americanness was lost in the insult.[39]

In short, an uneasy relationship existed between the company's troops stationed in Allahabad fort, and the sacred space stretched out below. William Tennant, a chaplain in the company, described the annoyance of the officers in the fort, who were disturbed by the 'midnight orisons of these devotees. Their howlings under the windows, rather resemble the noise of a madhouse, or the wailings of despair, rather than the aspirations of sober piety'.[40] And if the Europeans ventured down to the sangam during a mela, they were confronted with 'heat, dust, noise, confusion, and the insulting remarks of the fanatics assembled'—not an ideal environment for an important fort.[41] At the same time, the British came to appreciate the social and ritual importance of pilgrimage to the sangam in the subject population, and realised that the pilgrimage industry needed to be managed in order to build goodwill. In 1808, the company had waived pilgrim taxes for native soldiery wishing to bathe at Allahabad, with the expressed aim of 'strengthening their attachment and loyalty' to the British government.[42] It was sepoys such as these, drawn from agricultural families from Awadh and the NWP region, the 'peasants in uniform' described by Rudrangshu Mukherjee,[43] who rose up against their British officers in Allahabad, creating the opening for the Prayagwals to also rebel.

The Mutiny and Rebellion in Allahabad

The military mutiny in Allahabad began in the fort. After news of the initial outbreak in Meerut, the British residents of Allahabad were relieved to hear that the 6th Native Infantry, then quartered at Allahabad, had 'professed their utmost loyalty, begged to be led against their mutinous brethren, swore again and again they were, and would continue to be, "true to their salt"'.[44] However, on 5 June the sepoys of the 6th Native Infantry received information that troops of the 37th Native Infantry in Varanasi had been disarmed and massacred.[45] This provided the catalyst for the 6th to rise against fifteen of their officers in their mess-house, on 6 June, just after 9 p.m.—all were killed. The *sepoys* were joined by two troops of the 3rd Oudh Cavalry—except thirty-six men, who remained loyal—and together they took control of two nine-pounder cannons.[46] The rebels released the prisoners in the town's jail and set about attacking and burning elements of British infrastructure in the town, such as the collector's records, the railways and telegraph. Among the British dead, one of the most memorialised deaths was that of the ensign Arthur Cheek, who was only sixteen when he was killed by the rebels and who had arrived in India just two weeks earlier to be attached to the 6th Native Infantry.[47]

At the outbreak, any European civilians in the town took shelter in the fort, and all Indian soldiers were expelled, except the Sikh garrison.[48] The tension in the fort was too much for those who discovered 'an enormous depot of every description of liquor existed in the Government Stores Agency compound [and] the Christians and Sikhs soon found it out and universal drunkenness was the order of the time', leaving only a skeleton staff of four men to share in keeping watch while they awaited reinforcements; they were in no position for defensive action.[49] The fort would remain the focus of much of the conflict in Allahabad, and it was the only part of the town to remain in British hands throughout. Although the sepoys plundered its treasury, estimated at 30 lakhs of rupees,[50] distributing some of it to a group of holy men who prophesied success to the rebellion, the fort itself was 'saved by a very close shave'.[51]

Accounts referring to the 'Muslim nature of the Allahabad outbreak' refer chiefly to the contribution of maulvi Liaqat Ali, who, after the outbreak by the 6th, proclaimed himself governor of Allahabad under the King of Delhi and set up a rebel government under a green banner in Khusrao Bagh.[52] Supported by zamindars from Chail, the maulvi reigned for nearly a week 'during which, murder, rapine, and incendiarism were the order of the day'.[53] On 11 June, when General Neill burst into the town, the maulvi escaped and continued to elude the British for fourteen years. According to an article printed at the time of Liaquat's capture, the 'Moulvie headed the Muhomedons, while the Pragwal Brahmins carried with them the Hindu population. The troops fought on their own account.'[54] Contemporary sources also infer that the maulvi's leadership was not accepted by Hindu rebels in Allahabad, and so it seems that the rebellion in the town remained a disjointed affair.[55] It is true that the maulvi's proclamations were framed in explicitly Islamic discourses: 'This is a proclamation for Jehad (Mohammedan Crusade against the Christians) issued by the Imam named Leeaqut Ali of Allahabad, to both great and low men of the creed of Islam for massacring all the accursed Christians'.[56] Such a statement differs sharply from rebel statements which call for Hindus and Muslims to rise together, of which there are many.[57] For example, one Maulvi Syed Kootub Shah from Bareilly issued a proclamation which reasoned:

> Shastra declares that it is best to follow one's own religion and not to adopt others ... it is evident to all men that these English are perverters of all men's religion. From time immemorial they have endeavoured to contaminate the Hindoo and the Mahomedan religion by the production and circulation of religious books thro (sic) the medium of missionaries and by extirpating

such books as affords arguments against them.... I conjure the Hindoos in the name of Gunga, Toolsee, and Salikram and the Mahomedans in the name of the Koran, and we entreat them to join us in destroying the English for their mutual welfare.[58]

The Prayagwals issued no proclamations, and the only evidence we have of their actions in the rebellion is in the accusations made of them by the British, although Prayagwals today acknowledge that their forefathers did indeed take part in the *vidroh*.[59] Persian records from post-mutiny criminal proceedings held in the Allahabad Regional Archives charge Prayagwals with several misdeeds. One file names two Prayagwals—Rakshi Bhai and Tulsi—who were tried and hanged for rebellion in January 1858; another, Babu Pragwal of Kydganj, managed to escape and avoid charges—his arrest warrant and hanging order still lie in the file.[60] Acting upon the animosity they held for missionaries who competed at the sangam for the attention of pilgrims, Prayagwals targeted and destroyed the mission press and unspecified churches in Allahabad.[61] An American missionary, Reverend James Owen, alleged that the Prayagwals attacked the missionaries' homes, including his own, looting and burning, and that they stole a bell from a church in the town and installed it in a temple.[62] The Prayagwals also took control of the bridge of boats over the Ganga at Daraganj, which linked Allahabad to Benares, in an attempt to arrest the movement of communication and also the entry of troops to the town. They were not as well armed as Colonel Neill and the Madras Fusiliers, who promptly attacked them on their entry into Allahabad on 11 June.[63]

The violence of Neill's 'pacification' of the Doab is well known. Rosie Llewellyn-Jones remarks that Neill was 'the Victorian militant Christian personified, who believed that God had chosen him to take part in suppressing the revolt'.[64] It is said that in Allahabad alone, Neill killed as many Indians as English men, women and children were slain throughout north India in the rebellion; Sir John Kaye estimated that in the town 'six thousand beings had been thus summarily disposed of and launched into eternity'.[65] Suspected rebels were arrested and

four Commissioners, specially empowered for the purpose, dealt out the sternest justice with utmost rapidity. In three hours and 40 minutes, 634 persons were hanged on the trees near the Kotwali. Besides these, the soldiers and volunteers, believing everyone to be guilty, had shot down thousands of the townspeople.[66]

Prayagwal mohallas received special attention from Neill, not only in Daragunj, but also in Kydgunj, where a settlement on the Yamuna was fired at and many buildings destroyed, their inhabitants dispersed.[67] Prayagwal land in Kydganj in the immediate proximity to the fort was seized,[68] and an esplanade was created around the fort, clearing it of trees, to give a clear view of anyone approaching.[69] In his memoirs, the Bengali 'Hindoo' traveller and correspondent for the *Saturday Evening Englishman*, Bholanauth Chunder, reasoned that Prayagwals had been resentful of the 'restraints imposed upon their greed', and 'had too anxiously desired to get quit of the Sahibs, whose presence hampered the free exercise of their rapacity'. Chunder estimated that many of the Prayagwal population, which he put at nearly 1,500 families, were forced to flee Allahabad and live as beggars in obscure towns and in jungles to evade capture.

Within days of the outbreak, Chester Court, the magistrate and collector of Allahabad, recorded the guilt of the Prayagwals, writing that the Brahmins 'know that belief in their shastras is fast declining and they know that with its fall, they fall, and they are consequently interested in exterminating those who have spread amongst their ignorant co-religionists the spirit of enquiry and consequent departure from their precepts'.[70] The rationale that Hindu 'superstition' was being undermined by the spread of modernity was taken up by Sir John Kaye as one of the main causes of the rebellion. A combination of Western reason and technology 'put to shame the wisdom of the Brahmins, and seemed to indicate a command over the supernatural agencies of the Unseen World such as the Pandits of the East could never attain or simulate'.[71] Governmental circles also favoured the religion argument, in that it allowed them to imagine that the actions of missionaries had precipitated the rebellion, instead of administrative ingredients, such as the 'incompetent judges, cruel tax-gatherers, and over-bearing military officers' that helped to ferment the 'pickle' that the EIC found itself in during the Indian summer of 1857.[72]

It is true that the colonial impact on the religious landscape in Allahabad materially affected the Prayagwals, and this undoubtedly threatened to under-mine their power and status. The Prayagwals deployed the religious discourses and mechanisms at their disposal in order to undermine the British in Allahabad. However, to hold that the Prayagwals themselves did not attribute any reverence to the land on which they lived and worked, and which they sought to defend, is presumptuous. As the case of the Prayagwals shows, it is impossible to separate notions of religion from economy or power, particularly in a society in which religious actors and factors are popularly believed to have agency—recall the role of the original Prayagwal in allowing the fortification at the sangam. And while a history drawing on religious agency as the Prayagwals saw it may be largely unrecoverable, 'as the legacy of Enlightenment rationalism will always cut across it',[73] to refuse to accept such a position is to ignore an important and potent element of resistance against the British.

The question remains *why* the cry of 'religion in danger' was so meaningful to others, not just the rebels who framed their proclamations in religious terms, but also to the British themselves, that it is mentioned in so many accounts of the time, even as it is dismissed as 'false'. No doubt, part of the British discomfiture lay in the fact that they were, as a result of their imperfect knowledge of Indian religions, understandably nervous of any claims to religious offence or agency. Religious rationales had their own internal logic, which the British found hard to understand and predict. A pertinent example of this relates to an investigation carried out by British authorities in 1859, into the cholera epidemic that broke out in Fort Allahabad during the mutiny. A specialist on epidemics, Dr Dickson, had convinced the commissioner of Allahabad of the good sense in instituting a system of floating latrines on the Ganga. This would mean that human waste would immediately be carried away from the fort, and therefore prevent further cholera outbreaks: up to this point, the plan seemed like a perfectly workable solution. Subsequent consultations into the viability of the scheme revealed that 'Hindoos would never dream of polluting the waters of their holy stream at so sacred a place and in so open a manner'.[74] Despite the endeavours of orientalists and Indologists, the British in the mid-nineteenth century found that they were still unfamiliar with Hindu religious practices. Seeking to understand Hinduism through a Christian framework was always going to be an imperfect approach, and one which would have long-lasting repercussions for Hinduism.[75]

Writing for the centenary of the mutiny, the Marxist historian P.C. Joshi surmised that 'traditional religious-cultural concepts could not but be a very important constituent of the Indian ideological struggle against the foreigner's rule'.[76] More importantly, political actors such as Prayagwals seemed to realise the currency applied to the concept of a 'religious war' by the British, and they adapted and used that discourse, realising that religion was one of the fronts in which administrators erred with caution. The ethos in the subject population that religious freedom was important had been recognised by the company since its takeover. Observing the company's Indian soldiers bathing at Allahabad mela in 1837, Captain Mundy wrote that 'it is obvious to every one, that open and violent opposition to a rite so firmly rooted in the religious prejudices of the natives might shake the allegiance to our Hindoo sepoys, and thereby involve even the loss of India.'[77] The long-held notion in the Indian population that 'revolt in the defence of religion was the only legitimate form of revolt'[78] was reaffirmed by Queen Victoria's Proclamation in 1858.

The Proclamation, which purported to draw new limits upon the power of the British in India, contained a clause avowing abstinence from 'all interference with the religious belief or worship of any of our subjects'. Thus, after the rebellion, religion gained a new importance, as it became enshrined as a right of constitutional proportions. John Zavos has recently argued that

> [t]he 'right' of religious freedom confirmed by the Proclamation created the space for the articulation of religion.... As issues of religion became more prominent in this space during the second half of the nineteenth century, Hindus were increasingly required to articulate their concerns within this framework.[79]

One of the significant points that is often overlooked is that the post-mutiny moment represented a period of opportunity for Indian actors seeking to position themselves against the emerging Victorian state. With the rebellion, an epoch had ended, and along with it, records, people and administrative frameworks that held together the structures of the company's empire were partially destroyed.

In Allahabad, administrative records in the collector's office had been targeted and destroyed by the rebels, deliberately erasing and disrupting a vital element of the administrative memory in the town. In November 1858, when the time came to compile a coherent 'narrative of events' in Allahabad for the sake of posterity, the officiating commissioner of the district lamented that 'officers with a knowledge of the Allahabad disturbances had proceeded to Europe' or 'otherwise passed out of reach' without leaving any official statement of facts.[80] Chester, the collector and magistrate during the rebellion, had retired due to ill health, and a number of Europeans who had been based in Allahabad had rather wisely taken the opportunity to return to the safety of Britain. The transition to the new imperial order presented an opportunity for savvy indigenous actors to step in and take advantage of the disjuncture represented by the events of 1857–1858. It was this opportunity that remaining Prayagwals perceived as they rebuilt the pilgrimage trade, incorporating the Kumbh Mela tradition into the existing mela observances in Allahabad.[81] Concepts of 'religion' as a legitimate space of Indian sovereignty were pivotal in this.

Several decades of research have established that numerous different factors catalysed the rebellion, although in recent scholarship the emphasis has fallen on social and economic causes, leaving behind the religious motives that were attributed by more contemporary mutiny writers. For the latter, injecting 'religion' into their analysis of the rebellion had several advantages. It made the rebellion appear obscurantist and therefore illegitimate; and it gave the company an occasion to lay the blame at the feet of missionaries for their hubris and exuberance in spreading the Christian message. In mutiny eyewitness accounts, references to religious fanaticism serve as a gripping literary device, rendering the actions of the British survivors more heroic, and the deaths of the victims more tragic, as in the case of Ensign Cheek, memorialised as 'The Martyr of Allahabad'.

From the rebels' point of view, proclamations were either framed in explicitly religious terms, or drew on religious grievances as a rationale to oppose the British. Perhaps this was opportunistic, as some scholars have suggested, and drawing on a sense of besieged Hindu and Muslim religious identities became an expedient and effective way of forging rebel unity in the face of government oppression. Where, in historiography, religious motives can be equated to or subsumed by material ones, they have been largely due to a Eurocentric ideological scepticism accorded to claims to religious agency. Yet religious grievances were heeded by the new imperial order. One of the key promises made in the proclamation issued by Queen Victoria was that henceforth the government would abstain from 'all interference with the religious belief or worship of any of our subjects'. Thus, religion would become one of the foremost arenas in which Indians could legitimately contest British power in late-nineteenth century politics.[82]

Notes and References

1. C.A. Bayly, 'Religious Conflict in Twentieth-century India', in Judith Devlin and Ronan Fanning, eds, *Religion and Rebellion, Papers Read before the 22nd Irish Conference of Historians* (Dublin: University College Dublin Press, 1995), p. 194.
2. Diane L. Moore, 'Overcoming Religious Illiteracy: A Cultural Studies Approach', *World History Connected*, vol. 4, no. 1, 43 pars. (2006), http://worldhistoryconnected.press.uiuc.edu/4.1/moore.html (accessed 14 February 2007).
3. William Dalrymple, *The Last Mughal: The Fall of a Dynasty, Delhi 1857* (London: Bloomsbury, 2006), p. 23.
4. Gyan Prakash, 'Inevitable Revolutions', *Outlook*, 18 April 2007.
5. Chandra Mallampalli, 'Evaluating Marxist and Post-Modernist Responses to Hindu Nationalism during the Eighties and Nineties', *South Asia Research*, vol. 19, no. 2 (1999), p. 163.
6. A third level of analysis, which has been explored by postcolonial scholars in particular, is where people believe that Gods, divinities and spirits intervene in material affairs, and thus the course of history. See, for example, Ashis Nandy's work: 'History's Forgotten Doubles', in Philip Pomper, Richard H. Elphick and Richard T. Vann, eds, *World History: Ideologies, Structures and Identities* (Malden, Mass. and Oxford: Blackwell, 1998), pp. 159–178; and 'A Report on the Present State of Health of the Gods and Goddesses in South Asia', in *Postcolonial Studies*, vol. 4, no. 2 (2001), pp. 119–122.
7. For a lengthy description of rituals performed at the *triveni sangam*, see D.P. Dubey, *Prayaga: Site of Kumbh Mela* (New Delhi: Aryan Books International, 2001), pp. 74–102. 'Prayagwal' is a contraction of the word 'Prayagwallah', which translates as 'the one from Prayag'; in everyday usage, their name is shortened further to 'Pragwal'.
8. H.R. Neville, *Allahabad District Gazetteer* (Allahabad: Government Press, 1909), p. 67.
9. *Prayaga Mahatmya* (CV: 15), in Taluqdar of Oudh, trans., *The Matsya Puranam*, vol. 2 (Allahabad: Indian Press, 1916), p. 286.
10. Robert B. Minturn, *New York to Delhi, by Way of Rio de Janeiro, Australia and China* (NY: Appleton & Co., 1858), p. 157.
11. C.A. Bayly, 'From Ritual to Ceremony', in C.A. Bayly, ed., *The Origins of Nationality in South Asia: Patriotism and Ethical Government in the Making of India* (Delhi: Oxford University Press, 1998), p. 150.
12. 'Measures Adopted in Consequence of Numerous Applications from Persons of Rank for Exemption from the Tax on Pilgrims', OIOC, Board's Collections, F/4/421, 1812, no. 10371, 1814.
13. 'Fair at Hurdwar', *Asiatic Journal*, n.s., 13 (April 1834), p. 245.
14. Warren Edward Fusfeld, 'The Kumbh Mela in Allahabad: Networks of Communication in Nineteenth Century North India', M.A. diss., University of Pennsylvania, 1974, p. 20.

15. Letter, 20 May 1802, 'Allahabad to Be Grand Depot for All Military Stores', OIOC, Board's Collections, F/4/151, no. 2547.

16. William Tennant, *Indian Recreations: Consisting Chiefly of Strictures on the Domestic & Rural Economy of the Mahomedans and Hindoos* (Edinburgh: C. Stewart, 1804), vol. II, p. 247; Katherine Prior, 'British Administration of Hinduism in North India, 1780–1900', PhD diss., St Catharine's College, Cambridge University, 1990, p. 72.

17. Fanny Parkes, *Wanderings of a Pilgrim*, vol. I (London: Oxford University Press, [1850] 1975), p. 162.

18. James Pegge, *India's Cries to British Humanity Relative to Infanticide: British Connection with Idolatry, Ghaut Murders, Suttee, Slavery, and Colonisation in India* (London: Leicester, 1832).

19. Prior, 'British Administration of Hinduism', pp. 54, 72.

20. 'The Mela at Allahabad', sourced from the *Corr. Christian Advertiser*, 28 March, *Asiatic Journal*, n.s., vol. 32, no. 127 (July 1840), p. 194.

21. Letter from Spiers, Deputy Collector Allahabad to Stockwell, Commissioner of Allahabad, 22 September 1833. 'Evasion of Pilgrim Tax by the Son of the Rajah of Rewah', OIOC F/4/1573, no. 64239, 1835.

22. Letter from J. Wilson, 31 January 1839, quoted by Fusfeld, 'Kumbh Mela in Allahabad', p. 22.

23. 'Pilgrim Tax', *Asiatic Journal and Monthly Register*, n.s., vol. 28, no. 112 (April 1839), p. 258.

24. David Batavia, *The Missionary Register* (1836), p. 133; quoted in Geoffrey A. Oddie, 'Participant-Observers: Protestant Missionaries and the Kumbh Mela in the Nineteenth Century' (paper presented at ASAA Conference, Hobart, 2 July 2002, p. 13).

25. For example, see W.W. Hunter, *Imperial Gazetteer of India*, vol. 1 (London: Trubner, 1881), p. 151.

26. Some believe that one of Akbar's motives in building the fort was to put a stop to the practice of religious suicides in Prayag. Shaligram Shrivastav, *Prayag Pradip* (Allahabad: Hindustani Akademi, 1937), p. 236.

27. See D.P. Dubey, 'Historicity of Aksayavata', in *Prayaga: Site of Kumbh Mela* (New Delhi: Aryan Books International, 2001); Kama Maclean, *Pilgrimage and Power: The Kumbh Mela in Allahabad* (New York: Oxford University Press, 2008), chap. 2.

28. B.N. Pande, *Allahabad: Retrospect and Prospect* (Allahabad: Municipal Press, 1955), p. 34.

29. Shiv Nath Katju, 'The Eternal Tree of Creation', *Leader*, Kumbh Supplement (3 February 1954), p. vi.

30. C.A. Bayly, 'Pre-history of Communalism?', reprinted in Bayly, *Origins of Nationality* (2001), p. 219.

31. *Indian People*, 28 January 1906, in *Selections from Native Newspapers Published in the United Provinces*, no. 5 of 1906, p. 46. Technically, this was not a 'tax', although it was styled as such in the press. This particular incident referred to the collection of a small fee at the Akshaybat tree by European soldiers on the orders of the fort commandant. The fee was intended to defray the fort authorities for the sanitary expenses connected to allowing pilgrims access to the fort, but also to 'deter all but bona fide pilgrims from entering the Fort to visit the temple'. Memo from Major Douglas Smith, Brigade-Major, Allahabad, 26 March 1906, in 'Tax Levied on Pilgrims Visiting the Shrine at Allahabad fort', UPSA, 177/1906, GAD Box 171.

32. C.A. Bayly, *Empire and Information: Intelligence Gathering and Social Communication in India 1780–1870* (London: Cambridge University Press, 1996).

33. Henry George Keene, *Fifty-seven: Some Account of the Administration of the Indian Districts during the Revolt of the Bengal Army* (London: W.H. Allen & Co., 1883), p. 98.

34. M.P. Srivastava, *The Indian Mutiny 1857* (New Delhi: Chugh Publications, 1979), p. 68.

35. 'Petition of a Native of Allahabad Relative to the Belief That the British Government Intended to Forcibly Convert the Natives to Christianity', OIOC, F/4/2723, no. 197731, 15 May 1858.

36. *Delhi Gazette*, 22 January 1859, p. 77.

37. A Volunteer (W. O. Swanston 7th Madras NI), *My Journal, or, What I Did and Saw between the 9th of June and 25th November, 1857; with an Account of General Havelock's March from Allahabad to Lucknow* (Calcutta: CB Lewis, Baptist Mission Press, 1858), p. 18.

38. Letter from J. Warren, 20 October 1845, American Presbyterian Mission, Presbyterian Church in the USA (Pennsylvania), Board of Foreign Missions Correspondence and Reports, India Letters, Allahabad Mission, Microfilm Reel 5.

39. Sadhus also played an important role in the rebellion. See William R. Pinch, *Peasants and Monks in British India* (Berkeley: University of California, 1996), p. 8.

40. Tennant, *Indian Recreations*, vol. II, p. 247.

41. A Retired Officer of the Bengal Establishment, 'Suicides at Allahabad', *Asiatic Journal*, vol. 11 (April 1821), p. 326. An important part of this hostility most likely came from the various militant *akhara*s of sadhus who attended melas, or who were based in Allahabad in Daraganj, close to the point of the *sangam*.

42. 'Native Soldiery Exempted from Tax Levied on Pilgrims Bathing at the Confluence of the Jumna and Ganges', OIOC, Board's Collections, F/4/299, no. 5118, 1808.

43. Rudrangshu Mukherjee, 'The Sepoy Mutinies Revisited', in Kaushik Roy, ed., *War and Society in Colonial India, 1807–1945* (Delhi: Oxford University Press, 2006), p. 122.

44. Lt. Vivian Dering Majendie, *Up among the Pandies, or, A Year's Service in India* (Allahabad: Legend Publications, [1859] 1974), p. 96.

45. P.J.O. Taylor, ed., *A Companion to the Indian Mutiny* (Delhi; New York: Oxford University Press, 1996), p. 10.

46. Chester Court, 'Particulars of the Mutiny at Allahabad', Foreign sect Cens, July 1857, no. 94, reproduced in Pande, *Allahabad: Retrospect and Prospect*, pp. 24–25.

47. Letters to the Editor, *The Times*, 8 September 1857, p. 8; Reverend Robert Meek, *The Martyr of Allahabad: Memorials of Ensign Arthur Marcus Hill Cheek of the 6th NI, Murdered by the Sepoys of Allahabad* (London: James Nisbet & Co., 1858).

48. M.P. Srivastava, *The Indian Mutiny 1857* (New Delhi: Chugh Publications, 1979), p. 77. When Colonel Neill arrived with forty men to take the city on 11 June 1857, the Sikhs too were evicted.

49. Chester Court, 'Particulars of the Mutiny at Allahabad', Foreign sect Cens, July 1857, no. 94, reproduced in Pande, *Allahabad: Retrospect and Prospect*, pp. 24–25.

50. Sir William Muir, *Records of the Intelligence Dept of the Government of NWP of India during the Mutiny of 1857* (Edinburgh: Clark, 1902), p. 4.

51. Letter from Mr Court (*Rough Jottings*, 4 July 1857) in Muir, *Records of the Intelligence Department*, p. 436.

52. A.M. Monteath, 'A Supplement to the Narrative of Events in Allahabad District', in *Religious Character of the Revolution, 1857*, ARA, List no. 36, Inventory no. 34, Bundle A, Slip 3, p. 75.

53. H.L. Adam, *The Indian Criminal* (London: John Milne, 1909), p. 171.

54. Quoted from 'An Indian newspaper', in *Nelson Examiner and New Zealand Chronicle*, 4 November 1871, p. 6.

55. This is attested to in Henry George Keene, *Fifty-seven: Some Account of the Administration of Indian Districts during the Revolt of the Bengal Army* (London: WH Allen & co., 1883), p. 98; and Adam, *Indian Criminal*, p. 170. See also P.J.O. Taylor, *What Really Happened during the Mutiny: A Day-by-Day Account of the Major Events of 1857–1859 in India* (Delhi: Oxford University Press, 1997), p. 68.

56. Quoted in Taylor, ed., *Companion*, p. 195. However, it is interesting to note that the maulvi himself did not carry out his order to massacre 'all the accursed Christians' indiscriminately. The Christian convert Reverend Gopinath Nundy, along with his wife and three children, were

captured by rebels in Allahabad and taken to the maulvi but spared, despite being surrounded by 'no less than a hundred infuriated and savage-looking men with drawn swords'. Nundy felt that they were spared because his wife's farewells to their children were so piteous. 'The Rev. Gopenath Nundy', *Christian Missionary Gleaner*, July 1858, p. 76.

57. Nupur Chaudhuri and Rajat Kanta Ray, '1857: Historical Works and Proclamations' (paper presented at Mutiny at the Margins workshop on 'Historiography, Pedagogy and Future Histories of 1857', Royal Asiatic Society, London, 27 July 2007), http://www.csas.ed.ac.uk/mutiny/RoyalAsiaticWorkshop.html, p. 9.

58. 'Abstract translation of a circular letter regarding the 'Victory of Religion', Narrative of Events in the NWP for the week ending 14 Feb 1858, OIOC, L/MIL/17/2/496.

59. Discussion with the *pandas* of 'Panch Sipahi Talwardar', Allahabad, 12 February 2005.

60. 'State vs Babu Pragwal', 15 June 1860. ARA, ARA, Pre-mutiny Records, List 23, Basta 6, Serial 2, File 171, 4.8.1857.

61. 'Report of Kotwal about Pragwals of Keetgunj', ARA, Pre-mutiny Records, List 23, Basta no. 16, File 54, September 1857; and 'State versus Babu Pragwal'.

62. J. Owen, 'Narrative of the Outbreak in Allahabad, and of the Destruction of Mission Property', in M.A. Sherring, ed., *The Indian Church during the Great Rebellion* (London: James Nisbet & Co., 1859), p. 223.

63. Owen, 'Narrative of the Outbreak in Allahabad', pp. 215–216.

64. Rosie Llewellyn-Jones, *The Great Uprising in India, 1857–1858: Untold Stories, Indian and British* (Woodbridge: Boydell Press, 2007), pp. 155–156.

65. Quoted in Pande, *Allahabad: Retrospect and Prospect*, p. 24.

66. Pande, *Allahabad: Retrospect and Prospect*, p. 23.

67. Owen, 'Narrative of the Outbreak in Allahabad', p. 218.

68. Letter from J. Hawkins, Secretary, Judicial Department, 23 August 1860, in 'Confiscation of the Kydgunge Quarter', OIOC, P/235/26 Judicial (Criminal) Dept, NWP, progs no. 40 and 41.

69. Neill Papers, BL Mss. Eur. Photo. 422/5.

70. Letter from Court, 21 July 1857. *Character of the Outbreak at Allahabad, 1857: Political Character of the Revolution*, vol 4, List 36, Inventory 34, ARA. A similar line of argument is invoked by Meek, *The Martyr of Allahabad*, p. 25.

71. Sir John Kaye, 'The War as a Brahmanical Protest', in Ainslee Embree, ed., *1857 in India; Mutiny or War of Independence?* (Boston: Heath, 1963), p. 29.

72. Cf. Anonymous, 'How to Make an Indian Pickle', reproduced in Barbara Harlow and Mia Carter, eds, *Imperialism and Orientalism* (Malden, Mass. and Oxford: Blackwell, 1999), pp. 170–171.

73. See Dipesh Chakrabarty, 'Subaltern Histories and Post-Enlightenment Rationalism', in *Habitations of Modernity: Essays in the Wake of Subaltern Studies* (Chicago: University of Chicago, 2002), pp. 36–37.

74. Letter from W. Campbell, Magistrate, 26 August 1859. 'Improbability of a Place of So Much Sanctity as the Tribanee Being Habitually Defiled by the Hindoos Who Visit It', OIOC, P/215/70.

75. See Maclean, *Pilgrimage and Power*, chapter 4.

76. Joshi, 'A Social Revolution', in Embree, ed., *1857 in India*, p. 59.

77. Captain Mundy, *Pen and Pencil Sketches, Being the Journal of a Tour in India*, vol. II (London: Chatto and Windus, 1837), p. 255.

78. C.A. Bayly, *The Local Roots of Indian Politics: Allahabad 1889–1920* (Oxford: Clarendon Press, 1975), p. 7.

79. John Zavos, *The Emergence of Hindu Nationalism in India* (Delhi: Oxford University Press, 2000), p. 38.

80. E.C. Bayley to W. Muir, Secy to Govt NWP, 15 Nov 1858, 'Narrative of Events Attending the Outbreak of Disturbances and the Restoration of Authority in the District of Allahabad in 1857–1858', No. 2646 of 1858, OIOC L/MIL/17/2/496.

81. See Kama Maclean, 'Making the Colonial State Work for You: the Modern Beginnings of the Ancient Kumbh Mela', *Journal of Asian Studies*, vol. 62, no. 3 (August 2003), pp. 873–906.

82. Kama Maclean, 'Hybrid Nationalist or Hindu Nationalist? The Life of Madan Mohan Malaviya', in Kate Brittlebank, ed., *Tall Tales and True: India, Historiography and British Imperial Imaginings* (Melbourne: Monash Asia Institute, 2008).

10

⚛

THE MUTINY IN WESTERN INDIA
The 'Marginal' as Regional Dynamic*

Veena Naregal

Where was I to go? All the world said the English Raj had come to an end, and so being a quiet man, I thought the best place to take refuge was in my own home.[1]

THESE quietist sentiments, expressed by a deserter of the 27th Regiment of the Bombay army that mutinied in Kolhapur on the night of 31 July 1857, resonate with an eerie poignancy, seemingly at odds with the context of great historic accomplishment in which they were uttered. Gautam Bhadra notes how 'the idea of replacing the alien Raj by one that was the people's own—be it located in Delhi or nearer home at the seat of a rural insurrection—was very much in the air'.[2] While they echo the conviction of various, better-studied rebel groups elsewhere they had successfully overthrown the Raj, paradoxically, they also evocatively hint at the specifically constrained circumstances under which rebel activity proceeded in the Deccan/western India. Further, as noted for other provinces, in western India, perfectly ordinary ryots were transformed by the spirit of the times which allowed them to approximate the language of insurgency, even when they did not actually participate in it. For instance, a petition submitted by 'all the ryots of Satara' on 12 September 1857 expressed their strong moral objections to Rose's role in the ongoing counter-insurgency operations in the district. Rose, they said may be wise, but had 'now gone mad'. In no uncertain terms, they contended:

> Rose having listened to false information has killed some men here. This has been unnecessarily incurred. This is sure to lead to the overthrow of the government. For much sin has been committed. Before Rose's arrival here,

*Several people have helped me in accessing material for this chapter: my most sincere thanks to Crispin Bates, John Game, Eddie Rodrigues and Morina Carter for help at the India Office Library, and to the staff of the Bombay State Archives.

no one was (so) punished. He made a false representation to the government, killed some men, and brought himself to notice. This is sinful and has alarmed the *ryots*.[3]

The petition further held that having chosen to be instigated by the Satara people, and having had men killed, Rose 'will have to pay very dearly for this', reiterating with little prevarication that this would only lead to 'the early overthrow of the government ... [as] the *ryots* had no grievances before, but now they have many'.[4] Equally, there were instances of resolute defiance on the part of rebels who faced trial and immediate execution. A Rajput messenger who had been arrested in the lines of the 22nd Regiment for 'endeavouring to corrupt the Subedar, and through him, all Hindustani men of the regiment' continued to harangue the crowd gathered to witness his execution on 20 June 1857 and exhorted them as the 'sons of Hindus and Musalmans not to remain quiet ... [for] the English had a less hold on the country than when they set foot on it'.[5]

Very little work has been done on the extent and possible interpretations of regional patterns of anti-British military and civil activity in western India. Writing several years after 'the principal events in the countries under his military or political control', the specially appointed political commissioner of Kolhapur in 1857, Sir George Le Grand Jacob, thought it was remarkable that they should be so little known beyond the limits of the Bombay Presidency.[6] Sumit Guha has recently written on the relatively well-known travelogue of an impoverished *bhatji*, travelling from Konkan in search of alms, who found himself traversing central and north India in growing consternation, as the mutiny unfolded.[7] Yet in the literature on the mutiny, the situation that Jacob alluded to has not yet significantly altered. Nevertheless, the evidence suggests that there was neither a dearth of flashes of militancy, nor were rebels in western India devoid of a sense of the larger theatre of insurgent activity action through the subcontinent. Rango Bapuji, one of the principal organisers of rebel activity in western India, had seemingly been actively mobilising since December 1856. As rebel activity spread to north India, news from Meerut, Delhi and Awadh circulated through letters and messages sent by sepoys of the Bengal army; or through informal messages to kinsmen and contacts in native regiments from native soldiers in Bombay regiments dispatched to fight the rebels elsewhere in north India; through the trade and moneylending networks that passed through central India and even from reports in the vernacular press.[8] Some of these fascinating trails of circulating information that ended up as intercepted/planted excerpts within the colonial archive were my first glimpse into the hitherto largely unexamined record of the events of 1857–1858 in the Deccan and Bombay. A more systematic search revealed there had been three main, separate and prolonged episodes of insurgency that touched civilian populations and the native army in Satara, Kolhapur and Bombay city. These had reverberated widely within official and political circles and invited summary sentencing, resulting in several major public executions of dozens of mutineers and suspected rebels. Dinshaw Wacha recollects leaving the Elphinstone Institute as a high school student one afternoon to witness (on 15 October 1857) a grand ceremonial and spectacular display of violence as two suspected rebels were blown from the mouth of guns set in the midst of a packed maidan, which was lined with rows of foot soldiers, artillery and marine troops and spectators:

> The orders went out as we watched with throbbing pulses. The canons roared and the bodies of the men chained to those guns went up in smithereens. The stench of burning flesh filled our nostrils. It was all over.[9]

I come to the 1857 theme via my interest in the Marathi-speaking areas of western India and the emerging political formation there through the nineteenth century. Sudipta Kaviraj has written about how the colonial state deployed markedly different political registers as its mode of address towards different sections of native society. Although it adopted the language of ideological engagement with the new educated classes, it chose to deal with the rural peasantry and other subaltern groups primarily through coercive, often brutal means.[10] Elsewhere, I have explored one dimension of the somewhat schematic political equation that Kaviraj offers.[11] In exploring how colonial intellectuals in Bombay–Pune learnt to negotiate representative claims and a position of hegemonic significance from a numerically miniscule and 'middling' position, I emphasised 1857 as a key watershed in that process. However, in terms of the intelligentsia's self-awareness of their hegemonic potential, I argued that the emergence of Bombay University in 1857 was crucial in instituting the bilingual divide as a structural aspect of colonial society, and thus important in any calculations of cultural and political dominance.[12] While the colonial intelligentsia were themselves affected by the bilingual hierarchy, they remained the only group with the requisite cultural capital and linguistic skills to perform a mediating function within colonial society. Thus, as regional intelligentsias after 1857 realised their hegemonic potential within the structuring principles of the colonial world, their focus and self-perception underwent a crucial shift. From seeing their primary engagement as being one of 'dissemination' in the pre-1857 years, there was much evidence to show that after 1857, colonial intellectuals chose rather to focus on consolidating their representative position. If the emergence of a full university system in 1857 was the pivotal moment in instituting these changes with respect to the cultural sphere, the juncture was of structural political significance in other respects too. The mutiny and the responses of various social groups within the emerging regional formations to the challenge of 1857 was of primary importance to the subsequent distribution of power, both vertically, between different social layers and the colonial state, and spatially, between city and country in each presidency.

Additionally, spatial patterns underlying circuits of mobilisation harked back to the dynamic and terms through which the dismantling of the alliance of interests presided over by Peshwa rule, and the takeover of power by the

British after the decisive defeat of the Peshwa's forces in Khadki in 1818, had proceeded. While Satara and Kolhapur, until recently under Maratha princely rule, emerged as the main sites of mobilisation in the Marathi-speaking areas, the erstwhile rulers of Indore, Gwalior and the area around Sangli under the *chitpavan* Patwardhans—all stayed loyal to the British. A preliminary sketch of the three major locations of rebel activity in western India that this chapter will consider is in order at this point. Between January and June 1857, Satara district and the surrounding areas witnessed hectic attempts by the erstwhile Satara minister and ambassador, Rango Bapuji, to mobilise the civilian population in order to mount a simultaneous attack on Satara and Mahabaleshwar. The aim was to kill Europeans, plunder the government treasury and set free prisoners held at Satara jail—all to be carried out in the name of Pratapsingh, the erstwhile Raja of Satara, who had been exiled to Benares, where he died in 1848, but whose family had returned to reoccupy the palace in 1854.[13] The actual outbreak of insurgency in Satara was pre-empted, when seventeen of the suspected rebels were apprehended on 20 June 1857, apparently just a week before the imminent attack. They were put to death in a spectacular public execution on 8 September 1857 at the parade ground of the 22nd Native Infantry stationed at Satara.[14]

Between July and December 1857, Kolhapur witnessed two separate major events of rebellion, of which the mutiny in the 27th Native Infantry Regiment stationed in Kolhapur, which broke ranks on the night of 31 July 1857, was the first. The mutineers had expected support from the palace in allowing the city gates to stay open to admit them. However, that was not forthcoming, partly, perhaps, because the uprising had been hurriedly brought forward after apparently being timed for 10 August 1857, the day the new cartridges were to be introduced to the regiment. In any case, the apparent failure of the palace to keep to its word did not seem to have damaged its credibility in rebel eyes or their hopes that the princes would play a leading role in legitimising their cause. Thus, on the night of 5 December 1857, after days of rumours of an imminent rebel attack on the town, news reached Col. Jacob that a large band of men had marched into town from the nearby forests and occupied the palace. This seems to have been mainly a civilian action that had been planned through the implicit support and sympathy of an assortment of aristocratic agents (who had otherwise accepted treaties of understanding with the British). For example, Sardar Nimbalkar; some Kolhapur court officials; Chimasaheb, the younger prince; Nanasahib, the ex-Peshwa Bajirao's son; court agents from Gwalior and the Baroda Gaikwads (as the Kolhapur rani was a Baroda princess).[15] And yet, or perhaps *because* of the famous ambivalence of royal rebels, the consequences here were far more tragic. Having marched and entered the palace, the rebels were betrayed by the ruling family, who then opened the gates to allow Col. Jacob to enter under the pretext of making peace. Having assessed the situation, he proceeded to round up all the rebels, conduct a summary trial and enforce immediate punishment right there within the palace walls. Twenty-one and thirty-six insurgents, allegedly involved in the events of 31 July and the night of 5 December 1857, respectively, were put to death in two separate public executions carried out in the parade ground and within the palace within minutes of the verdict being pronounced.

In Bombay, skirmishes between British policemen and soldiers from the native infantry regiments stationed in Bombay broke out in September 1857, leading to the death of two native soldiers. In stark contrast with the fulsome assertions of loyalty from prominent inhabitants of Bombay in the form of separate petitions submitted on behalf of Hindus, Parsis, Jews, the Bombay Association and hundreds of Muslims in June and August 1857,[16] there had been rumours of an imminent uprising on the night of Muharram on 30 August 1857. That failed to materialise, only to lead to speculation about a similar plan scheduled to proceed under cover of Diwali celebrations in the city on the night of 16 October 1857. However, on the night of 12 October, the police broke into a rebel meeting and made several arrests. A hurried court martial led to two soldiers from the 10th and 11th Batallions, Mangal Gadre and Subedar Syed Hussain, being blown from guns in a public execution watched by hundreds of people in the Esplanade grounds in Bombay on 15 October 1857.[17] It was alleged that in the weeks leading to their arrest, these sepoys had been attending meetings among reformist circles of Bombay. Section IV discusses how these alleged links between native liberal circles and rebels in Bombay were amplified in subsequent events.

These sites and the sequence of mutiny action in western India, along with the social and spatial scale of mobilisation within these episodes of insurgency, contain important clues of the emerging political balance of forces in the Marathi-dominated areas of the Bombay Presidency. This preliminary sketch shows how the vital dimensions and limitations of the 1857 rebel imagination in other places were echoed in the unfolding of events, the contrasting character of the mutiny in the Bombay Presidency and the momentum it acquired in the Gangetic belt or in central India notwithstanding. The quietist note struck in the opening quotation, as well as the main contours of rebel action in Bombay Presidency during 1857–1858 outlined here, show that neither the scale of the insurgency nor the horror of the retribution visited upon Delhi after British forces had re-entered the city, or after the sack of Jhansi, were replicated in western India. Rather, as I will show, the colonial state in western India was able to renegotiate its dominance from a seemingly far weaker position. Thus, despite evident parallels with the underlying logic of rebel and counter-insurgency operations elsewhere, both the rebels and the colonial state in Bombay give the impression of acting within peculiarly hampered circumstances. So, in bringing this unexplored material within existing studies of 1857 to light, the plea is *not* a simple desire to put Bombay Presidency on the mutiny map. Rather, in trying to extend what we know about what the mutiny meant at its 'margins', it is 'critical' to thematise the difference in scale and the episodic nature of insurgent activity in western India around 1857. As we have learnt in other contexts, this might perhaps add critical insights into our understanding of the outcome of the mutiny and the balance of equations around colonial power emanating from its aftermath in its 'core' areas.

The social stratification of rebel activity and responses to the mutiny has always been an important concern for scholars of 1857. Akin to my attempt to investigate what the intelligentsia's negotiation of the bilingual divide could tell us about their ideological orientation and the structure of state-society in nineteenth century western India, my concern in engaging with the material on 1857 in the Deccan and Bombay is to see what light this pivotal event can throw on the emerging political equations within the regional dynamic. With this in mind, the rest of this chapter will elaborate on each of these episodes of rebel activity, the nature/lack of leadership therein, the social composition of rebel organisation, the connections between rebels, 'old' and 'new' elites and the colonial state, and the emerging regional balance of forces between Bombay as a presidency capital and its political hinterland. The final paragraphs will lay out lines for further enquiry into how the episodic character of rebel activity in western India may be embedded in the shifting basis of dominance through the historical redefinition of resource and political mobilisation in the region from the later Peshwa period to the mid-nineteenth century.

II

Hailing from a *kayastha prabhu* family that traced its lineage of court service to Shivaji's rule, Rango Bapuji, the dedicated, spirited and loyal vakil of the erstwhile Raja of Satara (Pratapsingh, who reigned between 1818–1839) was the chief catalyst and mobilising force in raising men to carry out the planned rebellion at Satara. Satara's significance derives from its creation by the British as a 'successor' state to the *peshwai* when they installed Pratapsingh, a nominal descendant of Shivaji Bhonsle, on the Satara *gadi* soon after defeating the Peshwa forces in 1818. In doing so, they were also hoping to exploit caste divisions and political rivalries between the Maratha royal family at Satara and the Brahmin Peshwas who had 'usurped' political power since the mid-eighteenth century. Rosalind O'Hanlon has provided a powerful account of how Pratapsingh's period in office initiated movements of upward social mobility among the Maratha caste cluster through the deployment of *varna* categories in political rivalries, which, in turn, had a profound impact on the emerging regional culture.[18] On the one hand, during these years Pratapsingh worked in a concerted fashion to counter attempts by the *chitpavan* Brahmin party of Pune and Sangli to restrict the authority of Vedic rituals to Brahmins; on the other, Pratapsingh mobilised efforts and made attempts to establish the Kshatriya and Rajput antecedents of the Bhonsle clan and other elite Maratha families. These efforts culminated in a major public debate, held in the Satara Sanskrit school in 1830, between pandits hired by both sides, followed in 1836 by a decision to replicate the coronation ceremony performed on Shivaji upon himself. Alongside this preoccupation over the restoration of his authority over *all* Hindus against the usurpers—namely, the Pune, Satara and Sangli *chiptavan* Brahmins—from 1832 onwards, he began contesting the Bombay governor's adverse rulings on the territories under his jurisdiction. By the late 1830s, relations had deteriorated to the extent that Pratapsingh was threatened with the loss of his kingdom unless he acceded to orders that would effectively curtail his rights to communicate independently with the Home authorities about his claims over lapsed *jagir*s as per the treaty of 1819.[19] Pratapsingh showed few signs of giving up, and in March 1839 he was deposed without a trial on charges of treason and conspiracy. Levied on the basis of much dubious evidence, these charges led to his being removed to Benares in September 1839.

At this point, the kingdom passed into the hands of his docile brother, Shahaji. The ex-Raja deployed the dedicated and faithful Rango Bapuji, his vakil of long standing, who had been in Bombay, to fight his case before the authorities in London. Rango Bapuji fought his master's case determinedly, lobbying in Parliament and the British press, publishing a book and several pamphlets, cultivating support and arranging public meetings through fourteen long years, even after his master's death in 1847, and long after all other envoys hired by the Raja had given in, apparently worn down by the court's prevarications and the expense of running an establishment in London.[20] In 1849, Satara passed to direct British control after Shahaji died in 1848, leaving only an adopted son, whose succession rights the British refused to recognise.

In 1853 Rango Bapuji returned home after signing a statement surrendering all claims against the government and agreeing to refrain from any future agitation in Britain or in India. Soon after Rango Bapuji's return to Satara from Bombay after hearing the news of the annexation of Jhansi and Nagpur in March 1854, Pratapsingh's second wife and adopted son, Shahuraje, came back to Satara in July 1854 to resume residence in the palace. These event-threads, highlighting the adversarial relation between Pratapsingh, Rangoji Prabhu and the British on the one hand, and Balaji Natu's circle of *chitpavan* Brahmin allies, (whose relation with the British, at this point, was one of tacit collaboration) on the other, exemplified the ways in which the core alliance in the Deccan between the Maratha *deshmukh*s and the literate *kayastha prabhu deshpande*s, undermined by the rise to political power and administrative prominence of the *chitpavan* Brahmins during the *peshwai*, was now being further defined through colonial manoeuvres and the new political norms. The reactivation and redefinition of these fault lines through the contestation sketched here had wide-ranging repercussions that resonated well beyond Satara in affecting the ground on which regional political alliances could emerge in the subsequent decades.

It is not simply coincidental that Rango Bapuji emerged as the only figure from the political elite in the Deccan to directly, if secretly, engage in mobilising rebel activity in 1857. Others, including the Kolhapur princes and the remaining erstwhile major Maratha sardars of central India, in accepting the protection treaties they had individually signed with the British, had clearly identified their optimal chances of political survival by throwing in their lot with the British. Even if they strongly sympathised with the rebel cause, these aristocratic elites were unlikely to jettison this alliance unless forced by pressure from below to do so.[21] The other major *jagirdar*s of Sangli and adjoining areas, the *chitpavan* Patwardhans, were unlikely to make common cause either with Rango Bapuji or the Maratha princes of Kolhapur. In contrast, ingenious, determined and loyal, Rango Bapuji had every intention of continuing his struggle against the British to restore the Satara monarchy to Pratapsingh's family. With little power of his own to protect, and with the added insights into the workings of colonial power accrued from his experience in England, it seemed inevitable that Rango Bapuji should fling himself into the task of gathering men into a rebel force. From January till the time when a contingent of his rebel associates, including his son, Sitaram, were arrested in June 1857, it seemed that Rango Bapuji was continuously on the move, most often in the Bhor province and in Belgaum district, trying to contact and cleverly cajole individuals to mobilise bands of men, find funds, check and secure arrangements, and provide ammunition and weapons for the rebel force that he was trying to cobble together.[22]

It is noteworthy that the record of rebel activity in Satara–Bhor shows little trace of links with the Nanansahib Peshwa camp, or even with other major princely courts of the Deccan. Rather, it seemed that Rango Bapuji legitimised his solo efforts by pretending that the late, ex-ruler Pratapsingh was still alive and had authorised him to mobilise men to work for the Raja's restoration. Among his key associates were Narain Pavuskar, a *sonar*, Shivram Babushroot, Munajee alias Bapoosaheb, a Maratha, Sakharam Kabhade, a *karkun* in the Satara *vazir*'s office (who eventually turned informer and key witness during the trial) and Ganesh Sakhram Karkhanis from the 22nd Native Infantry Regiment.[23] Rango Bapuji's nephew, Keshav Nilkanth Chitre, was another active conspirator. However, Rango Bhau's son, Sitaram, seems to have been a somewhat reluctant participant and not one of the most active mobilisers. In all, seventeen rebel prisoners (three *prabhu*s, *ramoshi*s, *kunbi*s each; two Brahmins; two *mang*s; one Maratha and one *sonar*) and an equal number of witness testimonies were presented during the trial (three *prabhu*s and Brahmins each; one *sonar*; three *kunbi*s; and a *ramoshi*, *musulman* and *purdesi* each).[24] These speak uniformly of Rango Bapuji's hectic, tenacious and seemingly tireless efforts to personally spread news of the progress of the mutiny, as well as coordinate plans for the intended attack.[25] It seems a rebel network existed across a 100-mile stretch between Bhor (just north of Satara) and Belgaum across Yanewada, Deour, Arabi, Kalambi, Karad, Phaltan and Pandharpur.[26] Rango's key efforts had been to work with a band of *prabhu*, Brahmin and *sonar* contacts to tap into immediate kin networks to mobilise men from *kunbi*, *ramoshi* and *mang* groups from neighbouring villages. Of the seventeen rebels on trial, Pavuskar, the *sonar*, was entrusted with the task of manufacturing ammunition—when the rebels were arrested, some 800 lead bullets were recovered from them.[27] However, Rango Bapuji certainly seemed strapped for cash and funds to pay advances for the services the conspirators were trying to mobilise. And so, despite weeks of intense preparations and despite—if the evidence recorded during the trial is credible—the last meeting before the rebels were captured being a gathering of approximately 2,000 men, the resources gathered were relatively modest and had been put together bit by bit after repeated rounds of painstaking negotiations. Both the testimonies of the *karkun* in the Satara *vazir*'s office and Rango Bapuji's key contact Sukharam Dajee Kabade, as prosecutor's witness, mention Rango Bhau claiming that the Governor Saheb had given him written orders to seize the *sahib log* in the Satara territory and use them as hostages to demand the restoration of the Satara Raja, failing which, compliance war, murder of the Europeans and plunder were to be order of the day.[28] Whatever the veracity of Sakharam's testimony, Rango Bapuji seems to have worked in a most clever and quick-witted fashion, often travelling with the district magistrate's touring camp on the pretence of other business so as to escape suspicion while secretly keeping in constant touch with his conspirators through months of preparation. Most business-like of the negotiations were talks to secure the cooperation of *ramoshi*s and *mang*s. Nania Wullud Narko Chavan, the elderly *ramoshi*, was told (in Nania's words) that the Raja of Benares was going to place himself on the throne and had given him (Rango Bapuji) orders to sustain men and was therefore asking him (Nania) to raise 400 or 500 men. Nania, it seemed, was no less clever and answered that he would do whatever he was asked if he was introduced to the raja and promised to raise men on an advance of ₹4,000 or ₹5,000. Further, when asked why he had not informed the sarkar, the wily Nana promptly responded that he could not do so without proof, and had therefore wanted to collect his money before reporting the matter![29]

The verdict of 7 September 1857 apportioned the seventeen captured Satara 'ringleaders' to be executed, but by different means. Whereas five upper-caste prisoners were sentenced to be hanged, one of the *prabhu*s (glossed here as a 'militant caste'), the Maratha-*kunbi*s and one of the *ramoshi*s were to be blown from guns, and the lower-caste prisoners were to be shot dead.[30] Rango Bapuji was apparently captured but escaped from the Gwalior prison on 5 July 1857. A reward of ₹5,000 was announced, but he eluded all attempts to apprehend him. Rumours circulated that he had become a wandering mendicant. Others speculated he had made his way to Telicherry where his close friend, Mr Brown, lived. The administrative or military labour market in the Deccan had been traditionally sustained around the dominance of *deshasth* Brahmins, who had effectively constituted the precolonial rural elite through their pan-regional control over the *deshpandeki* and *deshmukhi*, key positions of rural administration. It is most striking that Rango Bapuji's efforts to mobilise did not have recourse to tap into any of these wider social networks. Available trial testimonies suggest that the Satara mobilisational activity mostly proceeded through a handful of upper-caste individuals whose access to Maratha-*kunbi* networks was quite limited, suggesting that the changes instituted by the colonial administration had already significantly eroded earlier precolonial structures of dominance, while the above-mentioned ongoing processes of contestation had lent a sharper and more general anti-Brahmin edge to the emerging Maratha-*kunbi* identity. In conclusion here, its is noteworthy that the *mang* 'ringleaders' tried in the Satara case clearly enjoyed little influence within wider community networks, and had apparently agreed to service under Rango Bapuji with some reluctance.[31] Thus, the Satara events also underlined how caste groups like the *mahars* and *mangs*, with their history of distinguished and loyal military service in Deccan armies since Shivaji's time, also remained aloof from the mutiny action. Their loyalty was a strong residue of their resentment over how the late Peshwa state had tried to regulate their status and conduct by imposing humiliating restrictions on their movement, particularly, in urban areas. However, the cooperative links between the British and *mahar* and *mang* networks formed through the Anglo-Maratha wars leading to the Peshwa's defeat had, no doubt, been reinforced by the caste dynamics of the early colonial period in western India, especially, the political rivalry between the Maratha elite and *chitpavan* Brahmin factions.

III

The events in Kolhapur shared similarities, but also had important differences with the above-discussed trajectory in Satara. The resentment over Pratapsingh's removal was shared by people in Kolhapur. Additionally, there was bitterness over British moves to pre-empt the kingship from passing to either of the two princes on Raja Babasaheb's death in 1838. Available accounts indicate that levels of discontentment among the civilian population and the native army in Kolhapur ran high. Alluding to the latter half of 1857, Jacob tells us 'the state of the country ... grew more unsettled', and that there was a 'common sense of coming disturbance'.[32] These remarks need to be seen against the context of the *gadkari* (literally, fort-keepers) insurrection in 1844–1845, provoked by British efforts to deprive them of their traditional land grants in the areas around forts in the adjoining territory. That uprising had required the deployment of more than 10,000 troops and took nine months to quell.

The introductory account of the Kolhapur events show that they did not have a single catalyst or prime mover like Rango Bapuji. The incidents sketched there also show that despite multiple reasons for resentment against British policy, the chances of a real alliance of interests emerging between the rebels and the palace remained weak, playing out with starkly tragic consequences on the night of 5 December 1857. While the sequence of events showed that although the British were able to put a brutal end to the mutiny in the 27th Regiment, they could not root out the widespread disaffection and the hope of resisting the *firangi* Raj quite as easily. And yet, despite the concerted manoeuvres between several segments of the erstwhile ruling elite, the scale of mobilised resources may not have been dramatically higher than what Rango Bapuji had garnered. This disconnect again points to the erosion of possible links between the palace, an intermediary layer of landholders with revenue rights and cultivating/martial communities that may have yielded a wider alliance of material interests. Further, the record of negotiations over the capture and punishment of the Kolhapur rebels also reveals the important fissures between military and civil authorities in western India as they each attempted to outdo the other in their use of extra-legal measures. Motives here ranged across several paranoid desires including the need to restore normalcy and repair the damage to the image of the coloniser, combined with the career ambitions of individual officials.

The impetus for the attack on 31 July 1857 on the Kolhapur treasury, ammunition depot, cantonment bazaar and the jail had come from a group of native officers and spirited soldiers in the 27th Regiment who had learnt of the plan to introduce the new greased cartridges during a stint at the military training centre in Pune. This group included Subedar Imamkhan, Ramji Shirsat, Mahadev Chavan, Sabaji Pawar, Babaji Thankur, Mukund Sawant, all of whom then began to meet in secret at Subedar Beg's house.[33] Links had apparently been established with Chimasaheb, the younger prince, who was known to be sympathetic. The plan was for the regiments in Belgaum and Kolhapur to rise together on 10 August 1857; however, the threat of betrayal probably compelled them to act earlier than intended. From the depositions at the trial, it emerged that between 150 and 200 soldiers had broken ranks and, defying attempts to rally them, had marched from their lines to the cantonment where they attacked British officers and ransacked the treasury and bazaar leading to much chaos and terror among the British. The rebels then wanted to proceed to enter the city, but, finding the city gates shut, they were forced to take shelter in another outlying building. After a pitched battle which led to heavy British casualties, the mutineers were forced out of the city. This large contingent, which included several *purabiya*s as well as Maratha, *kunbi* and *mahar* soldiers, many of whom hailed from the Konkan, set out towards the coast. The plan was to find their way to Goa, and perhaps find an escape route via the sea to return to the Deccan. However, on hearing that the coast was heavily patrolled, many *purabiya*s turned back at Phonda Ghat, ostensibly to return to Kolhapur. At Solunkar village in Sawantwadi territory, just as they were talking to some villagers to arrange for some food, the remaining group—which included Ramji Shirsat—a spirited, stately looking, 29-year-old Konkani Maratha private who figures through the official record as a key ringleader, caught sight of three British officers, still in uniform, desperately trying to flee. Without any hesitation, the rebels unceremoniously shot them dead, and their bodies were quickly flung into the river. A smaller band that ostensibly hailed from the Konkan stayed on, moving through the Savantwadi jungles.

The case now became a matter of negotiation between the authorities in Kolhapur and the Savantwadi district magistrate culminating in Shirsat being shot dead in Pavshi village, apparently at point blank range, after a tip-off from a local Brahmin informant spying for the police.[34] Shirsat's death at the hands of Savantwadi police seems to have been the result of the decision of the Savantwadi district magistrate, Mr Turquand, not to 'return' any more rebels for trial at Kolhapur, apparently in the hope of making an impression with the Bombay administration. The record bears evidence of a protracted and ugly row between Mr Turquand and Col. Jacob who, as the recently appointed special commissioner, was keen to retain control over the trial and execution of captured soldiers in order, no doubt, to suitably enhance *his* reputation and establish personal authority over the civilian officer Mr Turquand. Thus, the two men squabbled over their respective 'rights' to boost their own personal tally of rebel executions they had overseen. Jacob had complained to the Bombay government that Turquand was being uncooperative, insulting and temperamental in refusing to make more arrests in the area under the latter's jurisdiction on the apparently 'irrational' grounds of insufficient evidence. Turquand, in turn, had responded with extended insinuations about Jacob's poor Urdu skills that, Turquand claimed, had led Jacob to commit gross errors while deciphering intercepted communication. Turquand thus attempted to project himself as the liberal official determined to thwart the military man's authoritarian tendencies and disregard for legal procedure. While refusing to return two mutineers captured by the Savantwadi police to Kolhapur, Mr Turquand insisted that it was far safer for Col. Jacob to dispatch the required evidence (including their abandoned uniforms and some ammunition that the men had buried before crossing into Savantwadi) so the trial and sentencing could proceed in Savantwadi. Interestingly, at this point, Turquand hastily summoned a commission, comprising mainly of military officers, to try the two men. However, the trial ended summarily after the first meeting when the commissioners refused to comply with Turquand's wishes that sentence be passed without the physical evidence. Unable to get the verdict he so desperately wanted in order to impress his superiors at Bombay, Turquand now railed against the unreasonable and uncooperative stance of the commission in insisting upon procedure and demanding evidence be produced before the men could be sentenced!

Nevertheless, reprimanded by the Bombay government, probably on account of Col. Jacob's greater familiarity with the Bombay office, Turquand could not escape instructions issued to arrange for an escort for the prisoners up to the Savantwadi border, after which Jacob's men would assume responsibility for conducting them further. It would seem that such internal squabbling, caused by the equally illiberal, self-aggrandising personal ambitions of civilian and military officials, was at least partly responsible for the manner in which Shirsat, the Kolhapur ringleader, met his death. Unsurprisingly, such differences, so faithfully amplified within the official internal archive, find no place in the aforementioned retrospective public recollection that Jacob authored for posterity. Yet the tension between the two official versions, one for internal consumption, the other for public circulation, seems potentially productive and may suggest the specific constraints that counter-insurgency measures and colonial state-formation were subject to in western India.

In a letter of 13 September 1857, Nanasahib chided Chimasaheb for his failure to rise to the occasion on the night of 31 July 1857, and urged him to compensate by showing his support for the rebels.[35] My analysis, in particular, of the events of the night of 5 December 1857, derives almost fully from Jacob's published account of 1872. On receiving news that rebels had marched into Kolhapur city and advanced straight towards the palace, Col. Jacob arrived with a small contingent of British troops at his disposal after a relatively easy battle to force the lightly guarded city gates. With the palace already in rebel hands, Col. Jacob decided to send in Captain Schneider as herald, waving a white cloth, to assess the situation inside the palace and dialogue with the princes. Schneider was willingly let in and found the palace 'full of hundreds of men, on roofs, windows, on every available standing place'.[36] On being approached, both rajas thanked Schneider for his visit, maintained that the town had been taken by escalade and claimed that the rebels had forced the rajas to surrender. On receiving this report, Schneider quietly accepted it and suggested that Jacob's troops be allowed into the palace square to begin disarming the insurgents. Prisoners were taken and 'then and there tried by drum-head court martial'. The president of the court martial, Col. Guerin, soon reported that there was no doubt about the complicity of thirty-six men who had pleaded guilty. As for the remainder, since they had not admitted guilt and 'as evidence on both sides had to be fully gone into', it was felt that 'the day might pass before they could arrive at a verdict; therefore thirty-six only were then tried and the rest removed for subsequent procedure'. While Col. Jacob was convinced that most of those inside were as guilty as the unfortunate thirty-six, the sentence against those who had pleaded guilty was carried out immediately, right against the outside front wall of the palace as a stern example 'to convince all of the folly of armed opposition to our Government'.[37]

IV

Both the arrest of the rebel soldiers from the house of Ganga Prasad in Sonapur gali where they had been gathering and the executions were widely reported in the Bombay and Poona English newspapers. While maintaining that the discontent remained confined to army units, newspaper reports alternately insinuated and denied the truth of strong rumours alleging the involvement of influential persons, including the powerful magnate Jagannath Shankarseth. While reporting that a prominent individual was under suspicion, the *Bombay Gazette* went on to maintain that the wealthy citizenry of Bombay would not harm their interests by such rash actions. However, the *Poona Observer* reported that this eminent and respectable person of the Hindu *samaj* had gone underground to ward off the possibility of arrest. The *Bombay Gazette* responded that these reports were baseless and the person in question was keeping up his regular routine and his public engagements. Eventually, it seems that the Police Chief Forjett helped clear Jaganath Shankarseth's name.[38]

Apparently, Nanasahib died on 6 October 1858 in Nepal. Yet, several years later, another round of serious allegations of treason against Jagannath Shankarseth, in the form of alleged attempts to finance rebel activity through *hundi*s drawn in favour of Nanasahib, were publicised in some Pune papers and the *Bombay Saturday Review* of 18 April 1863. These *hundi*s—and other documents—were said to have been found with Mahadevrao, who had been arrested by the Sholapur police and had confessed to being an agent of Nanasahib Peshwa. Within a few days, the *Times of India* carried an editorial stating that all the evidence found with Mahadevrao had been found to be planted by Nutall's men. Next, Shankarseth quite shrewdly took the matter up with the Bombay government through an open letter to the *Bombay Gazette* that began with a request for the matter to be brought to the governor's notice. Expressing great pain at the recently published allegations, the letter spoke of the gravest displeasure that such baseless and serious charges could be levied in court by Captain Nutall against a member of the Law Council (Shankarseth) without so much as an attempt to personally verify the claims with the affected individual. The letter went on to categorically state that he had never issued bills to Mahadevrao, nor to anyone else, in support of the rebellion. Further, it clarified that neither he nor his father, who had died forty years earlier, had ever had any financial dealings with Nanasahib or the Peshwa family.[39]

This interesting trajectory of events surrounding the question of (the lack of) evidence for Shankarseth's involvement in supporting rebel activity highlights, not only Shankarseth's importance in Bombay society, but the relationship between the Bombay administration and provincial officials. It also seems clear that Shankarseth had determined enemies, possibly among the anti-reform factions, who were determined to malign his public standing. Nevertheless, as a powerful seth, he enjoyed immense influence with the Bombay government and English circles in the city. This allowed him to dictate the terms on which the 1863 episode ended. Not only were the controversial allegations speedily dropped, but the alacrity with which the administration sprung into action to reassure Shankarseth of Nutall's errors was revealing. In a profusely apologetic letter to Shankarseth, written on 1 June 1863 from Jejuri, Commissioner Hart exonerated the Bombay magnate of all charges by referring to Nutall's clarification where he now recorded that he realised the charges to be untenable and false. Interestingly, Nutall's letter admitting to his error in initiating charges on unfounded suspicions was enclosed with Hart's reply with the plea that Shankarseth take, firsthand, note of Nutall's regret. The letter further added that, notwithstanding the unseemly haste of Nutall's earlier conclusions, the government would never harbour any suspicions about Shankarseth's loyalty. Shankarseth's reply was to cordially thank Hart for this communication. However, he noted that he was yet to receive a reply to his letter to the governor. Soon afterwards, the governor's office wrote to Shankarseth stating that Nutall had been asked to submit a full explanation, which would be forwarded to Shankarseth. Meanwhile, the letter expressed regrets over Nutall's testimony in court which, it said, had been investigated the moment it had come to the notice of the Bombay government. Now that Nutall had realised his errors, the letter ended with the assurance that his clarification and apology would be duly publicised widely in the newspapers without further delay.

Jagannath Shankarseth's importance clearly stemmed from his exceptional status as a Hindu seth who enjoyed extraordinary influence with the Bombay government. The precision and authority with which he was able to dispose of allegations made in a court of law, through the speedy intervention of sections of the Bombay English press and the governor's office, is most striking. However, the apparent schism between the Bombay administrations and the provincial authorities is important to note as it hints at a divergence of orientation, perhaps even of interest, between networks in the capital and its hinterland. It also highlights how the figure of Nanasahib Peshwa was kept alive in the colonial imagination as a name invoked by paranoid provincial authorities to prove the continuous possibility of treason, perhaps in the hope of winning official recognition. It is hard, however, to ascertain from the official record whether any funds surreptitiously flowed between the native elite of Bombay and the rebels in other parts of the presidency. Arguably, the evidence of a strong understanding between official circles in Bombay and Shankarseth can be juxtaposed with the aforementioned examples of provincial colonial officials like Col. Jacob, Turquand and Nutall jockeying for recognition from the Bombay administration. While Shankarseth had the Bombay government bending to his will to reprimand a major provincial official for having insulted a prominent native citizen by making baseless charges, Turquand and Jacob had to squabble for control over native rebels who would face summary execution on the basis of rudimentary evidence. The contrast in the way Shankarseth and ordinary rebels were treated is evident; the Bombay government's role in sanctioning the public discrediting of a high police official and the provincial judicial system is equally noteworthy. Such links between the Bombay government and the city's economic elite not only reflect the *bases* of the emerging authority of the colonial administration in Bombay, they also throw up questions about the political means available to *extend* that authority in the regional context, given the nature of Bombay's ties with the provincial hinterland. In choosing to implicate a person of his eminence, Nutall was perhaps trying to capitalise on Shankarseth's reputation to convince the court—although as a provincial official, he seems to have misjudged the clout that a native seth could enjoy with the Bombay government. The clues in the material here need to be followed up systematically, but, at this stage, it seems clear that they bear critical insights into how the dynamics of the colonial economy of the capital city played out within the regional political economy. They indicate a discernible variance in the rules of the game as they operated in the capital and elsewhere in the presidency, suggesting that politics was done differently in Bombay city as compared with how it was done in the interior. Surely, such gaps in the political field, as defined across the emerging relation between town and country, would also have been factors in attenuating sources of possible support for rebel alliances spread across a wider area in the region.

Conclusion

The three episodes dealt with here explore how the mutiny action unravelled across three locations in western India. What the events in Satara, Kolhapur and Bombay reveal about the possibilities of leadership and the basis of an alliance between erstwhile and current elites and ordinary disaffected rebels is noteworthy. While the Satara plans were drawn up with much assiduous effort and dexterity, the actual rebellion did not materialise; many rebels were punished and their leader, Rango Bapuji, escaped. The tragic disunity between the palace and subaltern rebels resulted in the ringleader being killed in a police ambush, several executions and the emergence of the special commissioner, Col. Jacob, as the official hero of the Kolhapur events. The constrained scope for mobilisation both in Satara and Kolhapur, and the fateful lack of unity between the Kolhapur palace and subaltern rebels seems to have played out in a different register, and on a different plane, in Bombay. While mutinying soldiers met a brutal death watched by hundreds, the prominent Hindu seth who was suspected of being in league with efforts to restore the Peshwa Dynasty, deftly mobilised the support of colonial officials and the English press to vindicate himself of allegations of supporting rebel activity.

Writing in 1919, Caldwell, the historian of the Bombay army, noted that, theoretically, there were several reasons that should have incited the Bombay army into revolting in a major way in 1857.[40] Maintaining that the distinctive feature of the Bombay army was the extent to which it remained free from the 'stain of insubordination', among the reasons that the contrary may well have been true, Caldwell firstly mentions that Bombay regiments had significant number of *purabiyas* and Hindustani Musalmans.[41] There was also much talk of an appeal for Nanasahib to be reinstated as the Peshwa, which could have captured the imagination of the Bombay army in a major way. Further, both the presence of several disaffected members within the sardar families, and the British strategy over the succession issue at Kolhapur, Nagpur and Satara would represent causes that would have struck a chord with the men of the Bombay army. However, as it turned out, Western India remained at periphery of the major action of 1857.

The analysis here suggests that the Bombay army did not necessarily remain free of insubordination. Rather, Caldwell's reading needs to be contextualised in terms of the disconnect between surface-level evidence of multiple sites of resentment and the erosion of the basis through which a larger, more inclusive alliance of interests emerged. The scale of rebel activity should be placed in the context of shifts as Shivaji's political vision, based on an inclusive ethos of military *naukari*, gave way to the exclusivist biases of the expansionist Peshwa regime and the manoeuvres of colonial transformation. This chapter has examined three main episodes of insurgency to show how political shifts through the eighteenth and nineteenth century had weakened power-sharing arrangements in the Deccan in ways that precluded a scale of mobilisation that, at best, yielded a few hundred insurgents. Nevertheless, limitations of space have not allowed a full contextualising of the developments discussed here against the shifts in arrangements to mobilise resources such as land, revenue and military labour through this period. That extended exercise will have to await another occasion.

Notes and References

1. This is what a soldier of the 27th Bombay Regiment is said to have replied on being questioned after being caught in his own village. See George Le Grand Jacob, *Western India before and during the Mutinies* (Delhi: Mayur Publications, 1985), p. 175. First published in 1872.
2. Gautam Bhadra, 'Four Rebels of Eighteen Fifty Seven', in Ranajit Guha, ed., *Subaltern Studies IV* (Delhi: Oxford, 1985), p. 252.
3. Secret Correspondence, no. 543 of 1857, Political Department (henceforth, PD), Bombay State Archives (henceforth, BSA), vol. 27 (1857), p. 179.
4. PD, BSA, vol. 27 (1857), p. 180.

5. James Campbell, *Bombay Gazetteer Series*, vol. 19 (Bombay: Central Press, 1885), p. 316.

6. Jacob, *Western India*, p. 236.

7. Godse Bhat, *Majha pravaas athvaa 1857 chya bandachi hakikat* (Bombay: Pratibha Pratisthan, 1992), first published 1909. The account was written around 1883, but fearing reprisal, was published only after the author's death.

8. Substance of a letter from Dajeenath, 27 July 1857 to Mhadnath Jemadar of the Fourth Company of the First Grenadier Regiment, residing at Broach. The letter mentions news that a battle is anticipated at Malwan, that the rebels were at Sanglee and Sheerwar, that the 29th Regiment had mutinied, while the 27th Regiment at Kolhapur was coming to Malwan, adding that that rice and *nachnee* had become very dear there. A communication from Col. Le Grand Jacob, Commanding Officer Kolhapur, to Lieutenant Col. Telley, Asst. Adjutant General Belgaum, 21 November, mentions the 'exaggerated reports of native newspapers that do much mischief in feeding the hope that sooner or later the time may come for a successful rising'. The letter adds that Col. Jacob has brought to the notice of the political secretary reports in the Bombay, Poona and Ratnagiri papers. It quotes the *Vartmandeepika* of 14 November as having reported that General Outram and General Havelock were wounded, the British army at Lucknow were in want of food and that the rebels were getting stronger everyday. All this information was attributed to the Calcutta Englishman. Similarly, the Vritssar of 16 November stated that communication between Calcutta and the upper provinces had ceased, owing to the rebels having carried off the post horses. Both these and other Bombay papers which circulated in Kolhapur carried persistent reports that Nanasahib would come as promised with a large army for the restoration of the Hindoo raj. See PD, BSA, pp. 598–599.

9. Dinshaw Wacha, *Shells from the Sands of Bombay: Being My Recollections and Reminiscences 1860–1875* (Bombay: K.T. Anklesharia, 1920), pp. 79–80.

10. Sudipta Kaviraj, 'On the Construction of Colonial Power: State, Discourse, Hegemony', in Engels and Marks, eds, *Contesting Colonial Hegemony* (London: 1994), pp.19–54.

11. Veena Naregal, *Language Politics, Elites and the Public Sphere: Western Indian under Colonialism* (Delhi: Permanent Black, 2001).

12. One indication of the importance of the bilingual divide was a shift in the nature of native press initiatives from the 1840s. See Naregal, *Language Politics*, chap. 5.

13. Witness testimonies and depositions included in 'Proceedings held before Charles Forbes, Lieutenant Colonel George Malcolm and Captain James Rose, Commissioner under the Provisions of Section VII Act XIV of 1857 for the Trial of Offenses against the State', 27 August 1857, vol. 29, PD 1857, BSA, pp. 303–360.

14. Vitthal Gopal Khobrekar, *Ingraji Sattaviruddha Maharashtratil Sashastra Uthava* (Bombay: Popular Book Depot, 1959), pp. 54–55; James Campbell, ed., *Bombay Gazetteer Series*, vol. 19 (Bombay: Central Press, 1885), pp. 315–319.

15. Vitthal Gopal Khobrekar, *Ingraji Sattaviruddha Maharashtratil Sashastra Uthava*, pp. 40–50.

16. These petitions strongly denounce rebel activity in Delhi and Meerut, etc., express their fullest confidence about the fidelity of the Bombay army and the loyalty of its inhabitants, and assure the governor of the fullest support and cooperation in ensuring that there would be no disturbances in Bombay. PD, BSA, vol. 13 (1857).

17. The alleged chief instigator, Gulmar Dube, a *purabiya*, was sentenced on 22 October to be hanged; however, the sentence was commuted to life imprisonment, for reasons that remain unclear. Similarly, *Hawaldar* Sumasingh and Naik Laxman of the Tenth Batallion were sentenced to life imprisonment and banishment, respectively, while one of the prime accused, Sheikh Rahman of the Eleventh Marine Batallion, was acquitted.

18. See Rosalind O'Hanlon, *Caste, Conflict and Ideology: Mahatma Jotirao Phule and Low Caste Protest in Nineteenth-century Western India* (Cambridge: Cambridge University Press, 1985).

19. A mere boy when he came to the throne, as he matured, Pratapsingh proved much too capable and independent-minded to accede to British designs to take over any lapsed *jagirs* that had hitherto formed part of the raja's territories. Pratapsingh's determination to approach the Home authorities directly to secure a just hearing led to charges of treason and conspiracy being levied against him, to prove which, much false evidence was supplied with the help of the Raja's enemies, including Balajee Punt Natu, the *chitpavan* Brahmin, who had rendered venerable service by defecting to the British camp and supplying valuable intelligence against the Peshwa in the last stages of Bajirao II's rule and, in fact, had hoisted the British flag over Pune after the final battle of Khadki in 1818. See R.D. Choksey, *Raja Pratapsingh of Satara 1818–1839* (Pune: Bharat Itihas Samshodak Mandal, 1970), pp. 1–22.

20. See Michael H. Fisher, *Counter Flows to Colonialism: Indian Travellers and Settlers in Britain 1600–1857* (Delhi: Permanent Black, 2004), pp. 275–296.

21. This has been widely documented, most famously in the case of Bahadur Shah Zafar, but also for Rani of Jhansi, Scindia. See William Dalrymple, *The Last Mughal: The Fall of a Dynasty, Delhi, 1857* (Delhi: Viking-Penguin, 2006); Tapti Roy, *Raj of the Rani* (Delhi: Penguin, 2007); Iqtidar Alam Khan, 'The Gwalior Contingent in 1857–58: A Study of the Organisation and Ideology of the Sepoy Rebels', *Social Scientist*, vol. 26, nos 1–4 (1998), pp. 53–75. As we shall see below, and closer to our context, the same held true for the intelligent and energetic Chimasaheb, the younger prince in Kolhapur.

22. PD, BSA, vol. 29 (1857), p. 297.

23. Ibid.

24. Ibid., p. 303.

25. Ibid., pp. 303–357.

26. Vitthal Gopal Khobrekar, *Ingraji Sattaviruddha Maharashtratil Sashastra Uthva*, p. 52.

27. PD, BSA, vol. 29, 1857, p. 317.

28. Witness testimony, Sakharam Kabhade, ibid., p. 307.

29. PD, BSA, vol. 29 (1857), pp. 335–336.

30. Ibid., pp. 354–357.

31. Ibid., pp. 346–348. For an excellent study of the importance of the military tradition of *mahar* and *mang* groups within the inclusive ethos of military service in the Deccan and how that changed through the colonial period, see Phillip Constable, 'The Marginalization of a Dalit Martial Race in Late 19th and Early 20th-century Western India', *Journal of Asian Studies*, vol. 60, no. 2, 2001, pp. 439–478.

32. *Western India before and during the Mutinies*, p. 178.

33. PD, BSA, vol. 24 (1858), pp. 245–250.

34. PD, BSA, vol. 31 (1857), p. 138.

35. P.D. BSA, vol. 30 (1857), p. 47.

36. Jacob, *Western India*, p. 190. Other estimates put the size of the rebel force that night at approximately 500 men.

37. Ibid.

38. For excerpted reports from the *Bombay Gazette* and *Poona Observer*, see P.B. Kulkarni, *Nana Shankarseth Yanche Charita* (Bombay: Marathi Sahitya Sangh, 1959), pp. 393–396. See letter dated 8 June 1863 to Comissioner Hart, quoted in *Nana Shankarseth Yanche Charita*, pp. 403–404.

39. The Marathi translation of this letter has been published, suggesting that the former may have been carried in some Marathi papers; however, there may be a discrepancy about the date when the *Bombay Gazette* carried the original letter, mentioned in Marathi as 3 July 1863.

40. Patrick Cadell, *History of the Bombay Army* (London : Longmans, Green and Co., 1938).

41. In 1852, according to Cadell, the number of Rajputs and Brahmins constituted nearly one-third of the Bombay infantry, excluding the Baluch regiments. Whereas Marathas numbered 8,037, the number of Rajputs and Brahmins stood at 6,928, and other castes stood at a combined 8,789. See Cadell, *History*, p. 200. Appendix V mentions the class compositon of the Twenty-seventh and Twenty-eighth Infantry regiments as follows: comprising four companies of Pathans, two Brahui companies and two Punjabi Mohammedan companies, see p. 330.

11

⁓⁓

WHAT CONSTITUTES A MARGIN OR MARGINS? THE POLITICS OF PERCEPTION AND THE REPRESENTATION OF POWER
The Insurrection of 1857 in Kolhan

Gautam Bhadra

SIR Ernest Gowers wrote rather sharply, 'Marginal has a number of useful jobs to do ... but in recent years marginal has come to be increasingly used to mean no more than small. This misuse has now reached the status of an epidemic.'[1] In fact, the Oxford dictionary has enumerated no fewer than five distinct usages of 'marginal' and six distinct usages of the term 'margin' in different contexts. Primarily though, the margin is a spatial concept. It points to the outer area bordering something, an area that is often distinct in appearance from what it encloses. As a category of spatial distribution, it also refers to an empty space that sets off and surrounds another entity. In this sense, the 'margin' can be meaningful only in reference to another space, a centre or an interior.

This implication of space extends to identify the excluded or non-integrated part and thereby indicates the group or men at the periphery. But the notion of space is never absent in its social nuance. Again, on a philosophical plane, Hegel has used the concept of the margin as a logical category to denote the limit of philosophical discourse. Philosophy, it has been said, 'insisted upon this: thinking its other'.[2] In the process of thinking, the limiting factor may not be always located on a borderline, but erupts within. That disturbs the accepted notion of boundary from spatial to moral. The centre would always try to have its mastery over the margin and would never be 'foreign to it'. The margin, through its own formation, may have an edge to pierce the centre, to dislocate it. Shifts in particular modes of marginal formations may also lead to displacements in the periphery conceived and recognised by the centre. 'Margin' versus 'Centre' and vice versa. It may not always be so. One also constitutes the other, changing relations may form new alignments, spatially and historically.

This chapter intends to focus on some of these issues which are implicitly connected with the notion of the margin in the context of the insurrection in Chotanagpore Division, specifically that in Kolhan, i.e., Singhbhum or the country of the Kols. This is neither a sequential narrative nor a causal analysis of the uprising. Much has been written on it, and I have myself conducted such an exercise elsewhere.[3] The objective of this chapter is to show how the notion of the 'margin' is explicitly or implicitly present in the fashioning and perceiving of local insurgency in the context of an uprising covering a large part of India. How do the local and supra-local interact? This question has been viewed from three vantage points—(a) the vision of the English administrators and commanders, (b) the perception of the insurgent chief Arjun Singh, raja of Porahat, Singhbhum and (c) the experience of the village vis-à-vis the local and supra-local polity.

The Margin in the Making: A Prose of Counter-insurgency

Sir Fredrick Halliday, the lieutenant governor of Bengal (and 'a musician of unusual capacity as an amateur'), authored a minute 'on the mutinies as they affected the lower provinces'. He argued that the provinces of Bengal and Bihar had been less affected, and thereby had naturally attracted less notice, whilst the events in upper and central India were 'all engrossing'.

The contemporary media's focus was on upper India, not on eastern India. Halliday wrote this minute to rectify this oversight in the focus. He introduced his subject with a crucial passage:

> It cannot, however, be supposed that these great provinces, connected in so many ways with the more disturbed districts, inhabited partly by a people cognate in manners, language, sympathy, and race with those of the North-Western provinces—*partly by tribes of ignorant and unenlightened savages*, and everywhere, to some context, occupied by portions of *that army* whose mutiny is at least the proximate cause of these disturbances—can have altogether escaped the wide-spread *contagion*.[4] (Emphasis added.)

It is interesting to note how Halliday envisages three axes around which a comparatively marginal area, in the context of the India-wide scale of 'engrossing events', is significant because 'contagion' spreads. The uprising discussed here ran from 30 July to 5 August 1857, when the Ramgarh Battalion and its detachments stationed at Hazaribagh, Ranchi-Doranda, Chaibasa and Purulia revolted and began to march in a similar pattern to the uprisings in the upper provinces. As eastern India is related to northern India through cultural networks, the spread of news and disturbance is not surprising. But Halliday employs an anthropological category of social Darwinism to inject a thin line of cultural marginality—the area inhabited 'by tribes of ignorant and unenlightened savages'. The savage, in this presentation, appears as a cutting edge to the rebellion, its dangerous margin. J.S. Davis, operating in Palamau—adjacent to Singhbhum, and, because of the combined uprisings of Chero and Bhogta tribe, another epicentre of civil upsurge of Chotanagpore Division—explained the slow progress of 'pacification' in the region as follows:

> The whole of the inhabitants without exception are, if not openly, on the side of the rebels who received every information of our movements whilst it is with the utmost difficulty that we are enabled to trace them—and then not perhaps till they have plundered and burnt some villages in the vicinity.

Not only was the whole community united against the British, but:

> The causes of the rebels having the country so entirely with them are many; the inhabitants generally are a *wild race* fond of marauding, they are held together by a clannish feeling and the common one of self-preservation as they have no sufficient confidence in the power of the government to protect them, should they act contrary, to the wishes or orders of the rebel chiefs.[5] (Emphasis added.)

Again, the rebels belong to a 'wild race' and are fond of plunder. Palamau and Singhbhum here are seen as dangerous marginal spaces, culturally antithetical to civilisation due to their cultural and political behaviour. On the uncivilised margin (which is populated by those driven by ethnic loyalty as well as political motivations), no rational negotiation or settlement is possible. In order to explain the limiting effects the Palamau insurgents had on the progress of the army, Davis conjures up a violent race, which is prone to plunder and is united in a 'clannish' loyalty inimical to their loyalty to the company bahadur. The necessity of the causal sequence demands the formation of a margin, both in an actual and metaphorical sense.

To Halliday, the dangers of the margins are obvious:

> It will be readily be understood that I became more than ordinarily anxious for the Province of Bihar, *bordering as it does on the actively disturbed parts of the country*, more than any one of his districts supplying soldiers for the army, the town of Patna, itself rightly or wrongly supposed to be hot bed of Mohammedan conspiracies and of course at this time an object of more than usual suspicion—which, however, I am bound to say, that events have not justified.[6] (Emphasis added.)

The perception of a region as a danger zone is clear. The location of a division bordering on a highly disturbed space, swelled by apprehension of a counter-ideology, leads the ruling power to surmise the imminent possibility of an outbreak. But it was not the area around Patna (except Sahabad) but another area that tested the resilience of the control of authority most seriously. Halliday began with a spatial description:

> During the whole period of outbreaks, the Division of Chotanagpore has been a source of anxiety and uneasiness, and from time-to-time of embarrassment and difficulty, and even of actual danger. In fact, *no division in the whole of Bengal had been subject to such continued disturbance* as this province. It extends along the whole length of Grand Trunk Road, from Raniganj to Shergate, a distance of no less than hundred miles. (Emphasis added.)

The Chotanagpore Division, thus, posed a threat throughout the course of the mutiny. The nature of the disturbances and their parallel location to the lines of communication rendered the area a margin that defined the limits of the state's authority. On this margin Halliday commented:

> Its population is composed chiefly of *half savages*, ignorant and *highly excitable*, with a number of petty chiefs able at any time to collect a rabble around them, and now formidable from the disaffection of the very troops intended to keep them in check.[7] (Emphasis added.)

The people ready for mobilisation are not educated *ashraf*s or Wahabis, 'fanatic' religious preachers, but the 'savages' who are beyond the pale of civilisation and education and to whom to the rules of ordered governance are anathema. The failure of governance and sudden abandonment of the city of Chaibasa by captain Sissmore, the assistant commissioner, makes the region volatile.[8] The presence of authority in the stationing of garrisons, 'scattered and not easily accessible', is seen as necessary because the physical presence of authority speaks to 'savages' in a way that reason and language cannot. As the anthropologist Sarat Chandra Roy has argued, for a considerable time, the location of margins as the residence of 'wild' tribes such as the Kols was crystallised to suit the needs of governance. While discussing the importance of a report sent by S.T. Cuthbert from Ramgarh to the government, in April 1827,[9] Roy states that the record-room of the local administrative office holds as many reports of ethnographic interest as it does of historical interest. To him, ethnographic details were crucial to the effective running of local government. Cuthbert was unable to write the 'different land tenures' and 'rights and privileges' of all classes of the division without a discourse on the people and its customs because custom is, to many, the foundation of tribal life and nation. K.K. Basu would have been of the same attitude. Discussing the memorandum of Major Roughshedge, the first official English report (1820) on the Larka Kols (the militant tribe or 'savages' that reside in Singhbhum and who fought for Arjun Singh, king of Porahat),

K.K. Basu paraphrased Major Roughshedge's initial reaction to a little-known border territory:

> The northern most Taluk of the Larkas named Adjoundea was separated from the civilised part of Singbhum by a small river ... on crossing it one comes across a singular spectacle of a well-cultivated country, studded with large villages, but inhabited by the people, who owned no law and were in a constant state of aggression and hostility with the rest of the world. It was with difficulty he could bring himself to believe that the smiling hamlets in view contained so ferocious and sanguinary a people as one forced them to be.[10] (Emphasis added.)

The image is of two spaces, civilised Singhbhum on the one hand and the land of the ferocious Larka Kol on the other, gravitating in opposite directions—an interpretation that runs against the prevailing imperial notion of economic activity.

In the fury of the post-pacification days, E.T. Dalton, commissioner and future ethnographer, had a similar vision of the area. On 'a protracted sojourn' in Singhbhum with his detachment, Dalton was satisfied with the submission of all classes and the villages at pargana of Porahat, the estate of Arjun Singh, which 'not only submitted but have gladly agreed to settling agreements for twenty years'. Due to his two months' operation, the villagers of the burnt villages returned, 'made considerable progress in building huts' and 'have also been briskly employed in the cultivation of rich rice lands of Porahat proper'. But he was ever-suspicious of the people of the area as a threat to normalcy, referring to them as 'the wild Kols of the high-ranges to the south, rude savages'. 'Wild', 'rude', 'savage'—the adjectives are, by now, familiar. Their placement and association with a specific race and locality are also predictable. He thus described the frontier between the peace zone and the receding zone of the rebellion:

> The remnants of the rebels with the Ex-Rajah are reduced to a pitiable condition. They have returned to the most inaccessible portion of the Porahat hill and jungles. All sources of supplies are cut off. They have nothing but wretched food supplied to them half savage hill Kols. A few of these Kols guard the ghats by which the Ex-Rajah's retreat is approached. The force of the Porahat insurgents is reduced to this, a handful of despicable savages and about a score of desolate characters in the district.[11]

With glee, Dalton expresses confidence that the centre is now enclosing the border itself, the plain has surrounded the hill and the forces of the state have cornered the forces of the rebellion. Yet the raja of Porahat is within its retreat, a zone protected and covered by a group of Kols belonging to the hilly area of South Singhbhum. They are few, yet stubborn, despicable and desolate savages. Dalton, the civilised anthropologist and the restorer of peace, is aware of the limit to his power, which is even now much reduced. He would prefer to withdraw to Chakradharpore and Chaibasa during the rainy seasons; he is not willing to take any risks. Halliday is similarly cognisant of the narrow margin of success. Describing a series of incidents here and there, he reported that tranquillity seemed to be, in great measure, restored, but 'some uneasiness however, continued to exist in the district'.[12]

The disturbed 'space' seemed to be a function of wild passion and savagery, a perpetual 'tribal' state of being.[13] This argument helped authority to locate a space which demanded special and direct attention from the centre; politics should look to culture to understand the alterity of civilisation, savagery. In the romantic ideology of Western civilisation, invocation of a 'wild area' may act as a place of retreat into which a defeated third person, often the noble and self-sacrificing victim of a triangular love, withdraws with the royal mission of taking up the white man's burden. *Jane Eyre* is not an atypical Victorian novel in this respect. But to the administrators of colonial India, the 'wild' and 'the savages' existed side by side with the peasant cultivator and the educated babus. There was a practical necessity for a space of alterity because of its contemporaneous and simultaneous presence with colonial modernity. Hence, there was a need to locate history within current practices regarding marginal areas; in fact, the marginality was distinctly marked by these practices, branded as peculiar and generic to the culture of the area. Ethnography and anthropology provided the necessary clues to understanding and linked political practices and a cultural theory of progress or noble isolation. In local reports or in general narrative, the points of marginality were thus mapped on the grids of moving power. Loss and re-appropriation determined the application of adjectives to the margin and marginal people within a scale of culture of governance, historical and anthropological. Geographical and cultural investment cannot be sustained without political power, and marginal space was almost encapsulated within the political desire and assertion of the ruling centre; yet there remained a 'margin', however small and insignificant, for generating uneasiness and anxiety.

Dual Faces of a Reluctant Rebel: Arjun Singh at the Margin

'The people belonged to God and the country to the King, and Urjoon Singh is ruler there of.'[14] In early September 1857, this was the proclamation heard at Chaibasa, marking a shift in the existing power structure at Kolhan. This was quite in tune with similar events in the cities and *qasbah*s of northern India. But in a sense, during its march towards Ranchi, the rebel army clearly understood that the situation was altogether different. Throughout the year of 1855 the same battalion had, with ruthless efficiency, crushed a mighty insurrection of the Santals, and was known over the region as 'Chota Burdwan ka Paltan',

as Burdwan was the centre of the sahibs who controlled the entire district of
South-west Frontier Agency within the Non-regulation Province.[15] Kolhan was
exempt from general civil regulations and, as a frontier area, was separately
administered by officers, selected generally from the army, 'with an aptitude for
civil business' and 'an acquaintance with vernacular'. Moreover, the area was,
on a local level, conceived as a conglomeration of *peers*, a collectivity of a few
villages with their *manki* or headman, responsible to authority for the conduct
of local affairs. Thus, the military officer in civil dress and local village headman
with his 'pugree', conjoined in a hierarchical reciprocity, were the chief features
of Charles Wilkinsons system.[16] Its intention was to neutralise the tension arising
from an evolving political system through the claims and actions of Rajput-
Bhumij chiefs, centring on the King of Singhbhum, or raja of Porahat, the rulers
of Seraikilla and Mayurbhanj, each house being related to the other. As the
Poltan had revolted, the pressure on the local polity evaporated, and Captain
Sissmore, a khaki man with the talent for civil duties, left Chaibasa on 3 August
1857, giving directions to the rajas of Porahat and Seraikilla, the rival houses, to
maintain law and order in the frontier agency.

The people at the frontier encircled a hitherto moving representative of the
centre, 'Chota Burdwan ka Poltan'. That was precisely the experience of a sepoy,
a member of the coercive rebel detachment of the Ramgarh Battalion in early
September, who wrote:

> The sepoys plundered the treasure and we marched West till we were stopped
> by a Nuddee, which we could not cross; we remained there four days; about
> five hundred or six hundred Coles surround us there; but no forces of any
> of the zamindars of the district were with them; during, that time we were
> starving.[17]

There was no civil rebellion consequent on the military rebellion; the tribes
were up against the rebel army. Here the raja of Porahat intervened, rescued
them and brought the detachment to his estate. In lieu of his temporary
protection, 'they consented to lodge their arm to the Rajah'. Dalton described
the ultimate fate of the members of the battalion when Arjun Singh of Porahat
met Captain Davis at Ranchi on 11 October 1857: 'When he (Davis) met the
party, he found the mutineers divided into four-bodies of twenty-five each,
all marching with intervals of a few hundred yards only between each body,
and each surrounded by a large force of armed men chiefly Cole-bow men.'
According to an estimate, three or four thousand Larka Kols of the Southern
Pirs 'volunteered to act as escorts'. Dalton reported the loyal action of the chief
of Kolhan in graphic detail:

> Urjoon Singh was on an elephant with a loaded gun himself engaged in guarding
> the mutineers, of whose escape he appeared to be very apprehensive.

Dalton, on the basis of Davis' report, went on to state:

> It seems a great relief to him [Arjun Singh] when they were all safely made over to Madras troops, every man with Urjoon Singh and he himself were ... engaged in guarding the mutineers or the arms and the treasure.[18]

Arjun Singh, the loyalist, handed over to the sahib 'one hundred mutineers as prisoners, one hundred stands of arms, a considerable quality of ammunition' and the sum of 19,000 rupees. Thus, the military mutiny was not taken up by a civilian population led by a local chief. They had, in fact, opposed it. The army represented the coercive power of the centre, and the Kols were not in sympathy with them. The Kols as a group surrounded the mutinous soldiers without the intervention of any higher local power. As Dalton himself remarked: 'The Coles of Chybussah neighbourhood assembled with wonderful alacrity and would not allow them to proceed.' There was a clear hiatus. The uprising of Ramgarh Battalion may have created a vacuum, but the civil rebellion at Kolhan had its own volition. It began as an act of opposition against the military rebellion and later assumed the character of civil rebellion because of the lack of recognition the Kols received for their service to the English authorities. The margin wanted to serve the centre, but the centre was suspicious.

The nature of local politics then became decisive.[19] The preference of the military official at Chaibasa for the raja of Seraikilla made Arjun Singh highly nervous, and he avoided meeting with Birch, the assistant commissioner at Chaibasa, despite several *purwanah*s of assurance. Juggu Dewan or Jagannath Patnaik formed a 'war party', was immediately arrested and hanged by the British and, as an exemplary punishment, his body was left exposed at 'the centre of Bazar' of Chakradharpur until dusk. On 20 October 1857, the troops, with the assistance of men from the raja of Seraikilla, confiscated Porahat estate and destroyed the fort. Arjun Singh was labelled an 'Ex-Rajah', everybody being convinced of his 'wavering vacillating conduct'. As a result, as Dalton reported, 'the South Colehan was now in open insurrection'.[20]

During this time, the civil rebellion generated a number of *Talpatras* or Tal-leaf letters. L.T. Birch made a sudden raid to the retreat of the ex-raja at Kooridah and seized a number of letters written on 'Tal-leaves'. A debate to determine the authenticity of this correspondence was a part of the judicial discourse. This debate reveals the extent of juridical weightage of responsibility placed upon the behaviour of Arjun Singh, '[w]ho played so confusing a part when the struggle just began'.[21] Arjun Singh challenged the authenticity of the correspondence, but Dalton was convinced that 'Once the Rubicon of rebellion was passed', Arjun Singh was encouraged to remain at revolt by 'too credulous acceptance of the false reports of designing men'.[22] *Talpatras* representing examples of these reports were presented as an 'appendix' to the trial charge sheet against Arjun Singh.

Arjun Singh knew two scripts well, Oriya and Nagri; he was fond of using various pens, and his scribes were encouraged to do the same. His signature for the English authority was written in the English alphabet. But his usual signature, inscribed on letters meant for his subjects and neighbours, was different and he 'used to add to the Ramnam two geese' probably because 'all the near relations of the Rajah signed their names Ramnam'. But after taking to the jungle he stopped this practice. The tactics of the raja seem to be transparent to the judicial authority.[23]

The letters belonged to two groups. One group relates to the correspondence between Arjun Singh and his brother Baijunath Singh, and another group refers to letters and reports sent by anonymous writers, as Damodar informs us, 'who was [sic] in habit of writing to raja Arjoon Singh, and giving him news from all parts'. In one of the letters to his brother, Arjun Singh states:

> He had sent a letter by Gopal and Phungur to the Badshah, and gives the news brought by these messengers that the 'Badshah' had thirty lacs of infantry, ten thousand guns, and thirteen lacs of cavalry. All the Rajahs of North-West had joined him, that Nana Sahib had twenty-two lacs of cavalry, that the 'Badshah' of Roum had sent the Badshah two thousand five hundred guns, seven thousand horses and a great body of infantry. That Jung Bahadur had joined with a large force. Kooer Singh had one thousand cavalry.[24]

In another typical *Talpatra*, 'in reply to a letter asking if the Badshah was coming' to Kolhan or not, an anonymous informer states: 'The Badshah [King of Delhi] has not come but is at Delhi, that a force has come as far as Cawnpore and that Koonwar Singh has come from Jugdeespore to Palamau with five hundred men. Koonwar Singh has a large force.'[25]

The two letters cited as illustrations show how people at the periphery perceived the movements of the rebels and assessed their power in core regions of the mutiny. The Badshah's arrival was expected, and this hope would have bolstered their confidence against the might of the company. The rebels at Kolhan were clearly contemplating a broader vision of political alliance, beyond their locality, against the English. The Kols relocated and redefined themselves with the Badshah and Kunwar Singh. The search for alternative centres of power were discernible in the 'news' being collected in the *Talpatras*. Thus, there was nothing arbitrary in Arjun Singh's choice. In order to maintain his very existence in local politics, he was serving two masters. He was aware of the Queen's Proclamation and, at the same time, was interested in the political and military progress of the rebel leaders at Delhi, Kanpur and Jagdishpur. In a political sense he was, vis-à-vis the English onslaught, undoubtedly on the margin. But in order to maintain his very marginal existence, he opted to position himself at the centre.

A Ho in Kolhan: The Man and His Margin

The Kols at Kolhan had two appellations, 'Larka' and 'Ho'. 'Larka', an adjective, was more frequently used by its neighbours in official documents, implying nature or essence and the militancy of the tribe. 'Ho' means 'man'—an innocuous common name, signifying a species. Dalton, the anthropologist, believed that 'Ho' was the term the people preferred and retained as their exclusive 'appellation'.[26] Kol as a single person is part of this exclusive name, a mark of his embeddedness in a clan or village for which a *manki*'s representation to the English authority would suffice. In fact, the company's rule had formalised the *manki-munda* system with an oath to the commissioner by which the headman and his assistants were made responsible for the payment of revenue and maintenance of peace in their village.[27] The increase in the number of annual visits of the *manki*s to the authorities at Chaibasa (the English headquarters) was considered an index of the prevalence of peace in the area. A *manki* was also a Ho, but the Ho alone had a status recognised by the state. Without this kind of sanction, a Ho would have been hardly visible, unless committing a violent act. Two illustrations may be cited to underline the tension between visibility and opaqueness, a feature suggesting the constant presence of a margin within any margin.

During the rebellion, Mora and Bya, two Hos, killed Toonya and Kunda: 'two *pykes* of Seraikillah, Rajah's contingent, recently serving in Singbhum against the insurgents of Porahat'.[28] They were at the rear of a party in charge of looking after the cattle following Birch's march to Burpeer, the most disaffected area of Kolhan. A party of insurgents fell on the escort. Rugu Dewan asked Bya, Moro, Kannoo and others, all Kols and cultivators, to hold the ghats and passes against the army and to cut off stragglers. Maro stated with a supposed frankness:[29]

> About a mile to the west of village Bankee, when about twelve *pykes* were coming along the road, we drew up and met them. They fired at us and then we let fly at them; they were all ready and so we were ready; at first discharge two of their men were struck and then all ran away leaving two of their number on the ground.

They cut the heads off the *pykes*, took away the cattle and divided them amongst themselves. Maro described his part in the incident as follows:

> [T]he party with me consisted altogether twelve. Of these myself, Jarka and Dooley from Agooroa, we are brothers. Kanu, Bya and Dergey came from Kooilenta and are also brothers, the remainder of them came from Byntorra Peer but I cannot give particulars of them.

He asserted:

> We *had no leader*. We all went together to cut off stragglers on the road to the Sahib's camp and we were all ordered to kill all the people we came across. (Emphasis added.)

It is a minor skirmish, even in the context of the revolt at Singhbhum. Yet, in this incident, neither Maro nor Bya recognised any leader. They themselves decided how to act during a violent and armed confrontation; common residence and blood relations are the bonds of action—'we are all brothers', the utterance was like a refrain. The collectivity dominated the particular act. It was again through violence that they asserted their marginality. At the same time, they were unaware of the particulars of some members of their own force; brotherhood in action appeared to be the only bond on which the collectivity had formed itself for the moment. 'We all went together.' This 'we' again, might be a melting point. As Bya said, 'We all went but the prisoners Jarka, Doley and Dergey fled when they saw *pykes*, we three Mora, Kanoo and I stood.'[30] Action is the moment when a 'Ho' could express himself as 'I' with an assertion of his particular responsibility for an act.

The second illustration has no direct causal relation with the rebellion, but may be related in character. Martoon of Pargana Porahat, by 'Cast Kol and by occupation a cultivator and brother of Boomya Cole', thus narrated his sad experience:[31]

> About the time the Ex-Rajah took the treasure to the treasury, I missed my brother. One day I had parted with him, in the morning before I went out to cultivation and when I returned in the afternoon, I could not find him.

On the basis of the information of Maddoo Cole, a fellow villager,

> I went in search of the body, and was four days looking for it; I then discovered it in the jungle about a quarter mile to the East of the village; the body was quite decomposed, too much so to enable me to remark any wound or signs of violence on it, but I would recognise it as the corpse of my brother.

On enquiry it was revealed that Doonga, 'The Moonda of village', had made a plan to kill Boomya Cole because he was insane. 'He went about naked', a villager said, and 'killed all the fowls in the villages'. Mora, a fellow villager, confirmed the situation: 'He had become a maniac and used to run about naked and always dancing and singing; the villagers all made up their minds to kill him, least he should do them injury.' Dongloo, another villager, reported, 'Boomea once set fire to his own house.' At the same time, 'he had a dispute with the prisoner Doonka', the principal accused, over a plot of land.

Doonka might have wished to do away with Boomya for purely material motives; the authority of government was shaken, and as Dalton, the commissioner, remarked, 'many considered themselves justified in taking the law into their own hands'. Doonka was successful in his project because the villagers shared his belief. Boomya, the Ho, had been recognised as a threat to the community. He was not normal, and hence, he existed at the margin, 'a dangerous maniac'. As a Ho, he went beyond the margins of the community, and was finally subjected to the wrath and retribution of the village. Considering the situation, Dalton, 'the just' commissioner, declared, 'I abstain from passing a capital sentence.'[32]

Dalton was eager to specify the *persona* of a Ho; the particular would always help him to judge and to distribute reward and punishment. At the same time, as an anthropologist with faith in the scale of civilisation, he was interested in the development of a community, a community consisting of few aspiring persons, eager for betterment, each for his own good. A Ho is in a fix between these two discourses: the judicial and the beneficial anthropological judgement. In the days of the pacification campaign, Dalton imposed a collective fine over the area and was perturbed by his failure to individualise the responsibility for the rebellion, as he wrote officially:

> It is a singular fact that in not one instance has the offer of the reward had the desired effect. Many of the delinquents have been captured it is true, but by military force or by police, not by the people. Thus, though a man may have committed a crime so atrocious as to lead us to expect that the society in which he lives would be most anxious to get rid of him and that all who know him guilty would for their own sake help to deliver him to justice, not a soul will move in the matter, even with the additional temptation of a large reward for doing so.[33]

The community Dalton desired was a 'civil' order, but its pre-civil behaviours obfuscated its persona before the searching eye of the state. At the same time, it was clear that the community has its own notion of marginality by which so-called delinquents should be judged and punished; the number of crimes increased because the community redefined its own margins vis-à-vis a particular Ho or Kol, conspicuous by his singular behaviour.[34] Yet this would not do for Dalton as it went against the norm of the state and put a limit on the 'rule of law'. Dalton, the practising ethnographer, believed the 'judicious management' of the officers of Kolhan. The law of progress was inexorable, he was convinced; the insurrection was a serious check, but of brief duration. The Ho in a village would be transformed into a loyal and law-abiding person; his behaviour would be particular and natural. In this way, a marginal area would be integrated into the core and the Hos would return to the authority of the English like 'lambs to the fold'.[35]

Conclusion

It ought to be clear from the above discussion that there is no a priori existence of the margin in historical discourse; spatially, politically and culturally,
it is a relational concept, evolving and reconfiguring from time to time. The
administrative exercises of a state, whether precolonial, colonial or modern, the
imperatives of regional politics, and the existential necessities of a community,
as well as the high practices of juridical, historical and ethnographical discipline
and mores, of course, tend to demarcate a space as a margin in need of stabilisation. At the same time, it seems that the margin has its own expectations from
a centre; its dissatisfaction might well affect the relation between the locale of a
margin and the core during a crucial 'event'; the event may itself be an assertion
of the margin, the self-expression of a political space. On a third level, the margin
is embedded in a culture of collectivity as opposed to the culture of individuality.
A particular within a collectivity may sometimes behave quirkily and may create
a thin marginal line within it. The margin and centre tend to stabilise each other
through a judicial balance of tensions. It is merely the possibility of occasional
mismatches and incongruities that transforms the study of the 'marginal' and
the margin from a subject of predicable boredom into a fascinating topic.

Notes and References

1. Sir Ernest Gowers, *Complete Plain Words* (London: Penguin, 1987), pp. 243–244.
2. Jacques Derrida, 'Tympan', in *Margins of Philosophy*, trans. Alan Bass (Chicago: University of Chicago, 1982), pp. 10–11.
3. On the insurrection of 1857 in Singhbhum, see P.C. Ray-Chaudhuri, *1857 in Bihar* (Patna: Government of Bihar, 1959); Purushottam Kumar, *Mutinies and Rebellions in Chotanagpur, 1831–1857* (New Delhi: 1999); M. Sahu, *The Kolhan under British Rule* (Jamshedpur, 1985). For a brief account of the rebellion in the whole of the division, see S.B. Chaudhuri, *Civil Rebellion in the Indian Mutinies 1857–59* (Calcutta: World Press, 1957), pp. 185–196; Gautam Bhadra, 'Chotanagpur in 1857', in O.J.P. Taylor, ed., *A Companion to the 'Indian Mutiny of 1857* (Delhi: OUP, 1996), pp. 83–85.
4. F. Halliday, 'The Mutinies as the Affected the Lower Provinces under the Government of Bengal, 1858', 30 September 1858. Published as appendix to C.E. Buckland, *Bengal under the Lieutenant Governors*, vol. 1 (Calcutta, 1902), p. 64.
5. J.S. Davis to Dalton, 23 December 1858, The Old English Correspondence, Ranchi; quoted in Chaudhuri, *Civil Rebellion*, pp. 186–187.
6. Halliday, 'The Mutinies', pp. 68–69.
7. Ibid, pp. 98–99.
8. Sahu, *The Kolhan*, pp. 84–85.
9. Sarat Chunder Roy, 'Ethnographical Investigation in Official Records', in *Journal of the Bihar and Orissa Research Society*, vol. VII, part IV (1921), pp. 1–27.

10. Reproduced in Dr K.K. Basu, 'Larka Kols of Singhbhum', *Journal of the Bihar and Orissa Research Society*, vol. XLIII, part 1–2, p. 75.

11. E. Dalton to Arthur Young, 2 September 1858. Judicial Consultation. MR No.120, Bihar State Archives, Patna (cited hereafter as BSA).

12. Halliday, 'The Mutinies', pp. 108–109.

13. The perceptive article by Prathama Banerjee, 'Culture/Politics: The Irresoluble Double-bend of the Indian Adivasi', *Indian Historical Review*, vol. XXXIII, no. 1 (January 2006), pp. 99–126. In the same issue, interested readers may also consult the pieces written by Sanjukta Dasgupta and Vinita Damodaran.

14. Deposition of Mouder son of Doudah, by caste, a Bhooya, and by occupation, a Chowkedar, 26 September 1857, sent by L.T. Birch and appended by Daltons' Report to Lushington on the trial of Arjoon Singh, 30 September 1859, Judicial Department, West Bengal State Archives, Calcutta (henceforth WBSA), 27 October 1859, no. 167.

15. N.K. Sahu, *Veer Surendra Sai* (Cuttack: Government of Orissa, 1985), pp. 132–133.

16. C.P. Singh, *The Ho Tribe of Singhbhum* (New Delhi, 1985), pp. 133–135.

17. Deposition of Beharee Lall, a resident of Mousa Amarood, Purgunnah Sherghotty, by caste, a Kayet, and by occupation, a sepoy, 24 February 1859, Judicial Department, WBSA, no. 5.

18. Dalton to Lushington, 30 September 1859, para. 23. Dalton, *Descriptive Ethnology of Bengal* (Calcutta, 1872; republished, Delhi: Cosmo Publications, 1973), p. 183.

19. The best available discussion of local politics is Nikhil Sur, 'Chotanagpur and the Rising of 1857', in *Bengal Past and Present* (January–December, 1986).

20. Dalton to Lushington, 30 September 1859, paras 29–34. R.C. Birch to A. Young, 23 November 1857, *Parliamentary Papers*, House of Commons, vol. 44, part IV, 1858–1859, no. 25, enclosure 17.

21. F.D. Bradley-Birt, *Chota-Nagpore: A Little-known Province of the Empire*, (London: Smith, Elder & Co., 1903), p. 220.

22. Dalton to Lushington, 30 September 1859, para. 49.

23. Deposition of Damodar, by caste, a Rajput, and by occupation, a landholder, 26 April, 1859, no. 34; Deposition of Mohan Lal, 10 May 1859, Judicial Department, WBSA, no. 37.

24. Arjoon Singh to Byjnath Singh, 17 November 1858, WBSA, no. 9, Appendix A.

25. To Byjnath Singh, 2 August 1858, WBSA, no. 59, Appendix B.

26. E.T. Dalton, *Descriptive Ethnology of Bengal*, p. 178.

27. For the written text of the oath taken by Manki or Munda see, P.C. Ray-Chaudhuri, *Singhbhum Old Records*, (Patna: Government of Bihar, 1958), pp. 54–55.

28. E.T. Dalton to H. Brown, 6 September 1859, Judicial Department, WBSA, 27 October 1859, No.176.

29. The Confession of Mora, 25 July 1859, Judicial Department, WBSA, 27 October 1859, No. 177.

30. Examination of Bya, 25 July 1859, Judicial Department, WBSA, 27 October 1859, No. 177.

31. Deposition of Martoon, 22 July 1859, attached to the letter from E.T. Dalton to H. Brown, 20 October, Judicial Department, WBSA, December 1859, pp. 32–34

32. Deposition of Martoon, 22 July 1859, attached to Dalton to Brown, 20 October.

33. Dalton to Young, 19 April 1858, Judicial Department, BSA, Patna, no. 67, para. 6.

34. For the increase and the nature of Crime in Singhbhum during the rebellion: A. Money to the Commissioner of Chotanagpur, 24 August 1860, Judicial Department, WBSA, August 1860, No. 331.

35. E.T. Dalton, *Descriptive Ethnology*, p. 184.

12

※※※

THE WAR OF INDEPENDENCE, 1857, AND SWAT*

Sultan-i-Rome

Introduction

UPRISINGS in India, against the English, were not rare phenomena. For example, in the pre-1857 period there occurred the sepoys' uprisings of Vellore 1806, Bareilly 1816 and Barrakpur 1824, and there were multiple Muslim movements and tribal and local peasant uprisings during the same period as well. These testify to the general ferment in the subcontinent in relation to English rule, but the Uprising of 1857 was the most severe as it rocked the edifice of English rule in India to its very foundations. The uprising of 1857 was neither planned solely by the sepoys nor remained a mere sepoy revolt. In its planning many other segments of Indian society apart from the sepoys were involved, and many who were not under English control played a role in the unfolding of events. Moreover, rulers of some Indian states and a segment of the intelligentsia and the common people—both Muslims and Hindus alike—joined the standard of revolt, due to which it became a mass uprising, though not throughout India, not well organised and, to a great extent, leaderless. These factors give the uprising the shape of a war of independence, although tragically unsuccessful in attaining its objective.

Although not part of the territories ruled and controlled by the English, and far from the centre of the uprising, Swat had a significant—albeit ambivalent—role to play in the war of 1857, both in terms of its causation and effect. Thus, Muhammad Anwar Khan asserts that since it was a 'south-sponsored movement', the Mujahidin of Swat and Sitana were intimately involved.[1] Based on archival records and published sources, this essay endeavours to evaluate and analyse this

*This chapter was presented in the 'International Conference on the War of Independence 1857' held in Bara Gali (University of Peshawar Summer Campus), on 18–19 August 2007; organised by Department of History, University of Peshawar, Pakistan, in collaboration with the Higher Education Commission, Pakistan.

role and the significance of Swat in relation to the War of Independence 1857 as well as the part played by the Akhund of Swat[2] and his policies, together with the effects of the war on the politics of Swat.

The English and Swat

Situated in the north-west of the subcontinent, the historic Swat valley retained its separate entity/status for most of its known history. In the sixteenth century the Yusufzai Afghan tribe occupied the valley of Swat and emerged as the dominant force but did not establish an organised state and government. In the meantime, the English came to the subcontinent in the seventeenth century initially for the purposes of trade. In the process of expanding their dominion in India, the territories of the Frontier plains—the then created districts of Hazara, Peshawar, Kohat, Bannu and Dera Ismail Khan—fell into their hands in 1849 'as the successors of the Sikhs'[3] in the upshot of the second Anglo-Sikh war and became part of the East India Company's Indian territories.

The Yusufzais did not recognise a sole person as their ruler or head and remained divided into two opposite blocks and factions called *dalas*—in Pukhtu (Pashto), singular: *dala*; plural: *dalay*—headed by their own Khans. However, they suspended their factional fighting, 'mutual rivalries and hostilities ... in cases of national emergencies'.[4] This virtue was noteworthy when the English occupied Peshawar in 1849 and led to punitive expeditions to Sam Baizai on the border of Swat.[5]

Positively responding to the threat to their independence, they agreed to make a common cause for defence under one responsible chief and to nominate a king for Swat. Although there were many claimants to the seat, the matter was settled amicably, and Sayyad Akbar Shah of Sithana was installed as the 'king of Swat', who was pointed out by the Akhund of Swat alias Saidu Baba as a man of energy, leadership abilities and true Islamic principles, and thereby best qualified for the position, with the additional advantage of being a Sayyad.[6] As far as the Akhund himself was concerned, 'during his lifetime there was no question of his assuming any degree of temporal power'.[7]

Sayyad Akbar Shah formed a friendship with the Hindustani followers of Sayyad Ahmad Shaheed Brailvi. At the death of Sayyad Ahmad at Balakot in 1831, while fighting the Sikhs, Sayyad Akbar Shah gave his surviving followers asylum in Sithana[8]—the place that defied Hari Singh and later Ranjit Singh himself, in 1824[9]—where he himself resided. On assuming charge as the king of Swat, Sayyad Akbar Shah made Ghaligay his capital. He evolved a crude administrative machinery of his own. He started to collect the revenue, i.e., *ushar*,[10] as agreed upon before his installation as the king, to meet the expenditure of war.[11] When his authority was better established, he set about collecting a standing army and guns.[12] He, thus, 'eventually managed to collect a force of 800 mounted men, 3,000 footmen and five or six guns'.[13]

As English rule was established in the Peshawar valley, so too did the state of Swat come into being, with Sayyad Akbar Shah as its king. Sayyad Akbar Shah pursued a vehemently anti-English policy. Thus, Swat became a refuge for outlaws and opponents of the colonialists from the English controlled territories, as well as a centre of anti-English sentiments. Swat, thus, served as an inspiration to Indians to rise against the English.[14] H.C. Wylly asserts that when Peshawar valley was annexed by the English 'then and thereafter the Swatis proved themselves bad neighbours' to them. 'Plunderers and marauders, mounted and on foot, issued from Swat, passed through Ranizai, and raided into' the English-held 'territory'. 'They kidnapped almost all classes except Pathans; and Swat became an Alsatia where evilly-disposed persons' and 'criminals of all shades', from the English perspectives, and 'people hostile to the British Government were readily granted help, asylum and countenance'.[15]

In December 1849, when Lt. Colonel Bradshaw led a punitive expedition against the villages of Palai, Zormandai and Sherkhana in Sam Baizai, people from Swat, numbering 5,000 to 6,000, rose to the assistance of their fellow tribesmen, but to no avail: a further 15,000 said to be still en route when the English expedition came to a close were thus unable to turn the tide of battle.[16] The Swatis even 'invited their fellow Pathans to throw off the British yoke and acknowledge a nominal allegiance to Swat'. For this purpose, they were ready to 'assemble troops' on the border and to 'send horsemen' into villages under colonial control 'partly as emissaries, and partly as representatives of [their] authority'.[17] In 1852 the colonial authority sent 'a conciliatory letter' to Sayyad Akbar Shah, but this was 'very rudely received and never answered'.[18] Even 'it was reported that the killing of the messenger' was debated so as 'to mark the King's determination not to hold any intercourse with the infidels'.[19] And when the colonial authorities imposed a fine of ₹5,000 on the people of Sam Ranizai, for their insolence, which the Akhund of Swat recommended should be paid, Sayyad Akbar Shah opposed him and urged the people to refuse payment.[20]

Again in May 1852 'some 4,000 foot and 500 horse' from the Swat valley assisted the people of Sam—the plain to the south and south-west of Swat—this time against the English forces led by Sir Colin Campbell, with Colonel Mackeson as political officer.[21] The colonial authorities remarked in the *Mutiny Reports* that it was well known that in the first years of English rule in the Peshawar valley, 'the border was chiefly disturbed by the hostility of the neighbouring country of Swat'[22] and that 'the King, to justify his own existence, made himself as bad a neighbour to the English as he could do without actually drawing down an expedition on his head'.[23] Swat was the fountainhead of offences against the English despite the fact that they 'never interfered' with the Swatis. The English, moreover, believed that the Swatis chose to make war upon them, simply because they were 'infidels by religion' and 'were the lords of a fair and fertile valley within reach of plunder'.[24] In such a tense situation of strained relations between the colonial rulers of India and the people and king of Swat, and anxieties arising from Sayyad Akbar Shah's anti-English background, the Uprising of 1857 commenced in the Indo-Gangetic plains to the south.

The War and Swat

As already stated, Sayyad Akbar Shah became king of Swat with local support due to fears arising from the English occupation of the valley. Although not yet part of the territories over which the English held sway in the subcontinent, Swat played a significant part in the 1857 War of Independence as a refuge for rebels. Its king was in communication with anti-English elements in the English-held territories to the south. Sayyad Akbar Shah of Swat was, thus, considered a dangerous enemy by the English and a potential source of unrest not only in the Frontier region but over the northern part of India as a whole.

Clear evidence of Swat and Sayyad Akbar Shah's connection with those who planned the uprising against the English in India came to the surface in reports published after the insurrection. Thus, 'it appeared', states one English official, that there had long been 'intrigues going on between the 55th and 64th Native Infantry and the 10th Irregular Cavalry' and the Hindustani 'fanatics in Swat and the neighbouring hills'; while two Hindustani Mawlwis 'in the collectorate' of Mardan 'were the hosts of the emissaries who passed to and fro'.[25] In addition, 'the most rancorous and seditious letters' had been intercepted from the Muslims of Patna and Thanisar to soldiers of the 64th Native Infantry, speaking of the atrocities committed on the Muslims there and rousing the sepoys to revenge. 'These letters also alluded to a long correspondence that had been going on, through the 64th Native Infantry, with the fanatics[26] in Swat and Sitana.'[27] A note in the *Mutiny Reports* mentions this correspondence between the Indian revolutionaries and Swat, stating that 'this is farther confirmed by Mahomedan [Muslims] correspondence [including] a rabid letter from a "Kuleefa Nathoo" at Thaneysur [Thanisar] to friends in Swat, through a Naik of 64th Native Infantry'.[28]

The pitch of communication from Swat with those planning rebellion in the English-held territories is further evident from this assertion of John Nicholson, made on 30 May 1857:

> I am strongly inclined to believe that we should not merely disarm but disband that corps [i.e. 64th Native Infantry] and the 10th Irregular Cavalry. There is no doubt that they have both been in communication with the Akhund of Swat.... I believe we did not pitch into the 55th one day too soon. That corps and the

64th were all planning to go over to the Akhund together. I have got a man who taunted my police on the line of march [for] siding with infidels in a religious war. May I hang him?[29]

This account reveals that not only were Sayyad Akbar Shah and other anti-English elements in Swat in league and communication with revolutionaries in north India but that the Akhund of Swat was as well. However, the Qandahari—the resident of Qandahar sent to Swat by H.G. Raverty—asserted that the Akhund

> has been said, at Peshawar, to possess the most despotic power over a most fanatical tribe; and even the old miscreant who lately set himself up at Delhi, had it proclaimed, that the poor old Akhund was coming to assist him with from 12,000, to 18,000 Ghazis at his back. I need scarcely add, that the whole is a mass of falsehood got up by interested parties. I will now endeavour to give a sketch of the Akhund as he appeared to us.[30]

And after giving his own sketch of the Akhund, he states that 'such is the true history, and such the faithful portrait of the terrible, fanatic, plotting Akhund of Suwat, the bugbear of Peshawar'.[31] Keeping aside the issue of determining the truthfulness or otherwise of the Akhund coming to the assistance of the Indian revolutionaries and his influence in Swat, the news itself was no minor incident as it generated enthusiasm and added fuel to the fire against the English in those regions. The explicit use of the Akhund's name in the affair, therefore, should not be underestimated. We may deduce more about his position by considering the role he later played when sepoys of the 55th Native Infantry reached Swat, and the course he adopted thenceforward.

Ansar Zahid Khan states that when 'working on Kotwal's Dairy',[32] he 'repeatedly found references that the Jihadis or Muslim Revolutionaries [in India] were repeatedly told that Wali [king] of Swat and Amir of Rabil were coming to their help'.[33] Keeping his past career and role in view, and his association, relations and communication with the anti-English element and Indian revolutionaries, it is not improbable that Sayyad Akbar Shah would have wished to come to the freedom fighters' help. Fortunately for the English, however, he died on 11 May 1857, the day when the news of the uprising in India reached Peshawar.[34] It is believed in some circles that he may even have been poisoned—probably at the instigation of the English.

Whatever the reason behind his death may be, Sayyad Akbar Shah's demise inhibited his men from taking immediate action. Thus, it was noted in the *Gazetteer of the Peshawar District* that the state of affairs in Swat 'prevented [Swat] from making those aggressions' on the English-occupied territories 'which might otherwise have been looked for'.[35] Hence:

> It might naturally have been expected therefore that this Padshah [king] of Swat would be at the head of all mischief when the troubles of 1857 overtook us. It

is a remarkable fact, however, that he died on 11th May, the very day that the first news of the mutiny reached Peshawur [Peshawar], so that Swat itself was simultaneously plunged into civil war and entirely pre-occupied with its own affairs.[36]

This, however, was not an end to the fears and troubles for the English arising from Swat, as defection occurred in the Frontier in the course of which sepoys of the 55th Native Infantry at Nowshera 'broke across the river', on 21 May so as to join the main body of their regiment at Mardan. And on 23 May it was reported to the colonial authorities that the 55th Native Infantry at Mardan were in a state of rebellion. Action against them was, therefore, deemed necessary, and forces were sent under the command of Col. Chute, accompanied by Col. John Nicholson as political officer. Upon the colonial forces nearing Mardan 'the 55th Native Infantry, with the exception of about 120 men, broke from the fort'.[37] The sepoys of the 55th Native Infantry, after their defection, asserts Lionel J. Trotter—the biographer of John Nicholson—'marched off with drums beating and colours flying towards the hills of Swat'.[38] Although urged that it was inadvisable and unfeasible, Col. Nicholson followed in pursuit of the rebel sepoys who, as Nicholson himself admitted in a private note to Edwardes, 'fought stubbornly "as men always do who have no chance of escape but by their own exertions"'.[39]

Meanwhile in Swat, a power struggle commenced between Sayyad Mubarak Shah, son of Sayyad Akbar Shah, and the Akhund of Swat to determine whether Mubarak Shah should succeed Sayyad Akbar Shah. Although Sayyad Akbar Shah was reportedly formally succeeded by his son, Mir Mubarak Ali Shah (or more commonly Mubarak Shah), it was said that the Swatis detested being under firm control and were reluctant to subject themselves to Mubarak Shah's rule.[40] Already having grown tired of tithes they paid to Sayyad Akbar Shah, the Swatis were reluctant to recognise Mubarak Shah as his successor as the king of Swat, and hence called on the Akhund of Swat to excommunicate him.[41] The Akhund was himself inclined to bring about the downfall of Mubarak Shah for his own reasons, hence 'after debate the people, under the Akhund's influence, rejected Mubarik'.[42] Therefore, 'both sides'--Mubarak Shah and his followers and the Akhund of Swat and his followers—'called in their friends and allies and prepared to settle' the issue 'by arms'.[43]

Amidst this scenario of strife and disorder in Swat, 500 of the rebel sepoys of the 55th Native Infantry[44] succeeded in crossing the border and arrived at Swat 'with their arms, ammunition and plundered treasure'.[45] The sources do not agree upon the number of sepoys who escaped to Swat. The *Military Report and Gazetteer on Buner and Adjacent Independent Territory* states the number as 600[46] and the *Mutiny Reports* gives the number as 500,[47] as also quoted above, 'upwards of 600' as they reached Swat,[48] and as 600 and 700 after their expulsion from Swat and crossing the Indus.[49] Whether five, six or seven hundred in number, the sepoys, on reaching Swat, brought a new dimension to the power struggle as, to the chagrin of the Akhund, they went to Mubarak Shah—the young king—and he immediately took them into his service. At this point, with the advent of trained rebel soldiers, Swat might have again become a centre of anti-English activities. Certainly it is reported that Mubarak Shah had raised an army for the purposes of war in Panjtar, but certain factors worked to the benefit of the English. On the one hand, because many Swatis refused allegiance and *ushar* to Mubarak Shah, he was short of armed local supporters and finances which made his position vulnerable. The instability of his rule also meant he could not venture far for fear of losing control of his kingdom. To pay the sepoys of the 55th Native Infantry, who sided with and fought for him in one battle, Mubarak Shah borrowed ₹1,000[50] from their leader, a grey-haired jamadar, but the sum was soon exhausted and he was unable to pay more. And without pay the sepoys were unwilling to fight for him. At the same time, the sepoys who had escaped to Swat were mostly 'high-caste Hindoos'. Remaining in a strange land amid tribal Muslims was difficult for them not only due to the lack of funds but also because they did not understand the language of the local people.[51]

The sepoy support for Mubarak Shah naturally displeased the Akhund of Swat who saw a threat to his own influence if Mubarak Shah gained a firm footing. He thus exerted his influence both against Mubarak Shah and the sepoys—perhaps making use of the sepoys' alien status—and siding with popular forces brought about the expulsion both of Mubarak Shah and the sepoys from Swat.[52] Thus was 'the first Islamic State of Swat'[53] brought to an end. In this way, the 1857 War of Independence played a great role and left its mark on Swati politics: the rule of members of an influential religious family, descendants of Pir Baba,[54] was terminated and the Akhund's status and position was strengthened and secured. The policy and course adopted by the Akhund of Swat at this juncture not only left its mark on the course of events, politics and history of Swat but also on that of India. By refraining from joining with the rebel and anti-English elements, despite his having been previously in communication with them, and refusing to declare war against the English, the Akhund rescued the Frontier from the threat of a general and mass uprising, a situation which was summarised by H.B. Edwardes, commissioner at Peshawar division, as follows:

> Had the Akhoond [Akhund] of Swat at this time, standing forward as the champion of the faith, preached a crescentade against us, and hushing intestine strife moved across the passes and descended into Peshawur [Peshawar] Valley, with all the prestige of the 55th Sepoys in his favour, I do not doubt, that he would have excited among our subjects that spirit of religious zeal which may be overlaid for a while, but never extinguished by material prosperity. Instead of this he suddenly sided with the popular party, dismissed the 55th Sepoys with guides to conduct them across the Indus and expelled the young King from Swat.[55]

'This conclusion', asserts Edwardes, 'assured the peace of our northern frontiers, and Colonel Nicholson with Colonel Chute's Moveable Column returned to cantonments in the second week of June'.[56]

Describing Edwardes' assertion as 'a correct assessment of the situation', S. Moinul Haq contends that 'there can be no doubt that with the departure of the sepoys of the 55th from Swat the course of the Revolution was changed in that region'.[57] Ghulam Rasul Mehr has contended that the rebel sepoys of the 55th Native Infantry reached Swat with the view that taking the Muslims of that place with them, they could attack the English with greater force and expel the English from the Frontier.[58] Lamenting the attitude adopted by the Akhund of Swat and the Swatis towards the sepoys, arising from petty local arguments about the payment of *ushar* and the succession of Mubarak Shah, Mehr says that had the Swatis or the Akhund Sahib considered the end result they would have realised that they could have fought and won a far greater prize. But the hearts and minds of the Swatis it appears failed to consider the wider possibilities of the situation.[59] S. Moinul Haq concludes that the decision of the Akhund Sahib determining Swat's attitude towards the revolution was apparently solely prompted by 'the local conditions which were uncertain'.[60]

Referring to the apathy of the tribes in not taking arms against the English and the course adopted by the Akhund of Swat, Munawwar Khan suggests that

> the tribes followed their tribal interests. Relegious [*sic*] doctors could unite the tribes for some purpose but unfortunately, the Akhund Sahib had been so impressed by British superiority in war, and so concerned with the independence of Swat and Buner, that he on this occasion decided to keep quiet.[61]

However, following this assertion Munawwar Khan states, in what may perhaps be a rejoinder or rebuke to Ghulam Rasul Mehr's views and lamentation, that

> it is bad logic in history to judge people and individuals according to one's own standards. The people of Swat had no knowledge of the Mughul ruler in whose name the rising took place. Swat had never been an integral part of the Mughul Empire, and anyway that empire had long ceased to exist. It would be too much to expect the tribes of Swat to be imbued with the spirit of nationalism and patriotism which did not exist ever in the rest of India. How else can one explain the few British crushing the whole of India with the help of Indian mercenaries? The one force which could be effective was tribal loyalty and religious appeal. The same Swatis *when properly led by religious leaders* [italics mine] put up a stubborn resistence [*sic*] to the British arms in 1863, 1895 and 1897.

> The policy of the Akhund of Swat was to protect the independence of Swat and Buner. He induced the tribesmen that the invasion was imminent, but was careful not to offend the [colonial] Government to such an extent that

an expedition would become inevitable. At the same time he would not create the impression that he was lagging behind in a religious rising against the infidels.[62]

Nonetheless it is clear that, even if the Akhund of Swat was himself not ready to lead them, the Swatis were willing to take up arms and fight the English outside Swat, if he enjoined so, whether Swat remained part of the Mughal Empire and whether that empire existed or not. Despite the fact that the Swatis owed no loyalty to the Mughal Emperor Bahadur Shah II, there were links between them and the Indian revolutionaries. Thus 'one letter from the *Akhund* [himself] authorised ... one Ajun Khan, to destroy all Europeans and Hindus in the Peshawar valley, and all Muhammadans in the British service; but enjoined him to spare all other Muhammadans'.[63] Munawwar Khan, too, has written of Ajun Khan, who used to raid the English-held territories, that when he 'went to Kabul via Jalalabad. Letters from the Akhund Sahib and Sayed Akbar were discovered among his papers'.[64]

Interestingly, when the rebel sepoys fled into Swat they remained as the Akhund's guests for a few days, as travellers generally do. However, the Akhund then advised them to leave Swat, although Sayyad Mubarak Shah 'wished them to remain'.[65] Raverty states that 'other mutineers also came from Murree, all of whom he [the Akhund] dismissed as quickly as possible to Kabul'.[66] From a British perspective, 'The whole tendency' of the Akhund's 'policy at this time' appeared to be 'distinctly peaceful'[67] and designed 'to protect the independence of Swat and Buner', and hence he 'was careful not to offend the [colonial] Government'.[68] At the same time, there is 'no doubt' that in the expulsion of both Mubarak Shah and the sepoys from Swat in 1857, he 'was partly actuated by motives of fear, lest [Mubarak Shah] the son of the late king of Swat, with the assistance of the sepoys, might be able to gain firm power in Swat and overshadow his, the Akhund's, authority'.[69] This assertion and conclusion concerning the Akhund's apprehensions about the Swati people is supported by the report of the deputy commissioner of Hazara who states that despite their having been expelled from Swat, the sepoys were not only guided across the Indus but the Akhund's 'confidential messengers' accompanied them with 'letters calling on all good Musulmans [Muslims] to aid and escort them, and excommunicating and denouncing as unbelievers all who should oppose them'.[70] And when on 5–6 July 1857 a combination of the natives took action against the sepoys at the village Guddarh on the edge of the Blue River in consequence of which 'many of the sepoys were killed or wounded, or drowned in the rapid stream', a Mulla from Palas had forbidden 'their further molestation', 'to whom' the Akhund 'commended them'.[71] The Mulla, moreover, then 'conveyed them to Kote Gullee, on the border of Chilass' from where 'they made for Durawah'.[72]

Thus, partly actuated by motives of fear that Mubarak Shah—with the assistance of the sepoys—might be able to gain power in Swat and overshadow his authority and partly so as not to provoke the English, the Akhund exerted his influence to expel them both. As a result, Swat remained aloof from the War of Independence of 1857, but this policy of the Akhund was clearly for reasons of local policy, 'not from love of the British Government'.[73] Had Sayyad Akbar Shah not died, and had Mubarak Shah and the sepoys had not been expelled from Swat, the course of events of the War or Uprising of 1857 would have certainly been different. Mubarak Shah himself took on the mission of his father and after his expulsion from Swat he went to Panjtar, just across the border from Swabi, and from that centre, 'reinforced as related by mutineers from the district, raised the Chamla tribes against the British'.[74] This, however, was by no means comparable to the threat that a revolt in Swat itself might have presented to the British authorities.

In conclusion, despite Swat being outside of the English controlled Indian territories, the state maintained close links with the Indian revolutionaries and those planning the uprising against English rule gained inspiration from religious and tribal leaders of that territory. Specifically, Sayyad Akbar Shah had encouraged anti-English elements in India and would most certainly, but for his untimely death, have moved to their assistance in the revolt. However, Swat did not join the war due to the death of Sayyad Akbar Shah and the course and policy adopted by the Akhund of Swat after Sayyad Akbar Shah's death and the arrival of the sepoys of the 55th Native Infantry in Swat. The policy and course of the Akhund of Swat, though mainly adopted for local and personal reasons, benefited the English at this critical time. The course that events took in Swat after the coming of the sepoys of the 55th Native Infantry and their siding with Mubarak Shah, to the chagrin of the Akhund of Swat, and the consequent course of action pursued by the Akhund are all too familiar in the historiography of the Indian Uprising. Unlike the colonialists themselves there was a complete absence of strategic leadership in the uprising and wider perspectives were too often subordinated to local rivalries and concerns. In this respect the events of 1857 in Swat tragically depict in microcosm the problems of anti-colonialism at this time in the subcontinent as a whole. However determined, inspired and inspiring anti-colonial sentiment may have been in the locality, local leadership ultimately failed to match up to the opportunities that the Sepoy Uprising had presented.

Notes and References

1. Muhammad Anwar Khan, *The Role of N.W.F.P. in the Freedom Struggle* (Lahore: Research Society of Pakistan, 2000), pp. 14–15.
2. For some detail about the Akhund of Swat see Sultan-i-Rome, 'Abdul Ghaffur (Akhund), Saidu Baba of Swat: Life, Career and Role' in *Journal of the Pakistan Historical Society* (Karachi), vol. 40, part 3 (July 1992), pp. 299–308.

3. Olaf Caroe, *The Pathans: 550 B.C.–A.D. 1957* (reprint, Karachi: Oxford University Press, 1976), p. 324.

4. Makhdum Tasadduq Ahmad, *Social Organization of Yusufzai Swat: A Study in Social Change* (Lahore: Panjab University Press, 1962), p. 33.

5. See T.J.C. Plowden, assistant commissioner in charge of Yusafzai, to deputy commissioner Peshawar, 8 February 1876, 'Report on the Leading Men and State of Factions in Swat', *Files of Tribal Affairs Research Cell, Home Department, Govt. of NWFP* [henceforward *TARC*], Serial No. 71/Swat, File No., 17-States I, 1932, p. 6; T.J.C. Plowden, *Report on the Leading Men and State of Factions in Swat* (reprint, Simla: Government of India Press, 1932), p. 9.

6. *(Confidential) Central Asia, Part I, A Contribution towards the Better Knowledge of the Topography, Ethnography, Statistics, & History of the North-West Frontier of British India* (henceforward *[Confidential] Central Asia*), compiled for military and political reference by C.M. MacGregor, vol. 3 (Calcutta: Office of the Superintendent of Government Printing, 1873), p. 155; *Confidential Gazetteer of the North-West Frontier: From Bajaur and the Indus Kohistan on the North to the Mari Hills on the South* [henceforward *Confidential Gazetteer of the North-West Frontier*], compiled for political and military reference in the Intelligence branch of the Quarter Master General's Department in India, completed and edited by A.L.E. Holmes, vol. 4 (Simla: Printed at the Government Central Branch Press, 1887), p. 1849; Plowden, 'Report on the Leading Men and State of Factions in Swat', *TARC*, p. 6; Plowden, *Report on the Leading Men and State of Factions in Swat*, p. 10. Also see Caroe, *The Pathans*, p. 363; W.W. Hunter, *The Indian Musalmans*, Introduction by Bimal Prasad (reprint, New Delhi: Rupa & Co., 2002), p. 11.

7. Caroe, *The Pathans*, p. 363.

8. Plowden, 'Report on the Leading Men and State of Factions in Swat', *TARC*, p. 6; Plowden, *Report on the Leading Men and State of Factions in Swat*, p. 10.

9. Caroe, *The Pathans*, p. 361.

10. According to Islamic law, Muslims are required to pay a portion of their land produce to the Islamic state at the rate of ten or five per cent, depending upon nature of the water given to the fields, which is called *ushar*. However, the heads under which the *ushar* is utilised and disbursed have also been specified.

11. Holmes, *Confidential Gazetteer of the North-West Frontier*, vol. 4, p. 1849; MacGregor, *(Confidential) Central Asia*, vol. 3, p. 154; *Tribes North of the Kabul River* (2nd ed. in Pakistan), India Army Intelligence Branch, *Frontier and Overseas Expeditions from India*, vol. 1 (Quetta: Nisa Traders, 1982), p. 343. Also see *Mutiny Reports from Punjab & N.W.F.P.*, vol. 2 (reprint, Lahore: Al-Biruni, n.d.), pp. 159–160; *Gazetteer of the Peshawar District, 1897–98* (reprint, Lahore: Sang-e-Meel Publications, 1989), p. 84.

12. H.C. Wylly, *The Borderland: The Country of the Pathans* (reprint, Karachi: Indus Publications, 1998), p. 125 cf. Holmes, *Confidential Gazetteer of the North-West Frontier*, vol. 4, p. 1850; MacGregor, *(Confidential) Central Asia*, vol. 3, p. 155; *Frontier and Overseas Expeditions from India*, vol. 1, p. 344.

13. Wylly, *The Borderland*, p. 125; Holmes, *Confidential Gazetteer of the North-West Frontier*, vol. 4, p. 1850; MacGregor, *(Confidential) Central Asia*, vol. 3, p. 155; *Frontier and Overseas Expeditions from India*, vol. 1, p. 344.

14. See A.H. McMahon and A.D.G. Ramsay, *Report on the Tribes of the Malakand Political Agency (Excluding of Chitral)*, Revised by R.L. Kennion (henceforward *Report on the Tribes of the Malakand Political Agency*) (Peshawar: Govt. Press, NWFP, 1916), pp. 33–35; Holmes, *Confidential Gazetteer of the North-West Frontier*, vol. 4, p. 1850.

15. Wylly, *The Borderland*, pp. 120–121. Also see *Frontier and Overseas Expeditions from India*, Vol. 1, p. 334; Holmes, *Confidential Gazetteer of the North-West Frontier*, vol. 4, pp. 1850–1851; MacGregor, *(Confidential) Central Asia*, vol. 3, pp. 155–1556.

16. See Wylly, *The Borderland*, p. 123; *Frontier and Overseas Expeditions from India*, vol. 1, pp. 337–338.

17. *Frontier and Overseas Expeditions from India*, vol. 1, p. 334; Holmes, *Confidential Gazetteer of the North-West Frontier*, vol. 4, p. 1850; MacGregor, *(Confidential) Central Asia*, vol. 3, p. 155.

18. McMahon and Ramsay, *Report on the Tribes of the Malakand Political Agency*, p. 34; A.H. McMahon and A.D.G. Ramsay, *Report on the Tribes of Dir, Swat and Bajour* [Bajawar] *Together with the Utman-Khel and Sam Ranizai*, edited with Introduction by R.O. Christensen (henceforward *Report on the Tribes of Dir, Swat and Bajour*) (reprint, Peshawar: Saeed Book Bank, 1981), pp. 71–72; Holmes, *Confidential Gazetteer of the North-West Frontier*, vol. 4, p. 1851.

19. *Frontier and Overseas Expeditions from India*, vol. 1, p. 348.

20. McMahon and Ramsay, *Report on the Tribes of the Malakand Political Agency*, p. 34; McMahon and Ramsay, *Report on the Tribes of Dir, Swat and Bajour*, p. 72; *Frontier and Overseas Expeditions from India*, vol. 1, p. 349.

21. McMahon and Ramsay, *Report on the Tribes of the Malakand Political Agency*, p. 34; McMahon and Ramsay, *Report on the Tribes of Dir, Swat and Bajour*, p. 72; *Frontier and Overseas Expeditions from India*, vol. 1, p. 350.

22. *Mutiny Reports from Punjab & N.W.F.P.*, vol. 2, p. 159.

23. Ibid., p. 160.

24. *Frontier and Overseas Expeditions from India*, vol. 1, pp. 352–353; Holmes, *Confidential Gazetteer of the North-West Frontier*, vol. 4, p. 1851.

25. *Mutiny Reports from Punjab & N.W.F.P.*, vol. 2, p. 152.

26. Munawwar Khan rightly points out the 'chivalry and bravery' of the tribesmen as 'fanaticism to the British historians.' See Munawwar Khan, 'Swat: Second Instalment', in *Peshawar University Review* (Peshawar), vol. 1, no. 1 (1974–1975), p. 67. H.G. Raverty also states, sardonically, that 'all are "fanatics", "rebels", or "dacoits", who fight against us according to some people'; Henry George Raverty, *Notes on Afghanistan and Baluchistan*, vol. 1, 2nd ed. in Pakistan (Quetta: Nisa Traders, 1982), p. 251.

27. *Gazetteer of the Peshawar District, 1897–98*, p. 80; *Mutiny Reports from Punjab & N.W.F.P.*, vol. 2, p. 141.

28. *Mutiny Reports from Punjab & N.W.F.P.*, vol. 2, p. 143, n 2.

29. Lionel J. Trotter, *The Life of John Nicholson: Soldier and Administrator Based on Private and Hitherto Unpublished Documents*, 1st ed. in Pakistan (Karachi: Karimsons, Jamshed Road, 1978), p. 217.

30. H.G. Raverty, 'An account of Upper and Lower Suwat, and the Kohistan, to the Source of the Suwat River; with an Account of the Tribes Inhabiting Those Valleys', *Journal of the Asiatic Society* (Calcutta), vol. 31, no. 3 (1862), p. 241.

31. Ibid., p. 246.

32. For the *Kotwal's Diary* see Sayyid Mubarak Shah (Kotwal of Delhi, 1857), *The Kotwal's Diary: (An account of Delhi during the War of Independence 1857)*, English translation by R.M. Edwards, edited by Ansar Zahid Khan (Karachi: Pakistan Historical Society, 1994).

33. Ansar Zahid Khan (General Secretary and Director of Research, Pakistan Historical Society, and Editor, *Journal of the Pakistan Historical Society*) to Sultan-i-Rome (the present author), 6 October 1996, Personal Collection of the Author, Village Hazara, Swat.

34. For Sayyad Akbar Shah's death on 11 May 1857, the day when the news of the uprising in India reached Peshawar, see Holmes, *Confidential Gazetteer of the North-West Frontier*, vol. 4, p. 1851; *Frontier and Overseas Expeditions from India*, vol. 1, p. 353; *Mutiny Reports from Punjab & N.W.F.P.*, vol. 2, p. 160; Wylly, *The Borderland*, p. 129; *Gazetteer of the Peshawar District, 1897–98*, p. 84. All other sources state that he died on 11 May 1857, but H.G. Raverty contends that he died in August 1857. For Raverty's contention see Raverty, 'An account of Upper and Lower Suwat', p. 246. Also see Raverty, *Notes on Afghanistan and Baluchistan*, vol. 1, p. 251.

35. *Gazetteer of the Peshawar District, 1897–98*, p. 84.

36. *Mutiny Reports from Punjab & N.W.F.P.*, vol. 2, p. 160. Also see Plowden, 'Report on the Leading Men and State of Factions in Swat', *TARC*, p. 6; Plowden, *Report on the Leading Men and State of Factions in Swat*, p. 10; *Frontier and Overseas Expeditions from India*, vol. 1, p. 353; Holmes, *Confidential Gazetteer of the North-West Frontier*, vol. 4, p. 1851.

37. *Mutiny Reports from Punjab & N.W.F.P.*, vol. 2, pp. 149–151.

38. Trotter, *The Life of John Nicholson*, p. 215.

39. Ibid; *Mutiny Reports from Punjab & N.W.F.P.*, vol. 2, p. 151.

40. H.W. Bellew, *A General Report on the Yusufzais*, 3rd ed. (Lahore: Sang-e-Meel Publications, 1994), p. 97.

41. *Mutiny Reports from Punjab & N.W.F.P.*, vol. 2, p. 160; *Frontier and Overseas Expeditions from India*, vol. 1, p. 353; Plowden, 'Report on the Leading Men and State of Factions in Swat', *TARC*, pp. 6–7; Plowden, *Report on the Leading Men and State of Factions in Swat*, p. 10.

42. Caroe, *The Pathans*, p. 364.

43. *Mutiny Reports from Punjab & N.W.F.P.*, vol. 2, p. 160; Plowden, 'Report on the Leading Men and State of Factions in Swat', *TARC*, p. 7; Plowden, *Report on the Leading Men and State of Factions in Swat*, p. 10.

44. *Mutiny Reports from Punjab & N.W.F.P.*, vol. 2, p. 160.

45. Ibid., p. 114.

46. See *Military Report and Gazetteer on Buner and Adjacent Independent Territory*, 2nd ed. (Delhi: Government of India Press, 1926), p. 7.

47. *Mutiny Reports from Punjab & N.W.F.P.*, vol. 2, p. 160. Also see *Frontier and Overseas Expeditions from India*, vol. 1, p. 353; McMahon and Ramsay, *Report on the Tribes of the Malakand Political Agency*, p. 34; McMahon and Ramsay, *Report on the Tribes of Dir, Swat and Bajour*, p. 74.

48. *Mutiny Reports from Punjab & N.W.F.P.*, vol. 2, p. 152.

49. See Ibid., p. 114.

50. The *Mutiny Reports* and T.J.C. Plowden state the amount borrowed by Mubarak Shah from the Jamadar of the sepoys as rupees 100 (one hundred) but *Gazetteer of Peshawar District* states it as rupees 1000 (one thousand) which seems correct, because rupees 100 were not sufficient for the one month pay of 500, 600 or 700 sepoys. See *Mutiny Reports from Punjab & N.W.F.P.*, vol. 2, p. 160; Plowden, 'Report on the Leading Men and State of Factions in Swat', *TARC*, p. 7; Plowden, *Report on the Leading Men and State of Factions in Swat*, p. 10 cf. *Gazetteer of the Peshawar District, 1897–98*, p. 84.

51. *Mutiny Reports from Punjab & N.W.F.P.*, vol. 2, p. 114.

52. *Gazetteer of the Peshawar District, 1897–98*, p. 84.

53. Muhammad Asif Khan, *The Story of Swat as told by the Founder Miangul Abdul Wadud Badshah Sahib to Muhammad Asif Khan* (Preface, Introduction and Appendices, Muhammad Asif Khan; and trans. Preface and trans., Ashruf Altaf Husain) (Peshawar: Ferozsons Ltd, 1963), p. xlviii.

54. For Pir Baba see Sher Afzal Khan Barikoti, *Pir Baba* (Mingawara, Swat: Shoaibsons Publishers & Booksellers, 1999); Abdur Rashid, *Islami Tasawuf aur Sufyay-e-Sarhad: Daswayn Sadi Hijri mayn Ilmi wa Adabi Khidmat* (Islamabad: Tasawuf Foundation, 1988); Hamesh Khalil, 'Hazrat Syed Ali Ghawas Tirmizi: (Pir Baba)', in Jalaluddin Khilji, ed., *Muslim Celebrities of Central Asia* (Peshawar: Area Study Centre [Central Asia], n.d.).

55. *Mutiny Reports from Punjab & N.W.F.P.*, vol. 2, pp. 160–161. Also see Plowden, *TARC*, p. 7; Plowden, *Report on the Leading Men and State of Factions in Swat*, p. 11; Munawwar Khan, 'Swat: Second Instalment', *Peshawar University Review* (Peshawar), vol. 1, no. 1 (1974–1975), p. 64; *Frontier and Overseas Expeditions from India*, vol. 1, pp. 353–354.

56. *Mutiny Reports from Punjab & N.W.F.P.*, vol. 2, p. 161.

57. Syed Moinul Haq, *The Great Revolution of 1857* (Karachi: Pakistan Historical Society, 1968), p. 262.

58. Ghulam Rasul Mehr, *1857: Pak wa Hind ki Pehli Jang-e-Azadi* (Urdu) (Lahore: Sheikh Ghulam Ali and Sons [Private] Limited, Publishers, n.d.), p. 418.

59. Ibid, p. 420.
60. Haq, *The Great Revolution of 1857*, p. 261.
61. Khan, 'Swat: Second Instalment', p. 64.
62. Ibid., pp. 64–65.
63. *Frontier and Overseas Expeditions from India*, vol. 1, p. 348.
64. Khan, 'Swat: Second Instalment', p. 63.
65. Raverty, 'An account of Upper and Lower Suwat', p. 246.
66. Ibid.
67. *Gazetteer of the Peshawar District, 1897–98*, p. 273.
68. Khan, 'Swat: Second Instalment', p. 65.
69. *Gazetteer of the Peshawar District, 1897–98*, p. 273.
70. *Mutiny Reports from Punjab & N.W.F.P.*, vol. 2, p. 116.
71. Ibid., pp. 118–119.
72. Ibid., p. 120.
73. *Imperial Gazetteer of India, Provincial Series, North-West Frontier Province* (reprint, Lahore: Sang-e-Meel Publications, 1991), p. 218.
74. Caroe, *The Pathans*, p. 364. Also see Bellew, *A General Report on the Yusufzais*, p. 97.

13

✄✄

SPATIAL MEMORIALISING OF WAR IN 1857
Memories, Traces and Silences in Ethnography[*]

Carol E. Henderson

Introduction

RURAL and non-elite personalities associated with the 1857 War have recently become a focus for the assertion of collective identity, the reclaiming of memory from diverse sources and its reconstitution within the national narrative of India's first war of independence. Studies of the movements associated with these claims suggest their significance as avenues for affirmation of non-elites within the nationalist paradigm of the anti-colonial struggle.[1]

Emphasis is on the congruence between these narratives and those of national identity, patriotic themes and idealised concepts of citizenship, action and sacrifice for the Indian nation. This chapter explores elements of an Indian rural memory landscape linked to the War of 1857 as it was constituted in the decade after independence in 1947. This period was just outside living memory of the war, yet people could still remember elders who experienced it. They could also recollect its memorialisation during the colonial era, when authorities might deem undue attention to such monuments to be seditious. The monuments in question utilise local cultural idioms and material forms to commemorate personalities and incidents. In this respect, they differ from

*I would like to thank for their suggestions, advice, diverse comments and ongoing suggestions on various aspects of this work: Ainslie T. Embree, Stanley A. Freed, Sumit Guha, Jayasinhji Jhala, Pauline Kolenda, Owen Lynch, Philip Oldenburg, Barbara J. Price, Frances Pritchett, Kenneth X. Robbins, Susan Wadley, Maxine Weisrau and Neil Whitehead, along with the very helpful discussion of an earlier version of this chapter by participants at the 'Mutiny at the Margins' conference. David Magier of Columbia University Library; Satish Bindra of the division of Asian Studies, Library of Congress; Catherine O'Sullivan of the National Anthropological Archives, National Museum of Natural History, Smithsonian Institution; and the library staff of the Prints and Photographic Division, Library of Congress, who kindly assisted in locating materials for the project.

monuments conceived within the symbolic apparatus of the modern nation state. The landscape to be examined provides evidence for the complex framing of memory, here regarded as a social process that incorporates multiple, often competing, discourses of events reflecting diverse relationships of power.

Rather than seamlessly reflecting the state's master narrative of patriotic activism, I shall argue that these local memories, as refracted in 1950s' ethnographic practice, give a contested view of the past. While generally congruent with the position that memorialisation allows a glimpse of past social fractures through the prism of current social relationships and struggle, this view is also complex. There are multiple points of conflict for the mobilisation of diverse claims. In the following discussion, the memorialisation of 1857, circa 1950–1955, renders not a univocal subalternity, but potential multiple discourses and points of contact among them.[2] As will be seen, there are several difficulties associated with unpacking such 'speaking'.[3]

In the arguments that follow, I focus on landscape as the centre or focal point of the memory of places associated with events deemed significant, *les lieux de mémoire*, or 'sites of meaning'.[4] Landscape here is understood to be the environment as mediated by human understanding and the practices associated with it.[5] Landscape is a nexus of worldview, physical attributes, events and memory that reflects an underlying set of related symbols and meanings that provide context for the realisation of specific memories.[6] Landscapes and the memories associated with them, especially of violent death, comprise focal points for the testimonies of survivors, witnesses and perpetrators. Elements of landscape may be materialised additionally through objects associated with physical remains, practices relating to death and memory, the cultural norms of behaviour at sites of death, naming, oral traditions and the praxis of individual encounters with these sites.[7] Landscape's characteristics may become politically and emotionally charged, even contradictory and contested ('*this* is where the Rani leaped to safety on her charger; *here* our hero fell; *there* is his grave or cremation spot; *that city* is where my grandfather saw fifty Indian men strung up on a single tree during the war of 1857').[8]

The present work is a component of a larger project that investigates the relationships of memory, violence and the War of 1857. This project focuses on the processes of creating memorial landscapes and the transformations of memories of violence associated with these landscapes. These colonial era monuments include both those constructed by the British and their supporters and Indian forms of spatial memorialisation—particularly those that can be documented in the colonial period. Unsurprisingly, the narratives associated with British-built monuments of 1857 appear supportive of the project of empire and of British identity.[9] The story of Indian monuments, at least in the present investigation, appears to suggest a different basis for, and trajectory of memorialisation that, in speaking in its own terms, incorporates and dialectically reworks itself in relationship to the state.[10]

This chapter uses an ethnohistoric and ethnographic approach to the spaces of memorialisation. It is fashionable to speak of the détente between history and anthropology; I favour this dialogue. Yet 'doing ethnography' is not, as popular accounts would have it, simply adding subaltern, gendered or marginal voices to social science discourse. Nor is it simply 'reading across the grain' of elite representations of non-elites to fill in the blanks about them. Ethnography reflects the biases, genres and modes of presentation of its practitioners.[11] Its claims to speak for or give voice to groups largely unrepresented in dominant discourses that must be scrutinised for such data is neither neutral nor independent of the processes through which 'data' come to be asserted in scholarly discourse. Ethnography's goal is explicit comparative analysis of diverse cultural entities, hence the effort to seek a value-free conceptual language. Yet this goal is often confounded by the historical and cultural specificity of phenomena that lose meaning if not articulated in their own terms. Setting ethnography in this framework foregrounds agency, social relations and the cultural framing of knowledge of diverse voices.[12]

This discussion first examines the background to the study of memory, landscape and monuments related to ideas of death, particularly in northern India. Second, I consider the 1857 memory landscape of a village in Saharanpur district of Uttar Pradesh circa 1950–1956. Background works consulted include newspapers, journals, diaries, photographs and published accounts of the area. The effort to examine a village's memorialisation of 1857 draws on a largely untapped source, which may prove useful for thinking about the war and its meanings.[13] This is ethnographic research data collected by anthropologists in northern India during the first half of the twentieth century. Some of this material was collected at the tail end of living memory of 1857, or from those who heard first-hand accounts of the war. Little of this research was carried out with any great interest in documenting the war's history. At this time, ethnographers had other concerns. Yet in a number of cases, ethnographers conducted research very close to places where, historical records say, violent events had taken place. The holistic interests of ethnography did produce oral histories of places, communities and personalities. My impression in reading these materials is that the war enters the ethnographic record almost despite the ethnographer's disinterest. What the war meant to those who participated in the ongoing construction of a memory landscape of 1857 in this village is explored here, with the caveat that both the approach and its conclusions are tentative.

War, Landscape and Memorialisation

Overall, the study of war monuments features the dynamics of representation and the process of memorialisation primarily in metropolitan European and North American settings.[14] Studies of monuments in colonial settings tend to emphasise the fate of monuments in the postcolonial era as these memorial spaces were reconfigured to represent new national interests. A much smaller number of studies attempt to document these monuments in specifically colonial time frames.[15]

The generalising context of these studies is the nation state, within which complex interactions exist in the conception, design, execution, use and subsequent histories of memorial sites.[16] A guiding interest is how war monuments embody nationalism and the idealised characteristics of the nation and its people.[17] One theme also taken up is local resistance to state hegemony, as in Anne Walthall's study of pre–Meiji era Japanese peasant memorials to insurgent leaders, which the Japanese state attempted to destroy.[18] Shrines were often disguised or misnamed in order to hide them from government attention. After the 1868 Meiji restoration, however, these monuments became valued symbols of peasant democracy. In contemporary Vietnam, Heonik Kwon has investigated the differences between local and state-sponsored forms of memorialisation of what is known there as the American War of the 1960s.[19]

A second important framework of investigation examines the intersections between cultural mediation and traumatic experience in the construction of memory. These studies focus on individual subjectivities (largely within state contexts), and memory within gendered, religious, ethnic and class- and age-specific groupings. Over time, the testimony of survivors, witnesses to violence, and perpetrators also become forms of memorialisation.[20] Here the individual is understood to be embedded in social networks, cultural expectations of discourse (especially where transgressive violence occurs), and the multiple forms through which memory may be expressed.[21] Occupational, gender and ethnic differences in these contexts intersect with subjectivity and the relationship to violence.[22]

At first glance, both the above-mentioned subject areas might seem to be somewhat distant from what could be recovered of rural memories of 1857 collected in the early 1950s by ethnographers. Ethnographers of this era were more likely to emphasise the distance between the localities that they studied and the state than to theorise the intersection between the two. The data also, as far as such remembrances are concerned and without further scrutiny that is outside the focus of this chapter, may permit little tracing of individual motivations, inner states and personal remembrances. In the ethnographic records to be discussed, the materials of memory are predominantly captured and presented in the form of collective, rather than individual, memories.[23]

In northern India, a broadly shared cultural understanding is that landscape is inescapably connected to the social lives and deaths of its people. Those who live on the land share in its transcendent supernatural qualities by virtue of consumption of its products and by contact with it. This sacred geography connects the social realm with the characteristics of the environment and particularly the overall balance of supernatural phenomena such as good, evil, auspiciousness and inauspiciousness.[24] The living and the dead alike share the supernatural characteristics of the landscapes that they occupy. Spaces associated with the that deaths of significant individuals may become marked as sacred, particularly if an individual continues to intercede with the living after death. Supernatural characteristics and personalities include the orientation of objects to one another and the manifestations of great Indian deities, tutelary deities, ancestral goddesses, border-protecting deities and saints whose attachment to persons and to place may call them forth at times of danger.[25] The deceased of a community or family may become important supernatural intercessors: an ancestor; a warrior or hero; a Sati (a woman who sacrificed herself to honour a close relative); a *pativrata* (a woman whose life exemplified that of the virtuous wife); or angry spirits such as women who hunger for the souls of children or men who died without heirs or family to venerate them. Those who died violently could become dangerous ghosts.[26] British comments in the mid-nineteenth century suggest that beliefs such as these were also present at this time.[27]

Physical spaces associated with memorial practices and beliefs include tombs and cenotaphs such as *chattris* and memorial stones. Commemorated sites could include the space where a person physically died, the cremation or burial site and the place where the deceased, now a spirit or a ghost, chooses to manifest itself. The various shrines and tablets of a single figure may serve different clients for example, members of upper-caste groups and Dalits (former untouchables) who conventionally (and particularly before post-independence reforms) did not enter one another's spaces.[28] Where these spirits powerfully interceded in people's lives, a monument might grow into a substantial shrine. Around Varanasi in eastern Uttar Pradesh, for example, diverse types of dead—Hindu and Muslim alike—were honoured with shrines. Those whose deaths occurred in fighting might become *Bir Babas*, warrior-deities to be venerated.[29]

Memorial practices of the major religious groups of northern India include cremation for Hindu adults and interment for Muslims and some Hindu saints. There are also later ceremonies such as death feasts, anniversary commemorations and annual family rituals which honour the spirits of the deceased.[30] The popular Sufi Islamic movements commemorate their saints' death anniversaries with special prayers, poetry, song and the distribution of alms. The tombs of Sufi saints, such as Mu'in al-Din Chisti in Ajmer, draw pilgrims from a wide spectrum of social and religious backgrounds who seek boons, come to share in worship at the shrine or give thanks for a successful intervention.[31] Saints' cults and death cults were also evident in the nineteenth century as evidenced by the American traveller Bayard Taylor, who noted in 1853 that the graves of saints and Mughal notables in northern and central India were freshly covered with elaborate, embroidered cloths and wreaths.[32]

Certain elements, such as commemorative feasting, erection of memorial stones and creation of charitable institutions, carried out in memory of the deceased cut across diverse religious groups. There would also be a mourning period, connected with rituals, to ease the passage of the soul to the afterlife. The complex of beliefs relating to ghosts, their embodiment in spirit possession and the elaboration of spaces associated with these spirits are other forms of memorialisation.

The generally beneficent character of the land is disrupted by contact with death and blood, for blood is a dangerous, ritually polluting substance.[33] Bloodshed does not sanctify in the Christian hermeneutical sense of sacrifice and ultimate redemption as recapitulated, for example, in Abraham Lincoln's 'hallowed ground' of the Gettysburg Address or Rupert Brooke's nostalgic space that is 'forever England'. In northern India, violence and untimely death produce unhappy spirits, the signal of an unsettled landscape. Violence and untimely death also may evoke protection by tutelary deities, warrior-heroes and saints.

Ethnography and Village 'Pasts'

Seen in this perspective, the War of 1857 should have produced many diverse supernatural manifestations, from angry ghosts to protective action by beneficent spirits.[34] British newspaper accounts published in London early in the war report summarise justice, mass hangings, the killing of prisoners, executions and the disposal of corpses in ways that often consciously violated the religious beliefs of the deceased and his family. For example, British forces burned Muslim bodies or had them, while living, 'blown from guns', so that there were no remains that could receive a proper burial.[35] Similarly, they might bury or expose the bodies of Hindus. The dead were left untended by roadsides to be eaten or dismembered by wild animals, tossed into rivers or wells, buried in makeshift graves or too hastily cremated.[36]

The landscape of memory examined here is that of the village Rankhandi, seven kilometres to the south of Deoband, site of the Islamic centre of learning that would importantly develop in the last half of the nineteenth century. Rankhandi is in the south eastern part of a local cultural region known as the *Katha* tract.[37] In the nineteenth century, Pundir Rajputs were the predominant landowners in the region. They were known as a troublesome lot. In the mid-twentieth century in Rankhandi, Pundirs were the dominant caste, quite proud of their martial heritage. In the 1950s, the police allegedly still regarded the place as one of criminals.[38]

Indian and American anthropologists initially studied Rankhandi as part of the Cornell-Lucknow University Project instituted in 1953.[39] The project, headed in the United States by John T. Hitchcock of Cornell University—himself in graduate school at the start of the project—included numerous students, who gained their first ethnographic research experience in Rankhandi.[40] Many of these young scholars subsequently went on to have distinguished careers in South Asian anthropology.[41] Research at Rankhandi would continue through the next several decades, although Cornell's formal support for the project ended in 1956. The project records held by Hitchcock were donated to archives at Cornell University and to the National Anthropology Archives at the Smithsonian Institution in Washington DC after his death in 2001.[42]

Ethnography in India in the early decades after independence largely focused on the identification of key elements of social structure with a particular interest in kinship and caste. Descriptions were phrased in the 'ethnographic present', which in practice could be either the period of the ethnographer's field research, or set in 'traditional times', usually—so far as these studies define what this means—some twenty to fifty years before the ethnographer's arrival. The basic unit of analysis was a large, multi-caste village, conceived as a relatively unchanging and self-contained unit. The prevailing theoretical model seen in these studies, structural functionalism, encouraged investigators to focus on the integrative and cooperative elements of rural life.[43]

So strong was this identification that the term 'village studies' swiftly came to identify the approach. The goal of anthropological holism meant collecting data on as many different aspects of culture and social life as possible, including history. In addition to genealogies and family histories, so important to producing a picture of social organisation, investigators interviewed their informants on local history. 'Traditional history', as this was sometimes called, tended to revolve around three subject areas: founding accounts of 'the village' (as the unit of analysis came to be known), stories associated with the origins of the village's different caste groups and striking incidents in the days of the village elders' youth.[44] In general, these ethnographers made light use of historical documents such as land settlement reports, district administration reports, diaries and journals. Their interests lay elsewhere in mapping extant social relationships, ideologies and behaviours. Congruent with these concerns was a strong interest in landscape, material culture and the uses of space. Ethnographers took photographs and mapped land uses and the locations of significant spaces, such as the neighbourhoods occupied by different social groups, shrines and tombs.

In the north Indian ethnographies of this period that I have reviewed to date, mention of the War of 1857 is minimal: a local ruler, whose head was displayed after he was executed; a man from Rajasthan who arrived in the Delhi area with a mutinied army unit made friends, settled and established a family; a deity, who protected villagers from harm; and the mass hangings of men.[45] The possibility of following up on these statements is complicated, especially in the case of the American ethnographers whose works have been reviewed for this research, by the convention of using pseudonyms for these spaces.[46] Indian ethnographic researchers were far less likely than the Americans to publish their results using a pseudonym for the villages that they studied.[47] It is therefore possible to find the same village reported in different publications under two different names.[48] Clearly, one must know what the people who live in a place call it, as well as how it is recorded in government and other documents, to locate historical records within a space. In the best-case scenarios, the anthropological village suddenly emerges as a space known in other records and databases, permitting a dialogue among these different types of knowledge.

A resident who is proud of his community's contributions to the Cornell-Lucknow University anthropological study identified Rankhandi on the Internet.[49] Recently, at least two Indian researchers who worked in Rankhandi some decades ago also posted Internet notes relating to their research there and added comments relating to the project.[50] Research on Rankhandi is published under both its real name and under the pseudonym 'Khalapur' or 'Khaalaapur', adopted by anthropologists in the 1950s.[51] Publications include works on the general social structure of Rankhandi, on gender, sociolinguistics, caste ideology and kinship.

Rankhandi's propinquity to Deoband provides its main link to historical records of 1857. Here, British forces chased down, captured and executed suspected enemies, commandeering food and supplies from villages along the way.[52] Saharanpur town, thirty miles or so to the north, was home to the headquarters of the Ganges Canal project, which began operating on the eastern side of the district in 1854. Saharanpur was also the location of a well known botanical garden established by the British and, from 1835, the site of an American Presbyterian mission.[53] Western sections of Saharanpur district had become irrigated by 1830 with reconstruction of the eastern Jumna [Yamuna] Canal. Canal irrigation was also beginning in the eastern sections of the district with the opening of the Ganges Canal. Land revenue settlement operations were in progress in the Deoband area just before hostilities began.[54] Eric Stokes, who wrote about Saharanpur district in his study of the war, notes that there had been lower rates of turnover in estates in the Deoband tehsil (subdistrict) than elsewhere in the district, but this evidently did not secure loyalty to the British, as fighting was fierce.[55] Nineteenth century English-language narratives of the 1857 War mentioned several events in the vicinity of Rankhandi. Most dramatically, the British burned villages on the southeast side of Deoband as retaliation for an alleged attack and looting of the market in Deoband.[56] Thirty-six villages belonging to Pundir Rajputs were confiscated and sold or given to British supporters.[57]

The ethnographic data collected by the team of anthropologists at Rankhandi in the 1950s included materials on beliefs about deaths and spirits. In general, these conform to north Indian norms. There were several forms in which the spirits of the deceased might appear in Rankhandi: as a *bhuut* (ghost), *preet* (the ghost of a dead boy), *uut* (ghost of a childless man), *churail* (ghost of a woman who died in childbirth or without children), *devpittar* (ancestor) or *piir* (Muslim saint).[58] Anthropologists in Rankhandi also collected stories, some of which are conflicting, set at the time of the war. In this chapter I discuss one set of stories that involves a saints' legend and stories told about parents and grandparents who experienced the war. One of the latter includes personal testimony, not of the war but of knowing persons who remembered the war. Some stories include more detail than others. Other stories appear to conflate events told as separate narratives by multiple informants. The oldest persons who told these stories were listed as being in their eighties. The eldest storyteller was stated to be ninety-seven years old in the mid-1950s when he was interviewed. Other statements by this individual recorded in field notes suggest that he was most likely born sometime between 1858 and 1870.[59] The stories evidently reflect their tellers' different social position and their kin groups' relationship to the events being told.[60]

A strict oral transmission of narratives cannot be assumed. At least one villager had read—in Urdu translation—a history of Rajasthan originally published in the early nineteenth century and referred to this material in talking with anthropologists.[61] Ethnographic practice gives preference to orally transmitted evidence, particularly that deemed most likely to disappear with the deaths of those who know the stories or due to a shift in preferences to mass media and text-based sources. In line with the effort to retrieve orally transmitted data, John J. Gumperz, who studied language and communication in Rankhandi, noted that while a few villagers were literate and had access to books and newspapers, the differences between standard Hindi and local dialects, general illiteracy, lack of interaction among different social groups (most notably between low-caste and high-caste people), and low mobility (including even travel to nearby Deoband) preserved this as a relatively socially isolated site.[62]

Memory and the War in Rankhandi

The relationship between Rankhandi and the War of 1857 appears in several versions of a story recorded in the village in the 1950s. This, in brief asserts:

> In a clearing in [Rankhandi] stands the Piir, the Mogul tomb of a saint named Darga. Both Hindu and Muslim villagers believe that Darga protects the village. One legend says that during the Indian rebellion of 1857, Darga appeared on his horse, wielding a sword, and prevented the British troops from entering [Rankhandi].[63]

Different ethnographers collected from various individuals a cluster of stories about the personality of the Muslim saint, known as the '*piir*', who protected Rankhandi in 1857.[64] Stories about parents and grandparents also referred to the war. This study first investigates the personality of the *piir* then turns its attention to family stories about the war. Stories of the *piir* include many different versions and variations. The field notes name him as the *piir*, as a fakir (Muslim holy man), as Kulka (a given name and an informal address, in this case by a twenty-year-old Chamar woman, a member of one of the village's lowest ranked caste groups) and as *darga*. This last is an interesting usage, as a *dargah* is the shrine complex of a Muslim saint.[65]

The founding myth of the *piir*'s relationship to Rankhandi consists of a miraculous story. In one version told by an eighty-year-old Rajput man, a traveller, who is identified as a Banjara (a travelling merchant), attempts to deceive the *piir* by telling him that he is taking salt, rather than sugar, to Jalalabad.[66] Jalalabad is a market town to the south-west of this region. When the Banjara arrives at the market, he opens one bag and discovers salt. Contrite, he returns to the *piir*, who magically restores the sugar. In gratitude, the Banjara builds the *piir*'s tomb with profits from its sale. These must have been good, for the *piir*'s tomb in Rankhandi is impressive and imposing. The field notes state that it is approximately twenty-five feet on one side and is built on a high platform with a dome.[67] This shrine clearly provides a focus for memory, both as a locus for stories told about the *piir* and as a place where rituals important to the villagers are carried out.

The origin myth of the *piir* is a conventional saint's legend where attempted trickery is magically revealed. It has several versions with slightly different details. Some versions of the origin myth state that the *piir* is from the Himalayas. A different version, told by an eighty-year-old man of the low-ranking Jhiinvar (water carrier or fisherman) caste, sets the story in the not-too-distant past. The merchant sells the sugar in Meerut to the British and makes an outrageously high profit.[68] Other narrators insist that the *piir* came to Rankhandi 600 years earlier, around 1350, well before any British colonial presence. The *piir* acts in many ways like a protective village deity, such as a Bhumiya, or an ancestral deity.[69] The *piir* is proud of his prerequisites and quick to punish the villagers with a hailstorm or to damage the rival Shiva temple as part of his ongoing feud with that Hindu deity.[70] Usually, the *piir* is known for keeping hailstorms and epidemics away from Rankhandi. Conventional elements of the tutelary village deity role also appear in the practices of bringing newlyweds to pay homage to the *piir* and the presenting of the sons of the village for their first tonsure ceremonies. The *piir* is very active: he appears to people in dreams and is especially present in Rankhandi on Thursdays. He is honoured with an annual festival and his shrine is tended by a family with hereditary rights to the position.[71]

The story of the *piir* appearing in ghostly form, clad in blue and riding on a blue horse, to stop the British soldiers from burning down Rankhandi in 1857 lies within the range of expectations of how village protectors should act in times of danger. The *piir* did this on other occasions too. On one occasion, he blocked the road with snakes, scorpions and spiders to keep the police from arresting a village leader suspected of murder.[72]

The second genre of stories about 1857 is family tales, usually told second- or third-hand, linking Rankhandi people to great deeds and family histories. A sample of these stories suggests that Rankhandi's people diverged in their loyalties during the war with some supporting and some opposing British rule. Some may have switched allegiances during the war, which might also confound recollection. The independence struggle and its attainment in 1947 may have further affected the telling and substance of these stories. Lastly, there is the question of the impact the mixed team of Indian and foreign, English-speaking ethnographers might have had on what was disclosed.

One senior story teller, a Rajput man in his eighties, assured the investigators that there was a rumour that the British were going to force them to eat leather, possibly a reference to the 1857 stories of beef and pork fat lubricated cartridges that often have featured in histories about the war.[73] However, this narrator stated Rankhandi's people did not oppose the British because their zamindars had been given one-third of the land.[74] The idea that those who received land title from the British would be less likely to oppose their rule is plausible.

Another story asserted that in 1857 Rankhandi people attacked and looted Ghalauli, Rankhandi's neighbour to the east. They escaped retribution, this narrator asserted, because they had British backing.[75] One man said that his grandmother used to have an old spinning wheel and a grain pounding stick, which, she told him, his great-grandfather looted from a neighbouring village.[76] This story, with the details of memories attached to material objects, would seem to corroborate claims of lack of opposition to the British. On the other hand, and complicating the question of whether (or to what extent) villagers supported anti- or pro-British fighters, the aforementioned eighty-year-old Jhiinvar man asserted that in 1857, the British aimed a cannon at the village. The gun failed to go off, reportedly because the *piir* interceded.[77]

Lastly, a long and complex story links Rankhandi to the events of 1857.[78] This story came from a Rajput man said to be ninety-seven years old in 1955, which locates his birth at earliest as sometime in the decade after the war. It braids together conventional folk motifs, family memories and personal memory. The story includes sections set before, during and after the war. In this tale, a handsome young village boy, a Hindu Rajput called Kunwar ('prince') becomes a protégé of the 'Nawab of Lucknow' (i.e., the king of Awadh). Hiding too long in a tree to spy on the Nawab, the boy wets himself and thereby comes to the attention of the Nawab. Impressed by the boy's personal qualities, the Nawab brings him up as his son and after the Nawab's own son is born, gives Kunwar an estate in 'Bandaa' district. Kunwar asks his family in Rankhandi to arrange his marriage, but they say that in order for them to do so, he would have to reconvert to Hinduism.[79] Kunwar replies that he has no faith, and he marries a Muslim girl from Panchli village in Meerut district.[80] He has eleven sons—six with a concubine, and five with his wife.[81] The number eleven, which recurs in the tale, is an auspicious number.

After Kunwar's death, his sons join the effort 'to make the Nawob [*sic*] Emperor of India by capturing the throne at Delhi for him. But the Nawob was captured and killed by the British'. Following this defeat, ten of the brothers escape to Rankhandi. The eleventh, Ramzaan Ali, instead helps a 'beautiful English woman' who, the story says, becomes his mistress.[82] Since the British don't know the ten brothers are hiding in their father Kunwar's home village of Rankhandi, they are safe. But the brothers soon spend all their money, become poor and must work for a living. The elderly storyteller in the field notes is quoted as saying in 1955, 'I can remember this very well. Then they began to work as labourers'.[83]

Eventually, the ten brothers buy back some of their land. Meanwhile, the story continues, Ramzaan Ali and his English mistress come before a committee in Lucknow to decide who should be punished and who should be rewarded after the war. Ramzaan Ali wins eleven rent-free villages for helping the English woman while she returns to her husband in England.[84] Ramzaan Ali's family also still owns its 'Bandaa' estates, so they appear to have substantially benefited. The components of this story range from assertions about plausible past events, legends and traditional motifs, such as the lucky number eleven, to eyewitness testimony. Instead of describing a supernatural being, the *piir*, who rescues Rankhandi, this story relates both the imagined wider community to which Rankhandi belongs and Rankhandi's imagined intimate community. Thus, for example, Rankhandi's initial identity is not as part of the British-controlled region to which it certainly belonged a generation before the war but as part of the lands of the Nawab of Awadh. This ruler also controls distant villages (if the identification of Bandaa as current 'Banda', is correct) that he may grant to his protégés. Banda was part of British India by the first decade of the nineteenth century. Yet, despite this temporal slippage with respect to geopolitical entities found in the first episodes of the story, overall, it possesses plausibility: Nawabs did have protégés, whom they gifted with means of support. Villagers did fight the British and find safe havens after the war. Some villagers provided help to British refugees during the war and were rewarded after the war with grants of villages, cash and other prerequisites by the colonial regime.

Most obviously, in the context of the post-Independence land reforms taking place in the region, the story—told by a Rajput—explains the relationship between Muslims and Hindus in the village. This matter is hardly an abstract concern to farmers, especially with the then recently passed Zamindari Abolition and Land Reforms Bill (1949). This law provided ceilings on land ownership: a matter of grave concern to large landowners who might lose lands under the law's provisions and a matter of great interest to poorer members of the communities who might stand to gain. Rankhandi's Muslims, the storyteller said, descend from the sons of Kunwar. But Kunwar had a brother who stayed in Rankhandi, and he is the ancestor of an important lineage of Hindu Rajputs in Rankhandi, in fact the storyteller's own.[85]

Landscape, Memory and the War

The issue for the present is not the truth value of the above stories, which may be explored at a different time, but rather how these saints' legends, miraculous events, legends and oral histories of Rankhandi are linked to understandings of 1857. The element of landscape provides contextual clues. Landscapes—sites of memory—appear at multiple points in the stories of the *piir* and in the stories told about villagers and the war. These stories claim for Rankhandi a relationship to a wider political and geographic universe, as well as to the mapping of social relationships and space within the community. Rankhandi appears both as a cosmopolitan space—no 'frogs in a well', here—and as an intimate space of home.

The *piir* comes from the Himalayas, abode of holy men and of great deities. Yet he chooses to make his home in Rankhandi, a small place, instead of making his way to one of India's great religious centres. His tomb in Rankhandi is built, not by a resident of Rankhandi, but by a member of an itinerant merchant group, whose members range across the north Indian landscape and connect distant and near spaces. Kunwar is plucked from obscurity by the 'Nawab of Lucknow' and gifted with a valuable estate within his realm. If 'Bandaa' indeed refers to contemporary Banda, this could only have been part of the Nawab's realm before the start of the nineteenth century, when the British acquired this territory.[86] Awadh is large indeed if this spatial claim is true.

Rankhandi's sons—grandsons really, the sons of Kunwar—fight in the war against the British, a war whose aim is to gain the Mughal throne for the Nawab. The Nawab is depicted here as a claimant to the paramount power. Another Rankhandi grandson provides help to a refugee from that war and is rewarded for his aid by the colonial regime. Interestingly, this award is from a court in Lucknow, the Nawab's capital, and not from the British provincial capital.[87] By claiming a privileged relationship to the events of 1857—even if displaced to grandsons who returned only after the war—Rankhandi is a player in the great events of the day. So too, are the legends of the *piir*'s engagement in 1857. The family stories of what happened in the war also link Rankhandi, in however contested a fashion, to the war.

The stories of memory emphasise local spaces. The *piir* is connected to his grand tomb, the Pipal tree under which he lived, a second tomb space where he is venerated and the places where he manifests himself to residents. He embodies himself within residents through spirit possession. When the ten sons of Kunwar come to Rankhandi, there is no question that they belong. No one turns them in to the British, despite substantial rewards for such actions (which go unmentioned in the story). Initial profligacy by the ten brothers is followed by hard work and a regaining of family land. Their rights as coparceners of Rankhandi's land are not in doubt. The story underlines this by noting these Muslim men's shared descent with Hindu Rajputs in the village.

At the outset of this chapter, I noted that studies of war memories in colonial settings have focused on the nation. This is seen in recent reframing of memorialisation to incorporate marginalised groups into the symbolic spaces of the national narrative or in the manner in which these studies have explored the cultural poetics and dimensions of subjectivity and subject position largely within a nation state context.[88] The *piir*'s story and the stories of Rankhandi's engagement in the war provide conflicting accounts of its allegiances to specific polities. At best, Rankhandi people both help and fight the British. The context is both an undisclosed, yet presumptively pre-colonial, era and the colonial period. In these stories the *piir* acts against the British, but as protector, not as anti-colonial leader. Local memorialisation is not stridently set against the 'state'; nor is it internally consistent with respect to claims.

The issue of the subject and trauma, a second site of recovery of local memorialisation, is equally problematic in these tales and spaces. Subjective trauma, if it exists, is displaced or denied. In the telling of these stories, Rankhandi's people deny that terrible things happened to them during the war. It is the nearby villages that were looted and burned. The Rankhandi people who fight the British live elsewhere. The British do not know that Rankhandi is their village, and so it is a safe haven. Other stories state that the Rankhandi people earned a victory of sorts over their neighbours, possibly an instance of 'revenge' for some unstated insult. The stories do not admit to loss. Most strongly evident in these collected tales are the emergent oral traditional elements and their links between space and genealogical relationships. This is congruent with the emphases of ethnography at this period. In the tales, kinship maps onto space. Space maps into memory. Physical spaces, such as the *piir*'s shrine, may be amenable to further investigation. The stories of 1857 that are associated with these spaces are embedded in a cultural discourse that does not resemble the imperialist narratives of the British monuments. They are intimate stories about homeland and the quintessential links among ancestors, land and kinship, relationships that constitute Rankhandi's people. And a story about homeland is a powerful thing.

Notes and References

1. See, for example, Badri Narayan, *Women Heroes and Dalit Assertion in North India: Culture, Identity and Politics* (New Delhi: Sage Publications, 2006), and also Badri Narayan Tiwari, 'Reactivating the Past: Dalits and Memories of 1857', *Economic and Political Weekly*, 12 May 2007, pp. 1734–1738.
2. Two articles that are important in this discussion are Gautam Bhadra, 'Four Rebels of Eighteen-Fifty-Seven', in Ranajit Guha and Gayatri Chakravorty Spivak, eds, *Selected Subaltern Studies* (New York: Oxford University Press, 1988), pp. 129–175; Ranajit Guha, 'The Prose of Counter-Insurgency', in Ranajit Guha and Gayatri Chakravorty Spivak, eds, *Selected Subaltern Studies* (New York: Oxford University Press, 1988), pp. 45–86.

3. Gayatri Chakravorty Spivak, 'Can the Subaltern Speak?' in Cary Nelson and Lawrence Grossberg, eds, *Marxism and the Interpretation of Culture* (Urbana: University of Illinois Press, 1988), pp. 271–313.

4. Pierre Nora, 'Between Memory and History: *Les Lieux de Memoire*', *Representations* vol. 26, no. 26 (Spring, 1989), pp. 7–25.

5. David Harvey, *Justice, Nature and the Geography of Difference* (Cambridge, MA: Blackwell Publishers, 1996), pp. 210–212, 304–306; Pierce Lewis, 'The Monument and the Bungalow', *Geographical Review*, vol. 88, no. 4 (1998), pp. 507–527.

6. On war and landscape, see Jay Winter and Emmanuel Sivan, eds, *War and Remembrance in the Twentieth Century* (Cambridge: Cambridge University Press, 1999).

7. Maurice Halbwachs, *On Collective Memory* (Chicago: University of Chicago Press, 1992).

8. The Rani of Jhansi supposedly leaped her horse off the battlements of Jhansi fort to escape attacking forces. Monuments mark the places where she died and where she was cremated. On the memory of the fifty executed men, see John T. Hitchcock Papers [JTH], Box 11, File 173. 17 'History', National Anthropology Archives, Smithsonian Institution, Washington DC.

9. See, for example, Manu Goswami, '"Englishness on the Imperial Circuit": Mutiny Tours in Colonial South Asia', *Journal of Historical Sociology*, vol. 9, no. 1 (March 1996), pp. 54–84.

10. For example, Nandini Sundar discusses how the local representations of rebellion in Bastar district suggest complex interaction processes between the state and local people as to how the state and its impact are represented. Nandini Sundar, 'Debating Dussehra and Reinterpreting Rebellion in Bastar District, Central India', *Journal of the Royal Anthropological Institute*, vol. 7, no. 1 (March 2001), pp. 19–35.

11. This question has generated a massive discussion within anthropology. See, for example, James Clifford, *The Predicament of Culture: Twentieth Century Ethnography, Literature, and Art* (Cambridge, MA: Harvard University Press, 1988); John and Jean Comaroff, *Ethnography and the Historical Imagination* (Boulder, CO: Westview Press, 1992); Nicholas B. Dirks, *Castes of Mind: Colonialism and the Making of Modern India* (Princeton: Princeton University Press, 2001); and Saloni Mathur, 'History and Anthropology in South Asia: Rethinking the Archive', *Annual Review of Anthropology*, vol. 29 (2000), pp. 89–106.

12. In the present instance, for example, the phenomenon being investigated is the memorialisation of the War of 1857. Ethnographers regard 'war' as collective violence in which armed territorially based groups fight other such groups. In the effort to talk about both British and Indian conceptions of the events of 1857, I use this terminology in the effort to incorporate as generally as possible the wide range of meanings, intentions, goals and understandings of the war by a variety of personnel. Insofar as possible, value-neutral language will be used in describing personnel, events and actions.

13. This constitutes an additional possible data source for examining Indian responses to the war, following Pankaj Rag's call for more sources. See Pankaj Rag, '1857: Need for Alternative Sources', *Social Scientist*, vol. 26, nos 296–299 (1998), pp. 113–146.

14. Winter and Sivan, *War and Remembrance*.

15. The post-colonial dynamics of monuments have been studied, for example, by Jonathan Golden, 'Targeting Heritage: The Abuse of Symbolic Sights in Modern Conflicts', in Yorke Rowan and Uzi Baran, eds, *Marketing Heritage: Archaeology and the Consumption of the Past* (Walnut Creek, CA: Altamira Press, 2004), pp. 183–202. Also, Katherine Verdery, *The Political Lives of Dead Bodies: Reburial and Postsocialist Change* (New York: Columbia University Press, 1999).

16. Benedict Anderson, *Imagined Communities: Reflections on the Origin and Spread of Nationalism* (London: Verso, 1983), pp. 9–10; Alex King, *Memorials of the Great War in Britain: The Symbolism and Politics of Remembrance* (Oxford: Berg, 1998).

17. Peter H. Hoffenberg, 'Landscape, Memory and the Australian War Experience, 1915–18', *Journal of Contemporary History*, vol. 36, no. 1 (2001), pp. 111–131; Catherine Speck,

'Women's War Memorials and Citizenship', *Australian Feminist Studies*, vol. 11, no. 23 (1996), pp. 129–145.

18. Anne Walthall, 'Japanese Gimin: Peasant Martyrs in Popular Memory', *American Historical Review*, vol. 91, no. 5 (1986), pp. 1076–1102.

19. Heonik Kwon, *After the Massacre: Commemoration and Consolation in Ha My and My Lai* (Berkeley: University of California Press, 2006).

20. Dominick LaCapra, *Writing History, Writing Trauma* (Baltimore: Johns Hopkins University Press, 2001), p. 23; Mark Sanders, 'Ambiguities of Mourning: Law, Custom, and Testimony of Women before South Africa's Truth and Reconciliation Commission', in David Eng and David Kazanjian, eds, *Loss: the Politics of Mourning* (Berkeley: University of California Press, 2003), pp. 77–98.

21. Veena Das, 'Our Work to Cry: Your Work to Listen', in Veena Das, ed., *Mirrors of Violence: Communities, Riots, and Survivors* (Delhi: Oxford University Press, 1990), pp. 345–398; and Veena Das, 'Language and Body: Transactions in the Construction of Pain', in Arthur Kleinman, Veena Das and Margaret Lock, eds, *Social Suffering* (Berkeley: University of California Press, 1997), pp. 67–91.

22. Alexander Laban Hinton, ed., *Annihilating Difference: The Anthropology of Genocide* (Berkeley: University of California Press, 2002); Andrew Strathern, Pamela J. Stewart and Neil L. Whitehead, eds, *Terror and Violence: Imagination and the Unthinkable* (London: Pluto Press, 2006); Neil L. Whitehead, ed., *Violence* (Santa Fe: School of American Research, 2004); Lisa Yoneyama, *Hiroshima Traces: Time, Space, and the Dialectics of Memory* (Berkeley: University of California Press 1999).

23. A similar limitation on the extant data is evident in Tapti Roy's interrogation of the ideas held by anti-British fighters, in attempting to uncover these through sources that are largely British. Roy gives a close reading of the events in Bundelkhand and the points of difference and similarity among these individuals, looking closely at their diverse positions with respect to the colonial state. See Tapti Roy, 'Visions of the Rebels: A Study of 1857 in Bundelkhand', *Modern Asian Studies*, vol. 27, no. 1 (February 1993), pp. 205–228.

24. C.A. Bayly speaks of the 'humoral balance', for example, of linkages among the supernatural characteristics of the land's fertility, the ruler's qualities and actions, and those of people and other supernatural agents connected with it. See C.A. Bayly, *Origins of Nationality in South Asia: Patriotism and Ethical Government in the Making of Modern India* (New Delhi: Oxford University Press, 1998), pp. 12, 19. On sacred geography generally, see Diana L. Eck, *Darsan: Seeing the Divine Image in India* (Chambersburg, PA: Anima Books, 1981).

25. John E. Cort, 'Devotees, Families and Tourists: Pilgrims and Shrines in Rajasthan', in Carol E. Henderson and Maxine Weisgrau, eds, *Raj Rhapsodies: Tourism, Heritage and the Seduction of History* (Aldershot, England: Ashgate Publishing Ltd, 2007), pp. 165–181; C.J. Fuller, *The Camphor Flame: Popular Hinduism and Society in India* (Princeton: Princeton University Press, 1992), pp. 39–50; Leigh Minturn, *Sita's Daughters: Coming Out of Purdah* (New York: Oxford University Press, 1993), pp. 161–162.

26. C.A. Bayly, 'From Ritual to Ceremony: Death Ritual and Society in Hindu North India Since 1600', in Joachim Whaley, ed., *Mirrors of Mortality: Studies in the Social History of Death* (New York: St. Martin's Press, 1981), p. 155; Ruth L. Freed and Stanley A. Freed, *Ghosts: Life and Death in North India* (New York: American Museum of Natural History [No. 72], 1993); David Knipe, 'The Night of the Growing Dead: A Cult of Virabhadra in Coastal Andhra', in Alf Hiltebeitel, ed., *Criminal Gods and Demon Devotees: Essays on the Guardians of Popular Hinduism* (Binghamton, NY: State University of New York Press, 1989).

27. H. Dundas Robertson, *District Duties during the Revolt in the North-West Provinces of India in 1857* (London: Smith, Elder & Co, 1859), pp. 62–63.

28. Cort, 'Devotees, Families and Tourists'.

29. Diane M. Coccari, 'The Bir Babas of Banaras and the Deified Dead', in Alf Hiltebeitel, ed., *Criminal Gods and Demon Devotees: Essays on the Guardians of Popular Hinduism* (Binghamton, NY: State University of New York Press, 1989), pp. 251–269.

30. Lindsay Harlan, *Religion and Rajput Women: The Ethic of Protection in Contemporary Narratives* (Berkeley: University of California Press, 1992). Freed and Freed, *Ghosts.* Also see Stanley A. Freed and Ruth S. Freed, *Hindu Festivals in a North Indian Village* (New York: Anthropological Papers of the American Museum of Natural History [No. 81], 1998), pp. 256–257.

31. Usha Sanyal, 'Tourists, Pilgrims and Saints: The Shrine of Mu'in al-Din Chisti of Ajmer', in Carol E. Henderson and Maxine Weisgrau, eds, *Raj Rhapsodies: Tourism, Heritage and the Seduction of History* (Aldershot, Hampshire: Ashgate Publishing Limited), pp. 183–201.

32. Bayard Taylor, *A Visit to India, China and Japan in the Year 1853* (New York: P. Putnam & Co, 1855), p. 135.

33. Lawrence A. Babb, *The Divine Hierarchy* (New York: Columbia University Press, 1975), pp. 204–205.

34. In like vein, Kwon in *After the Massacre* writes of the disruptions of death rituals during the war in Vietnam and problems that survivors faced after the war in locating their dead, who were not able to receive the proper rituals.

35. 'The Indian Mutinies', *Times* (London), 21 August 1857, p. 7; *Times* (London), 18 August 1857, p. 3; 'An Indian Execution', *Times* (London), 3 December 1857, p. 7.

36. For examples, see Bholanauth Chunder, *The Travels of a Hindoo to Various Parts of Bengal and Upper India* (London: N. Trubner & Co, 1869), pp. 324–325, 365; Henry Wylie Norman and Mrs Keith Young, *Delhi, 1857: The Siege Assault and Capture As Given in the Diary & Correspondence of the Late Colonel Keith Young. C.B., Judge-Advocate General, Bengal* (London: W&R Chambers, 1902), pp. 103, 144, 291; Robertson, *District Duties*, p. 159; John Walter Sherer, *Daily life during the Indian Mutiny: Personal Experiences of 1857* (Allahabad: Legend Publications, 1974), p. 61.

37. Also spelled 'Khatah' in nineteenth century sources.

38. Edwin T. Atkinson, *Statistical, Descriptive and Historical Account of the Saharanpur District* (Allahabad: North-Western Provinces Government Press, 1875), p. 186. John T. Hitchcock, 'The Idea of the Martial Rajput', *Journal of American Folklore*, vol. 71, no. 281 (July 1958), pp. 216–223. Leigh Minturn and John T. Hitchcock, *The Rajputs of Khalapur, India* (New York: Wiley, 1966), pp. 14–15.

39. 'Guide to the Cornell Rankhandi Project Records, 1953–1984', Division of Rare and Manuscript Collections, Cornell University Library. Available at rmc.library.cornell.edu/EAD/htmldocs/RMA02787.html (accessed 3 December 2008).

40. *American Journal of Sociology*, 'Doctoral Dissertations in Progress, 1955', vol. 62, no. 1 (July 1956), pp. 8393, lists Hitchcock as working on 'An Ethnography of the Rajputs, a Landowning Caste of Village Rankhandi, U.P., India', at Cornell University.

41. A list of the scholars involved in the studies in Rankhandi, based on the collection of notes in John T. Hitchcock archives at the National Anthropological Archives in Washington, and on published works includes, besides Hitchcock, Brij Raj Chauhan, S.C. Dube, John Gumperz, Pauline Kolenda, J. Michael Maher, Leigh Minturn, Rudra Datt Singh, Robert T. Smith and others.

42. Records at the National Anthropological Archives, Smithsonian Institution include original typed field notes, photographs, maps and other materials from the Rankhandi project, along with Nepal field research notes. The papers are filed as the John T. Hitchcock papers.

43. For an example, see McKim Marriott, ed., *Village India: Studies in the Little Community* (Chicago: University of Chicago Press, 1955).

44. For a discussion of the concept of traditional history at this time, see Bernard S. Cohn, 'The Pasts of an Indian Village', *Comparative Studies in Society and History*, vol. 3, no. 3 (April 1961), pp. 241–249.

45. Richard G. Fox, *From Zamindar to Ballot Box: Community Change in a North Indian Town* (Ithaca, NY: Cornell University Press, 1969), p. 74; Freed and Freed, *Hindu Festivals*, p. 178. Morris E. Opler, 1956. 'The Extensions of an Indian Village', *Journal of Asian Studies*, vol. 16, no. 1 (1956), p. 7. Rudra Datt Singh, *Family Organization in a North Indian Village: A Study in Culture Change*, Ph.D. Thesis, Cornell University, p. 27.

46. Anthropologists with whom I have discussed the use of pseudonyms often cite the potential for dramatic harm to communities and individuals if real names are revealed. In the present case, data are fifty-four to fifty-six years old. Nearly all persons who were affected by, or who participated in, the 1950s Rankhandi project are deceased. In this work, I have not revealed the names of persons who told these stories to the ethnographers, and used instead, a general description of their social identity.

47. The Indian ethnographers' efforts were often linked to the felt urgent need for research to contribute to the nation's rural development efforts. Knowledge of specific communities, in this context, might be essential.

48. Brij Raj Chauhan details the double names of many of these villages in his *Rural Life: Grass Roots Perspectives* (New Delhi: Concept Publishing Company, 2009).

49. See the entry for 'Rankhandi' at: en.wikipedia.org/wiki/Rankhandi (accessed 14 November 2012). Field notes for the project in the National Anthropological Archives uniformly refer to the site as Rankhandi. Published works by anthropologists in the 1950s and 1960s refer to the site primarily by its pseudonym, 'Khalapur' or 'Khaalaapur', though it is possible to find research papers also under 'Rankhandi'.

50. Naresh Singh Pundir, 'Rankhandi: Putting the Old Threads Together', posted on the Internet at: boards.tiscali.ancestry.co.uk/surnames.pundir/2/mbashx (accessed 14 March 2008). There was also a Rankhandi Resurvey Project in 1984. See http://rmrims.org.in/scientist profile/ Enarendrakumar.html (accessed 02 January 2013).

51. For example, Leigh Minturn, 'Changes in the Differential Treatment of Rajput Girls in Khalapur; 1955–1975', *Medical Anthropology*, vol. 8, no. 2 (1984), pp. 127–132; Morris E. Opler, 'Rankhandi: Change in Education' in Mario D. Zamora and Zeus A. Salazar, eds, *Anthropology: Range and Relevance* (Quezon City, Kayumanggi Publishers, 1975), and Rudra Datt Singh, 'The Unity of an Indian Village', *Journal of Asian Studies,* vol. 16, no. 1 (1956), pp. 10–19.

52. Robertson, *District Duties*, pp. 157–163.

53. Atkinson, *Statistical, Historical and Descriptive Account*, pp. 126, 191.

54. Atkinson, *Statistical, Historical and Descriptive Account*, p. 219. Stokes, 'Rural Revolt in the Great Rebellion of 1857: A Study of the Saharanpur and Muzaffarnagar District', *The Historical Journal*, vol. 12, no. 4 (1969), p. 610.

55. Eric Stokes 'Rural Revolt'.

56. Atkinson, *Statistical, Historical and Descriptive Account*, pp. 180, 231, 267.

57. Atkinson, *Statistical, Historical and Descriptive Account*, pp. 180, 231.

58. Pauline Mahar Kolenda, 'Religious Anxiety and Hindu Fate', *Journal of Asian Studies*, vol. 23, no. S1 (June, 1964), pp. 76–77.

59. In the absence of corroborating birth records it would be difficult to get an exact age for this last person. One piece of evidence that tends to suggest that this person was in his eighties or nineties is the man's assertion that his father fought in the Sikh wars of the 1840s. It is also possible that his age could be noted exactly, if the family recalled that he was born 'the year after the war' and this was recalled and passed down in the family. Unfortunately, the data do not record such family traditions.

60. For a discussion of the problems and varieties of orally transmitted tales, see Jan Vansina, *Oral Tradition as History* (Madison: University of Wisconsin Press, 1985).

61. Hitchcock, 'The Idea of the Martial Rajput', p. 222. The book was most likely an edition of James Tod, *Tarikh-i Rajasthan, Musammabih Tadnamah-yi Rajasthan* (Lucknow: Munshi Naval

Kishor, 1877), Urdu translation of James Tod's *Annals and Antiquities of Rajasthan*, originally published in two volumes in 1829 and 1832.

62. John J. Gumperz, 'Religion and Social Communication in Village North India', *Journal of Asian Studies*, vol. 23, no. 1 (June 1964), pp. 89–97; and John J. Gumperz, 'Linguistic and Social Interaction in Two Communities', *American Anthropologist*, vol. 66, no. 6 (1964), pp. 137–153. This position would be less likely to be sustained in contemporary ethnography, with its turn toward the use of historical sources and the development of history.

63. The quote is from Leigh Minturn, *Sita's Daughters* (New York: Oxford University Press, 1993), p. 183. Rankhandi is identified in this work as 'Khalapur'. See also Leigh Minturn and John T. Hitchcock, *The Rajputs of Khalapur, India* (London: John Wiley & Sons, 1966). It should be noted that in general usage, a '*piir*' or *pir* is the term for a Muslim holy man, and the *dargah* is the shrine complex associated with him.

64. For a general description of the *piir* and his relationship to the villagers see Minturn, *Sita's Daughters*, pp. 183–184.

65. Published sources generally refer to the *piir* as '*darga*'. Field notes refer to him as the '*piir*' and as '*darga*'. Least-used is the personal name, 'Kulka', about which there is no other information. Interestingly, none of these names as recorded in fieldnotes includes the conventional honorifics that would respectfully be appended to the name of a personage (or supernatural figure) of such exalted status. See JTH Archives, Box 1, 'File 778, Sacred Objects and Places', interview, 2 December 1954. On Muslim saints' shrines and place names, see Sanyal, 'Tourists, Pilgrims and Saints', p. 185.

66. JTH Archive, Box 1, File '17 History', interview, 9 February 1956. Banjaras, according to nineteenth-century British sources, had a bad reputation and were listed as a 'criminal tribe' under the Criminal Tribe Act of 1871. By the early 1950s, the occupation of travelling merchant-cum-transporter was being replaced by trucks. The identification of this merchant as a Banjara might add a flavour of olden times to the story.

67. The single photograph I have found in the archive that possibly shows the tomb is entitled simply a 'shrine'. It matches, however, written descriptions in the notes.

68. JTH Archive, Box 1 File '77/78 Religion', interview, 11 February 1956; JTH Archive, Box 1, File '17 History', interview, 9 February 1956.

69. See also Minturn, *Sita's Daughters*, pp. 183–844.

70. JTH, Box 18, File 'Piir', interview, 18 February 1955.

71. JTH Archive, Box 1, File 'Holy Spots', interview, 1 April 1954; JTH Archive, Box 1, File '778. Sacred Objects and Places', interview, 2 December 1954. JTH Archive, Box 18, File 'Piir', interview, 18 February 1955. JTH Archive, Box 1, File '778: Sacred Objects and Places: Piir', interview, 29 November 1954; See also Minturn, *Sita's Daughters*, p. 184.

72. JTH Archive, Box 1, File '778: Sacred Objects and Places: Piir', interview, 29 November 1954; JTH Archive, Box 18, File 'Piir', interview, 18 February 1955.

73. The cartridges story is widely discussed in historical treatments of the war, with the weight given to this varying by the author's consideration of causal factors. See, for example, Christopher Hibbert, *The Great Mutiny: India 1857* (London: Penguin, 1978); John William Kaye, *Kaye's and Malleson's History of the Indian Mutiny of 1857–58* (Westport, CT: Greenwood Press, Publishers, 1971 [1897–1898]); R.C. Majumdar, *The Sepoy Mutiny and the Revolt of 1857* (Calcutta: Mukhopadhyay, 1957); Surendra Nath Sen, *Eighteen Fifty-Seven* (Delhi: Publications Division, Ministry of Information & Broadcasting, Govt. of India, 1957).

74. JTH Archive, Box 1, File '17 History', interview, 9 February 1956.

75. JTH Archive, Box 1, File '17. History', interview, 9 February 1956.

76. This incident is recounted in JTH Archive, Box 18, File 'Piir', interview, 18 February 1955.

77. JTH Archive, Box 1, File '77/78 Religion', 11 February 1956.

78. JTH Archive, Box 11, File 'Traditional History, Family History', interview, 7 January 1955. The storyteller is identified as a Rajput man, age not given, but this man is identified elsewhere in the files as ninety-seven years old.

79. That is, the family could only arrange a match within its own marriage circle or network, people with whom interdining is possible and who are linked through concepts of descent and of the exchange relationships of marriage.

80. Panchli or Panchali village today is celebrated as the home of Kotwal Dhan Singh Gurjar, who led initial actions against the British in Meerut in May 1857.

81. The numbers of sons born to Kunwar's wife and to his mistress may humorously suggest how he felt about each.

82. 'Ramzaan (or Ramzan) Ali' is a common name. In seeking cultural resonances, however, it might be noted that this is one of the given names for the youth declared king in summer 1857 by the Awadhi leadership, known as 'Ramzan Ali Khan Mirz Birjiz Kudr Bahadur', according to P.J.O. Taylor, ed., *A Companion to the 'Indian Mutiny' of 1857* (New Delhi: Oxford University Press, 1996), p. 54.

83. JTH Archive, Box 11, File 'Traditional History', 7 January 1955. This quote is recorded in English.

84. The record of this story in field notes does not comment if it resonates with any popular novel or cinema treatments of 1857 that were current in the early 1950s, and that this storyteller might have known.

85. On the theme of shared descent of Hindus and Muslims in Rankhandi, see also Minturn and Hitchcock, *The Rajputs of Khalapur*, p. 64.

86. Banda District was south of the Jumna river in the southern part of the then North-west Province. Rankhandi lay in the north-western part of North-west Province.

87. Jurisdiction is unclear, but the nearest court that collected testimony on events in 1857–1858 was at Saharanpur. Testimony was also collected at Agra (capital of the North-west Province). Testimony relating to Banda, the other relevant named locale was made in the court at Lucknow. Testimony relating to court cases in these regions may be found in S.A.A. Rizvi and Motilal Bhargava, eds, *Freedom Struggle in Uttar Pradesh*, vols 2 and 5 (Lucknow, Uttar Pradesh: Information Department, 1957–1960).

88. Narayan, *Women Heroes and Dalit Assertion in North India.*

About the Editor and Contributors

Editor

Crispin Bates is Reader in Modern South Asian History in the School of History, Classics and Archaeology and Director of the Centre for South Asian Studies at the University of Edinburgh. His publications include *Subalterns and Raj: South Asia since 1600* (2007); *Beyond Representation: Constructions of Identity in Colonial and Postcolonial India* (2005); and (with Subho Basu) *Rethinking Indian Political Institutions* (2005). Between 2006 and 2008 he was the Principal Investigator in a major AHRC-funded research project concerning the Indian Uprising, based at the University of Edinburgh.

Contributors

Gautam Bhadra is a former Lecturer in History at Calcutta University and Professor of History at the Centre for the Study of Social Sciences in Calcutta. He is a founding member of the Subaltern Studies collective and has researched and published extensively, in both English and Bengali, on peasant rebellions in Mughal and colonial India.

Chhanda Chatterjee was educated at Presidency College and Calcutta University; her doctoral thesis was published by the Asiatic Society, Kolkata, as *Punjab and Awadh: Ideology, the Rural Agrarian Structure and Imperial Rule, 1849–1887* (1999); she teaches history in Visva-Bharati, Santiniketan.

Mahmood Farooqui studied History at the Universities of Delhi, Oxford and Cambridge. He is the author of the acclaimed *Besieged: Voices From Delhi, 1857* (2010) and the co-director of the internationally acclaimed film *Peepli Live*. Over the last six years he has effected a major revival of the lost art of Urdu storytelling, Dastangoi, which is his principal occupation at present.

Carol E. Henderson is Research Associate and part-time Lecturer in the Department of Sociology and Anthropology, Rutgers University-Newark. Books include *Raj Rhapsodies: Tourism, Heritage, and the Seduction of History* (2007) co-edited with Maxine Weisgrau; and *Culture and Customs of India* (2002). Her current research interests include violence and memory in South Asia.

Rakshanda Jalil is a Senior Associate Fellow at the Indian Council for Social Development. She has edited two collections of short stories; written a collection of essays on the little known monuments of Delhi, called *Invisible City* (2008, revised edition in 2011); and co-authored two books with Mushirul Hasan, *Partners in Freedom: Jamia Millia Islamia* (2006) and *Journey to a Holy Land: A Pilgrim's Diary* (2009). She has also published eight works of translations, recently submitted a PhD on the Progressive Writers' Movement and has guest edited two special theme issues, one on Progressive Literature for *The Book Review* (April 2011) and *Delhi 100* (Forthcoming).

Dirk H.A. Kolff is Emeritus Professor of Indian History at Leiden University, the Netherlands. Among his publications are *Naukar, Rajput and Sepoy: The Ethnohistory of the Military Labour Market in Hindustan, 1450–1850* (1990 and 1990); *Grass in their Mouths: The Upper Doab of India under the Company's Magna Charta, 1793–1830* (2010); several articles on Indian law and on Johan Huizinga as Indologist; and (edited with Jos J.L. Gommans) *Warfare and Weaponry in South Asia, 1000–1800* (2001).

Tom Lloyd completed his PhD at the University of Edinburgh. His doctoral thesis studied the creation of extra-legal spaces and state power during counter-insurgency initiatives in British India, Ireland and Kenya, circa 1810–1960.

Kama Maclean is Senior Lecturer of South Asian and World History at the University of New South Wales, Sydney, and editor of *South Asia: Journal of South Asian Studies*. Her research interests range across a broad range of themes relating to history, politics and religion in nineteenth and twentieth century north India. Her book, *Pilgrimage and Power: The Kumbh Mela in Allahabad*, was published in New York in 2008.

Andrea Major is a former Leverhulme Early Career Fellow, working on British attitudes to slavery in India, and is now a Lecturer in Wider World History at the University of Leeds. Her doctoral thesis, completed at Edinburgh University (2004), explored british interpretation of Sati (widow-burning) in India. She has written extensively on British engagements with gender and social issues in colonial India. Her publications include *Pious Flames: European Encounters with Sati 1500–1830* (2006); *Sovereignty and Social Reform: The British Campaign Against Sati in the Princely States* (2010); *Sati: A Historical Anthology* (2007); and *Slavery, Abolitionism and Empire in India, 1772–1843* (2012).

Amaresh Misra is an independent historian and author. Currently resident in Mumbai, he is also a freelance journalist, political commentator, columnist on foreign policy and a political and civil rights activist. He has lectured widely in Indian and American universities on 1857 and the roots of peasant turbulence. His publications include *War of Civilizations: India AD 1857*, volumes 1 and 2 (2007); *Mangal Pandey: The True Story of an Indian Revolutionary* (2005); and *Lucknow: Fire of Grace—The Story of Its Renaissance, Revolution and the Aftermath* (1999).

Veena Naregal is Associate Professor at the Institute of Economic Growth, Delhi. Having published extensively on the cultural and political history of western India, she is currently heading a collaborative three-language research and translation project on regional theatre histories in India. Besides, she is also involved in a collaborative research project on the history of the social sciences in post-1947 India. Her first book, *Language Politics, Elites and the Public Sphere: Western India under Colonialism*, was published in 2001.

William R. Pinch is Professor of History and Chair of the Department of History at Wesleyan University. He earned his PhD in History at the University of Virginia in 1990. He is the author of *Peasants and Monks in British India* (1996) and *Warrior Ascetics and Indian Empires* (2006), and the editor of *Speaking of Peasants: Essays in Indian History and Politics in Honor of Walter Hauser* (2008). His articles have appeared in *Past & Present, History and Theory, The Indian Economic and Social History Review, Modern Asian Studies* and *Counterpunch*, and he has authored numerous book chapters for edited volumes. Professor Pinch's teaching focuses on South Asian history, world history, religion and history and maritime history.

Sultan-i-Rome is Assistant Professor of History in Government Jahanzeb Postgraduate College, Saidu Sharif, Swat, Pakistan. Hailing from Hazara village in Swat, he obtained his Master's degree in General History from University of Karachi, and PhD in History from the University of Peshawar. His publications include *Swat State (1915–1969): From Genesis to Merger; An Analysis of Political, Administrative, Socio-Political and Economic Developments* (2008); *The North-West Frontier (Khyber Pukhtunkhwa): Essays on History* (Forthcoming); *Land and Forest Governance: Transition from Tribal System to Swat State to Pakistan* (Forthcoming); and *Mataluna* (a book of Pashto proverbs, Forthcoming).

Index